OXFORD STUDIES IN BYZANTIUM

OXFORD STUDIES IN BYZANTIUM

Oxford Studies in Byzantium consists of scholarly monographs and editions on the history, literature, thought, and material culture of the Byzantine world.

Writing and Reading Byzantine Secular Poetry, 1025–1081
Floris Bernard

The Byzantine–Islamic Transition in Palestine
An Archaeological Approach
Gideon Avni

Shaping a Muslim State
The World of a Mid-Eighth-Century Egyptian Official
Petra M. Sijpesteijn

Niketas Choniates
A Historiographical Study
Alicia Simpson

Byzantines, Latins, and Turks in the Eastern Mediterranean World after 1150
Edited by Jonathan Harris, Catherine Holmes, and Eugenia Russell

Debating the Saints' Cults in the Age of Gregory the Great
Matthew Dal Santo

The Embodied Icon
Liturgical Vestments and Sacramental Power in Byzantium
Warren T. Woodfin

'We have no king but Christ'
Christian Political Thought in Greater Syria on the
Eve of the Arab Conquest (*c.*400–585)
Philip Wood

Tilling the Hateful Earth
Agricultural Production and Trade in the Late Antique East
Michael J. Decker

The Chronicle of Morea
Historiography in Crusader Greece
Teresa Shawcross

The Trophies of the Martyrs
An Art Historical Study of Early Christian Silver Reliquaries
Galit Noga-Banai

A Byzantine Encyclopaedia of Horse Medicine
The Sources, Compilation, and Transmission of the Hippiatrica
Anne McCabe

George Akropolites: The History
Introduction, translation, and commentary
Ruth Macrides

Holy Fools in Byzantium and Beyond
Sergey A. Ivanov and translated by Simon Franklin

Basil II and the Governance of Empire (976–1025)
Catherine Holmes

Law, Power, and Imperial Ideology in the Iconoclast Era

c.680–850

M. T. G. HUMPHREYS

OXFORD
UNIVERSITY PRESS

OXFORD
UNIVERSITY PRESS

Great Clarendon Street, Oxford, OX2 6DP,
United Kingdom

Oxford University Press is a department of the University of Oxford.
It furthers the University's objective of excellence in research, scholarship,
and education by publishing worldwide. Oxford is a registered trade mark of
Oxford University Press in the UK and in certain other countries

First Edition published in 2015

Impression: 2

Published in the United States of America by Oxford University Press
198 Madison Avenue, New York, NY 10016, United States of America

British Library Cataloguing in Publication Data
Data available

Library of Congress Control Number: 2014949668

ISBN 978–0–19–870157–6

Printed and bound by
CPI Group (UK) Ltd, Croydon, CR0 4YY

For Beth

Preface

In the process of researching and writing this work, I have been acutely aware of three things. Firstly, how I came to the subject of law and Byzantium, and the huge role that chance and tangential research has played in shaping my enquiries. My academic studies began with iconoclasm, and in particular how and why three distinct (but to my mind interlinked) societies—Byzantium, the Caliphate, and the Carolingians—came, around the same period, to discuss the issue of religious imagery. Underpinning this was a greater issue: how from the corpse of the Roman Empire three divergent, religio-political societies emerged; how these utilized and contested their shared inheritance; and how they related to each other. While thinking about this, I made the surprising discovery—surprising at least to me—that one seemingly priceless lode of material had fallen by the wayside of historical research, namely the legal sources. I found this particularly odd for Byzantium, which for the period in question is hardly overloaded with sources. Moreover, I had formed the suspicion that there was far more to the eighth century than iconoclasm, a suspicion that has been reinforced and substantiated by some excellent recent scholarship, and that there must be another way into the era, one that could complement and contextualize iconoclasm. I decided that the legal material was perhaps that new way, and I hope that the reader will at the least be challenged and stimulated to think about the age in a new light.

However, I am also aware of what this book is, what it is not, and what has been left out. The present work is a mixture of close reading of some well-established texts, and a prolonged analysis of other, more numerous legal works, whose origins, meanings, and context are far murkier and highly contested. As such, this study not only is not a replacement for a general history of the period, but also is not a full legal history either. Much more can be said, and needs to be said, about the Byzantine legal order, how it fitted into the rest of Byzantine society, and how Byzantine law shaped and was shaped by the society, economy, and culture in which it operated. Such a work, however, would be impossible without first working on the legal texts whose study must form the foundations of future research. There was the option to withhold publication of the present work until such time as that research was completed. However, not only would such a study be a hefty tome indeed, but also I am not gifted or arrogant enough a scholar to deem that my work is the end of the matter. Rather, my intention is to reignite debate, and I hope to enrich my previous and future work through the dialectical process. Furthermore, as part of that spur to debate, and the third element in the trilogy of work proposed, I am preparing a translation of most of the texts contained herein for the *Translated Texts for Byzantinists* series at Liverpool University Press, and I sincerely thank them, the board of Oxford Studies in Byzantium, and Oxford University Press for permitting the overlap of these works. Many of the translations found in the present study are early versions of those that will appear in the book for *TTB*, although, as ever in scholarship, much might change between the two.

Finally, and in many ways most importantly, I owe several huge debts of gratitude. Firstly, to the board and editorial team of Oxford Studies in Byzantium for their support and help. Furthermore, in the writing of this book, I have often felt that to a great extent, academic work is always seeing further by standing on the shoulders of giants. As such, I feel particular admiration for the huge quantity and quality of work that has gone into the coalface of Byzantine legal studies, the codicological and philological effort that has created the critical editions, primarily under the aegis of the *Forschungen zur byzantinischen Rechtsgeschichte* series, without which none of my work could be possible. More particularly, the works, words, and encouragement of James Howard-Johnston and Rosamond McKitterick have been greatly appreciated. The incisive analysis and support of Jonathan Shepard and Mark Whittow, both during the viva voce of the thesis on which this book is based and since, have been truly invaluable. The comments and suggestions of my two anonymous readers have also distinctly improved this work. Above all, I owe Peter Sarris, who set me on my course long ago as an undergraduate, and deftly guided me through both my Master's and PhD, a huge thank you for all his aid, knowledge, and wisdom. Much that is good in this work belongs to the above; all the mistakes belong to the author. I also thank the Master and Fellows of Pembroke College, Cambridge for providing the ideal setting for the generation of the thesis, and the Master and Fellows of St John's College, Cambridge for the Research Fellowship that permitted the transformation into the present work. I have also been blessed to have been surrounded by a vibrant graduate community, who made the past years not only productive but also highly enjoyable. Finally, my family have been constant supports, especially my wife Beth, who has been there since this project's conception, throughout all its trials and tribulations, about whom no words can express my gratitude, and to whom I fondly dedicate this work.

Mike Humphreys

St John's College, Cambridge
December 2013

Contents

List of Tables

List of Abbreviations

ACO	*Acta conciliorum oecumenicorum*
AE	*Appendix Eclogae*, ed. L. Burgmann and S. Troianos, *FM* III (Frankfurt, 1979), 24–125.
B/BS	*Basilika*, ed. H. Scheltema et al., *Basilicorum libri LX*, Series A (Text), 8 vols, Series B (Scholia), 9 vols (Groningen, 1953–88).
BMGS	*Byzantine and Modern Greek Studies*
BZ	*Byzantinische Zeitschrift*
C	*Codex Iustinianus*, ed. P. Krüger, vol. 2 of *Corpus iuris civilis* (11th edn., Berlin, 1929).
C(s)	Canon(s)
Coll. Trip.	*Collectio Tripartita*, ed. N. Van der Wal and B. Stolte, *Collectio Tripartita: Justinian on Religious and Ecclesiastical Affairs* (Groningen, 1994).
D	*Digest*, ed. P. Krüger and T. Mommsen, vol. 1 of *Corpus iuris civilis* (16th edn., Berlin, 1928).
DOC	P. Grierson, *Catalogue of the Byzantine Coins in the Dumbarton Oaks Collection and in the Whittemore Collection, II: Phocas to Theodosius III, 602–717*, 2 vols (Washington DC, 1968); *III: Leo III to Nicephorus III, 717–1081*, 2 vols (Washington DC, 1973).
DOP	*Dumbarton Oaks Papers*
E	*Ecloga*, ed. L. Burgmann, *Ecloga: Das Gesetzbuch Leons III. und Konstantinos V.* (Frankfurt, 1983).
EA	*Eisagoge Aucta*, ed. K. Zacharia von Lingenthal, *IGR* IV 180–370 = Zepos, *IGR* VI 57–216.
ED	*Ecloga Derivative*
EHB	A. Laiou et al. (eds), *The Economic History of Byzantium*, 3 vols (Washington DC, 2002).
Eis.	*Eisagoge*, ed. K. Zacharia von Lingenthal, *Collectio librorum juris Graeco-Romani ineditorum* (Leipzig, 1852), 61–217 = Zepos, *IGR* II, 236–368.
EP	*Ecloga Privata*; see L. Burgmann, *Ecloga: Das Gesetzbuch Leons III. und Konstantinos V.* (Frankfurt, 1983), 51–2.
EPA	*Ecloga Privata Aucta*, ed. K. Zacharia von Lingenthal, *IGR* IV, 7–48 = Zepos, *IGR* VI, 12–47.

EPAs *Ecloga Privata Aucta Sinaitica*, ed. D. Simon and S. Troianos, 'EPA Sinaitica', *FM* III (Frankfurt, 1979), 168–77.

EPrM *Ecloga ad Prochiron mutata*, ed. K. Zacharia von Lingenthal, *IGR* IV, 49–170 = Zepos, *IGR* VI, 217–318.

FM *Fontes Minores*

I *Institutes*, ed. P. Krüger and T. Mommsen, vol. 1 of *Corpus iuris civilis* (16th edn., Berlin, 1928).

IGR K. Zacharia von Lingenthal, *Jus Graeco-Romanum*, 7 vols (Leipzig, 1856–1884).

JHS *The Journal of Hellenic Studies*

K *Krisis peri gambrōn stratiōtōn*, ed. D. Simon, 'Byzantinische Hausgemeinschaftsverträge' in F. Baur, K. Larenz, and F. Wieacker (eds), *Beiträge zur europäischen Rechtsgeschichte und zum geltenden Zivilrecht: Festgabe für J. Sontis* (Munich, 1977), 91–128, text at 94.

LBG *Lexikon zur byzantinischen Gräzitat:* besonders des 9.–12. Jahrhunderts, ed. E. Trapp et al., 7 vols to date (Vienna, 1994–).

Mansi J. Mansi (ed.), *Sacrorum Conciliorum nova et amplissima Collectio* (Florence–Venice, 1759–98).

MS(S) Manuscript(s)

N *Novellae*, ed. R. Schöll and G. Kroll, vol. 3 of *Corpus iuris civilis* (6th edn., Berlin, 1928).

NG *Nomos Georgikos*, ed. I. Medvedev et al., *Vizantiĭskiĭ zemledel'cheskiĭ zakon* (Leningrad, 1984).

NM *Nomos Mosaikos*, ed. L. Burgmann and S. Troianos, *FM* III (Frankfurt, 1979), 126–67.

NN *Nomos Rhodion Nautikos*, ed. W. Ashburner, *The Rhodian Sea-Law* (Oxford, 1909).

NS *Nomos Stratiotikos*, ed. W. Ashburner, 'The Byzantine Mutiny Law', *JHS* 46 (1926), 85–109.

ODB A. Kazhdan et al. (eds), *The Oxford Dictionary of Byzantium*, 3 vols (Oxford, 1991).

PD *Prochiron Derivative*

PG *Patrologia cursus completus: series graeca*, ed. J.-P. Migne (Paris, 1857–66).

PLRE *Prosopography of the Later Roman Empire*, ed. A. H. M. Jones et al., 3 vols (Cambridge, 1971–92).

PMBZ *Prosopographie der mittelbyzantinischen Zeit*, ed. R.-J. Lilie et al., I *(641–867)*, 6 vols (Berlin, 1998–2002).

Pr. *Prochiron*, ed. K. Zacharia von Lingenthal, *Ho Procheiros Nomos* (Heidelberg, 1837).

RHBR L. Burgmann et al. (eds), *Repertorium der Handschriften des byzantinischen Rechts: Teil I Die Handschriften des weltlichen Rechts* (Frankfurt, 1995). A. Schminck and D. Getov (eds), *Teil II Die Handschriften des kirchlichen Rechts I* (Frankfurt, 2010).

Zepos, *IGR* I. Zepos and P. Zepos, *Jus Graecoromanum*, 8 vols. (Athens, 1931).

ZV G. Zacos and A. Veglery, *Byzantine Lead Seals*, vol. 1 (Basel, 1972).

Note on Language and Tables

In order to ease understanding and accessibility of this work for non-specialists, all the Greek has been transliterated. Diacritical marks have been left out, but bars are used to distinguish *ēta* from *epsilon* and *ōmega* from *omicron*. Further, *bēta* is transliterated as a 'b', and *upsilon* as a 'u'. All translations are the author's own, unless indicated. Names have been given in their established anglicized form, so Nicephorus not Nikephoros, and *Ecloga* not *Eklogē*.

The reader should also note that all references to the Old Testament refer to the *Septuagint*, which although highly similar to other (perhaps more familiar) versions, does employ a slightly different ordering.

Further, this book contains multiple tables of manuscripts. The vast majority of the information is derived from the *Repertorium der Handschriften des byzantinischen Rechts: Teil I Die Handschriften des weltlichen Rechts*, ed. L. Burgmann et al. (Frankfurt, 1995), *Teil II Die Handschriften des kirchlichen Rechts I*, ed. A. Schminck and D. Getov (Frankfurt, 2010), or *RHBR* for short, but checked against and supplemented by information from the relevant editions. These appear in two different forms. Tables 2–4 give the relevant contents of particular manuscripts. As such, they list the number given to each manuscript in the *RHBR* which contains the particular text in question. The number after the decimal point refers to a text's order in that manuscript, also as given in the *RHBR*. So, anything listed as .1 (Text) means that the text is the first item in the manuscript. Some of the texts contain others within them, and this is represented in the tables by a [–x], indicating that everything up to that number is contained within the first text. This fuller, but slightly ungainly, system has been adopted, as these three tables are relatively short, simple, and above all contain content that is referred to in the main argument, namely the precise ordering of certain manuscripts.

Tables 9–14 grouped in the Appendix, on the other hand, are too complex for such a system. Instead, they give the *RHBR* numbers of the manuscripts for the particular text under discussion, including the number for where that text appears in that manuscript. So *RHBR*.1.1

means that it is the first manuscript recorded in the *RHBR*, and the first text in that manuscript. The presence of other texts is indicated by an 'x', and the totals given at the bottom of the table. Since, on some occasions, this would misleadingly give an impression of association, when in reality there was scant codicological closeness between the two, an (x) indicates an insignificant association. This is an inherently subjective exercise, but in an attempt to include a measure of objectivity, the following rule was applied in measuring insignificance: whether a text was 50 folios or 20% of the manuscript (whichever was greater) distant from the text in question, or from an associated text-group. This is clearly arbitrary, but hopefully does weed out the most obvious outliers.

List of Maps

Maps

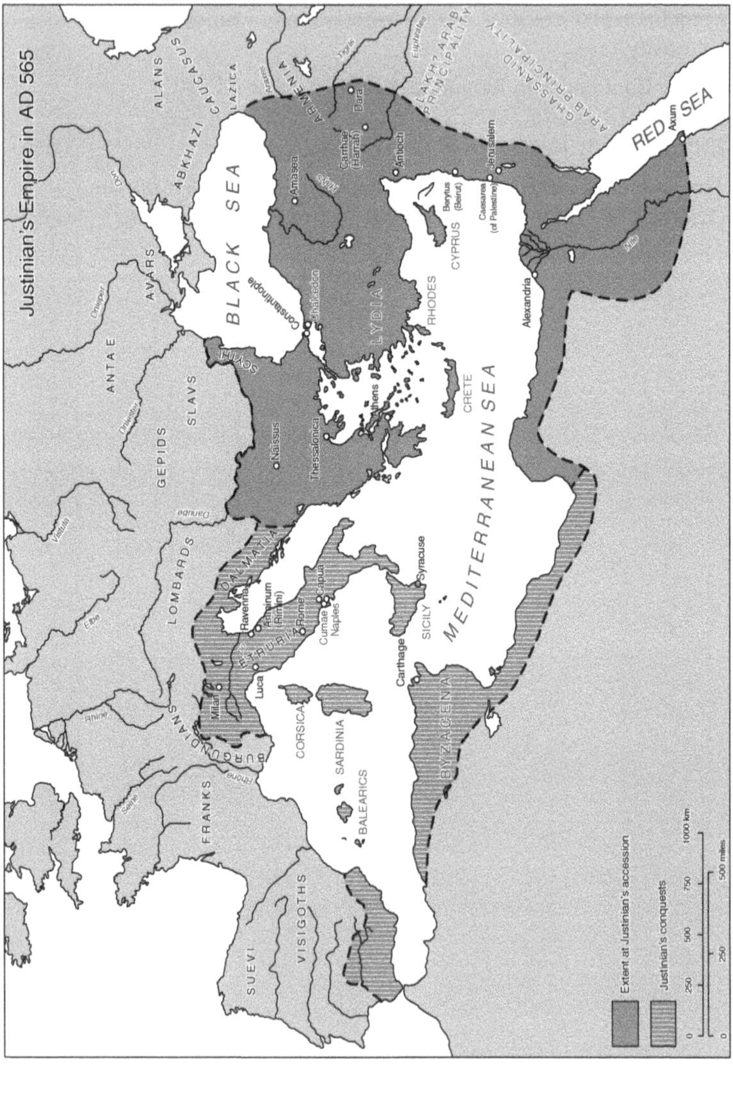

Map I. Justinian's Empire in AD 565

Map II. Theme Commands in Byzantine Asia Minor around 720

Map III. The Empire in 780

Introduction

Roman Law and Imperial Ideology from Justinian to Heraclius

The aim of this book is to examine the legal sources of the 'Iconoclast era', *c.*680–850, in order to reintegrate their evidence into the mainstream of Byzantine scholarship for Byzantium's formative period.[1] In particular it will focus on the light shed by the legal material on the ideological system and 'symbolic universe' of that age.[2] For this was the era in which the vast, complex inheritance of late antiquity was perforce recast, following the collapse of the late antique Roman world, when war and plague created socio-economic, political, and cultural dislocation and decline. Above all, the seventh century witnessed unprecedented change and challenge, especially in the form of the rise of Islam, a uniquely dangerous threat to the Roman world combining a polity that vied for, and eventually won, hegemony over the Mediterranean, and a different explanation of divine dispensation.[3] From this crucible a new society was forged,

[1] I have taken this period from the recent and excellent work by L. Brubaker and J. Haldon, *Byzantium in the Iconoclast Era, c. 680–850: A History* (Cambridge, 2011), which builds on the work done by L. Brubaker and J. Haldon, *Byzantium in the Iconoclast Era, c. 680–850: The Sources* (Aldershot, 2001).

[2] For this term see E. Cassirer, *An Essay on Man: An Introduction to a Philosophy of Human Culture* (New Haven, 1944), 25. Cf. C. Geertz, *The Interpretation of Cultures* (New York, 1973).

[3] See J. Haldon, *Byzantium in the Seventh Century: The Transformation of a Culture* (rev. edn., Cambridge, 1997). See also M. Whittow, *The Making of Orthodox Byzantium* (Basingstoke, 1996), esp. 38–193. For particular emphasis on the sources and the role of conflict between Rome/Byzantium and Islam, see J. Howard-Johnston, *Witnesses to a World Crisis: Historians and Histories of the Middle East in the Seventh*

named by modernity medieval Byzantium to distinguish it from ancient Rome.[4]

The causes, nature, and extent of that transformation are, to put it mildly, disputed academic territory. Perhaps even more controversial is the age that followed, named for a religio-political controversy, 'iconoclasm', literally the destruction of religious images.[5] A flood of scholarly ink has explored the period through the prism of this debate, rather than vice versa. Only recently have historians attempted to write a history of the period that includes iconoclasm, but is not determined by it.[6] This is vital, for this was the era that set the pattern for Byzantium until at least the eleventh century. Yet the iconoclast controversy provides manifest evidence that this was a contested, fluctuating, and uncertain process. Indeed, the whole age could be described as one of prolonged identity crisis, as the structures of the Byzantine imagination were remoulded and contested as profoundly as those of the state and society—perhaps even more so.

However, one priceless lode of material has been systematically underused or misused in the study of the period, namely the law.[7]

Century (Oxford, 2010). For the special threat of Islam see P. Crone, 'Islam, Judeo-Christianity and Byzantine Iconoclasm', *Jerusalem Studies in Arabic and Islam* 2 (1980), 59–95.

[4] For a discussion on general periodization in Byzantine history, see J. Shepard, 'General Introduction', in J. Shepard (ed.), *The Cambridge History of the Byzantine Empire c.500–1492* (Cambridge, 2008), 2–95, esp. 21–52. For the broader changes across the entirety of the post-Roman world see C. Wickham, *Framing the Early Middle Ages: Europe and the Mediterranean, 400–800* (Oxford, 2005); and C. Wickham, *The Inheritance of Rome: A History of Europe from 400 to 1000* (London, 2009); J. Herrin, *The Formation of Christendom* (Oxford, 1987); and for a particular emphasis on Byzantium, see M. Angold, *Byzantium: The Bridge from Antiquity to the Middle Ages* (London, 2001).

[5] Brubaker and Haldon, *History*, is now the best introduction to the controversy, but A. Bryer and J. Herrin, *Iconoclasm: Papers Given at the Ninth Spring Symposium of Byzantine Studies, University of Birmingham, March 1975* (Birmingham, 1977); and E. Martin, *A History of the Iconoclastic Controversy* (London, 1930), remain useful. See also S. Gero, *Byzantine Iconoclasm During the Reign of Leo III with Particular Attention to the Oriental Sources* (Louvain, 1973); and S. Gero, *Byzantine Iconoclasm During the Reign of Constantine V with Particular Attention to the Oriental Sources* (Louvain, 1977).

[6] See in particular the works of M.-F. Auzépy, especially her collected essays, *L'histoire des iconoclastes* (Paris, 2007); and above all her superb 'State of emergency', in J. Shepard (ed.), *The Cambridge History of the Byzantine Empire c.500–1492* (Cambridge, 2008), 251–91.

[7] For instance, although Brubaker and Haldon, *Sources*, 286–93 analyses and details the legal material, only the *Ecloga* and *Farmer's Law* make it into the

This is not due to scarcity, for numerous and varied legal texts have survived.[8] True, it is a complex corpus, rendered especially problematic by much of it being undated, and to a degree even un-datable. Yet much the same could be said of hagiography, which has produced countless studies.[9] Moreover, since the 1970s a wave of new critical editions, predominantly produced by German scholars, especially under the aegis of the *Forschungen zur byzantinischen Rechtsgeschichte* series, have re-examined and reproduced these texts and their complex manuscript traditions. This has culminated in the creation of the *Repertorium der Handschriften des byzantinischen Rechts* (*RHBR*), a catalogue of all extant Byzantine legal manuscripts.[10] Combined, these present the opportunity for unprecedented assessment, both in breadth and depth, of the legal sources.

Ironically, the very processes of academic specialization that propelled these achievements are also to blame for their lack of impact on broader Byzantine studies.[11] For history and law, once inseparable, have become distinct disciplines over the course of the twentieth century, with historians largely uninterested in legal history, and

bibliography of sources in Brubaker and Haldon, *History*, warranting (according to the index) 910, a grand total of 12 mentions between them across 799 pages of detailed and first-rate scholarship. This is not to single out for criticism what is an excellent work, but to highlight the widespread disuse of the legal material despite penetrating and extended analysis of the age. The general lack of interest in Byzantine law by general Byzantinists is well measured by the fact that in three recent (and generally excellent) overviews of the discipline, namely E. Jeffreys et al. (eds), *The Oxford Handbook to Byzantine Studies* (Oxford, 2008); L. James (ed.), *A Companion to Byzantium* (Oxford, 2010); and P. Stephenson (ed.), *The Byzantine World* (London, 2010), only one chapter is dedicated to Byzantine law, to wit B. Stolte, 'Justice: legal literature', in Jeffreys (ed.), *Handbook*, 691–8. Thus, Byzantine law occupies a grand total of eight pages out of 1,840!

[8] For good overviews see P. Pieler, 'Byzantinische Rechtsliteratur', in H. Hunger (ed.), *Die hochsprachliche profane Literatur der Byzantiner*, 2 vols (Munich, 1978), vol. 2, 341–480, esp. 429–44; N. Van der Wal and J. Lokin, *Historiae iuris Graeco-Romani delineatio: les sources du droit byzantin de 300 à 1453* (Groningen, 1985), 71–7; and S. Troianos, *Oi Pēges tou Vyzantinou dikaiou: eisagōgiko voēthēma* (Athens, 1986), 63–92.

[9] For instance see A.-M. Talbot (ed.), *Byzantine Defenders of Images: Eight Saints' Lives in English Translation* (Washington DC, 1998).

[10] L. Burgmann et al. (eds), *Repertorium der Handschriften des byzantinischen Rechts: Teil I Die Handschriften des weltlichen Rechts* (Frankfurt, 1995); A. Schminck and D. Getov (eds), *Teil II Die Handschriften des kirchlichen Rechts I* (Frankfurt, 2010).

[11] B. Stolte, 'Not new but novel: notes on the historiography of Byzantine law', *BMGS* 22 (1998), 264–79; and B. Stolte, 'Balancing Byzantine law', *FM* XI (Frankfurt, 2005), 57–75.

vice versa.[12] This process is most marked and surprising in Byzantine history, whose modern study originated with classicists immersed in Roman law. Yet as Byzantine studies distinguished itself from Classics, and Byzantine legal historians from Roman lawyers, the two discourses emerged disconnected and unaligned.

A similar development occurred in Roman history, where a subject dominated by scholars steeped in Roman law, from Theodor Mommsen[13] to A. H. M. Jones,[14] gave way to cultural history pioneered by Peter Brown.[15] However, recent scholars such as Harries,[16] Humfress,[17] Matthews,[18] and Sirks[19] have reapproached the immense corpus of legal evidence from late antiquity to ask it new questions, especially social and political ones. For instance: what does the law reveal about social praxis and power relations? In what ways, and to what extent, did law order social realities or reflect the thought-world of late antiquity? How was the law used in the competing claims of the state and powerful elites? How did the law project the ideology and policies of the imperial system?

Such questions are rarely raised (even more rarely answered) in Byzantine studies. Indeed, Alexander Kazhdan's 1989 call for a new legal history, in particular to tackle the social questions in which he was primarily interested, has mostly remained unanswered.[20] There

[12] Stolte, 'Not new but novel', 265–8; Stolte, 'Byzantine law', 58.

[13] See esp. T. Mommsen, *Römisches Staatsrecht*, 3 vols (Leipzig, 1871–88); and T. Mommsen, *Römisches Strafrecht*, 2 vols (Leipzig, 1899). For the general overview of law and history within late antique studies, including the role of Mommsen, see J. Matthews, 'Roman law and Roman history', originally in D. Potter (ed.), *A Companion to the Roman Empire* (Oxford, 2006), 477–91; reprinted in J. Matthews, *Roman Perspectives: Studies in the Social, Political and Cultural History of the First to Fifth Centuries* (Swansea, 2010), 291–310.

[14] A. H. M. Jones, *The Later Roman Empire, 284–602: A Social Economic and Administrative Survey*, 2 vols (Oxford, 1964).

[15] See inter alia P. Brown, *The World of Late Antiquity* (London, 1971); and P. Brown, *The Rise of Western Christendom: Triumph and Diversity, AD 200–1000* (2nd edn., Oxford, 2003).

[16] J. Harries, *Law and Empire in Late Antiquity* (Cambridge, 1999).

[17] C. Humfress, *Orthodoxy and the Courts in Late Antiquity* (Oxford, 2007).

[18] J. Matthews, *Laying Down the Law: A Study of the Theodosian Code* (London, 2000).

[19] B. Sirks, *The Theodosian Code: A Study* (Friedrichsdorf, 2007).

[20] A. Kazhdan, 'Do we need a new history of Byzantine law?', *Jahrbuch der österreichischen Byzantinistik* 39 (1989), 1–28. Kazhdan was particularly challenging the lack of any replacement for the magisterial work of. K. Zacharia von Lingenthal, *Geschichte des griechisch-römischen Rechts* (Berlin, 1892). This study formed the

are good reasons for this, including the relative dearth of documentary evidence, which for the Iconoclast era, at least, does appear almost total. More significantly, historians and lawyers have been motivated by fundamentally different interests.[21] In general, the former are concerned with what the law 'actually was' or 'law in action'—that is, what happened on the ground—while the latter explore what the law 'should be' or 'law in books'—that is, the normative system of legal texts.[22] This has led Byzantine lawyers primarily to focus on the sources of law, namely the examination of individual texts as repositories of law, which can then be extracted, posited on an arc of development, and judged accordingly.[23] For the sources we shall explore, this has repeatedly led to the same narrow question of whether the law they contain can be described as Justinianic—that is, adhering to the principles and dictates of the great legal codifications promulgated by Justinian I (r.527–65), or not. Moreover, even within the discipline of legal history, the Iconoclast era is generally perceived as a transition point, either a lamented coda to the great Justinianic legal outpouring, or the dismal background from which the Macedonians reanimated Roman law.[24] One result of this perception is that no study has ever been dedicated solely to the legal sources of the period, despite the impressive work undertaken on individual texts.

Meanwhile, Byzantinists, when they do study the legal evidence, do so overwhelmingly from a socio-economic perspective. In particular the *Nomos Georgikos* or *Farmer's Law* has been quarried and interpreted in numerous conflicting ways, revealing as much about the methods and politics of the examiners as about Byzantine agriculture,

apotheosis of nineteenth-century Byzantine legal scholarship, largely succeeding in replacing the previous works of J. Mortreuil, *Histoire du Droit Byzantin*, 3 vols (Paris, 1843–6); and G. Heimbach, *Anekdota*, 2 vols (Leipzig, 1838–40); and G. Heimbach, 'Griechisch-römisches Recht im Mittelalter und in der Neuzeit', in J. Ersch and J. Gruber (eds), *Allgemeine Encyclopädie der Wissenschaften und Künste in alphabetischer Folge. Section I Pt.86* (Leipzig, 1868), 191–471.

[21] J. Crook, 'Legal history and general history', *Bulletin of the Institute of Classical Studies* 41 (1996), 31–6.

[22] Stolte, 'Not new but novel', 265.

[23] Stolte, 'Not new but novel', 267–9.

[24] For instance compare H. Scheltema 'Byzantine law', in J. Hussey (ed.), *The Cambridge Medieval History Vol. IV* (Cambridge, 1967), Pt. 2, 55–77, with Pieler, 'Rechtsliteratur', 429–44. For the whole question of the periodization of Byzantine law see D. Simon, 'Die Epochen der byzantinischen Rechtsgeschichte', *Ius Commune* 15 (1988), 73–106.

let alone Byzantine law.[25] In contrast, political and cultural historians have shown nugatory interest in the law of the period, concentrating almost entirely on the texts generated by the iconoclast controversy. This has led to some notable and rectifiable oversights. For instance, the *Logos Prosphonetikos* of the Council in Trullo in 691/2 and the *prooimion* to the *Ecloga* of 741 represent by far the longest, extant, continuous statements issued directly by their respective regimes, and indeed are two of the richest sources for the whole period, yet remarkably, neither has been studied in depth as works of political rhetoric.[26] Furthermore, while countless articles have been written on the financial and military structures of the state, barely a word has been expended on the judicial system.[27]

More broadly, these divisions are underpinned by the shifting tectonic plates of scholarship. Since at least the 1970s, under the influence of the 'Cultural Turn', historians have increasingly focused on the nebulous field of culture, to the relative decline of Marxist history, and the full-blown retreat of institutional history. Law, it is fair to say, has been more resistant to these siren calls from anthropology, sociology, and philosophy. It is true that Legal Anthropology has emerged as a fascinating field of study, yet overall the impact of the social sciences on Law has been far more limited than on History.[28] As such, lawyers and historians are frequently not just asking different questions, but often speaking different scholarly languages and inhabiting different mental worlds.

This work aims to fill several of these scholarly interstices and establish a few bridges between increasingly separate academic

[25] See the salient warnings of over-interpretation in Whittow, *Making of Byzantium*, 115–17. For the NG, see Chapter 5.

[26] See respectively Chapters 1 and 2.

[27] The best and fullest account of seventh- and eighth-century legal administration is Haldon, *Seventh Century*, 272–6. This is in turn highly reliant on Jones, *Later Roman Empire*, vol. I, 470–522, for late antiquity; and J. B. Bury, *The Imperial Administrative System in the Ninth Century, with a Revised Text of the Kletorologion of Philotheos* (London, 1911); and N. Oikonomidès, *Les Listes de préséance byzantines des IX*e*–X*e *siècles* (Paris, 1972), for later developments. See also H. Saradi, 'The Byzantine tribunals: problems in the application of justice and state policy (9th–12th c.)', *Revue des Études Byzantines* 53 (1995), 165–204. It must be admitted that the present study will, due to the pressures of space and structure, not tackle the legal order head-on, but various sections will touch on the issue; see esp. Chapter 2, 85–8, 107–13, Chapter 5, 218–22, and Conclusion 250–3.

[28] For an introduction see S. F. Moore (ed.), *Law and Anthropology: A Reader* (Oxford, 2005).

arenas.[29] Firstly, it will seek to enhance legal historical scholarship by providing the first study dedicated solely to the legal sources of the 'Iconoclast era', *c*.680–850. Such an overview offers the opportunity to compare and contrast the individual works, in the hope of highlighting any connections or differences, and, by contextualising and reassessing them, open the possibility of more securely dating these difficult texts. This reappraisal shall argue that there was a deliberate programme of legal codification and reform in the eighth century, under the aegis of the Isaurian emperors (r.717–97), extending their central work the *Ecloga*. Further, this rich vein of material shall be subjected to historical questions, in particular political ones, to elucidate how the law was utilized to project imperial ideology and how it reflected the thought-world of Byzantium in its formative period, and how the position of law within the symbolic universe of the Byzantines altered. Finally, the evidence gleaned from the legal sources shall be, briefly, combined with and compared to the narrative drawn from the non-legal material. For the legal evidence provides a perspective on this crucial era external to the prism of iconoclasm, supplying much-needed nuance to the recent insights into an age masked by the miasma of iconophile polemic.[30]

This book does not in any way aspire to comprehensiveness, an especially vain ambition here given the difficulties of the source base, with which much of the work will contend. Rather it confines itself to a particular class of source, to wit legal texts. By their very nature they can offer only limited insight as to how law operated in reality. They are more records of the aspirations and thoughts of their authors, and how they saw society and the function of law within it.[31] A social history of the law in the period would perforce have to employ a far wider range of material.[32] Here the focus is instead on the ideological function of law, how it was conceived, how it structured identities,

[29] For a similar account of the growing differences between Roman Law and Roman History, and a self-described attempt to bridge the two, see E. Meyer, *Legitimacy and Law in the Roman World: Tabulae in Roman Belief and Practice* (Cambridge, 2004).

[30] For the degree of distortion in the sources due to the iconophiles, see P. Speck, *Ich bin's nicht, Kaiser Konstantin ist es gewesen: die Legenden vom Einfluss des Teufels, des Juden und des Moslem auf den Ikonoklasmus* (Bonn, 1990).

[31] See Jones, *Later Roman Empire*, vol. I, viii.

[32] Kazhdan, 'New history', 28. See also B. Stolte, 'The social function of the law', in J. Haldon (ed.), *A Social History of Byzantium* (Chichester, 2009), 76–91.

projected imperial propaganda and reflected a shifting symbolic universe. As such, the normative nature of the legal texts is ideally suited to our purpose.

Moreover, this work does not and cannot stand for a general history of the period. Even if this study could explore every aspect of law and the legal order, that is only one thread in a broader tapestry.[33] That thread, this scholar believes and this book argues, is a rich one, whose study does much to illuminate the overall picture, even to the extent of fundamentally altering our understanding of the whole. Yet it is inescapably woven with other themes, and the overall design is greater than law alone. Indeed, a central tenet underpinning this study is that law has never been and can never be an autonomous field, whatever the pretensions of some of its practitioners and theorists, but is rather an integral part of a society and culture.[34] However, because that is so, it is impossible to understand the law without its context, and so this will always be held close to the material examined. Furthermore, because law is immanent, it is never wholly inert or irrelevant to the rest of society.[35] Therefore, it is impossible to understand Byzantine society fully without some appreciation of its law and legal order. Hence an effort is made throughout both to contextualize the legal evidence and draw forth some conclusions about the society in which it operated. Given the limits of time and space, law's reciprocal relationship with power and imperial ideology is highlighted, but again it should be noted that these are only parts of a greater whole.

Furthermore, this study is not a classical legal study. In-depth analysis of important issues such as the law of dowry and inheritance has been left to legal specialists. This is unashamedly an historical study of Byzantine law, and although it is hoped to have interdisciplinary

[33] For the general concept of a 'legal order', incorporating rules, institutions, and processes, see W. Chambliss and R. Seidman, *Law, Order, and Power* (2nd edn., Reading MA, 1982).

[34] For an introduction into study of law as part of a greater cultural matrix, see inter alia S. F. Moore, *Law as Process: An Anthropological Approach* (2nd edn., Hamburg, 2000); N. Rouland, *Legal Anthropology* (London, 1994), trans. P. Planel; L. Rosen, *The Anthropology of Justice: Law as Culture in Islamic Society* (Cambridge, 1989); and L. Rosen, *Law as Culture* (Princeton, 2006).

[35] As C. Geertz, *Local Knowledge: Further Essays in Interpretative Anthropology* (3rd edn., New York, 2000), 218 expressed it, 'law is local knowledge, not placeless principle and it is constructive of social life not reflective, or anyway not just reflective, of it.'

merit, it must be admitted that it is written from the vantage-point of a particular discipline. One of the consequences is that the principal concern of legal scholars as to what extent the law of this period deviated from that of Justinian, and whether this should be classified as 'vulgar', 'provincial', or somehow affected by foreign influences, especially in the nebulous form of custom, is of only secondary interest here.[36] As it is, this author tends to the argument that the law of this period was generally that of Justinian, holding much in common with the legal practice of late antiquity, although simplified and moderated through centuries of change. However, this work argues that what was far more significant were several interlocking changes in focus within the legal discourse, in particular towards criminal law and delict; in the style and format through which those interests were expressed; and in the ideological and rhetorical architecture that framed and justified those changes.

For the authors of our texts were explicitly aware that they were operating within an established discourse, one dominated by the figure of Justinian I. Indeed, they deliberately sought to legitimize and justify their own works through reference to that great imperial legislator.[37] Moreover, these texts were self-proclaimed selections, not aiming towards comprehensiveness. What they chose to select and what they chose not to, therefore, reveals much about the relative interests of the compilers. That does not mean that the law not chosen was absent from society's legal practice, only that the authors of the legal texts thought other legislation was more important or relevant, whether for practical or ideological reasons. This process of selection and reference to past authority, therefore, illuminates continuities and changes in attitudes across the period.

Furthermore, other discourses were also shaping their work, just as they had Justinian's, and indeed all law, operating as it does within a moral, socio-economic, and cultural matrix, and not separated

[36] For the slippery concepts of 'vulgar', 'provincial', or other terms, see D. Simon, 'Provinzialrecht und Volksrecht', *FM* I (Frankfurt, 1976), 102–16; and D. Liebs, 'Roman vulgar law in late antiquity', in B. Sirks (ed.), *Aspects of law in Late Antiquity* (Oxford, 2008), 35–53. See also the classic L. Mitteis, *Reichsrecht und Volksrecht in den östlichen Provinzen des römischen Kaiserreichs* (Leipzig, 1891); and E. Levy, *West Roman Vulgar Law* (Philadelphia, 1951). For custom and law, see A. Rio (ed.), *Law, Custom, and Justice in Late Antiquity and the Early Middle Ages* (London, 2011).

[37] The vast majority of the texts examined in Chapters 2–5 describe themselves as selections from an established source, normally Justinian.

from it.[38] Above all, Christianity in general and the Old Testament in particular held sway over the law of the Iconoclast era, moulding its content, expression, and purpose.[39] Moreover, none of these discourses was static, but were evolving internally and in relation to each other, and were highly mutable in the ways they were woven together within an individual text, created in a specific time and context. For instance, both the Council in Trullo and the *Ecloga* are suffused in biblical thought and laden with exegetical quotations, yet they utilize different elements of Scripture to form markedly different ideological constructs. What discourses impinged on these texts and how they were meshed together thus further highlights the multifaceted nature of the legal evidence and the world that generated it.

The organization of this book is essentially chronological. Chapter 1 examines the Council in Trullo convoked by Justinian II in 691/2, a synod that produced the surviving kernel of orthodox canon law, and which ideologically straddles the divide between late antiquity and medieval Byzantium. Moving forward to 741, Chapter 2 explores the *Ecloga*, a new form of law-book, cast as an anthology of Justinianic law and testament to the Isaurian reimagining of their subjects as the New Israelites. Chapters 3–5 study those undated texts that have a disputed association with the *Ecloga*, arguing that they were indeed products of the half-century following its promulgation, the works being divided between those that are considered extensions of the *Ecloga*, and those argued to be complementary but separate codes.[40] Chapter 6 then briefly explores the only other legal texts definitively dated to the period, the Novels of Irene and Leo V, as evidence for the potency of the legal programme created under the

[38] See p. 8, n. 34.

[39] P. Magdalino and R. Nelson, 'Introduction', in Magdalino and Nelson (eds), *The Old Testament in Byzantium* (Washington DC, 2010), 1–38, esp. 18–22. For the significance of the Old Testament in general in Byzantine law, see P. Pieler, 'Das Alte Testament im Rechtsdenken der Byzantiner', in S. Troianos (ed.), *Analecta Atheniensia ad ius byzantinum spectantia* (Athens, 1997), 81–113. For the west, cf. R. Kottje, *Studien zum Einfluss des Alten Testaments auf Recht und Liturgie des frühen Mittelalters* (2nd edn., Bonn, 1970). For its general significance in the Iconoclast era, see G. Dagron, *Emperor and Priest: The Imperial Office in Byzantium* (Cambridge, 2003), trans. J. Birrell, 158–91.

[40] Chapters 4 and 5 are divided solely due to considerations of space, with chapter 5 dedicated solely to the *Nomos Georgikos* because of the sheer volume of scholarship dedicated to it, unlike the *Nomos Mosaikos* and *Nomos Rhodiōn Nautikos* examined in chapter 4.

Isaurians; then the Macedonian reforms, which opened a new era in legal and Byzantine history, are also discussed in a similar manner. Finally, the Conclusion seeks to summarize the function and evolution of law, both practically and symbolically, in the Iconoclast era, and then to integrate the narrative of ideological reconfiguration garnered from the legal sources with the picture conveyed by the non-legal sources. Due to the varied nature of these diverse sources, chapters 1, 2, and 6, with their relatively securely dated texts gravid with rhetoric, are examined differently from those of chapters 3–5, with their undated and more practical works. By necessity, significant space is dedicated to the task of demonstrating association between the texts of chapters 3–5 and the *Ecloga* and in positing plausible dates, an ambition that it is hoped is sufficiently achieved as to provide stable data for comparison.

However, before that is possible, one must establish what material the iconoclast age was working with, and in the case of law that means briefly surveying the legal programme of Justinian I, who utterly reworked Roman law and brought it within an imperial Christian paradigm. Finally, this introduction shall end with investigating the apparent mummification of that system under the emperor Heraclius (r.610–41), as the Roman world system, and its socio-economic, political and cultural underpinnings, buckled under the stresses of the seventh century.

THE ROMANS, THEIR LAW, AND THE JUSTINIANIC REVOLUTION

Perhaps no other society in the ancient world placed such a premium on law as the Romans.[41] To Cicero a *sine qua non* of civilization and statehood was the possession of law.[42] Moreover, the Romans thought they had created the best law, which was the crowning

[41] M.-T. Fögen, 'Reanimation of Roman law in the ninth century: remarks on reasons and results', in L. Brubaker (ed.), *Byzantium in the Ninth Century: Dead or Alive?* (Aldershot, 1998), 11–22, esp. 22.

[42] Cicero, *De legibus*, 2:12, ed. C. Keyes, *De re publica, De legibus* (Loeb Classical Library, London, 1928).

achievement in their own special arts of government that legitimized their universal rule; for as Virgil declared:

> Remember, Roman, that it is for you to rule the peoples beneath your sway! These shall be your arts: to impose peace and the rule of law; to spare the conquered and battle down the proud.[43]

Further, law was conceived as a divine institution, inherently rational, the force that governed and ordered the natural world.[44] Lack of law or illegality were therefore impious, irrational, and unnatural, the traits of barbarism. Hence, Roman civilization, the antithesis to barbarism, and Roman identity were defined to a great extent through Roman law.[45] For instance, citizenship was a legal category that carried the right to be judged under Roman law by Roman magistrates.[46] Patently, law to the Romans was inherently bound to a nexus of religion, culture, and society.

Unsurprisingly therefore, it formed a vital component in the ideological armature of the state and a seminal interface between it and the ruling elites. Power and law inhabited shared conceptual space. The holders of official power, *imperium*, were Roman magistrates who combined military, fiscal, and judicial functions; thus *imperium* was conceived as incorporating judicial authority and duties.[47] As the empire expanded, so did the reach of Roman law, as provincial governors and other magistrates brought a degree of access to the Roman legal system to the provinces.[48] Meanwhile, as the profile and power of the supreme magistrate—the emperor—increased, so did his legal and judicial role, and commensurately the more important law became as a legitimising authority for imperial power. Already in the early principate, emperors spent much of

[43] Virgil, *Aeneid*, 6.851–53; trans. C. Day Lewis (Oxford, 1986).

[44] Cicero, *De legibus*, 2:8.

[45] G. Dagron, 'Lawful society and legitimate power', in A. Laiou and D. Simon (eds), *Law and Society in Byzantium: Ninth–Twelfth Centuries* (Washington DC, 1994), 27–51, esp. 28. See also C. Ando, *Imperial Ideology and Provincial Loyalty in the Roman Empire* (London, 2000), 49; and C. Ando, *Law, Language, and Empire in the Roman Tradition* (Philadelphia, 2011).

[46] P. Garnsey, 'Roman citizenship and Roman law in the late empire', in S. Swain and M. Edwards (eds), *Approaching Late Antiquity* (Oxford, 2004), 132–55.

[47] P. Magdalino, 'Justice and finance in the Byzantine state, ninth to twelfth centuries', in Laiou and Simon (eds), *Law and Society*, 93–115, esp. 96.

[48] For the significance of hearing cases for the average governor in the Republic and early empire, and the emergence of provincial assize circuits, see G. Burton, 'Provincial procurators and the public provinces', *Chiron* 23 (1993), 15–28.

their time hearing cases.[49] Ever more pleas for guidance and judgement flooded towards the imperial centre from nervous provincial governors, reciprocated by a steady flow of rescripts, written imperial responses to specific cases, and points of law.[50] The traffic would only increase after the extension of citizenship, and therefore access to Roman law, to all freemen in 212.[51] Thus, the very mechanics of the Roman legal and administrative system, combined with the interaction of social praxis and acculturation of provincials, created a strong centripetal force that demanded law and justice from the imperial centre.[52]

Further, the centre proactively supplied law, for both symbolic and practical reasons. In particular, legislation was used to enforce, or at least pronounce, the emperor's religious and moral duties, and thereby to secure the *pax deorum*, the peace of the gods, that in Roman thought underpinned imperial success. Thus, Augustus (r.27 BC–14 AD) sought to reform the (supposedly laxer) morals of contemporary citizens through legislation encouraging marriage and children, and punishing adultery, forming a precedent for imperial marriage legislation that generations of Roman emperors would follow.[53]

[49] F. Millar, *The Emperor in the Roman World: 31 BC–AD 337* (London, 1977), 228–40.

[50] For the rescript system, and its steady growth, see T. Honoré, *Emperors and Lawyers* (London, 1981). A remarkable vista onto this constant stream between governors and emperors survives in Pliny the Younger, *Letters*, trans. P. Walsh (Oxford, 2006), Book X, where Pliny (as governor of Bithynia-Pontus) informs, badgers, and flatters Trajan over a huge array of administrative, political, judicial, and personal issues. For some of the breaks on transmission of Roman law to the provinces see, H. Galsterer, 'Roman law in the provinces: some problems of transmission', in M. Crawford (ed.), *L'impero Romano e le strutture economiche e sociali delle province* (Como, 1986), 13–27.

[51] T. Honoré, 'Roman law AD 200–400: from Cosmopolis to Rechtstaat?', in Swain and Edwards (eds), *Approaching Late Antiquity*, 109–32, esp. 113–16.

[52] For this gradual acculturation of at least provincial elites, and the complex role of law within that process, see G. Woolf, *Becoming Roman: The Origins of Provincial Civilization in Gaul* (Cambridge, 1998).

[53] S. Treggiari, 'Social status and social legislation', in A. Bowman et al. (eds), *The Cambridge Ancient History, Vol. X: The Augustan Empire, 43 B.C.–A.D. 69* (Cambridge, 1996), 873–904, esp. 886–93. Cf. J. Evans Grubbs, *Women and the Law in the Roman Empire: A Sourcebook on Marriage, Divorce and Widowhood* (Abingdon, 2002), 83–7. See also J. Evans Grubbs, *Law and Family in Late Antiquity: The Emperor Constantine's Marriage Legislation* (Oxford, 1995).

The expansion of the imperial office from the third century greatly strengthened these processes.[54] In particular, Diocletian (r.284–305) and the other emperors of the Tetrarchy ushered in an age of imperial legal activism, with a steep increase in the number of imperial laws, in all their manifold forms.[55] Similarly, the number of provinces multiplied, as therefore did the number of governors who formed the normal court of first instance.[56] Even then, governors' caseloads were immense, leading to the creation in the fourth century of the office of *defensor civitatis*, an official who heard the minor cases of his city.[57] Meanwhile, a complex appellate system emerged, with fluctuating lines of appeal to proconsular judges of *spectabilis* rank, or to the *vicarii* who headed the dioceses into which provinces were grouped, then to the *praetorian prefects* who oversaw multiple dioceses, and finally to the emperor himself.[58] Thus, both demand and supply of Roman law grew rapidly during late antiquity, its tentacles delving ever deeper into provincial life.[59] These developments did not preclude the continuing existence of customary law and regional variations in practice, but the balance tilted ever further towards Roman law.[60] More sweepingly, the conception of what law could do became ever more ambitious, famously symbolized in the *Edict on Prices*,

[54] For a general overview, see C. Kelly, 'Emperors, government and bureaucracy', in A. Cameron and P. Garnsey (eds), *The Cambridge Ancient History, Vol. XIII: The Late Empire, A.D. 337–425* (Cambridge, 1998), 138–83; and A. Cameron and P. Garnsey, *Ruling the Later Roman Empire* (London, 2004).

[55] S. Corcoran, *The Empire of the Tetrarchs: Imperial Pronouncements and Government, AD 284–324* (rev. edn., Oxford, 2000). See also M.-T. Fögen, 'Legislation in Byzantium: a political and bureaucratic technique', in A. Laiou and D. Simon (eds), *Law and Society in Byzantium: Ninth–Twelfth Centuries* (Washington DC, 1994), 53–70. For a good general overview of the different forms of law in late antiquity, and their marked increase to the point of confusion, see Harries, *Law and Empire*, 9–26.

[56] Jones, *Later Roman Empire*, vol. I, 479–84. For their functions and the significance of their judicial and police role, see C. Roueché, 'The functions of the governor in late antiquity: some observations', *Antiquité Tardive* 6 (1998), 31–6. For the general background, pressures, and performance of late antique judges, see J. Harries, 'Constructing the judge: judicial accountability and the culture of criticism in late antiquity', in R. Miles (ed.), *Constructing Identities in Late Antiquity* (London, 1999), 214–33.

[57] See Jones, *Later Roman Empire*, vol. I, 479–80.

[58] Jones, *Later Roman Empire*, vol. I, 481–4.

[59] See D. Liebs, 'Roman law', in A. Cameron et al. (eds), *The Cambridge Ancient History, Vol. XIV: Late Antiquity: Empire and Successors, A.D. 425–600* (Cambridge, 2000), 238–59.

[60] Liebs, 'Roman law'. See also C. Humfress, 'Law and custom under Rome', in Rio (ed.), *Law, Custom, and Justice* (London, 2011), 23–47.

which tried through sheer imperial fiat to determine maximum prices across the empire.[61] That it failed is a testament to the limitations of imperial power; that it was attempted in the first place evinces the almost unlimited bounds accorded to imperial authority, and how law was used to articulate its will.

With law more and more the game and language of power, the elites increasingly participated. A legal education became a favoured avenue of career advancement for late antiquity's burgeoning aristocracy of service.[62] Elites also maintained the concept of lawful power to circumscribe, obfuscate, and occasionally condemn the power of the state.[63] The 'good' emperor was supposed to obey established law, which supported the position of the established elites, not because he was forced to—for no earthly power could constrain the emperor—but because he chose to constrain himself, in good Stoic mode, respecting legal authority.[64] Emperors, who needed elite cooperation to govern such a vast empire with limited communications, engaged with this rhetoric, which was a thoroughly conservative conceit that privileged law hallowed by tradition.[65]

Furthermore, Law was imbued still further with moral and religious imperatives. Thus Diocletian used it to punish deviants who undermined the *pax deorum*.[66] With the conversion of Constantine I (r.306–37), one of those deviants, Christianity, became first the

[61] Corcoran, *The Empire of the Tetrarchs*, 205–33.

[62] For the rise of an aristocracy of service in late antiquity, see P. Heather, 'New men for new Constantines? Creating an imperial elite in the Eastern Mediterranean', in P. Magdalino (ed.), *New Constantines: The Rhythm of Imperial Renewal in Byzantium, 4th–13th Centuries* (Aldershot, 1994), 11–44; and P. Heather, 'Senators and senates', in A. Cameron and P. Garnsey (eds), *The Cambridge Ancient History Vol. XIII: The Late Empire, A.D. 337–425* (Cambridge, 1998), 184–210. For the economic and monetary aspects of this, see J. Banaji, *Agrarian Change in Late Antiquity: Gold, Labour, and Aristocratic Dominance* (2nd edn., Oxford, 2007).

[63] For examples in the reign of Justinian, see p. 18 n. 84. In general see Harries, *Law and Empire*, 25–6.

[64] See e.g. Agapetus, *Ekthesis*, ed. R. Riedinger, *Der Fürstenspiegel des Kaisers Justinianos* (Athens, 1995), 1, 27. For a good discussion of Agapetus and his sources, see P. Bell, *Three Political Voices from the Age of Justinian* (Liverpool, 2009), 27–49.

[65] For the need for cooperation between elites and the state, see P. Brown, *Power and Persuasion in Late Antiquity* (Madison, 1992), esp. 3–32; and Kelly, *Ruling the Later Roman Empire*.

[66] For an example, see S. Corcoran, 'The sins of the fathers: a neglected constitution of Diocletian on incest', *The Journal of Legal History* 21 (2000), 1–34.

favoured imperial cult and then the official state religion.[67] On one level, this merely rearticulated the fundamental notion that the Roman state was founded on the goodwill of the divine.[68] Yet the gradual and piecemeal Christianization of society and imperial rhetoric progressively impinged on Roman law.[69] Whole new fields of social action opened with the rise of the Church, sucking in the emperor and his legal apparatus to regulate ecclesiastical and monastic life.[70] The Church also acted as an interest group, demanding imperial action on its favoured policies. Moreover, Christian rhetoric, both in a generalized form and in specific exaltation of a new repository of ideas and expressions, viz. the Bible, exerted a gravitational pull that slowly but surely dragged Roman society and the imperial system within its own paradigm.[71] Roman law, deeply ingrained as it was in classical thought, retained a degree of ideological autonomy, yet it could not help but be affected to some degree.

By the sixth century, these interlocking processes had cemented Roman law as a vital constituent part of Roman political, social, and cultural discourse.[72] Yet its very success had given rise to problems. In particular, the ever-expanding mass of imperial constitutions and disagreement over juristic authorities threatened to sink Roman law under its own weight. Already under Diocletian this had led to the

[67] For a general introduction to Constantine's reign, see N. Lenski (ed.), *The Cambridge Companion to the Age of Constantine* (Cambridge, 2006); see especially the chapter by C. Humfress, 'Civil law and social life', 205–25.

[68] For the measure of continuity versus change in late antique religion and politics, see J. H. W. G. Liebeschuetz, *Continuity and Change in Roman Religion* (Oxford, 1979), esp. 291–304.

[69] For the piecemeal process and impact of Christianization, see R. MacMullen, *Christianizing the Roman Empire (A.D.100–400)* (New Haven, 1984); and R. MacMullen, *Christianity and Paganism in the Fourth to Eighth Centuries* (New Haven, 1997). For the Christianization of imperial rhetoric, see A. Cameron, *Christianity and the Rhetoric of Empire: The Development of Christian Discourse* (Berkeley, 1991). For the broader impact of monotheism on imperial culture and ideology, see G. Fowden, *Empire to Commonwealth: Consequences of Monotheism in Late Antiquity* (Princeton, 1993).

[70] For the pivotal role of bishops in particular, for the reign of Constantine see H. Drake, *Constantine and the Bishops: The Politics of Intolerance* (Baltimore, 2000); for late antiquity in general see C. Rapp, *Holy Bishops in Late Antiquity: The Nature of Christian Leadership in an Age of Transition* (Berkeley, 2005).

[71] See in particular, R. Markus, *The End of Ancient Christianity* (Cambridge, 1990).

[72] For different measures of the extent to which Roman law had become ingrained in late antique Roman society, see R. Mathisen (ed.), *Law, Society and Authority in Late Antiquity* (Oxford, 2001).

Gregorian and *Hermogenian* codifications, comprised primarily of imperial rescripts.[73] Then, under the auspices of Theodosius II (r.408–50), the more famous and ambitious *Theodosian Code* was compiled between 429–38, collecting and arranging imperial constitutions dating back to Constantine I.[74] This was the first time the imperial government had attempted publicly to collect its laws.[75] Moreover, by deliberately beginning with the first Christian emperor, the *Theodosian Code* burnished its Christian credentials, made the more explicit in the culminating sixteenth book of the code, dedicated entirely to religious law.[76] Roman imperial power was thus intimately combined with both law and Christianity. Yet this great achievement had originally been designed as a grander project, the reduction of both *ius*—legal principles established mainly by a variety of jurists in the early empire—and *leges*—primary legislation—into one definitive work.[77] That task proved too great, but the *Theodosian Code* would become a model followed by emperors and kings, and would be the principal repository of Roman law for the post-Roman west until the eleventh century.[78]

Interestingly, the potency of the law as a politico-cultural system is perhaps best revealed in the fragmentation of the western empire in the fifth century, where Roman elites had to manage a transference of political power to 'barbarian' kings.[79] One central coping mechanism was to attempt to bind the new powers within the ideological structure of Roman law.[80] For instance, Orosius narrates the famous scene that the Gothic leader Athaulf in the early fifth century had once planned to replace *Romania* with *Gothia*, but had come to realize:

[73] See Corcoran, *The Empire of the Tetrarchs*, 25–42.

[74] *Codex Theodosianus*, ed. T. Mommsen and P. Meyer, *Theodosiani libri XVI cum constitutionibus Sirmondianis*, 2 vols (Berlin, 1905).

[75] Matthews, *Laying Down the Law*, 17.

[76] For the *Theodosian Code*'s link with Christianity, see J. Harries and I. Wood (eds), *The Theodosian Code: Studies in the Imperial Law of Late Antiquity* (2nd edn., London, 2010), 95–158.

[77] Harries, *Law and Empire*, 22.

[78] See the varied papers in Harries and Wood, *Theodosian Code*, 159–216.

[79] For the general process, see G. Halsall, *Barbarian Migrations and the Roman West, 376–568* (Cambridge, 2007). Cf. P. Heather, *The Fall of the Roman Empire* (London, 2005).

[80] P. Wormald, 'Lex scripta and verbum regis: legislation and Germanic kingship, from Euric to Cnut', in P. Sawyer and I. Wood (eds), *Early Medieval Kingship* (Leeds, 1977), 105–38.

> that the Goths, because of their unbridled barbarism, were utterly incapable of obeying laws, and yet believing that the state ought not to be deprived of laws without which a state is not a state, he chose to seek for himself the glory of restoring the renown of the Roman name by the power of the Goths . . .[81]

This deal between regional, Roman elites and barbarian warlords, where the latter offered protection in return for the legitimizing support of the former, was replicated across the west, and in the field of law led to the creation of numerous law codes, the successor kings imitating Roman emperors by bringing good law to their subjects.[82]

Thus when Justinian I became emperor in 527, he was presented with a complex legal situation.[83] The potency of law as an imperial symbol was unquestionable. Indeed, it was perhaps the pre-eminent language of power in the Roman imperial system. Yet it retained a degree of ideological autonomy, especially in the uncodified *ius*, which separated it from the emperor, and could be used to circumscribe and criticize him. Indeed, in the contemporary works of John Lydus and Procopius, it was used in such a way, indirectly and hesitantly in the former, blatantly in the latter.[84] Moreover, Roman law was a discourse encroached upon by an increasingly dominant landed-elite within the empire, and, to Justinian's mind, upstart barbarians in the fallen west. Further, its autonomy was also bound

[81] Orosius, *History Against the Pagans*, ed. C. Zangemeister, *Pauli Orosii Historiam adversam Paganos* (Vienna, 1882), 7.43; trans. I. Raymond, *The Seven Books of History against the Pagans* (New York, 1936), 395–6, reprinted in M. Maas, *Readings in Late Antiquity: A Sourcebook* (Abingdon, 2000), 303. Cf. the similar and contemporary sentiments of Rutilius Namantianus, *De reditu suo*, ed. and trans. A. Duff, *Minor Latin Poets* (Loeb Classical Library, London, 1934), I: 63–6.

[82] See Wormald, 'Lex scripta'; and J. Matthews, 'Roman law and barbarian identity', originally in S. Mitchell and G. Greatrex (eds), *Ethnicity and Culture in Late Antiquity* (London, 2000), 31–44, reprinted in Matthews, *Roman Perspectives*, 327–42.

[83] The best descriptions of Justinian's legal programme are T. Honoré, *Tribonian* (London, 1978); and C. Humfress, 'Law and legal practice in the age of Justinian', in M. Maas (ed.), *The Cambridge Companion to the Age of Justinian* (Cambridge, 2005), 161–84.

[84] For Lydus, see M. Maas, *John Lydus and the Roman Past: Antiquarianism and Politics in the Age of Justinian* (London, 1992). For Procopius see A. Kaldellis, *Procopius of Caesarea: Tyranny, History, and Philosophy at the End of Antiquity* (Philadelphia, 2004), 150–9, 223–8. Cf. A. Cameron, *Procopius and the Sixth Century* (London, 1985), esp. 242–60.

to its classical, pagan heritage, and although Christianity had shaped legal discourse, it had never fully integrated and subjugated it within its own paradigm. Finally, it yet again groaned under the accumulated weight of legislation added since the *Theodosian Code*, allowing confusion and therefore increasing the opportunity for elite obfuscation.[85] To the Christian autocrat Justinian, who sought to reassert imperial power against barbarians and overweening elites, none of this was acceptable.[86]

Justinian's response was immediate. In 528 he empanelled a commission tasked to integrate the *Gregorian*, *Hermogenian*, and *Theodosian Codes*, and all subsequent constitutions, into one work; to remove antiquated and contradictory legislation; and to promulgate the product 'under our auspicious name'.[87] All previous legislation was replaced by this *Codex Justinianus*, which homogenized imperial law into one voice and will, that of Justinian. Indeed, Justinian explicitly had an eye on exceeding the work of his predecessors, announcing that:

> Those things which seemed to many former Emperors to require correction, but which none of them ventured to carry into effect, We have decided to accomplish at the present time with the assistance of Almighty God; and to diminish litigation by the revision of the multitude of constitutions . . .[88]

Illuminatingly, imperial pretension and divine aid came before practicality. That is not to say that the revised code was not designed with a practical aim, for it manifestly was. Indeed, Justinian justified his programme by arguing that making the law clearer and more accessible, through reducing scattered works into one text, would ease the wheels of justice and fulfil his duty of care towards his subjects.[89] Yet a self-declared aim was also to associate all previous constitutions with Justinian's own name, indeed almost to subsume their authority into Justinian's own. Thus, individual constitutions would carry the name and the authority of the emperors who promulgated them, but they would now also be under the name of Justinian, who would

85 C. *Const. Haec*, pr.

86 For a good overview of Justinian's reign and the character of his rule, see J. Evans, *The Age of Justinian: The Circumstances of Imperial Power* (London, 1996).

87 C. *Const. Haec*, pr.

88 C. *Const. Haec*, pr.; trans. S. Scott, *The Civil Law*, 17 vols (Cincinnati, 1932), vol. 12, 3.

89 C. *Const. Haec*, 3.

gather, reshape, and correct them, turning the babble of legislation into a harmony conducted by Justinian. From the outset, then, Justinian sought not just to organize and restore the past and the glories of his predecessors, but to surpass them.

The commission managed to produce a first edition of the *Justinianic Code* in little over a year, ready for promulgation in 529.[90] This remarkable speed was an undeniable propaganda coup for Justinian and encouraged the next and far more ambitious stage in the programme.[91] For in 530 a second commission was empowered to collect, edit, and reduce the massive and variegated bulk of *ius* into a delimited, unified, and definitive collection called the *Digest*.[92] Anything not included was invalidated and inadmissible in court. We are told that the commission inspected 3,000,000 lines of Latin contained in 1,500 books—that is, the subdivision of texts rather than whole works, which was then replaced by the 150,000 lines in the 50 books of the *Digest*.[93] This was a vast achievement; indeed the *Digest* is the longest single work that survives from antiquity.[94] What is even more remarkable was the speed of composition, taking little more than three years, a swiftness that Justinian ascribed to divine intervention.[95] Through this act, Justinian had symbolically transformed an autonomous discourse composed over centuries into a branch of the imperial will.[96] The contents of the *Digest* were given the force of imperial law, for they had:

> as much authority as if . . . [they] had been uttered by our own inspired mouth; for we ascribe everything to ourselves, since it is from us that all their authority is derived; and one who amends something that is not done accurately deserves more praise than the original author.[97]

[90] *Codex Iustinianus*, ed. P. Krüger, vol. 2 of *Corpus iuris civilis* (11th edn., Berlin, 1929).

[91] Indeed it is the only element in Justinian's legal programme that repeatedly breaks into the literary sources of the period, e.g. John Malalas, *Chronicle*, ed. H. Thurn, *Chronographia* (Berlin and New York, 2000), 18.38.

[92] *Digest*, ed. P. Krüger and T. Mommsen, vol. 1 of *Corpus iuris civilis* (16th edn., Berlin, 1928).

[93] *Digest Const. Tanta*, 1. For the possible method of the *Digest*'s construction see T. Honoré, *Justinian's Digest: Character and Compilation* (Oxford, 2010).

[94] For comparison, it dwarfs in size both the Bible and the Koran.

[95] *Digest, Const. Tanta*, pr.–1.

[96] C. Pazdernik, 'Justinianic ideology and the power of the past', in Maas, *Age of Justinian*, 185–212, esp. 200.

[97] *Digest, Const. Tanta*, 6., trans. A. Watson, *The Digest of Justinian* (Philadelphia, 1985).

To ensure continued imperial control over interpretation, commentaries and paraphrases were prohibited, and translations (for the explication of the Latin *Digest* to a predominantly Greek-speaking world) were permissible only if they followed the word order of the original. Thus through the *Codex* and the *Digest*, both primary legislation and judicial thought were thereafter ineluctably defined by and conjoined to the imperial office in general, and Justinian in particular.

Moreover, the Justinianic programme extended into legal education, which was thoroughly overhauled and branded with the emperor's name.[98] Law students were even rechristened 'New Justinians'.[99] As an introductory text, Justinian ordered the creation of a textbook, the *Institutes*, 'the cradle of the law', which also enjoyed the force of law.[100] Together with the *Codex* and the *Digest*, these three works comprised the entirety of set material for five years of legal study, as they encompassed:

> The whole of [law] from beginning to end . . . this single branch of knowledge, issuing from us at the present time, will achieve an admirable perfection, a thing which has happened in almost none of the other branches of learning, the number of which is infinite, however worthless some may be.[101]

Justinian thus trumpeted his achievement as almost outdoing the whole of human intellectual endeavour. That programme reached full circle with the release of a second edition of the *Codex* in 534, which incorporated the unprecedented flood of legal change that had threatened to render it obsolete, although it was scarcely a few years old.

In the space of six years Justinian had revolutionized Roman law, substantively, stylistically, and ideologically. Moreover, having created a purified imperial tool, he used law to attempt to reshape the Roman state and society, issuing a prolific stream of novels, covering everything from public administration and monastic regulations to homosexuality and the price of vegetables.[102] In the end, that effort

98 *Digest, Const. Omnem*. See Humfress, 'Law and legal practice', 171–6.

99 *Digest, Const. Omnem*, 2.

100 *Institutes*, ed. P. Krüger and T. Mommsen, vol. 1 of *Corpus iuris civilis* (16th edn., Berlin, 1928). Quote from *Const. Imperatoriam*, 3; trans. P. Birks and G. McLeod, *Justinian's Institutes* (London, 1987), 33.

101 *Const. Tanta*, 5; trans. Watson, *Digest*.

102 *Novellae*, ed. R. Schöll and G. Kroll, vol. 3 of *Corpus iuris civilis* (6th edn., Berlin, 1928). For the above examples, see inter alia N.8, 4, 77, 64. For that reform programme and its essential continuity with the codifications that preceded it, see

foundered on the rocks of the Persian War and plague, yet Justinian's combined works, known from the eleventh century as the *Corpus iuris civilis*, transformed Roman law and forever imprinted Justinian's name on it.[103]

The particularities of the substantive alterations introduced by Justinian are beyond the scope of this enquiry, besides noting the obvious but important point that Justinian did not confine himself to the rearticulation of an intellectual discourse, but in numerous ways altered legal education and the justice administration, and designed the whole legal apparatus towards affirming his own power and position, and for reforming Roman society practically and morally. The more pertinent changes to this study concern the ideological transformation of Roman law within the symbolic universe of late antiquity and how the law was utilized as a medium of imperial representation.

Several significant tropes can be found throughout Justinian's laws, in particular emphasizing the Roman past and the importance of Roman law within it.[104] A repeated topos, especially prevalent in the early legislation, is the duopoly of war and law, most famously expressed in the *Constitution of Imperial Majesty* confirming the *Institutes*, which began with the declaration:

> Imperial majesty should not only be graced with arms but also armed with laws, so that good government may prevail in time of war and peace alike.[105]

M. Maas, 'Roman history and Christian ideology in Justinianic reform legislation', *DOP* 40 (1986), 17–31.

[103] For the eventual failure of Justinian's reform programme, see P. Sarris, *Economy and Society in the Age of Justinian* (Cambridge, 2006), 219–22. For the importance of warfare between Rome and Persia in shaping this period, see J. Howard-Johnston, 'The two great powers in late antiquity: a comparison', in A. Cameron (ed.), *The Byzantine and Early Islamic Near East II: States, Resources and Armies* (Princeton, 1995), 157–226.

[104] See Maas, 'Roman history and Christian ideology'. For a systematic analysis of the tropes of Roman law, see H. Hunger, *Prooimion: Elemente der byzantinischen Kaiseridee in den Arengen der Urkunden* (Vienna, 1964). For the importance of legal prologues, see M.-T. Fögen, 'The legislator's monologue: notes on the history of prologues', *Chicago-Kent Law Review* 70 (1994–5), 1593–620. For the general importance of Roman law in imperial rhetoric, see W. Voss, *Recht und Rhetorik in den Kaisergesetzen der Spätantike* (Frankfurt, 1982).

[105] *Institutes, Const. Imperatoriam*, pr., trans. Birks and McLeod, 33. For this dichotomy of war and law, see D. Simon, 'Legislation as both a world order and a legal order', in Laiou and Simon, *Law and Society*, 1–25, 1.

In this, Justinian was fulfilling the established, classical model for emperors to provide good justice and victory. He deliberately coupled his military and legal exploits as part of a programme of *renovatio imperii*, 'imperial restoration', a well-worn imperial trope stretching back to Augustus.[106] Thus, Justinian sought to revive Rome's glorious past, and thereby exceed the deeds of his immediate predecessors who had allowed that glory to slip, through decline in the law and the empire's military prowess. Indeed, he attempted to commandeer both legitimizing discourses, almost to the point of monopolizing them. In the legal sphere, at least, this attempt was broadly successful, reaching a crescendo when Justinian declared himself the *nomos empsuchos*, 'the living law', to which God had subjected all law, an old Hellenic concept never before claimed by a Roman emperor.[107] In doing so, Justinian completed his appropriation of Roman law to the imperial office in general, and himself in particular. Roman law had essentially become the word of Justinian.

Furthermore, Justinian grounded both his conception of the imperial office and his reformed Roman law within an explicitly Christian framework.[108] Divine intervention was given the credit for both the initiative and completion of the reforms.[109] Emperor and law were divinely instituted, God having established Justinian to rule through law.[110] Heaven had also ordained a world in a state of constant flux, necessitating reciprocal imperial action from an ever-watchful and caring emperor, fulfilling his duties through the medium of law.[111] Thus, Justinian positioned himself and his reforms as the fulcrum in Providence's terrestrial plans. Signalling this, imperial legislation concerning the Church and dogma was gathered in the first book of the *Codex*, symbolically founding the rest of the text on Christian underpinnings. Further, the *Digest* collated the substantive principles of Roman law, and although not altering them, harmonized them within a work constructed by divine aid, for a divinely

[106] Honoré, *Tribonian*, 18–19.

[107] N.105.4.2. For the development of this term, see F. Dvornik, *Early Christian and Byzantine Political Philosophy*, 2 vols (Washington DC, 1966), vol. 2, 716–22.

[108] Humfress, 'Law and legal practice', 167–71; Maas, 'Roman history and Christian ideology', 18.

[109] Humfress, 'Law and legal practice', 168.

[110] Pazdernik, 'Justinianic ideology', 200.

[111] Pazdernik, 'Justinianic ideology', 201.

appointed lawgiver, and issued in Christ's name.[112] Having affirmed the law's Christian credentials, Justinian used it to assert his authority within the Church, and over the moral and religious lives of his subjects. A flood of legislation affected ecclesiastical and monastic life, and would indeed eventually become part of eastern canon law, while the canons of the first four ecumenical councils were given the force of civil law.[113] Manifestly, Justinian felt able and duty-bound to regulate both *imperium* and *sacerdotium*, and that civil law was the medium to use.[114]

As Justinian's reign progressed, Christian rhetoric and themes increasingly dominated a shrinking legal outpouring. The classicisms contained in the prologues to Justinian's initial works, and oft attributed to his *quaestor* Tribonian, faded with the latter's death in 542.[115] The number of novels issued decreased dramatically in the 540s as, due to circumstances, Justinian was constantly fire-fighting, which left little time or political capital for reform.[116] Those novels that were promulgated focused predominantly on the Church and religious affairs. Indeed, the latter half of Justinian's reign saw imperial legitimacy drawn ever more from ceremonial and patronage over church and sacred materials, a movement followed and deepened by Justinian's successors.[117] Finally, in the reign of Heraclius (r.610–41), the flow of novels appears to have ceased altogether.[118]

Yet before we turn our attention to that transformation, we should summarize the effects of the Justinianic legal revolution. Firstly, Roman law became indelibly associated not just with the imperial office but also with the figure of Justinian himself. For the Byzantines Justinian was *the* Roman lawgiver, the analogue to the biblical Moses, and any later imperial legislator was perceived as following in his footsteps.[119] Furthermore, Justinian's codifications successfully delimited what was

[112] Humfress, 'Law and legal practice', 168. [113] N.131.1.

[114] See N.6.pr. For the stridency of *imperium*'s domination over *sacerdotium*, see Dvornik, *Byzantine Political Philosophy*, vol. 2, 817; for general interaction of the two concepts, see 724–850.

[115] Honoré, *Tribonian*, 251–4. Cf. Maas, 'Roman history and Christian ideology', 27.

[116] Only 31 extant edicts or novels date from 544–65, compared to 142 for 533–43, see Sarris, *Economy and Society*, 219 n. 107.

[117] A. Cameron, 'Images of authority: elites and icons in late sixth century Byzantium', *Past and Present* 84 (1979), 3–35.

[118] Haldon, *Seventh Century*, 255.

[119] G. Prinzing, 'Das Bild Iustinians I. in der Überlieferung der Byzantiner vom 7. bis 15. Jahrhundert', *FM* VII (Frankfurt, 1986), 1–99, esp. 54–67.

Roman law. The *Corpus* thereon comprised the bedrock texts of legal study and practice—at least theoretically.[120] Moreover, Roman law was now definitively incorporated under a grander Christian paradigm, ultimately drawing its moral authority from it and not the classical world.

However, in many respects this was an unfinished revolution with unintended consequences. Justinian never gathered his own novels—an enterprise left to a succession of private initiatives—nor incorporated them into a new *Codex*. Indeed, there was no defined *Corpus*, for Justinian's laws were dispersed across multiple texts, in both Latin and Greek. Further, the *Corpus*' very scale would have generated numerous difficulties, even had it been collated into one text in one language. In an effort to overcome the linguistic and textual barriers, a succession of sixth-century lawyers, called the *antecessores*, despite prima facie prohibitions, proceeded to create commentaries, translations, and paraphrases to aid in the teaching of law students.[121] These works, written in Greek and designed for ease of use and therefore tending to simplify Justinianic law and provide concrete examples to explain it, increasingly became the law that was practised rather than the difficult *Corpus*.[122] Thus, in a process of legal exegesis, Justinianic law was translated, modified, and disseminated among a huge variety of texts. Ironically then, the Justinianic revolution's codification and appropriation of law, explicitly designed to clarify the legal situation, over the following two centuries led to a private reworking and scattering of Justinianic law. All the while, however, the central figure of Justinian was affirmed, and the *Corpus* remained the pivot of legal endeavour, just as Scripture was the lodestar of theology. Indeed, there was a growing conservatism within the legal discourse, just as there was in the rest of late sixth-century Roman society, one that emphasized collection and preservation over innovation.[123] By the early seventh century, that process culminated in the embalming of the Justinianic system, the mechanics and significance of which we shall now turn to.

[120] Scheltema, 'Byzantine law', 55.

[121] For the best account of this, see Scheltema, 'Byzantine law', 55–60.

[122] Scheltema, 'Byzantine law', 60. See also L. Burgmann, 'Die Gegenwart der Vergangenheit im Byzantinische Recht', *Settimane di studio del centro italiano di studi sull'alto medioevo* 46 (1999), 591–612, esp. 591–2.

[123] For a similar contemporary process in theology, see P. Gray, 'Through the tunnel with Leontius of Jerusalem: the sixth-century transformation of theology', in P. Allen and E. Jeffreys (eds), *The Sixth Century: End or Beginning?* (Brisbane, 1996), 187–96, esp. 195–6.

THE NOVELS OF HERACLIUS AND THE SYMBOLIC FOSSILIZATION OF THE JUSTINIANIC SYSTEM

> Neither the purple nor the ruling Sceptre can embellish imperial majesty as much as pious deeds, which are inherently praiseworthy. For that attribute alone renders both greater honour to the rulers, and provides the common interest for the good inhabitants.[124]

This declaration of Heraclius' Novel IV marks a legal and political watershed.[125] This novel, promulgated on 24 April 629, is the last extant until the reign of Irene (797–802).[126] The apparent ending of a hitherto fundamental aspect of lawmaking and tool of imperial power would be important in itself. However, this novel also includes the first indisputable use of the title *Basileus* in any official media.[127] Indeed, the dispute over the significance of this title has completely overshadowed any consideration of the content of both this novel and the three that preceded it.[128] Yet the collection provides a rare glance at the slow evolution of imperial rhetoric under Heraclius, and more especially its inherent conservatism and continued dependence on the system established by Justinian. Thus, the legal evidence neatly fits the broader picture of an emperor who is increasingly seen as conservative, attempting to preserve and restore the old regime, with change forced from without, not only by the natural progression of time (a theme acknowledged in the novels themselves), but also by

[124] Heraclius, *Novel* IV.9–12; ed. J. Konidaris, 'Die Novellen des Kaisers Herakleios', *FM* V (Frankfurt, 1982), 33–106; *Novel* IV 84–94.

[125] Normally these novels are allotted a nondescript place in the secondary literature as appendices to Justinian, before a new legal age with the *Ecloga*. The unspoken assumption is that they are unimportant parts of the Justinianic age.

[126] See Chapter 6.

[127] A fact first noted by L. Bréhier, 'Le protocole impérial depuis la fondation de l'empire Romain jusqu'à la prise de Constantinople par les Turcs,' *Comptes-rendus des séances de l'Académie des Inscriptions et Belles-Lettres* 1 (1905), 177–82; expanded in L. Bréhier, 'L'origine des titres impériaux à Byzance', *BZ* 15 (1906), 161–78.

[128] For example, the recent scholarly, and generally excellent, biography by W. Kaegi, *Heraclius: Emperor of Byzantium* (Cambridge, 2003), mentions the adoption of the title (186), but nothing about the other novels. Konidaris' edition is listed only as a secondary source. The point is not to criticize this useful work, but to highlight the general lack of use—balanced by occasional misuse—of law in general Byzantine history, where one aspect of a source has been extracted from its context.

the extreme pressures of Heraclius' reign.[129] Therefore, before examining the issues of titulature and the apparent cessation of imperial legislation, the novels themselves shall be briefly surveyed and analysed.

Novel I was issued on 1 May 612, only two years after Heraclius had seized power.[130] He was therefore still cementing his position, something made more critical and difficult by the rapidly deteriorating Persian War.[131] This is reflected in the novel, for the rhetoric is highly conventional and aimed at the Church. The addressee, as in all the novels, is the Patriarch Sergius, a key member of Heraclius' regime, and the topic is ecclesiastical. The novel simply reaffirms a decree of Sergius regarding the number of clergy in the Hagia Sophia and the church of the Theotokos on the Blachernae. Essentially both the novel and Sergius' decree dealt with the regulations of Justinian's N.3, a point explicitly stated, which needed amendment due to natural evolution.[132] Apparently too many clergy had managed to find employment in the principal churches of Constantinople, the same issue as Justinian's legislation, but by 612, the possibility of reducing numbers to the Justinianic stipulations was considered impossible. Therefore, the novel altered the permitted numbers slightly upwards, while also regulating the Blachernae.[133] The issue was thus a minor technical change, initiated by the patriarch, with the novel's principal purpose to support and legitimize the patriarch's actions, and to alter a legal restriction that had become outdated. Rhetorically the novel was couched in traditional ideas of maintaining good order and removing confusion.[134] In particular, it was necessary for the Church to be well ordered to ensure the well-being of the State.[135] In this, Heraclius was fulfilling the imperial role established by Justinian, essentially mildly modifying the established corpus as needed, while specifically cementing the vital political relationship of a usurper with the patriarch.

[129] For an excellent recent study, with this theme as its recurring leitmotif, see the collection of G. Reinink and B. Stolte (eds), *The Reign of Heraclius (610–41): Crisis and Confrontation* (Leuven, 2002).

[130] Konidaris, 'Novellen', 62–72; discussion 94–9.

[131] For Heraclius' early moves to cement his position, see Kaegi, *Heraclius*, 58–99.

[132] Heraclius, *Novel* I.39–42.

[133] Konidaris, 'Novellen', 98 provides a comparative table of numbers between Justinian's and Heraclius' ordinances.

[134] Heraclius, *Novel* I.12–15.

[135] Heraclius, *Novel* I.15–18.

Novel II, promulgated in 617, continued these themes.[136] Again, it self-consciously regulated an aspect of Justinian's N.3, this time the issue of clerics illegally transferring to positions in the capital or holding multiple posts. The concerns are the same: the potential financial burden on the Church; the illegality of pluralism and unauthorized transfers; and the potential degradation in the status of clerics and monks undermining their prime utility to the state, namely prayer. The only real difference is the context of those fleeing the advancing Persians seeking a secure living in Constantinople. The worry of fleeing ecclesiastics or, worse, fraudulent impostors using bribery, threats, or intrigue to gain office was highlighted, and entwined with the threat of disorder. As a remedy, the novel proclaimed that no clerics should come to Constantinople without the patriarch's permission, stipulating a penalty of five pounds of gold and suspension for those who flouted the decree. Again, the patriarch's authority over clerics is emphasized. Like Novel I, this represented mere maintenance of the established order, if in straitened and deteriorating circumstances.

Novel III of 619 is even less radical, returning to the same topic as Novel I.[137] Seemingly, various practical problems had arisen in the intervening seven years. Clerics were resisting attempts to swap them between churches, while worthy applicants for places were discouraged by threat of dismissal. In essence, the attempt to cut costs through legislation was recognized to have failed, and Heraclius gave the patriarch total discretion over personnel, thus effectively abrogating Novel I.[138]

These three novels tell a common story. There was a steady rise of personnel in the principal churches of the capital, no doubt attracted by the security of tenure and legal privileges in a time of growing uncertainty. The effort to staunch the flow was led by the patriarch, with the emperor providing legal support when required. Time and circumstance were rendering the specifics of particular Justinianic regulations obsolete, necessitating imperial patching. There is here no trace of imperial activism. Rather, the activism of Justinian had brought imperial regulation so firmly into the heart of ecclesiastical affairs, especially those of the capital, that in the early seventh century, reform at the least had to be affirmed through

[136] Konidaris, 'Novellen', 72–8; discussion 100–102.
[137] Konidaris, 'Novellen', 80–4; discussion 99–100.
[138] Konidaris, 'Novellen', 100.

imperial legislation. Fundamentally these novels tell of an emperor uninterested in wide-scale reform, but rather looking to obtain the aid of the Church to secure his base, and hopefully the help of heaven, while trying to limit growing costs.[139]

Ideologically, Heraclius fulfilled the role constructed by Justinian of the constant legislator, keeping the law relevant, if now primarily focused on the well-being of the Church. Indeed, the only mention of any emperor in the body of the novels is that of Justinian twice, Heraclius thus deliberately underlining his function as preserving the great emperor's legal endeavours.[140] Therefore, as Stolte states, this was 'routine maintenance of the Justinianic building, for which the tool of the novella constitutio in its various forms is selected as a matter of course'.[141] Indeed, Heraclius, a usurper, may well have been deliberately promoting an aura of conservatism to downplay his own novelty, and connect himself with the legitimacy of the past, something more noted by scholars concerning his appropriation of Constantine I.[142] In the medium of law, that meant posing as the upholder of the Justinianic tradition.

Novel IV, issued a decade later in 629, does, however, represent change. Although dealing with issues regulated by Justinian, these are not mentioned.[143] More importantly, the novel concerns a far broader remit than the previous three, viz. the *praescriptio fori*, the clergy's right to be judged by ecclesiastical courts.[144] In civil cases, Justinian had granted clerics broad privileges, which were here affirmed and widened. Clerics and monks of the diocese of Constantinople could still only be judged by the patriarch or his nominee. Now, however, clerics or monks of other dioceses, who happened to be in Constantinople, were no longer required either to return to their diocese or to

[139] For Heraclius as essentially conservative, with the times forcing a degree of change, see J. Haldon, 'The reign of Heraclius: a context for change', in Reinink and Stolte (eds), *The Reign of Heraclius* (2002), 1–16.

[140] Justinian is mentioned at I.39 and II.24.

[141] B. Stolte, 'The challenge of change: notes on the legal history of the reign of Heraclius', in Reinink and Stolte (eds), *The Reign of Heraclius* (2002), 191–204.

[142] Famously he named his first son Heraclius new Constantine. See Nicephorus, *Breviarium*, ed. C. Mango, *Nikephoros, Short History* (Washington DC, 1990), 5. For the role of Constantine in Roman and Byzantine imperial ideology, see Magdalino (ed.), *New Constantines*.

[143] N.83 and 123.

[144] For the great extension of this right to special courts by various social groups, see Jones, *Later Roman Empire*, vol. I, 484–94.

be judged by the prefect of the east; instead they were to be judged in Constantinople by the patriarch, the prefect, or the emperor. The chain of jurisdiction and appeal was clarified, with bishops to be judged by their metropolitan, and metropolitans by the patriarch. More importantly, criminal cases now also came under the automatic authority of the patriarch or his nominee, unless he wished to refer them to the civil court. As before, if charges were proved, the guilty were to be punished by both canon and civil law, yet ecclesiastical judges were now given competence to enforce civil punishments. Together, these represent a significant, if hardly radical, widening of the Justinianic system.

The manuscript tradition underlines these themes.[145] The normal ordering is IV-I-III-II.[146] This is the natural order, for Novel IV is by far the most important and general of the novels. Moreover, I–III effectively form a unit as both deal with the same issue, with III essentially abrogating I. Furthermore, the novels overwhelmingly survive in manuscripts of canon law, often as an appendix to the *Collectio Tripartita*, a collection of Justinianic law broadly pertaining to ecclesiastical and religious matters, probably compiled in the late sixth century.[147] In addition, the *Collectio 87 capitulorum* and *Collectio 25 capitulorum*, both also being collections of Justinianic law touching on ecclesiastical issues but earlier than the *Collectio Tripartita*, are frequent companions.[148] Evidently, for the compilers of these manuscripts, the Heraclian novels were seen as the adjuncts and minor amendments to the Justinianic corpus that they were.

However, Novel IV's broader, if hardly revolutionary, changes were expressed through rhetoric far more strident than in the previous novels. As cited above, pious deeds were highlighted as the preeminent adornment for emperors. This novel was a 'starting point or foundation for our pious legislation', acting as a gift to God.[149] The

[145] Konidaris, 'Novellen', 35–9. [146] Konidaris, 'Novellen', 34.

[147] *Collectio Tripartita*, ed. N. Van der Wal and B. Stolte, *Collectio Tripartita: Justinian on Religious and Ecclesiastical Affairs* (Groningen, 1994).

[148] *Collectio 87 capitulorum*, ed. I. B. Pitra, *Iuris ecclesiastici graecorum historia et monumenta*, vol. 2 (Rome, 1868), 385–405; *Collectio 25 capitulorum*, ed. G. Heimbach, *Anekdota*, vol. 2 (Leipzig, 1840), 145–201. For brief introductions, see the entries 'Collectio Tripartita', 'Collectio 87 capitulorum', and 'Collectio 25 capitulorum' in the *ODB* (all entries by A. Schminck).

[149] Heraclius, *Novel* IV.15–16.

protection and patronage of clergy and monks was posited as vital to imperial success. This novel presented itself as both a renewal of the old state and the beginning of a new one.

The confident tone of renewal and refoundation was echoed in the change in titulature employed by Heraclius. As is repeatedly noted in general studies, this novel included the first extant use of the phrase *pistoi en Christō Basileis*, 'faithful in Christ, Emperors', to describe Heraclius and his co-emperor Heraclius neos Constantine.[150] While *basileus* had long been used informally, in official documents the Greek *autokratōr*, from the Latin *imperator*, had been retained, frequently conjoined with such ancient titles as *Caesar* and *Flavius*.[151] Similarly *aeisebastos Augoustos*, the Greek rendering of *semper Augustus* was employed on coins and seals until the reign of Leo III, most often providing the denouement of a long list of accolades, included in all Heraclius' previous novels. Moreover, Heraclius also maintained several victory epithets, finally set by Justinian in 534, and the more religious titles such as *euergetēs* and *eirēnikos*, 'beneficent' and 'peaceful', which had flourished from the late sixth century. This rich juxtaposition of accolades and titles, many reaching back centuries, emphasized the multifarious strands of imperial authority: the tradition of Caesar and Augustus, military victory, and religious virtues.

Heraclius' decision to simplify imperial titulature radically was, therefore, important, but its precise significance is disputed. Ostrogorsky argued that the simplification and Hellenization of imperial titles marked a broader revival of Greek culture.[152] Shahid, however, correctly highlighted that *basileus* was a fundamentally different title from *imperator*, with obvious Christian resonances.[153] *Basileus* was the title used for both the Old Testament kings, especially David, famously depicted in the contemporary David Plates, and for Christ.[154] The Christian emphasis was underlined by the phrase *pistoi*

[150] The seminal study in imperial titles of this period is G. Rösch, *Onoma Basileias: Studien zum offiziellen Gebrauch der Kaisertitel in spätantiker und frühbyzantiner Zeit* (Vienna, 1978).

[151] Rösch, *Onoma Basileias*, 108.

[152] G. Ostrogorsky, *History of the Byzantine State* (2nd edn., Oxford, 1968), 106–7.

[153] I. Shahid, 'The Iranian factor in Byzantium during the reign of Heraclius', *DOP* 26 (1972), 293–320.

[154] For the David Plates see, inter alia, S. Spain Alexander, 'Heraclius, Byzantine imperial ideology and the David Plates', *Speculum* 52 (1977), 217–37. For a

en Christō. The new titulature, therefore, represented the emergence of Christianity as the hegemonic ideological force in imperial ideology.[155] Chrysos, however, postulated a less elevated interpretation, with the recent defeat of the Persians permitting the Byzantines officially to use the title by which they had long been known both by their subjects and foreign potentates.[156]

What all agree on is the importance of the date. In 629, Heraclius had finally defeated the Persians and stood at the apogee of his reign.[157] Imperial ideology across all media proclaimed the costly imperial success. George of Pisidia, Heraclius' court poet, glorified his patron in his poem the *Hexameron*, comparing Heraclius' six-year campaign to the six days of Creation, followed by the seventh of rest.[158] Combined with the celebratory poem *Restitutio in Crucis*, George departed from his early propaganda, which had compared Heraclius to a gamut of biblical and classical heroes, especially Heracles.[159] Instead of this sophisticated mixing of literary traditions, Heraclius was now above all the Christian monarch. The symbolism of this, and the renewal of the regime, was displayed by his restitution of the Cross to Jerusalem in 630.[160] Meanwhile, *c*.629–31, Heraclius attempted to reform the empire's coinage.[161] The badly debased copper *follis* was restored, briefly, to the weight found at the beginning of Heraclius' reign, which had been broadly stable from the latter half of the sixth century. On the obverse, Heraclius was clad in military garb for the first time on any of his coins, clasping a

stimulating recasting of the Plates as evidence of a broader Christianization of the secular, see R. Leader, 'The David Plates revisited: transforming the secular in early Byzantium', *Art Bulletin* 82 (2000), 407–27.

155 Shahid, 'Iranian factor', 302–3.

156 E. Chrysos, 'The title Βασιλεύς in early Byzantine international relations', *DOP* 32 (1978), 29–75.

157 Kaegi, *Heraclius*, 192–228. For the significance and transforming effects of Heraclius' campaigns, see J. Howard-Johnston, 'Heraclius' Persian campaigns and the revival of the East Roman Empire, 622–630', *War in History* 6 (1999), 1–44.

158 For George, see the many works of Mary Whitby, especially her 'George of Pisidia's presentation of the Emperor Heraclius and his campaigns', in Reinink and Stolte (eds), *The Reign of Heraclius* (2002), 157–73.

159 For George's use of biblical and classical models, see Ma. Whitby, 'A new image for a new age: George of Pisidia on the Emperor Heraclius', in E. Dabrowa (ed.), *The Roman and Byzantine Army in the East* (Krakow, 1994), 197–225; and J. Frendo, 'The poetic achievement of George of Pisidia', in A. Moffatt (ed.), *Maistor* (Canberra, 1984), 159–87.

160 Kaegi, *Heraclius*, 205–7.

161 See *DOC* I, 22–4.

sword hilt in his left hand, and in the right holding a long cross, and flanked by his adult son Heraclius Constantine, wearing the civilian *chlamys*.[162] The image was of dynastic power, military victory, and Christian piety. More famously, the, contested David Plates perhaps reflect imperial propaganda, with Heraclius compared to David slaying Goliath. Indeed, Old Testament imagery, long a constituent of imperial rhetoric, came to the fore in Heraclius' reign, from the celebratory poem of Theodore Syncellus, given after the successful rebuffing of the siege of Constantinople in 626, that pronounced the Romans a New Israel and the capital a New Jerusalem, to Heraclius naming his son David in 630.[163]

Therefore, the adoption of the title *basileus* was only one component of a fervent ideological campaign to celebrate victory and proclaim a stridently Christian version of *renovatio imperii*. Similarly, the extension of the *praescriptio fori* was also meant to acclaim this revival and ensure the continued maintenance of good, Christian order. Through the stresses of near defeat and the intoxication of victory, imperial ideology, although aimed at the reanimation of the empire bequeathed by Justinian, had become simpler and indisputably religious in inspiration. However, any dreams of quick imperial renewal came crashing down in the travails of the following years, in particular the rise of Islam. The seemingly decisive achievement of Heraclius melted away, as did the phrase *pistoi en Christō Basileis*. *Pace* the repeated assumptions of scholars, this titulature did not become once and for all time the title of Byzantine emperors.[164] Heraclius himself complicated it by adding *en Iēsō Christō tō theō* in the *Ekthesis* of 638.[165] By the reign of Constantine IV (r.668–85), both *autokratōr* and *Flavius* had returned.[166] Indeed, it is only with

[162] *DOC* I, Class V Heraclian follis, 295.

[163] For the general rise in the importance of the Old Testament in imperial rhetoric, reaching a crescendo in Heraclius' reign, see C. Rapp, 'Old Testament models for emperors in early Byzantium', in P. Magdalino and R. Nelson (eds), *The Old Testament in Byzantium* (Washington DC, 2010), 175–97. For Theodore Syncellus, *Sermo* I, ed. L. Sternbach, *Analecta Avarica* (Kraków, 1900), 298–320, see Howard-Johnston, *Witnesses to a World Crisis*, 146–7. For Heraclius naming his son David, see Theophanes, *Chronicle*, ed. C. De Boor (Leipzig, 1883–5), 335.

[164] For example, Kaegi, *Heraclius*, 194: the new title 'signified a permanent Hellenization of titulature'.

[165] Heraclius, *Ekthesis*, ed. R. Riedinger, *ACO* 2.1 (Berlin, 1984), 156–62, signature 162.

[166] See Rösch, *Onoma Basileias*, 108.

the Isaurians that uniformity across media was established, with the *Ecloga* describing Leo III and Constantine V as *pistoi basileis*, repeated on coins, and moderately altered to *basileis Rhōmaiōn* on imperial seals.[167] Heraclius' innovation was, therefore, to drop the Victory accolades permanently and adopt *basileus*, yet the picture of imperial ideology from imperial titles across the seventh century is far more complicated than normally assumed. In the end, the importance of the change in title used in Novel IV is closer to the legal change enacted, a moderate reform budding naturally from the Justinianic system, couched in rhetoric whose components of piety and order espoused through law had not changed, but whose triumphant tone was a product of a fleeting period of victory.

If Heraclius were determined to maintain and renew the old regime, and had used novels as part of a strategy of self-representation, why did the tradition of legislation by novel cease? The first solution to the conundrum would be that emperors did not stop legislating. Manifestly fundamental alterations to the Roman state occurred in the seventh century, which must have necessitated some legal response. The fact that we do not have extant records might then be a product of chance survival.[168] Moreover, one must consider the survival pattern of ancient legislation, with the vast majority of novels only surviving when subsumed into collections. Indeed, Heraclius' novels only survive as they were absorbed into the canon law tradition. Perhaps the caesura is, therefore, a mirage created by chance and codification. Yet this seems unlikely to be the whole story. Even given those pressures, it is implausible that so little trace of novels, or indeed any legislative activity, would have survived if there had been significantly more. Maybe, then, the seventh century did witness a significant downturn in imperial legislation. Why?

Firstly, it must be remembered that lawmaking is neither a constant, nor indeed a necessary function of government. Rather, lawmaking is a luxury, generated through an oscillating dynamic of symbolism and practicality. It also involves both restatement and innovation. On all four counts, the seventh century was an inauspicious time.

[167] Rösch, *Onoma Basileias*, 113.

[168] For instance, Stolte, 'The challenge of change', 192 n. 7 notes that F. Dölger, *Regesten der Kaiserurkunden des oströmischen Reiches von 565–1453*, 5 vols (Munich 1924–65), 167, 173, 174 are brief appearances in the literary sources of now-lost laws concerning non-ecclesiastical issues.

After the monumental success of Justinian's legal work, there was little individual glory in restatement; the body of law, both as a symbol and reality, already existed. An emperor could not fundamentally deviate from it. Minor alterations were permitted, but the chief role for the emperor was to maintain the system. As Haldon has persuasively argued, as the seventh century rumbled on and reality fell further away from imperial rhetoric espoused through the legal material, the prime response was to try to fit reality to the law, not the other way round.[169] Furthermore, to institute innovation requires political capital and time, all consumed by constant warfare. Any attempt to change the majority of law, primarily concerned with private matters of marriage, inheritance, and contract, was therefore hardly high on the list of imperial priorities, and with political capital entirely tied to survival, it was impossible anyway. The great administrative changes were probably ad hoc, and did not fundamentally affect the legal status of the Church or landowners, the two groups most likely to preserve law. These interlocking factors had made the traditional novel ever less important as an imperial tool and less likely to be preserved.

Moreover, law was losing ground in both the Byzantine symbolic universe and in the imperial ideological armoury. Underpinning this was the ever-rising importance of Christianity. Increasingly, emperors—through court ceremonial, coinage, panegyric, titles, personal piety, dogmatic dispute, and the patronage of churches, ascetics, and relics—sought to expand the Christian sphere and magnify their own position within it as the pivot between heaven and earth.[170] Within this, the old duopoly of law and victory ceded ground to Christianity, but were also redefined by it.

These processes reached a tipping point in the reign of Heraclius, reflected in the caesura in issuing novels, which had ceased to be a useful tool, either symbolically or practically. This did not mean the sudden end of Roman law, either as a cultural construct or as judicial practice. Courts still sat, cases were settled, and lawyers trained. The great Justinianic *Corpus* endured, if increasingly scattered in the works of the *antecessores*. Further, Roman law remained a symbol of Roman power, glory, and identity. Nor did civil law become practically immutable, but the momentum for change was firmly

169 Haldon, *Seventh Century*, 256–61.

170 Haldon, *Seventh Century*, 348–55, 436–43.

passed, for the moment, to legal scholars and judges, who had always reinterpreted the law.

Yet in the stresses of the seventh century, emperors increasingly turned to other legitimizing discourses. Therefore, civil law was not abandoned, but on an imperial level symbolically embalmed, metaphorically placed in cold storage alongside much of the imperial edifice refashioned by Justinian, to be brought forth once more when late antique normality was restored, and the forces of Islam overcome, as the reversible chastisement sent by God as punishment for Roman-Christian sin that it was contemporaneously conceived to be. That conception of the empire's ills and its fated recovery, once it had purged the sin that had caused divine wrath, would frame imperial ideology and policy for the remainder of the seventh century.

Within that paradigm, imperial legal activity, or at least what survives of it, was aimed solely at propitiating Heaven. Thus the three extant imperial edicts concern the compromise Christological formula of monotheletism, namely the *Ekthesis* of 638 that proposed it, the *Typos* of 648 that banned all discussion on the subject, and the edict of Constantine IV enforcing the Sixth Ecumenical Council's condemnation of the doctrine.[171] These fluctuations in imperial religious policies were intimately intertwined with the ideological and geopolitical struggle between declining Rome and the emergent Islamic Caliphate for hegemony over the Near East. We shall now turn to the final step in that religio-political and legal dance, namely the reign of Justinian II (r.685–95, 705–11), and more particularly his convocation of the Council in Trullo of 691/2. For this council represents both the culmination of several late antique trends, but also the beginnings of a new conceptual paradigm that would underpin the Isaurian legal world of the eighth and ninth centuries.

[171] Heraclius, *Ekthesis*, ed. R. Riedinger, *ACO* 2.1 (Berlin, 1984), 156–62; Constans II, *Typos*, ed. R. Riedinger, *ACO* 2.1 (Berlin, 1984), 208–10; *The Council of Constantinople III of 680–1: The Sixth Ecumenical Council*, ed. R. Riedinger, *ACO* 2.2, 3 vols (Berlin, 1990–95), Edict vol. 2, 832–56. For an overview of these shifting imperial positions, see J. Meyendorff, *Imperial Unity and Christian Divisions: The Church 450–680 A.D.* (Crestwood NY, 1989), 333–73. See also P. Booth, *Crisis of Empire: Doctrine and Dissent at the End of Late Antiquity* (London, 2014).

1

The Council in Trullo

The decades following Heraclius' final novel in 629 witnessed some of the most dramatic events in Roman history. Heraclius' dearly bought victory against the Persians was set at naught when the Arabs, unified and driven by the new religion of Islam, swept into Palestine in 634. Within a decade Rome had once more and forever lost Egypt, Syria-Palestine, and Mesopotamia, and with them the bulk of imperial tax revenues.[1] Roman power, whose reality had structured the Eastern Mediterranean since at least the days of Pompey the Great, was incontrovertibly and manifestly diminished. Moreover, the struggle was far from finished. The Romans believed in and plotted for their eventual reconquest, while the leaders of the new empire and faith intended and predicted that their final triumph and the fulfilment of their providential mission would come with the taking of Constantinople. Thus began a struggle not just for superiority but survival, fought not only on the battlefield, but on diplomatic and cultural fronts.[2]

These ructions and tensions generated new and urgent questions that neither the Roman state nor the institutional Church could easily answer.[3] The spectacular rise of Islam, with its early emphasis on

[1] In an oft quoted assessment, M. Hendy, *Studies in the Byzantine Monetary Economy, c.300–1450* (Cambridge, 1985), 620 estimated that the empire may have lost three-quarters of its revenues.

[2] In general for this struggle, see Howard-Johnston, *Witnesses to a World Crisis*, esp. 461–516; and P. Sarris, *Empires of Faith: The Fall of Rome to the Rise of Islam, 500–700* (Oxford, 2011), 226–306.

[3] For an overview of the Church and belief in this period, see Haldon, *Seventh Century*, 281–375. This should be set in the context of increasing intransigence between the Christological communities of late antiquity, and the imperial search for unity, for which see Meyendorff, *Imperial Unity and Christian Divisions*.

pietism and the imminence of the end of days, fundamentally challenged the assumptions and structural underpinnings of the Roman world.[4] In this age of crisis and uncertainty, responses to the diminution in Roman power varied according to context, and especially religious and political affiliation.[5] Yet it is increasingly evident that the imperial authorities' expectation of a swift reversal of fortune and restoration of the empire was no mere imperial myopia, but represented majority opinion, even among the empire's persecuted and marginalized religious minorities, and is a defining feature of contemporary literature.[6] Simply too much political, social, and cultural capital had been invested, for too long, by too many in the Eusebian conception of the Christian Roman Empire (divinely ordained to last until the end of time), to allow quick abandonment of the ideal.

Furthermore, the eventual victory of Islam was not a foregone conclusion, and the Roman Empire remained a serious contender for Mediterranean hegemony right until the end of the seventh century. Battered and bruised though it might have been, the empire still commanded significant resources and respect. Moreover, as meteoric as the Caliphate's rise had been, Muslim control over the lands they had conquered was tenuous. Nor was the House of Islam a harmonious unity, but prone to fractiousness and division, leading to two full-blown civil wars, or *fitnas*, in the half-century after Muhammad's death. Indeed, the tide seemed to have turned decidedly in New Rome's favour in the 670s, when an Arab assault aimed at

[4] For the nature of early Islam, see F. Donner, *Muhammad and the Believers at the Origins of Islam* (London, 2010).

[5] See R. Hoyland, *Seeing Islam as Others Saw It: A Survey and Evaluation of Christian, Jewish, and Zoroastrian Writings on Early Islam* (Princeton, 1997); D. Olster, *Roman Defeat, Christian Response, and the Literary Construction of the Jew* (Philadelphia, 1994); D. Olster, 'From periphery to centre: the transformation of late Roman self-definition', in R. Mathisen and H. Sivan (eds), *Shifting Frontiers in Late Antiquity* (Aldershot, 1996), 93–102; and D. Olster, 'Ideological transformation and the evolution of imperial presentation in the wake of Islam's victory', in E. Grypeou et al. (eds), *The Encounter of Eastern Christianity with Early Islam* (Leiden, 2006), 45–71.

[6] For the surprising tenacity of Roman imperial ideology in forming the worldview of Jewish communities, see A. Sivertsev, *Judaism and Imperial Ideology in Late Antiquity* (Cambridge, 2011); cf. for the Miaphysite communities P. Wood, *'We Have No King But Christ': Christian Political Thought in Greater Syria on the Eve of the Arab Conquest (c.400–585)* (Oxford, 2010). For these manifold satellite cultures of the Roman world forming a 'First Byzantine Commonwealth', see Fowden, *Empire to Commonwealth*, 100–37.

Constantinople itself was decisively repulsed. Relieved, the Empire went on the offensive, unleashing irregular forces, called the Mardaites, who caused terror and confusion across Syria-Palestine. Forced to buy peace, the Caliphate soon descended into division, rebellion, and civil war. Heaven at last seemed to be coming down on the side of the Romans.[7]

CONSTANTINE IV AND THE BACKGROUND TO TRULLO

It was in this context of confidence renewed that Constantine IV (r.668–685), the hero of the hour who had thrown back the Arabs, convened the Sixth Ecumenical Council in 680/1.[8] Its purpose was to cap and secure this transformation in imperial fortunes by finally settling the vexed question of Christ's natures, wills, and energies, the latest round in the seemingly interminable controversies emerging from the Council of Chalcedon in 451. Thereby Constantine hoped to unify his newly confident realm and bring peace to the Church through the establishment of doctrinal orthodoxy. Thus he would fulfil a central function of imperial rule and secure that most vital element for all Roman/Byzantine rulers: divine goodwill.

However, the politics of the situation were complex. The imperially sponsored formula of monotheletism, originally designed to find a compromise with the Miaphysites who dominated the Churches of Syria and Egypt, had strong support in Anatolia and also in Syria. However, the West, and in particular Rome and the African Churches, were staunchly dyothelete. The intricacies of the Council

[7] For the above, see in particular Howard-Johnston, *Witnesses to a World Crisis*, esp. 488–501.

[8] *ACO* 2.2. More precisely, the Council met in 18 sessions between 7 November 680 and 16 September 681. For the Council and the controversy in general, see Meyendorff, *Imperial Unity and Christian Divisions*, 333–73; for the Council and the reign of Constantine IV, see Herrin, *Formation of Christendom*, 274–82. See also W. Brandes, 'Orthodoxy and heresy in the seventh century: prosopographical observations on monotheletism', in A. Cameron (ed.), *Fifty Years of Prosopography: The Late Roman Empire, Byzantium and Beyond. Proceedings of the British Academy* 118 (Oxford, 2003), 103–18. For the date of 669 when Constantine IV became emperor following the assassination of his father Constans II, see Howard-Johnston, *Witnesses*, 491.

are beyond our remit, but three elements must be noted. Firstly, the Council would see the Western position triumph and monotheletism condemned. Pope Agatho was lauded as St Peter's imitator and successor, and handed almost equal honours to the emperor in the successful establishment of true doctrine.[9] This would mark the high point of imperial–papal relations, and represented a remarkable imperial volte-face from the days of Constans II, Constantine's father, who had arrested and condemned a previous pope to exile. New Rome must have felt assured of Old Rome's allegiance following such an outcome.

Secondly, the Council was the culmination of a degree of ideological repositioning that took place during Constantine's reign. Heretofore, the Heraclian dynasty had in their rhetoric emphasized Constantine the Great and the Old Testament, particularly the model of David.[10] In contrast, perhaps Constantine IV's first act as emperor was to break three generations of precedent and call his son not Constantine, but Justinian.[11] Constantine IV's coinage and seals also broke the established Heraclian mould, and reverted to an iconography not seen since the early sixth century; they even restored, briefly, the much-debased copper *folles* to a heavy type introduced by Justinian I in 538.[12] Constantine also attempted in 680 to depose his two brothers as co-emperors, thereby moving away from the model of collegiality that had been part of Heraclian dynastic practice and a prominent feature of Roman ideology and governance more generally since Tiberius II became co-emperor with Justin II in 574. Meeting

[9] In particular note *ACO* 2.2, vol. 2, 816.19–818.1.

[10] See p. 33.

[11] Constantine IV's father, known as Constans II, was officially named Constantine. Constans in turn was the son of Heraclius *neos* Constantine—Heraclius new Constantine—Heraclius' eldest son. Heraclius also named another son who died young Constantine (*PLRE* III, Constantinus 34). For the fluctuating use of Constantine I and Justinian I in the seventh century, see J. Haldon, 'Constantine or Justinian? Crisis and identity in imperial propaganda in the seventh century', in P. Magdalino (ed.), *New Constantines: The Rhythm of Imperial Renewal in Byzantium, 4th–13th Centuries* (Aldershot, 1994), 95–107. Haldon is sceptical about the degree to which names signified anything more than the demands of a particular moment. This author would suggest that the change seems more significant than Haldon allows, but accepts that there is a limit to its importance. More importantly, it must always be remembered that both Constantine and Justinian were constant legitimate referents, revered by all their successors. However, like many aspects of ideology, shifts in emphasis are important and revealing.

[12] Solidi *DOC* Class II–IV, Folles *DOC* Class I–V. See P. Grierson, *Byzantine Coins* (London, 1982), 96–7, 113–14. For the seals see *ZV* 21–3.

resistance from the Anatolikon theme, Constantine prudently backed down, but having rounded-up the leaders of the revolt and successfully concluded the Ecumenical Council, he once more deposed and mutilated his brothers. Henceforth a single imperial image was projected on Constantine's coins.[13]

Convening an Ecumenical Council continued this theme of a return to older aspects of imperial ideology. It allowed Constantine to draw legitimacy from a source established by his namesake at Nicaea in 325, whereas his forebears had studiously avoided calling such a Council. Moreover, at its conclusion Constantine was praised as a New Marcian and a New Justinian, the conveners respectively of the Fourth and Fifth Councils, explicitly linking him with their prestige and lineage.[14] Furthermore, Constantine IV was a visible and active participant in proceedings, underscoring the extent to which this was his Council, in which he, along with the gathered bishops, was ensuring true doctrine. This is highlighted by Constantine's innovation in signing the produced declaration of faith after the bishops, unlike any of his predecessors.[15] It was also underlined by taking place in the imperial palace at Constantinople, the first time an Ecumenical Council had convened in a palace since Nicaea. Cumulatively, this marks a significant intensification in the importance attached within imperial ideology to direct imperial support of doctrinal orthodoxy, even to the extent of significant imperial intervention within the workings of the Church. The rhetoric employed reinforces this claim with Constantine the 'emperor, autocrat' resolving the issue with 'your co-ruler the Almighty', *tō sumbasileuonti pantokratori basileus autokratōr sunepsēphizou su.*[16] Imperial authority was here inextricably bound with heavenly support and orthodoxy. Taken together, this suggests that Constantine and his advisors were deliberately seeking to reconfigure imperial ideology in response to the immense challenges facing the empire, offering a new 'package' of a supreme emperor, after the model of the great Justinian, who co-ruled with Christ, and who once and for all established the true doctrine of His nature.

The third item to note is that this package, although broadly successful, was not universally popular. Monotheletes would not disappear after 50 years of imperial support simply because that

[13] Solidi *DOC* Class IV, Folles *DOC* Class V. [14] *ACO* 2.2, vol. 2, 798.10–11.
[15] *ACO* 2.2, vol. 2, 796.26–27. [16] *ACO* 2.2, vol. 2, 818.2.

support had been withdrawn.[17] The seemingly total repudiation of monotheletism is belied by the striking increase in the numbers of participants at the Council only once its outcome was clear. Evidently the vast majority of the episcopacy would trim their sails to whichever way the political winds blew.[18] In 681, that gave the impression of monotheletism's total defeat, but should the winds change, then its restoration was possible. Indeed, the fact that Philippicus Bardanes (r.711–13) would restore monotheletism is an indication that the doctrine continued to have some support.[19] Therefore, by placing even more emphasis on the importance of doctrinal purity as the *sine qua non* of imperial success, it made any reversal of imperial fortunes inextricably tied to its theological policy. This was no mere abstract risk, for even while the Council sat in 681, a new threat appeared in the Balkans in the form of the Bulgars. Constantine himself led a considerable army to counter this danger, but the expedition ended in a fiasco and Constantine buying peace.[20] Hence, the Council's credibility, and the edifice of imperial legitimacy bound up with it, was undermined, with surely more than the dejected monotheletes holding the Council discredited by divine judgment on the battlefield.

Of course, emperors and the court at Constantinople were never acting in an ideological vacuum, nor were they the sole actors in the drama. The whole cultural realm is naturally too vast to examine here, but three genres are especially pertinent to what follows. The first is canon law. Whereas civil law even during Justinian's reign entered into a period of decline, and in the seventh century was effectively put into stasis, canon law witnessed a marked effervescence.[21] More precisely, the momentum imparted by the prolific ecclesiastical, monastic, doctrinal, and more generally moral legislation of Justinian was maintained. Indeed, Justinian I could be described as the greatest canonist in the Orthodox tradition. During the later sixth century,

[17] Brandes, 'Prosopographical observations on monotheletism', 116 notes monotheletism had sympathizers among the highest military commanders, and in the imperial and patriarchal bureaucracy.

[18] Brandes, 'Prosopographical observations on monotheletism', 117.

[19] Theophanes, 382.

[20] For the Council and the Bulgars, see Haldon, *Seventh Century*, 66–9; W. Treadgold, *A History of the Byzantine State and Society* (Stanford, CA, 1997), 327–9.

[21] Stolte, 'The challenge of change', 195–201; Van der Wal and Lokin, *Historiae*, 51–4, 60–2.

relevant material from the *Corpus* was extracted and arranged into three extant works.[22] Meanwhile, Justinian's example in codifying civil law led to John Scholasticus' *Synagoga in L Titles*, which imposed a thematic order on the canonical corpus primarily emanating from the fourth century.[23] Finally, there arose that most quintessential of Byzantine collections, the *Nomokanones*, which combined canons proper (*kanones*) with imperial legislation (*nomos*) and arranged them thematically, the most famous of which was the *Nomokanon in XIV Titles* that Stolte argues was composed in the reign of Heraclius.[24] This peculiar format emphasized the extent to which *imperium* and *sacerdotium* were intertwined in the Roman/Byzantine world—theoretically, legally, and practically—especially after the legal outpouring and ideological repositioning of Justinian I. All this spoke of an urge to collect and codify.

Secondly, apocalyptic literature flourished, most famously seen in the huge popularity in multiple versions of the *Apocalypse of Pseudo-Methodius*, created *c*.691.[25] This reflected the anxiety of the era, in particular the revolutionary arrival and disruptive evolution of Islam, which had both swiftly overturned the political order of the Near East and preached the imminence of Judgement Day. Moreover, apocalyptic literature represented the struggle between Islam and Christianity over conflicting claims to inheritance of the biblical past, the present divine dispensation, and their future role in eschatological history.[26] However, despite the tone and focus on the immediacy of the end of time, these apocalypses accepted—indeed virulently

[22] See Introduction, 30 n. 148.

[23] John Scholasticus, *Synagoga L Titulorum*, ed. V. Beneševič (Munich, 1937).

[24] *Nomokanon in XIV Titles*, ed. I. B. Pitra, *Iuris ecclesiastici graecorum historia et monumenta*, vol. 2 (Rome, 1868), 433–640. For its origin in the time of Heraclius, see Stolte, 'The challenge of change', 195. For the genre, see A. Schminck, 'Nomokanon of fourteen titles', in *ODB*, vol. 3, 1491.

[25] Ps.-Methodius, *Apocalypse*, Syria version ed. G. Reinink, *Die syrische Apokalypse des Ps.-Methodius* (Louvain, 1993); Greek and Latin version ed. W. Aerts and G. Kortekaas, *Die Apokalypse des Pseudo-Methodius. Die ältesten griechischen and lateinischen Übersetzungen* I–II (Louvain, 1998). For analysis see G. Reinink, 'Ps.-Methodius: a concept of history in response to the rise of Islam', in A. Cameron and L. Conrad (eds), *The Byzantine and Early Islamic Near East I: Problems in the Literary Source Material* (Princeton, 1992), 149–87. See in general P. Alexander, *The Byzantine Apocalyptic Tradition* (London, 1985).

[26] See in particular P. Magdalino, 'The history of the future and its uses: prophecy, policy, and propaganda', in R. Beaton and C. Roueché (eds), *The Making of Byzantine History* (Aldershot, 1993), 3–34.

asserted in the face of the Islamic challenge—the starring role of the Roman Empire in cosmological history and its destined reconquest of the Near East, if only as a prelude to the Second Coming.

Thirdly, *Question and Answer* literature proliferated, where enquiries were posed to those imbued with spiritual authority.[27] Of particular note is the work of Anastasius of Sinai, like Ps.-Methodius a product of the late seventh century, from which significant changes in popular concerns and ecclesiastical interests can be charted.[28] For instance, the once-dominant Christological disputes have here receded in prominence, replaced by questions on religious rites and personal morality.[29] Evidently the tribulations of the times, combined with the threat of a new religion placing an onus on pietism, had shifted attitudes towards issues of practice and ethics, as individuals alongside institutions and states sought to ensure heavenly aid on earth and the promise of salvation.

At the confluence of all these trends stood Justinian II (r.685–95, 705–11). Inheriting an empire on the rise, Justinian's reign would be a crossroads in Roman history, witnessing the final serious attempt to wrest back hegemony of the Eastern Mediterranean from the Islamic Caliphate.[30] Following in his father's footsteps and as a crescendo to his putative campaign of rejuvenation, Justinian II convoked the Council in Trullo in 691/2 to maintain the divine support that was seen as the root of imperial fortune.[31] The ensuing council and its 102 canons remain the foundation stone of Eastern Orthodox canon

[27] For the general genre, see A. Kazhdan, 'Erotapokriseis', in *ODB*, vol. 1, 727.

[28] Anastasius of Sinai, *Questiones et Responsiones*, ed. M. Richard and J. Munitiz (Turnhout, 2006). For analysis see J. Haldon, 'The works of Anastasius of Sinai: a key source for the history of seventh-century East Mediterranean society and belief', in A. Cameron and L. Conrad (eds), *The Byzantine and Early Islamic Near East I: Problems in the Literary Source Material* (Princeton, 1992), 107–47; J. Munitiz, 'Anastasius of Sinai: speaking and writing to the people of God', in M. Cunningham and P. Allen (eds), *Preacher and Audience: Studies in Early Christian and Byzantine Homiletics* (Leiden, 1998), 227–45; and J. Munitiz, 'Anastasius of Sinai's teaching on body and soul', in L. James (ed.), *Desire and Denial in Byzantium* (Aldershot, 1999), 49–56.

[29] For Christological conflicts, see Meyendorff, *Imperial Unity and Christian Divisions*.

[30] Howard-Johnston, *Witnesses to a World Crisis*, esp. 488–501. Cf. M. Humphreys, 'Images of authority? Imperial patronage of icons from Justinian II to Leo III', in P. Sarris, M. Dal Santo, and P. Booth (eds), *An Age of Saints? Power, Conflict and Dissent in Early Medieval Christianity* (Leiden, 2011), 150–68, esp. 155–60.

[31] The standard edition of the council is that of P.-P. Joannou, *Discipline génerale antique*, vol. 1 (Grottaferrata, 1962), 101–241. This text was improved and given a

law.[32] Through them, Justinian sought to maintain divine support and deepen his own legitimacy by tying himself to his father's legacy, and to silence any critics of it by linking the doctrinal orthodoxy expounded at the Sixth Council with practical measures aimed at moral reformation proposed at Trullo. Furthermore, Justinian sought to yoke contemporary apocalyptic and concerns over rite and morality, and thereby garner support from the whole Christian world towards the imperial ambition of realizing the rhetoric and expectations of reconquest.

Yet too often Trullo has been studied and understood only through the narrow prism of canon law, and then distorted by centuries of polemic, especially concerning the ecumenicity of the council and the so-called 'anti-Roman' canons.[33] Even modern scholarship that does treat the council on its own terms has principally quarried it for markers of divergent rite and belief between east and west, and thus focused on issues such as clerical celibacy, or evidence of 'pagan' survivals, thus placing it within the long narrative of Christianization of Roman society.[34] In contrast, the council's role as a vehicle for imperial ideology and articulation of identity, and the vital questions of Justinian's role and ambitions for the council, have been virtually ignored.[35] This chapter shall attempt to redress the balance by

matching English translation in G. Nedungatt and M. Featherstone (eds), *The Council in Trullo Revisited* (Rome, 1995). A new edition with minor alterations to the Greek has appeared, with a German translation, by H. Ohme, *Das Konzil Quinisextum* (Turnhout, 2006). Ohme had earlier provided the first critical edition of the bishops' signatory list, in H. Ohme, *Das Concilium Quinisextum und Seine Bischofsliste* (Berlin, 1990).

[32] I have chosen to use the name Council in Trullo or Trullo for short, rather than Quinisext or Penthekte. Although these names neatly convey the intentional link to the Fifth and Sixth Ecumenical Councils, they were a neologism of the twelfth century and presuppose the ecumenicity of the council, something that has been contested since 692. See G. Nedungatt and M. Featherstone, 'Presentation', in Nedungatt and Featherstone, *The Council in Trullo Revisited* (Rome, 1995), 7–14, esp. 7–8.

[33] See H. Ohme, 'Die sogennanten "antirömischen" Kanones des Concilium Quinisextum', in Nedungatt and Featherstone, *Trullo Revisited* (1995), 307–21.

[34] For a good example, see the generally fine work of C. Gallagher, *Church Law and Church Order in Rome and Byzantium: A Comparative Study* (Aldershot, 2002), which uses certain issues such as a clerical celibacy as markers of divergent attitudes. Most generalist historical, rather than primarily canon law studies, also demonstrate this tendency; for example, see Haldon, *Seventh Century*, 73–4, 317–18.

[35] Although the most general political elements, such as the council acting as method for prestige-garnering for Justinian, have been noted far and wide—see for example A. Louth, 'Byzantium transforming', in J. Shepard (ed.), *The Cambridge*

exploring each component of Trullo in turn, for each had a specific function within the overall programme, and reveal different facets of imperial ideology and the late seventh-century world in which it operated.

THE *LOGOS PROSPHONETIKOS* AND THE RECASTING OF IMPERIAL RHETORIC

Trullo opens with a *Logos Prosphonetikos*, purportedly a loyal address from the bishops beseeching imperial confirmation, but which in all probability was a creation of the court.[36] Remarkably understudied, the *Logos* forms, alongside Cs.1 and 2, an introductory complex that provides the intellectual armature underpinning the ensuing canons.[37] Indeed, without an in-depth analysis of the *Logos* and its extraordinarily rich rhetoric, study of the canons alone is fundamentally insufficient to understand the purpose of Trullo or the world made known through it.

History of the Byzantine Empire, c.500–1492 (Cambridge, 2008), 221–48, esp. 244—a detailed study of the political and ideological role of the council has never been undertaken. The nearest has been the various works of Trullo's most recent editor Heinz Ohme, especially his identifying of Justinian's peculiar role and the conciliar theory espoused at the council; see especially his 'The causes of conflict about the Quinisext council: new perspectives on a disputed council', *The Greek Orthodox Theological Review* 40 (1995), 17–43.

[36] It is always impossible to know the extent to which ecumenical councils were planned in advance and controlled during session. Even where we have the *Acta*, these are not neutral documents. There was always potential for later editing and pre-arranged agreements; for the potential of this at the Sixth Council, see Brandes, 'Prosopographical observations on monotheletism', 112. Trullo's *Acta* do not survive, perhaps biasing our view, but everything that does survive gives the impression of a highly orchestrated synod.

[37] *Trullo Revisited*, 45:12–55:7. I have taken this phrase to describe the *Logos* and canons 1 and 2 from D. Wagschal, *The Nature of Law and Legality in the Byzantine Canonical Collections 381–883*, doctoral thesis, Durham University (2010). Available at Durham E-Theses Online: <http://etheses.dur.ac.uk/468>, 103–7. This excellent thesis offers one of the few extended discussions on the ideological and legal anthropological elements of Trullo, or indeed any focus on the *Logos* whatsoever. The relative dearth of study on the *Logos* can be measured by the fact that Ohme's edition, in what could be considered relatively long coverage, dedicates fewer than two pages on the subject compared to 122 pages on the canons; see Ohme, *Konzil Qunisextum*, 30–1, cf. 35–157. The eight essays in *Trullo Revisited* do not mention the *Logos* at all.

The first notable factor of the *Logos* is its length. It declares itself descended from the address used at the Second Ecumenical Council of Constantinople of 381—indeed it concludes with an almost verbatim citation of it.[38] Yet Trullo's *Logos* utterly dwarfs its proclaimed model. The *Logos* of the Sixth Ecumenical Council of 680/81, which the council in Trullo was designed to supplement, is far closer in length but employed more traditional rhetoric and focused far more on the precise doctrinal situation that had warranted the synod's convocation.[39] True, several of the themes explored below find correspondents in the *Logos* of 681—for instance, in Satan's war on mankind necessitating Christ to raise defenders,[40] and the prominence and praise of the emperor and his association with the Almighty.[41] However, Trullo's *Logos* marks a significant intensification, striking a far more radical style and tone beyond anything seen heretofore in the canonical tradition, and situates Council, emperor, and people within the grander vista of cosmological history.[42]

The *Logos* is composed of three sections. Section one, Trullo:46.1–48.12, proffers a synopsis of salvation history. The first part, 46.1–47.10, narrates the triumph of Christianity: divine grace through the Incarnation has illumined the world, while the Devil has been cast down. Correct worship is ordained and Communion given for the sanctification of the people. Then 47.11–48.12 describes how, due to the Devil's continued assaults on the faithful, God raises up in every generation men armed 'with the weapons of piety' to fight against the Devil, and luminaries to light the narrow way to heaven.[43] The middle section, 48.12–51.12, and thus literally the centre and fulcrum of the text, is devoted to Emperor Justinian II. For sloth had

[38] *Trullo Revisited*, 54:8–55:7. Cf. the *Logos Prosphonetikos* of Second Ecumenical Council, Mansi III:557.

[39] *ACO* 2.2, vol. 2, 804–20. To give a rough indication of the differing emphases of the two, the *LP* of the Sixth Council at a conservative reckoning spent 808.13–812.4 narrating the heresies countered by the preceding five councils, and then 812.5–816.16 explaining the current debate and the council's decision, around half of its total length. For the Trullo the respective sections are, on a more liberal reckoning, *Trullo Revisited*, 51:13–52:7 and 53:6–54:20, or around one-quarter of its total length.

[40] *ACO* 2.2, 808.1–2. [41] *ACO* 2.2, 818.2–820.17.

[42] The introductions to the preceding 'private' canon law codes of John Scholasticus, *Synagoga L Titulorum* and the *Nomokanon in XIV Titles*, offer some comparable themes and images, especially the former, but are far shorter affairs. See Wagschal, *Law and Legality*, 90–102.

[43] *Trullo Revisited*, 48:8–9, *hoplōn tēs eusebeias*.

enervated the people's moral guard, so Christ had appointed Justinian, adorned with an adulatory amalgam of Christian and Hellenistic tropes of pious rule, to lead the people back to piety. It is only in the culminating section, 51.13–55.7, that the precise occasion for the calling of Trullo, the provision of disciplinary canons that the Fifth and Sixth Ecumenical Councils had not supplied, was stated.[44] Even here, the prime focus was the emperor and his attributes, with future redemption and glory as prevalent as present problems. Thus, the general structure of the *Logos* serves a deliberate political purpose by not only lauding Justinian II, but also situating him within cosmological history as Christ's vicegerent on earth at a vital moment of moral reformation.

The themes and imagery employed represent a refined mixing of ancient Christian and Hellenistic ideas, a level of interpenetration unsurprising given centuries of interrelation, but which firmly position Trullo at the end of a distinctly late antique arc of thought.[45] Indeed, the central recurring theme is thoroughly Socratic: ignorance, *agnoia*, led to moral decline.[46] Thus, the righteous had to make 'straight the ways of the Lord for the peoples, lest through ignorance of good they should be pushed to the precipice of iniquity and slip away'.[47] Frequently, ignorance was paired with sloth and neglect, with disastrous consequences:

> Wherefore, as we conduct our lives in great sloth and slumber in the idleness of our thoughts, so that the waylaying enemy can come upon us unawares, little by little stealing away our virtue and substituting within us iniquity in its place . . .[48]

Countered to ignorance was knowledge, *gnōsis*, and wisdom, *sophia*. For Wisdom herself had borne and educated Justinian in all virtues.[49] Prompted by this, the *Logos* introduced its final crescendo, and the immediate premise for the convocation of the council, with Justinian

[44] Fifth Ecumenical Council, ed. J. Straub, *ACO* 4:1 (Berlin, 1971).

[45] The seminal study is still Dvornik, *Byzantine Political Philosophy*. See also C. Rowe and M. Schofield (eds), *The Cambridge History of Greek and Roman Thought* (Cambridge, 2000); and J. Burns (ed.), *The Cambridge History of Medieval Political Thought* (Cambridge, 1988), esp. chs. 1–7.

[46] T. Penner, 'Socrates', in C. Rowe and M. Schofield (eds), *The Cambridge History of Greek and Roman Thought* (Cambridge, 2000), 165–89, esp. 165.

[47] *Trullo Revisited*, 48:17–19.

[48] *Trullo Revisited*, 49:13–19. Cf. with the very similar image of 52:13–15, 'having slipped away from the achievements of virtue through ignorance and neglect'.

[49] *Trullo Revisited*, 50:7–10.

having been swayed by the biblical injunction, 'He who seeks the Lord will find knowledge with righteousness' (Prov. 16:5).[50] Just as the *Logos* ends with the theme of Justinian finding knowledge and righteousness through God, it begins with Christ saving the world through knowledge, thereby underscoring the imperial mirroring of Christ. Here, the dichotomy of ignorance versus knowledge is elucidated through light imagery and embedded in a broader biblical discourse of justice and Salvation through a subtle rephrasing of Isaiah 9:2 that deliberately paired knowledge with light, and ignorance with darkness:

> Now that the ineffable divine grace of our Redeemer and Saviour Jesus Christ has compassed all the earth and the life-giving preaching of the truth has been sown in the ears of all, 'the people who sat in the darkness' of ignorance 'have seen the great light' of knowledge and have been delivered from the bonds of error.[51]

The light metaphor recurs twice more, firstly with 'the luminaries and Doctors of the Church, illumining our steps toward God', and then more verbosely attached to Justinian: '[Wisdom] has made you the eye of the universe, you who brightly illumine your subjects with the pureness and splendour of your mind.'[52] Here one can see the combination of Scripture, a more generalized common Christian trope, and an ancient Hellenistic description of kingship, quarried for similar imagery on a joint theme.[53] Moreover, it highlights and unites three actors, Christ, Church, and emperor, with the first and last the more emphasized.

A more peculiarly Christian discourse employed is that of lost sheep and the good shepherd. This makes a brief initial appearance as a description of the faithful who lead the fight against evil, 'becoming leaders of the flocks [*hodēgoi tōn poimniōn*]', perhaps an oblique reference to bishops or clergy, but, considering the later reference to the 'luminaries and Doctors of the Church' and general context, more probably refers specifically to the Church Fathers, whose canons were

[50] *Trullo Revisited*, 53:8–10. [51] *Trullo Revisited*, 46:1–9.

[52] *Trullo Revisited*, 49:6–10; 50:10–13.

[53] For instance, eye imagery is used in a Christian rulership context by Agapetus, *Ekthesis*, 46. Further, Persian diplomacy had described Rome and Persia as the 'Two eyes of the earth', e.g. Theophylact Simocatta, *History*, ed. C. de Boor and P. Wirth, *Theophylacti Simmocattae Historiae* (Stuttgart, 1972), 4.1 1.2–3; trans. Mi. and Ma. Whitby, *The History of Theophylact Simocatta* (Oxford, 1986).

here affirmed and collated.[54] A far fuller allusion, however, is used for Justinian. Firstly, corresponding to the image of the Church Fathers, the emperor had 'chosen to lead [his] flock away from iniquity and corruption'.[55] Thus Justinian was elided with episcopal and patristic authority and the general tradition of righteous Christian leadership, but given personal leadership over *the flock* rather than either one of many or a conglomeration of all. A more startling claim is then made:

> It was your great desire, therefore, after the example of Christ, the good Shepherd, searching for the sheep lost in the mountains, to bring together this holy nation, as a special people, and return it to the fold and convince it to keep the divine commandments and statutes, through which we desist from dead deeds and are given life.[56]

This extended metaphor is the first extant application of Christ the Shepherd imagery to any Roman or post-Roman ruler in legal literature.[57] It is an explicit piece of *mimēsis* with the association of Christ and Justinian underlined linguistically with the deployment of the key word shepherd, *poimēn*, whereas the Fathers are just generic leaders, *hodēgoi*.[58] Justinian was thus Christ-like in protecting, guarding, and guiding the Christian people, bringing them back from sin to grace. It may also be implicitly invoking that other biblical shepherd-king, and a favoured trope for the Heraclian dynasty, David, although this is definitely subsidiary to the prime model of Christ.[59]

Further, the *Logos* situates Justinian II and his flock in an explicitly martial setting. The overarching narrative was the universal battle between God and the Devil, the latter having been made a prisoner of war, as 'the swords of the enemy have utterly failed' (Ps. 9:6).[60] However, the Devil maintained his rebellion, 'throwing darts of malice and wounding the faithful with passions [*pathos*]', a term deliberately chosen for its ambiguity, meaning both misfortunes or calamities falling upon the collective, and the emotional, impure

[54] *Trullo Revisited*, 48:15; 49:7–8.

[55] *Trullo Revisited*, 50:19–51:1.

[56] *Trullo Revisited*, 52:20–53:6.

[57] The image is ultimately drawn from Mt. 18:12/Lk. 15:4.

[58] In total contrast, in the *Synogoge in L Titulorum* it is the bishops who are called shepherds, an attribute repeated in the ninth-century *Eisagoge* ed. K. Zacharia von Lingenthal, *Collectio librorum juris Graeco-Romani ineditorum* (Leipzig, 1852), 61–217 = Zepos, *IGR* II, 236–368. See Wagschal, *Law and Legality*, 91.

[59] See Introduction, 33.

[60] *Trullo Revisited*, 46:18–20.

passions of an individual's soul, therewith underscoring the link between the two.[61] Therefore, God raised up those who were armed:

> with weapons of piety and will join the war against him [the Devil]. Drawing forth 'the Sword of the Spirit which is the Word of God' (Eph. 6:17), and thus engaging the evil one in battle, they have abolished his tyranny over us.[62]

This theme is then associated with the Christian empire. The opening salutation points the way by employing the now traditional description of Constantinople as *theophulakton kai basilida polin*, 'this God-guarded imperial city'.[63] More idiosyncratically, Justinian is then given the mantle of pious warlord in this comparison drawn from Numbers 25:1–15:

> In the fervour of your desire for God you have surpassed the zealot Phinehas and have transfixed sin with the power of your piety and understanding . . .[64]

This allusion is one of the most revealing and significant sections in the *Logos*. Its significance is evinced by its strategic placement in the text, for it bridges the long exultation of imperial virtues that culminated in God entrusting Church and people to Justinian, and the first ascription of the shepherd metaphor to the emperor.[65] By simple textual association, then, this passage is associated with the central themes of a providential plan to establish Justinian II as Christ's vicegerent on earth for the moral reformation of the people and the purgation of their sins. In this schema, Phinehas was a potent model.[66] For the Book of Numbers records that near the end of the Israelites' wanderings and the settlement of the Promised Land, the Israelites had begun to worship idols, and were generally adopting foreign customs and committing sexual sins. Therefore, God had punished them by sending a plague. Undeterred, the Israelites continued sinning, culminating with an Israelite copulating with a Midianite

[61] *Trullo Revisited*, 47:20–48:1. For the rich range of meanings of *pathos* in patristic literature, see G. W. H. Lampe, *A Patristic Greek Lexicon* (Oxford, 1961–8), 992–4. A similar elision occurs in George of Pisidia, *Heraclias*, ed. A. Pertusi, *Giorgio di Pisidia. Poemi I: Panegirici epici* (Ettal, 1959), 240–61, 2.34–82.

[62] *Trullo Revisited*, 48:8–14.

[63] *Trullo Revisited*, 45:22–3.

[64] *Trullo Revisited*, 50:18–21.

[65] *Trullo Revisited*, 49:13–51:12.

[66] Indeed, Phinehas as a model of zeal can be found in both George of Pisidia and Theodore Syncellus; see Howard-Johnston, *Witnesses to a World Crisis*, 147.

woman. Seeing this, Phinehas took his spear and ran both through. God's ire was raised, the plague ended, and Phinehas and his heirs were promised peace and perpetual priesthood. Thus, in Phinehas there was an Old Testament exemplar for Justinian: a zealous leader, purging his kinsmen from sin, and especially 'pagan' practices, thereby propitiating divine wrath. That the punishment had taken the form of a plague must have resonated with a late seventh-century audience, which had lived with the ravages of the disease from the first outbreak in 541, and would until the last in 747.[67] Yet the exemplar is even more revealing, for Phinehas was then given command of the divinely proclaimed mission to conquer the Midianites. Given that the Arabs and the Midianites were frequently conflated in Byzantine literature, this is highly suggestive.[68] Furthermore, the army that Justinian sent against the Arabs in the same year as the Council was christened *periousios laos*, 'the chosen people', the very same phrase that in the *Logos* describes his people.[69] The message is clear. Justinian, the new Phinehas, having crushed internal sin would then annihilate the new Midianites and so fulfil God's promise of a new kingdom, a rejuvenated and reconquered Roman Empire dedicated to Christ.

This highlights a broader issue, namely Trullo's use of Scripture. Perhaps surprisingly, previous canonical literature had made scarce direct use of Scripture.[70] In complete contrast, Trullo's *Logos* and canons are suffused with it. Indeed, the *Logos* is almost exegetical, weaving together biblical ideas, images, and phrases. In this it ranges from direct appropriation and inspiration, such as the Phinehas example, through to generic concepts, and from acknowledged long quotation to small but verbatim phrases, to looser tonal and stylistic similarities.[71]

67 For the economic impact of the plague, see A. Laiou, 'The human resources', in *EHB*, 47–55, esp. 48–9.

68 See for instance, Alexander, *The Byzantine Apocalyptic Tradition*, 18.

69 Theophanes, 366; *Trullo Revisited*, 52:20–1. For the link, see Magdalino and Nelson, 'Introduction', 19.

70 See discussion and literature in Wagschal, *Law and Legality*, 95–9. For instance, the introduction to the *Nomokanon in XIV Titles* does not cite biblical authority on the nature of law, but Demosthenes through, most probably, the *Digest*, see Wagschal, *Law and Legality*, 97–9.

71 Altogether, there are 26 references in Ohme's new edition of the *Logos*, of varying relevance, and indubitably more could be found. Of these, there are some 14 direct quotations, long and short, ascribed and not.

Further, these were not haphazardly chosen for either aesthetic qualities or mere ideological concurrence, but were carefully selected from crucial passages of Scripture. Behind this was the rise of the Bible as the central text in Roman culture, with the Psalter in particular becoming the principal primer for education.[72] This intensive engagement with the text meant that the audience for the plethora of biblical phrases and images were already primed to receive favourably the notions expounded, and also to ground them in their original textual contexts and a wider web of exegesis. For instance, we have already noted the subtle alterations to the first scriptural citation in the *Logos*, Isaiah 9:2, yet the broader significance of this quotation is raised by its original context; for it is the pivot between Isaiah 8 where God punished the Jews, through the instrument of the Assyrians—with the Devil described a few lines later in the *Logos* as the Assyrian—to the brink of destruction, and the remainder of Isaiah 9 that foretold the coming of the Messiah to sit on David's throne and the destruction of Israel's enemies.[73] Thus, from the outset, the central tenet of the *Logos* that Trullo marked the redemption of the Romans and the imminence of their victorious revival was foreshadowed. The concluding triplet of references in the *Logos*' introductory paragraph reinforced the message. For it is because *latreia logikē*, 'reasonable worship' (Romans 12:1), had been universally established that redemption has arrived, with the whole story of the Bible fitted into this meta-narrative with the 'garden of delight' (Gen. 3:25), from which man had been expelled, reopened and 'everything is made new' (Rev. 21:5).[74]

The overwhelming majority of the scriptural references come from analogous contexts conveying a consistent idea of the future coming of a leader who would purge sin and restore Israel. The *Logos* identifies Justinian II as that foretold leader, through an extraordinarily thick knot of exegesis that forms the backbone of his imperial virtues:

> You who dispense your words in discernment, 'safeguard truth always' (cf. Ps. 145:7), 'render judgement and justice upon earth' (1 Kings = 1 Sam. 2:10) and 'walk in the blameless path' (cf. Ps. 118 [119]:1) . . . To

[72] See C. Mango, *Byzantium: The Empire of the New Rome* (London, 1980), 136. Cf. Haldon, *Seventh Century*, 427–9; Markus, *The End of Ancient Christianity*, 225; R. Markus, *Gregory the Great and His World* (Cambridge, 1997), 34–50.

[73] *Trullo Revisited*, 46:6–7, 14.

[74] *Trullo Revisited*, 46:20; 47:8, 9–10.

> you [Wisdom] has entrusted her Church and has taught you to 'meditate on her law day and night' (Ps. 1:2) for the correction and edification of the peoples subject to you.[75]

Again, all these references emanate from passages exalting just rulers obeying and enforcing the law of God, thereby ensuring terrestrial success. The theme suitably culminates with the final citation. Prima facie, the explicitly attested quotation from Jeremiah 36:13–14, 'For you will seek me with your whole heart, and I will appear to you', might seem generic almost to the point of irrelevance.[76] Yet Jeremiah 36 was aimed at the exiled community that was being tempted by false prophets, who claimed their words came from God, and it prophesizes that after 70 years, the exiles would return. Such a paradigm and timescale fitted the contemporary geopolitical situation perfectly, 692 being exactly 70 years after the emergence of that most threatening 'false prophet', Muhammad. Here, the *Logos* was appropriating contemporary expectations of imperial reconquest contained in apocalyptic literature and grounding that prediction in exegesis. Overall then, this sophisticated, multilayered employment of the Bible represents a wholesale scripturalization of imperial rhetoric.[77]

Yet this was not a total scripturalization of imperial ideology. Many of the ideas and images of kingship evinced were Hellenistic in origin. Moreover, much was generically Christian, and more particularly its late antique, imperial version. The concept of the emperor as the vicegerent of God on earth, leading his people to righteousness within a Christianized time frame, can be traced back to Eusebius.[78] Conversely, the richest, most obvious, and most historically common biblical storehouse of kingship imagery and concepts, viz. the Old Testament, is notable for its relatively low profile. Indeed, there is little systematic employment of Scripture for models of kingship, identity, or law. What Trullo proffers is an imperial Christian–Roman discourse that was fundamentally anchored in the late antique

[75] *Trullo Revisited*, 50:2–7, 13–17. Quotation marks are not in the original Greek but are added to ease recognition of different references.

[76] *Trullo Revisited*, 54:4–7, 1–4.

[77] For similar developments in the contemporary west, see collection of essays in A. Thacker (ed.), *The Power of the Word: The Influence of the Bible on Early Medieval Politics. Early Medieval Europe* 7:3 (1998).

[78] For the general importance of Eusebius in Byzantine thought, see D. Nicol, 'Byzantine political thought', in J. Burns (ed.), *The Cambridge History of Medieval Political Thought* (Cambridge, 1988), 51–79, esp. 51–4.

world, even if the Christian element was now hegemonic. Its true novelty was that the prime medium of articulating that discourse was now exegetical. However, this was manifestly more significant than the Bible becoming merely the favoured repository of quotations. Throughout Trullo, there is an underlying need to justify itself and its canons in relation to Scripture. This had become the ultimate referent, an authority greater than all others, if not the sole one. Thus, Scripture was not only a useful legitimizing tool, but a numinous well of knowledge which had to be consulted on all things.

Furthermore, Trullo did not use nor was suffused in Scripture equally, but rather was dominated by extracts from the New Testament rather than the Old. In both the *Logos* and the canons it was the New Testament that provided the majority of references, while most of those from the Old Testament either were from the Wisdom literature—and thus easily appended to Hellenic and New Testament notions—or were passages that had long been explained as foreshadowing Christ. Moreover, the biblical figure that towers over the *Logos* is Christ. It is to Christ that Justinian is explicitly and repeatedly linked, to such an extent that one could describe the model of government elucidated as Christocentric monarchy.[79] The only Old Testament models of leadership are implicitly David and explicitly Phinehas, interestingly both in the imperial symbolic arsenal since Heraclius, the one a priestly king, the other a warrior priest. Similarly, the definition of the people was Apostolic, a 'holy nation, the royal priesthood' (1 Peter 2:9), a 'special people' (Titus 2:14).[80] Thrice, the community was described as a flock(s).[81] The people were also those who partake of Communion gathered in the church, and more generally described as 'the faithful'.[82] Perhaps the only fleeting reference to 'Roman' is the phrase that God had 'converted our race', *hēmeteron genos metapoiēsanta*, who now had 'their citizenship [*politeuma*] in heaven' (Phil. 3:20).[83] Yet this is distinctly minor.

[79] For this concept the seminal work remains E. Kantorowicz, *The King's Two Bodies: A Study in Medieval Political Theology* (Princeton, 1957), who attributed it first to the tenth-century Ottonian rulers of the Holy Roman Empire. See also H. Mayr-Harting, *Ottonian Book Illumination* (London, 1991). Cf. N. Staubach, *Rex christianus: Hofkultur und Herrschaftspropaganda im Reich Karls des Kahlen* (Cologne, 1993), who prefers a Carolingian context for its emergence.

[80] *Trullo Revisited*, 52:7–8, 20–1.

[81] *Trullo Revisited*, 48:15; 50:22; general notion in 52:20–53:3.

[82] *Trullo Revisited*, 46:20–47:4; 47:21.

[83] *Trullo Revisited*, 49:3; 49:10–12.

Rather, Christian and Roman have become so conflated that the former has effectively engulfed the latter. This reflects not just the constraints of genre, nor the general decline in the potency of the identifier Roman; it is also a deliberately ecumenical, indeed imperial identity.[84] Multiple peoples were united by their faith, but also by the divinely appointed leadership of Justinian II.[85] Thus, the *Logos* was staking a claim for legitimate rule over all Christians by the emperor in Constantinople, for whom this council would provide a unified rite and canonical corpus. By embedding its rhetoric so firmly in the New Testament, Trullo proclaimed the common identity and unity of the Christian *oikoumenē*, who, now purified, could rebuke the heathens sent to chastise them. In short, it was a rhetoric, identity, and mode of rulership designed for reconquest.

Connected to this rhetoric is the *Logos*' conception of law and justice. Here it was an exclusive imperial prerogative and duty to render earthly justice and judgement.[86] Justinian II, after the model of David, was to meditate on Church law day and night.[87] Remarkably, there is very little else concerning law, *nomos*. There is little focus on God the judge, even less on God the lawgiver. There is no Law of Moses to act as a guide for mankind. Instead, it was righteous individuals, ultimately culminating in Justinian II, who acted as guides and leaders to the people. It was ignorance that led to lawlessness, *anomia*, and preaching, teaching, and illumination the solution, rather than the stern application of divine law. Further, the *Logos* is very careful in specifying that the council's purpose was to issue canons, *kanones*, a term that had from its origins been imbued with ascetic tones of moral rigour and regulation, and which by the seventh century had developed a definite technical difference from *nomos*, whether it was Roman or Mosaic Law.[88] Moreover, the focus on Scripture implies a desire to align canon law with divine law, or more plausibly to reassert that they were already aligned. However, it is again the new Christian covenant that is in view, not the old based on the Law. Careful analysis of the scriptural citation that recapitulates the central contention that the lack of canons from the Fifth and

[84] For the decline in the use of 'Roman' from the mid-sixth century, see Cameron, 'Images of authority', esp. 24–9.

[85] *Trullo Revisited*, 50:17.

[86] *Trullo Revisited*, 50:4–7.

[87] *Trullo Revisited*, 50:14–15.

[88] See Wagschal, *Law and Legality*, 132–45 for overview and literature.

Sixth Councils had led to a decline in discipline, morality, and unity clearly reveals this.[89] For it cites Hebrews 10:29:

> They have spurned the Son of God, profaned the blood of the covenant through which they were sanctified, and outraged the Spirit of Grace.[90]

The whole thrust of this passage in Scripture is that the Law of Moses was a mere shadow of the new covenant of Grace. So, when Justinian took up the task of returning the people 'to the fold and convince it to keep the divine commandments and statutes, through which we desist from dead deeds and are given life', in the vaguest echo of Moses, his stated aim was to return people to the righteousness demanded of Christians.[91] Canons were the tool to achieve this, 'through which people might desist from their less noble and lowly conduct, and might be brought to a better and loftier life'.[92] Canon law was thus the crook by which the Christian flock were ordered and reformed. Its purpose was exhortatory, to guide people to a better life, rather than punishment for past sins. The canons' ultimate point was one of cleansing and purgation, as expounded in the final image proffered in the *Logos*:

> You ordained the gathering of this holy and God-chosen ecumenical council, in order that through the consent of many gathered together your purpose might be fittingly accomplished; but that if any remnant of pagan or Jewish perversity should be mixed in with the ripe grain of truth, it might be taken out by the root as a tare, and the corn-field of the Church be made clean.[93]

The *Logos*, therefore, elucidated a rich ideological paradigm that structured the canons that followed, whose interplay with the above themes we shall now examine.

THE APPROPRIATION OF THE CHRISTIAN PAST AND THE FUNCTION OF CANON LAW

Canons 1 and 2 continue many of the themes of the *Logos*, forming with it an extended introduction, separated from the remainder of the canons by rubric, length, and significance. C.1 narrates the doctrinal

[89] *Trullo Revisited*, 52:1–20. [90] *Trullo Revisited*, 52:16–20.
[91] *Trullo Revisited*, 53:1–6. Cf. Deut. 30:15–20.
[92] *Trullo Revisited*, 52:2–7. [93] *Trullo Revisited*, 53:11–54:1.

decisions of the preceding six ecumenical councils, and C.2 the composition of the canonical corpus. As such they form with the *Logos* three descending but interlocked paradigms, namely the cosmological history of the *Logos*, the evolution of Christian dogma, and finally the creation of canon law. Thereby, they situate Trullo within those pasts, and thus seek to legitimize its proceedings and glorify its convenor, Justinian II.

C.1 commences, literally, with order, for it begins by quoting Gregory Nazianzen saying, '[*Taxis aristē*] It is the best rule, when beginning any speech or action, to begin with God and to end with God.'[94] C.1 thus proclaimed the best order as one encompassed by God. Therefore, Trullo's canons and the Church itself, both constituents of that order, have 'Christ for its foundation'.[95] For this reason, it was vital for the council to declare its loyalty to the 'preservation inviolate and without innovation of the faith handed down to us by the eyewitnesses of the Word, the God-Chosen Apostles'.[96] Thereby, C.1 positioned Trullo within the tradition that stretched back to the foundation of the Church. It then proceeded to connect the definitions of the six ecumenical councils to that apostolic inheritance. More immediately, it connected Trullo to that tradition through the Sixth Council of 681. For it says that 'now that true piety is proclaimed by us clearly', implying the renewal of orthodoxy in 681, it was therefore possible to state the faith as the root of their 'sacred discourses'.[97] Further, due to the very nature of their subject, i.e. an immutable God, these theological and Christological decisions are repeatedly presented as unalterable truth. Therefore, dogma was raised in the conclusion of C.1 to the level of divine law in an echo of Moses: 'for we are resolved and cannot, for any reason whatsoever, either add anything or make any deletion from that which has been previously decreed.'[98] The discourse of doctrine, the proclaimed foundation of the succeeding canons, was declared complete and unchangeable.

To demonstrate their loyalty to that tradition, the history of the ecumenical councils was narrated and their decisions confirmed. The prime actors portrayed in this drama were the emperors.[99] They assembled the councils, and it was under their authority that the

[94] *Trullo Revisited*, 55:13–15.
[95] *Trullo Revisited*, 55:19–20.
[96] *Trullo Revisited*, 56:4–9.
[97] *Trullo Revisited*, 55:16–18; 56:3.
[98] *Trullo Revisited*, 64:8–12.
[99] The only person mentioned who is not an emperor, bar a multitude of heretics, is Gregory Nazianzen.

councils defined dogma. This overwhelming stress on the emperors furthered the image constructed in the *Logos* of the Church entrusted to imperial stewardship, and therefore he being responsible for the illumination of the Christian people. Just as in the *Logos*, the church per se is less an actor, far less the actor, in the formulation of dogma, or more broadly in the moral leadership of the people, but rather the stage on which pious ecclesiastics, gathered and nurtured by the emperor, defined and maintained the faith. Instead, the principal font of activity presented was indubitably imperial.

Moreover, among those emperors it is Justinian I and Constantine IV, respectively the conveners of the Fifth and Sixth Councils, who are specially mentioned. For whereas the previous four emperors were ascribed the rather bland description *tou genomenou hēmōn basileōs*, 'our former emperor',[100] Justinian was described as *tou tēs eusebous lēxeōs genomenou hēmōn basileōs*, 'our former emperor of pious memory',[101] and Constantine IV as *tou en theia tē lēxei genomenou hēmōn basileōs*, 'our former emperor, deceased in God'.[102] Furthermore, these epithets were recycled from the *Logos*, except the descriptions of Justinian and Constantine are reversed.[103] This served the dual purpose of underlining the significance of the Trullo's immediate synodical forebears, but also associated Justinian and Constantine IV as mirror images of each other.

C.2 introduces the third and lowest plane in the introductory schema: the narrow paradigm of canon law. The immediate pretext for the canon was a specific problem, the authenticity of the *Apostolic Constitutions*. Since the late fourth century, the *Apostolic Canons* had been a somewhat disputed element of the canonical corpus, whose primary utility was to connect the late antique Church with the apostles, thus legitimizing their own canons through imitation.[104] But whereas by the seventh century, the *Apostolic Canons* were firmly part of the corpus, the broader *Constitutions* which the canons endorsed were more suspect. As C.2 relates, 'certain spurious passages, foreign to true piety, have been inserted to the detriment of the Church by heretics, obscuring from us the comely beauty of divine

[100] *Trullo Revisited*, 56:13–14; 57:12–13; 58:14; 59:11.

[101] *Trullo Revisited*, 60:15–16.

[102] *Trullo Revisited*, 61:16–17.

[103] *Trullo Revisited*, 51:17–19.

[104] H. Ohme, 'Sources of the Greek canon law to the Quinisext Council (691/2): councils and Church Fathers', in W. Hartmann and K. Pennington (eds), *The History of Byzantine and Eastern Canon Law to 1500* (Washington DC, 2012), 24–114, 28–33.

doctrines.'[105] Therefore, C.2 rejected the *Constitutions* while affirming the *Canons*, so to keep pure the Apostolic teaching and for the general edification and security of the Christian flock.[106]

In the process of doing so, the canon defined the functions of canon law. It was a law that taught and enlightened, while saying little on punishment. The most important aspect, however, is that canons were *pros psuchōn therapeian kai iatreian pathōn*, 'for the healing of souls and the curing of passions'.[107] This healing imagery picked up a theme from the *Logos* where the Devil 'wounds the faithful with passions',[108] while C.1 declared that the faith handed down by tradition was *aparatrōton*, 'without wound'.[109] We have already noted the ambiguity inherent in the word *pathos*, combining both the idea of external misfortune and inward passion, and how the linkage between the two underpinned Trullo's goal in banishing the misfortunes of the collective through treatment of the individual's soul. Moreover, the concept of the sickly soul made ill through internal passions, necessitating rigour and rules, has long antecedents in Graeco-Roman thought, especially in the Stoic tradition.[110] Indeed, health and piety shared a conceptual space greater than simple imagery. In essence, classical thought held that disease and immorality were creations of the internal world. However, in Jewish thought, sin and disease were external afflictions.[111] Here, the two are combined, although the latter is dominant; it is wounds inflicted and passions aroused by the Devil and heretics that needed to be healed through canons. Canon law is presented as a tool and medicine, of secondary importance to the teacher and doctor administering it. Certainly, it is not presented as a new divine law, similar to Mosaic Law, which formed the basis of a community. Rather, it is simply a collection of guidelines and exhortations handed down by the Apostles and the Fathers for the edification of the people who were defined by faith, that is the realm of the *Logos* and C.1.

Canon law's relative subservience was also reflected in the history presented. For compared to the epic narrative of the *Logos*, and the

[105] *Trullo Revisited*, 65:10–15.
[106] *Trullo Revisited*, 65:16–23.
[107] *Trullo Revisited*, 64:20–65:1.
[108] *Trullo Revisited*, 47:21–48:1.
[109] *Trullo Revisited*, 56:5.
[110] See M. Schofield, 'Stoic ethics', and R. Hankinson, 'Stoicism and medicine', both in B. Inwood (ed.), *The Cambridge Companion to the Stoics* (Cambridge, 2003), respectively 233–56 and 295–309.
[111] Haldon, 'Anastasius of Sinai', 143–4.

lengthy laudations of C.1, C.2 is little more than a list of councils and fathers. Whereas the *Logos* began with Christ and C.1 immutable Orthodoxy dogma, C.2 commences with the Apostles, and then an interloper into the tradition. Importantly, there was no mention of emperors. The precise formation of canon law was portrayed as beneath their elevated status as God's chosen shepherd. Consequently, there was no notion of the emperor or indeed God as legislator. It was councils and fathers, in imitation and continuation from the prototype of the Apostles, who devised canons for the healing of souls. Further, unlike divine law, canon law was mutable. The only element that C.2 declared closed was the inherited corpus, now definitively purged of the *Apostolic Constitutions*.[112] Canon law was, therefore, the third and least of the paradigms offered in Trullo's introductory complex, but it directly emanated from the other two and through them was raised into an implement that could achieve the proclaimed goal of moral cleansing and imperial rejuvenation.

The subordination of canon law is far less surprising than the fact that Trullo's principal business was canon law. All previous ecumenical councils, which Trullo incessantly claimed to be, had dogma as their predominant concern. The generation of disciplinary canons had always been a secondary function. Rather, it was at local synods that the majority of the canonical corpus had been formulated, supplemented by patristic sources. Over time, the canonical corpus, in particular the numbering of legitimate councils, solidified so that even local synods could not create canons, or more precisely canons with universal application. Thus, the most recent authorities, conciliar and patristic, cited in C.2 were from the fifth century. Moreover, the *Logos* had castigated this inactivity as the source of the empire's moral dissipation and decline.[113] Trullo's extensive additions were, therefore, a radical reanimation of conciliar legislation and an upgrading in the importance of canon law into the principal function of an ecumenical council. Further, given this inherent innovation, Trullo had to cloak itself in legitimizing tradition, thus C.2's citation and affirmation of canonical history.

The actual documentation of the history of canon law given is in fact rather terse, presented almost as an afterthought to the

[112] *Trullo Revisited*, 68:17–69:9. [113] *Trullo Revisited*, 52:1–15.

adjudication on the *Apostolic Constitutions*.[114] Yet it represents the first and last 'official' (i.e. conciliar) listing of canonical authorities, and has become the foundation stone of eastern Orthodox canon law. The only precedent was Chalcedon C.1, whose one sentence proclaimed the general affirmation of previous canons. In its choice it was not radical, essentially repeating the contemporary standard list. This is hardly surprising, for the canonical corpus was a conservative genre, with the bulk of canons agreed across Christendom.[115] It would be barely conceivable, therefore, had Trullo offered anything more radical. Indeed, the principal purpose of the canon was not to form an official list of canonical sources, but to affirm Trullo's loyalty to a pre-existing tradition and thereby to situate their canons within its trajectory. However, as the dispute over the *Constitutions* shows, the canon was being interpolated in the seventh century. By cleansing it, Trullo was not just affirming the true and hallowed tradition, but staking its right to be the authority that could cleanse canon law. Further, C.2 might add little new, but it did sanction and delimit the corpus that had emerged, and stamped it with the authority of an ecumenical council. Finally, it pronounced Trullo's—and through it Justinian II's—authority to decide what was and what was not canon law. In short, C.2 established Trullo's legitimacy to codify what there was, and to legislate what there was not. Having established their legitimacy, and the function of canons as healing, what precisely did the Trullan canons prescribe?

THE CANONS: CODIFICATION, MORAL REFORMATION, AND IMPERIAL RESTORATION

The first notable aspect of the Trullan canons is their structure, for unlike the canons of preceding councils, they actually had one. Canons had normally been issued in a distinctly unsystematic way,

[114] See Wagschal, *Law and Legality*, 30–78 for the slow growth and organization of the corpus, and the role of Trullo 2 in that process. See also for canon 2 and the issue of codification Ohme, *Konzil Quinisextum*, 32–4.

[115] Wagschal, *Law and Legality*, 78–82. For a good overview of the emergence of variations between east and west over the canonical corpus, see Gallagher, *Church Law*. It must be stressed, however, that by the time of Trullo in 691/2, the overwhelming majority of the canonical material was shared between east and west.

different councils varying wildly in the scope, number, and focus of their canons. Indeed, it was the very unwieldiness of the growing corpus, along with imitation of the contemporary codifications in civil law, that prompted the first systematic canonical collections in the sixth century.[116] The Trullan canons are ordered into three distinct and explicitly stated groupings, within which there is a loose ordering by association—that is, similar topics are found together.[117] Canons 3–39 are grouped under the heading 'concerning priests and clerics',[118] 40–49 'concerning monks and nuns',[119] and 50–102 'concerning laymen'.[120] This is a deliberate structuring of material by religious role, with the three orders of clergy, monks, and laity.[121] Thereby, Trullo was rhetorically encompassing the entirety of Roman society, not just churchmen and ascetics, in an all-embracing legislative schema. Further, this was not a random number, for as Louth has expounded, the 'century' was by the seventh century a popular genre of monastic literature, a type of florilegium of moral principles and ascetic rules.[122] The appropriation of a popular contemporary genre further evinces Trullo's embedment in seventh-century culture. More importantly, it reveals an underlying function of these canons. They were a form of *askēsis* for all Justinian II's subjects.

Trullo is also extraordinary for its length, containing almost twice as many canons as issued by all preceding ecumenical councils.[123] This length supported considerable and unprecedented variety. Typical topics such as clerical celibacy (C.3), ecclesiastical organization (e.g. Cs.8, 15, 16), and monastic purity (C.40) cohabit with more

[116] See in general Gallagher, *Church Law*, 20–9.

[117] Numerous examples are evident from the exploration of the canons by theme given below. This associative principle will be a recurrent feature of nearly all the legislation explored in this work.

[118] *Trullo Revisited*, 69:10. [119] *Trullo Revisited*, 119:1–2.

[120] *Trullo Revisited*, 132:1.

[121] For the same division in the thought of Augustine and Gregory the Great, see Markus, *Gregory the Great*, 27–8.

[122] A. Louth, 'St John Damascene as monastic theologian', *The Downside Review* 125 (2007), 197–220. It is also interesting that the 'century' is composed of almost equal sections of 50 canons, following the numbering of the *Synagoga* and of course the *Digest*, one for the clergy and monks, one for the laity.

[123] The precise number of canons is a vexed issue. However, there were *c*.460 canons issued before Trullo by those authorities recognized by Trullo C.2, including the 85 Apostolic canons, many repetitious, so Trullo represents an expansion of more than 20% over (supposedly) the previous six centuries of legislation.

eccentric items, such as a prohibition on Bibles being destroyed or cut up for perfumers (C.68), civil law students dressing inappropriately and going to the theatre (C.71), and men plaiting their hair (C.96). This scope is Trullo's leitmotif. Its canons are all-encompassing, touching upon every aspect of Christian life. In a word, they are ecumenical.

Their relationship to the pre-existing canonical corpus is complex, ranging from repetition to innovation. Several canons are verbatim and explicitly ascribed citations of previous canons.[124] Others are uncited recapitulations or paraphrases.[125] Some use generalized quotes from the Fathers to support their legislation, such as C.24 instructing neither clergy nor monks to go to the races or the theatre.[126] Yet others are compilations of multiple canons.[127] That Trullo contained much that was unoriginal is hardly surprising, for it neither sprang *ex nihilo* nor claimed to be bringing new law; rather it set out to restore and restate the old. Each repetition connected Trullo to the established corpus. Further, as canon law had been elevated in the introductory complex into the cure for empire's sins, repeat prescription of sanctified and hallowed rules was a deliberate remedy. For it was not that the canons were wrong, but that people failed to follow them. Ergo, a *selection* of the most relevant canons, including the elegant weaving of multiple texts, to avoid the canonical corpus' own unwieldiness and repetitiousness, would aid the cleansing of cleric and layman alike. Thus Trullo produced not a jumble of existing canons, but an officially sanctioned selection from an authorized set of sources, designed and organized systematically; that is, Trullo was codifying in a manner highly reminiscent of Justinian I's codification of civil law.[128]

An adjunct to codification was adjudication, between contradictory canons and those canons which were either obsolete or objectionable. For instance, C.29 invalidated Carthage C.41 in favour of Laodicea C.50. Further, C.8 updated the repeated canonical instruction for regional synods of bishops to meet twice a year under the authority of their metropolitan, which due to barbarian incursions was now impractical, and so the requirement was reduced to one annual

[124] E.g. C.36, cf. Chalcedon C.28. [125] E.g. C.92, cf. Chalcedon C.27.
[126] Cf. Laodicaea C.54. [127] C.54, cf. Basil Cs.27, 68, 75, 76, 79, 87.
[128] For this principle in general, see Louth, 'Byzantium transforming', 244.

meeting.[129] This updating of the corpus is accompanied by more radical interventions. For instance, C.12 explicitly overturned the African custom of allowing bishops to cohabit with their wives after ordination, even though it was supported not just by local custom (Carthage Cs.3, 4, 25) but also by the fifth Apostolic canon, for:

> We say this not for the abolition and overthrowing of Apostolic ordinances, but in order to provide for salvation and progress of people towards better things, and that no reproach may attach to the sacerdotal state.[130]

This ruling was justified through a lengthy scriptural citation that demanded Christians not to give offence and to imitate Christ.[131] Here, Trullo was prepared to overrule ancient practices, supported by unquestionably legitimate canons, not just for the sake of a unified code, but to purify the clergy and so aid the salvation of the people, and to match a Scriptural injunction.

Trullo not only codified the existing, but also created completely new canons. For example, as Brubaker has noted, Trullo provided the first canonical regulations concerning art.[132] Most famously, due to its implications in the iconoclast controversy, C.82 declared that Christ should no longer be presented as a lamb but in figural form. This was truly radical, overturning a tradition-hallowed practice in the pursuit of a purer and more perfect form of Christianity. Further, C.73 ordained that the 'life-giving cross' should not be disrespected by being portrayed on floors where it could be trodden on.[133] Both canons indicate a new general desire to protect and promote certain symbols, and therefore a new sensitivity to how Christianity, and particularly Christ, was presented.[134] Almost certainly this sensitivity was linked to the rise of Islam, one of whose central precepts was to stress the unity of God and therefore deny the Incarnation, a message

[129] *Trullo Revisited*, 79:15. Cf. Nicaea I C.5, Chalcedon C.19; Apostolic Canons C.37; Antioch C.20. This is a prime example of (a) the canonical corpus repeating itself and (b) the seriousness of the 'barbarian invasions' to occasion the abandonment of a rule supported in four councils.

[130] *Trullo Revisited*, 83:4–10.

[131] *Trullo Revisited*, 83:11–18; quoting 1 Cor. 10:31–11:1.

[132] L. Brubaker, 'In the beginning was the Word: art and orthodoxy at the Council of Trullo (692) and Nicaea II (787)', in A Louth and A. Casiday (eds), *Byzantine Orthodoxies* (Aldershot, 2006), 95–101.

[133] *Trullo Revisited*, 155:4.

[134] In general see L. Brubaker, 'Icons before iconoclasm', *Settimane di studio del Centro italiano di studi sull'Alto Medioevo* 45 (Spoleto, 1998), 1215–54.

being more stridently proclaimed than ever before in this period.[135] Moreover, considering the constant verbal linkage of Justinian II and Christ in the *Logos*, an image reified in Justinian's coins, patently Justinian was confronting the challenge from Islam head-on by intimately associating the image of Christ with his own.[136] The final canon concerning art, C.100, is the most sweeping of all, declaring:

> Wisdom commands: *Let your eyes look directly forward* and *keep your heart with all vigilance* (Prov. 4:25, 23); for the sensations of the body all too easily influence the soul. Therefore, we command that henceforth absolutely no pictures should be drawn which enchant the eyes, be they on panels or set forth in any other wise, corrupting the mind and inciting flames of shameful pleasures. If any dares to do this, he shall be excommunicated.[137]

In a typical piece of rhetoric, the canon is framed by Scripture, thereby casting it as fulfilling divine instructions. Further, it expands on the theme of external influences corrupting the soul. Indeed, the entire issue of correct and incorrect art is subordinated to a grander narrative of purity of practice and people.[138]

This reflects a paradigm shift at the heart of Trullo. Dogmatic controversy was declared closed. What mattered at Trullo were questions of practical morality. In that schema, clergy and monks were vital instruments, but not the beginning and the end as they generally had been heretofore in canon law. Instead, it was the *haplousteroi*, the 'more simple-minded', and therefore those most at risk from the darkness of ignorance denounced in the *Logos*, who needed shielding, purifying, and illuminating.[139] It was they who were to be protected from the deceit of diviners (C.61), those feigning possession (C.60), false martyr stories (C.63), and participation in pagan rites (C.62). This radical refocusing is evidenced by the fact that the majority of the section concerning the laity, which at over half the canons is vastly

135 Donner, *Muhammad and the Believers*, 212–14.

136 For Justinian II's reformed coinage, see J. Breckenridge, *The Numismatic Iconography of Justinian II* (New York, 1959). For further and a proposed date of 690 for this reform, see M. Humphreys, 'The "war of images" revisited. Justinian's coinage reform and the Caliphate', *The Numismatic Chronicle* 173 (2013), 229–44.

137 *Trullo Revisited*, 180:17–181:10. Italics are in the original text.

138 Brubaker, 'In the beginning', 97–8.

139 *Trullo Revisited*, 141:11. See J. Herrin, 'The Quinisext Council (692) as a continuation of Chalcedon', in R. Price and M. Whitby (eds), *Chalcedon in Context: Church Councils 400–700* (Liverpool, 2009), 148–68, esp. 163.

more than in any previous council, had no canonical precedent whatsoever. Therefore, whereas those canons concerning clerics and monks can be described as primarily a codification, those concerning the laity represent new legislation for moral reformation.

The recurring theme underlying all the canons is purity and purification. The initial component of this is clerical purity. The first, and by far the longest, canon of the century, C.3, concerns that repeat canonical bugbear of clerical marriage. It begins:

> Whereas our pious and Christ-loving emperor, in his address to this holy ecumenical council, has requested that it should make pure and faultless ministers of those enrolled in the clergy who transmit divine things to others, so that they might be worthy of the spiritual sacrifice of the great God who is at once sacrifice and high priest, and that it should cleanse the defilement which has attached to them through unlawful marriages.[140]

Thus, the drive to cleanse the priesthood was framed as an imperial and divine priority. That prominence flowed from the prime stated role of the clergy, the celebration of Communion, the central symbol of the new covenant with Christ. Therefore, those who administered the sacrament needed to be beyond reproach, in the eyes of both heaven and the world. This opening statement should be seen as announcing the principal purpose of the whole, namely the formation of a pure clergy. This idea was based on, and culminated with, the quoted maxim of St Basil that 'it is incongruous that one who must tend his own wounds should give blessing to another'.[141]

Expanding on the theme, C.4 punished sexual impurity, specifically deposing clerics who had sex with a woman dedicated to God, and excommunicating any layman who did so. Similarly, C.5 enlarged the established canonical restrictions on women cohabiting with clergy into a blanket ban on keeping any woman or maidservant. More broadly, Trullo also attacked clerical participation in any inappropriate or unseemly activity. Ergo, clerics could not own taverns (C.9), receive interest (C.10), or interact with Jews (C.11). Clerics should not be ordained for money (C.22), go to the races or the theatre (C.24), or wear improper clothes (C.27). Nor should clergy only be drawn

[140] *Trullo Revisited*, 69:17–70:8.

[141] *Trullo Revisited*, 71:10–13; cf. Basil C.22.

from a priestly family, as was done in Armenia following Jewish custom (C.33).

A proper clergy should be an ordered clergy. Therefore, seating preferences were a recurrent issue (Cs.3, 7, 26), the age of ordinations was stipulated (Cs.14, 15), and the number of deacons discussed (C.16). Clerics should only be transferred with the permission of the bishop (C.17). The only exception was those who had fled the barbarian incursions who could remain only until the (implied imminent) return of political normality.[142] Similarly, barbarian incursions were invoked to justify the ordination and administration of bishops of sees who could not take up residence, as they canonically should, so that 'the heathen depredations should in no wise have a harmful influence on ecclesiastical law'.[143] These canons project an impression of marked disorder caused by warfare, and considering the grave moral—indeed almost cosmological—imputed consequences of disorder, re-establishment of proper order was by implication a moral crusade.

More prosaically, bishops were not to preach in another bishop's city (C.20), while the authority of bishops over village parishes was reaffirmed (C.25). C.36 restated, as Constantinople saw it, the ranking of the patriarchates and the equality of privileges afforded between old and new Rome. C.38 reiterated the stipulation that the organization of bishoprics should follow the civil organization, underlying the interpenetration of the two. This, along with C.37, framed C.39, which established the bishop of Cyprus at Nea Justinianopolis in the Hellespont, the city that Justinian II had founded for Cypriots he had transferred.[144] The canon also raised the bishop to metropolitan rank, and in the signatory list he was placed above all other metropolitans, thereby enhancing further the status and prestige of Justinian's new city. This transfer was more than a simple civil and ecclesiastical reorganization in the face of outside pressure. For, as Theophanes records, Justinian had deliberately transferred part of the population of Cyprus in violation of the treaty with the Arabs, who shared the revenues of the island with the empire.[145] This canon then was bestowing ecumenical legitimacy and justification to a strategic

[142] C.18. [143] C.37, *Trullo Revisited*, 115:19–21.

[144] For discussion of this policy, see P. B. Englezakis, *Cyprus Nea Justinianoupolis* (Nicosia, 1990).

[145] Theophanes, 365.

redeployment of the empire's resources, whose significance would be partially responsible for the resumption of hostilities. Instead of imperial provocation, the canon has the bishop fleeing of his own accord from the:

> inroads of the barbarians and in order to place himself solely under the sceptre of the most Christian empire, fleeing the aforesaid island, through the providence of God and the efforts of our pious and Christ-loving emperor.[146]

Thus, the old Roman/barbarian division had been elided and almost completely replaced by the Christian/heathen dichotomy. The empire is Christian, the emperor Christ-loving. This canon is the summation, literally and metaphorically, of all the canons on the clergy. For it presents the priesthood, tattered and shaken by war, fleeing to the Christian emperor for protection. Yet, as Cs.37 and 39 make clear, those bishops in no way abdicated their authority over their sees, despite being temporarily sundered from them by heathen barbarians. The whole thrust of the section is that the priesthood belonged to the Christian empire, whose ecumenical synod Trullo was, and which therefore had the right and duty to legislate for the whole empire, including those areas that had fallen and would be restored.

The purified clergy's prime duty was to administer the Eucharist. Therefore, ritual purity, above all the sanctity of Communion, was central to Trullo's agenda. Communion was not to be tainted by the custom of mixing the wine with an offering of grapes, as it was 'for their [the people's] vivification and the pardon of their sins'.[147] Likewise, milk and honey could not be offered at the altar (C.57) and water had to be mixed with the wine (C.32). Nor could the Armenian practice of offering cooked meat to the altar and the priests, 'after the manner of the Jews', be permitted for 'preserving the pureness of the Church' (C.99).[148] No layman could give himself the divine Mysteries if a member of the clergy was present (C.58), while clerics were prohibited from selling Communion (C.23). The divine Eucharist was also not to be tainted by association with death, so could not be given to the deceased (C.83).

The canons also frequently concern the Christian calendar, and especially the arrangements for Lent that fell upon clergy and lay

[146] *Trullo Revisited*, 117:8–16.
[147] C.28, *Trullo Revisited*, 103:4–6.
[148] *Trullo Revisited*, 180:3–5.

alike. The date for the mass of the Presanctified during Lent was set (C.52), and Lent fasting on Saturdays and Sundays was prohibited (C.55). C.56 condemned the Armenian custom of eating eggs and cheese on Saturdays and Sundays in Lent. This dietary diatribe was justified through the resolution that 'throughout all the world the Church of God should follow one order of fasting'.[149] Again, Trullo's ecumenical authority and intent were revealed, along with the presumption that a uniform Christian rite regulated by a united canon would win divine approval.

The priesthood was also there to teach. C.19 in particular exhorts that the:

> Superiors of the Churches must instruct all their clergy and their people in true piety every day, but especially on Sundays, choosing for them from divine Scripture the thoughts and judgements of truth and following unswervingly definitions already set forth and the tradition of the God-bearing Fathers.[150]

Instruction was aimed at both clergy and people, and supposed to be constant and based on Scripture. Moreover, no one was to interpret Scripture beyond the doctrines given in C.1 or the tradition of the Fathers. Theology was a closed discourse, to be trumpeted as widely as possible in order to educate the masses:

> For through the teachings of the aforementioned Fathers the people are given knowledge of important things and virtues, and of unprofitable things and those to be rejected; thus they reform their lives for the better and escape being taken captive by the emotions of ignorance; giving heed to this teaching they incite themselves to avoid succumbing to evil and work out their salvation in fear of the punishments which hang over them.[151]

The implicit purpose of these canons was therefore to pronounce the traditions of the Fathers and to form a clergy that would carry the message of reform to combat sin-inducing ignorance.

Further ordinances regulate the interrelation of cleric and lay, including the stipulation that baptism, the 'immaculate illumination',[152] should not be performed in a private oratory but in their parish church (C.59), that laymen could not enter the sanctuary

[149] *Trullo Revisited*, 137:13–16.
[150] *Trullo Revisited*, 94:15–95:3.
[151] *Trullo Revisited*, 95:13–96:2.
[152] *Trullo Revisited*, 139:10.

(C.69), and that no layman could teach or lecture on dogma (C.64). There is here an evident desire to demarcate clergy from laity, and holy from profane.[153] This extended to the church buildings, as no one was to eat in them (C.74), undertake any kind of commerce in the precincts (C.76), or 'otherwise heedlessly profane sacred places and conduct themselves contemptuously' in them.[154]

Purity was guarded to enable spiritual cleansing. The lay were enjoined to regular church attendance (C.80), especially during Easter week, when games were to be banned (C.66). All those to be baptized had to learn the creed and recite it before bishops or presbyters (C.78). Anything that might cause doubt in the Truth of Christ, such as the writing or reading of fake martyrologies (C.63), was proscribed; any who mocked it, such as by feigning possession by demons (C.60), were punished. The key linkage, however, comes again in the Eucharist, which is given a final flourish in canon 101. It begins, in typical fashion, with Scripture: '*Body of Christ* and *temple* (1 Cor. 12:27; 3:16): so does the divine Apostle loudly proclaim man, created in God's likeness.'[155] Immediately the amalgam Christ, sacrifice and priest, is joined to Christ's people. It continues:

> Transcending, therefore, all perceptible creation, he who has achieved heavenly rank through the passion of the Saviour, eating and drinking Christ, is made fit forever for the life everlasting, sanctified in soul and body by his participation in divine grace.[156]

The Eucharist is posited as the conduit to salvation, the *sine qua non* of the good Christian life. Therefore, true Christians were not to receive it in vessels of gold or silver, 'since they prefer inanimate and subordinate matter to the image of God', but in their hands.[157] Christ's people were to accept humbly Christ's sacrifice given by the divinely ordained, and newly reformed, clergy.

More general moral reformation was also advanced. Dice-playing was proscribed (C.50), as was attendance at mimes, wild-beast fights, and theatrical dancing (C.51). Pimps were excommunicated (C.86), as were those who used pagan oaths (C.94). Women who took drugs that caused abortion were to be treated as murderers (C.91). A group of canons concern marriage. C.53 proscribed marriage between

[153] See Ohme, *Konzil Quinisextum*, 101–7.
[154] C.97, *Trullo Revisited*, 178:19–179:2.
[155] *Trullo Revisited*, 181:15–18.
[156] *Trullo Revisited*, 181:18–182:3.
[157] *Trullo Revisited*, 182:15–17.

godfathers and the widowed mothers of those children they had sponsored. The canonical stipulation on prohibited degrees of relations for marriage was clarified, with marriage between first cousins, father and son with mother and daughter, and two brothers with two sisters explicitly condemned for the first time, in order to prevent the previous canonical silence leading to sin (C.54). Further, the orthodox could not marry heretics, 'for one must not mix things which are pure, nor join a wolf to a sheep and the portion of Christ to the lot of sinners'.[158] This canon thus combined purity, ritual, and the imagery of Christ the Shepherd. Further, the canonical penalty for various forms of adultery was stated (Cs.87, 93), likewise for those who had married someone betrothed to another (C.98) or had abducted a woman on the pretext of marriage (C.92). Again these canons were protecting a central sacrament of the Church, often with frequent recourse to Scripture, in a manner that fitted both the general trajectory of Trullo, but is also exceedingly similar to the civil legislation that we shall explore in later chapters.[159]

Interwoven through these themes is the language of illumination and knowledge versus darkness and ignorance. Moreover, there are recurrent images of cleansing and purging. Yet the culminating theme of the canons is healing, with C.102 thereby expanding the theme first explored at length in C.2 as the very purpose of canons. In essence, C.102 was a restatement of the principle of economy, *oikonomia*, that the Church should be flexible in the application of its strictures and penalties according to the stance of the sinner, first enunciated by St Basil, whose canon is quoted at the end.[160] However, there is a marked degree of embellishment. Sin is defined as an 'illness', which should be treated by those 'who profess the science of spiritual healing'.[161] The whole point of canons was to cure the sinner, not to punish for the sake of punishment. Indeed, canons were as much exhortations to good conduct and spiritual health as a treatment. Healing is then combined with sheep imagery:

> For the entire concern of God and of the one entrusted with pastoral authority is to bring back the lost sheep and heal the serpent's bite:

[158] C.72, *Trullo Revisited*, 153:18–154:3.

[159] A further similarity is in the interest in testamentary witnesses. E.g. C.85 legislates that the emancipation of slaves, a thoroughly civil law issue, should take place before two or three witnesses, following Mt. 18:16.

[160] Basil C.3.

[161] *Trullo Revisited*, 183:16; 184:4–5.

> neither pushing the sufferer to the precipice of despair, nor giving him rein to lead a dissolute or contemptuous life, but by one or another means . . . to stay the suffering [*pathos*].[162]

Considering the imagery of the *Logos*, 'the one entrusted with pastoral authority' was probably not, or not only, priests but Justinian II himself. Thus, both God and his chosen emperor desired the return of the lost sheep and the healing of the people. Trullo's canons present themselves as the hoped-for tool of the *Logos*, designed for the reformation of the Christian people as a prelude to the restoration of the Christian empire.

THE SIGNATORY LIST AND THE ECUMENICAL COUNCIL

The final element of Trullo is its episcopal subscription list. Like any signatory list, its primary function was to legitimize proceedings through the documenting of approval from appropriate authorities, and to explicitly demonstrate the signatories' consent to both substance and process. Reciprocally, inclusion on the list implied authority to confirm. In the specific context of an ecumenical council, this was reinforced by the conception that only a synod of bishops could issue canons, and only an ecumenical council could legislate for the entire Christian world. The definition of what constituted ecumenical had shifted as part of the general evolution of the Church, yet by the time of Justinian I, the essential criterion was agreement from the pentarchy, the five patriarchs under whom ecclesiastical administration of the Orthodox was divided.[163]

It was therefore essential to Trullo's legitimacy to garner as great an episcopal participation and consent as possible. Indeed, Justinian needed Trullo's status as ecumenical to be confirmed, both to guarantee the prestige accruing to an emperor of holding an ecumenical council, and above all to ensure that the proffered canonical codification, the prescribed medicine for imperial ills, was accepted and administered. Moreover, as the enforcement of canon law was primarily an episcopal responsibility, widespread support was required if this tool of reformation was actually to be employed, and God's aid

162 *Trullo Revisited*, 184:17–185:4, 7.

163 A. Papadakis, 'Pentarchy', in *ODB*, vol. 3, 1625–6.

won thereby. Further, it is possible that bishops were invited to raise (or raised anyway) several of the issues regulated by the canons, offering the potential for Justinian to acquire episcopal support for his wider agenda through responding to episcopal concerns.[164] More plausibly and significantly, episcopal participation provided an audience of important powerbrokers, both in the terrestrial and divine economies, to whom imperial ideology could be imparted, and who would then transmit it to their sees.

It is therefore significant that numerous bishops from across the empire did subscribe. In total there were 227 episcopal signatories, 190 from the patriarchate of Constantinople, ten from eastern Illyricum, the patriarch of Alexandria, 24 Antiochenes and two representatives from Jerusalem.[165] Considering the communication problems relayed in many of the canons, this represents a relatively large delegation, with the four eastern patriarchates represented. That the see of Constantinople dominated and western representation was limited was not unusual for an ecumenical council. Moreover, a further six places were left blank for the anticipated signatures of various western sees, above all Rome.

From this, several significant points can be deduced. Firstly, substantial and extensive agreement had been both sought and granted to support Trullo. Secondly, the imperial authorities went to considerable lengths to affirm Trullo's ecumenical status. On manifold occasions, Trullo trumpeted its claim to ecumenicity, which, by subscribing, the signatories tacitly accepted. Further, the mostly successful attempt to gather subscriptions representing all five patriarchates reinforced its assertion. Moreover, the subscription list underlined Trullo's repeated association of itself with the unquestionably legitimate Fifth and Sixth Ecumenical Councils in the first instance through a considerable personnel overlap with the latter synod. Indeed, Ohme convincingly argues that these bishops were required to sign using exactly the same formulars as they had at the Sixth Council, further reinforcing its connection with Trullo.[166] This

[164] Herrin, 'The Quinisext Council', 163.

[165] Ohme, 'Sources', 79. For in-depth analysis of the episcopal subscriptions, see Ohme, *Bischofsliste*.

[166] For overlap of personnel and similarity in formulars, see Ohme, *Bischofsliste*, 316–20. This led to the peculiar case of Basil of Gortyna, who signed saying he was a representative of Rome when he clearly was not, because he had so signed at the Sixth Council. See Ohme, *Bischofsliste*, 235–51.

was also strengthened by meeting in the exact same hall of the palace in which the Sixth Council had met. Furthermore, several of the six sees left blank for future subscription were distinctly peripheral, whose only significance was that they had also subscribed to the Sixth Council.

This constant insistence on Trullo's ecumenical status bespeaks of a degree of anxiety, probably generated from the lack of papal representation. However, given that relations with the papacy had been high since their victory in 681, Constantinople must have predicted Old Rome's support, at the very least after some diplomacy. In the event, it would only be after prolonged negotiation that a pope finally offered conditional assent in 710. Usually, this papal intransigence is explained by Trullo's inclusion of several canons that rejected Roman practice. Yet as Ohme powerfully argues, the lack of initial papal acceptance of Trullo had little to do with the 'anti-Roman' canons.[167] Firstly, many of those canons were in fact compromises or even actually support the basic Roman position.[168] Furthermore, Trullo drew from a canonical corpus whose overwhelming bulk was shared by the western and eastern churches. Similarly shared was the focus on issues of personal morality and correct rite. Thus, as Herrin forcibly expounds, 'the issues that most worried the bishops of 692 were shared with most of the Christian authorities in the West . . . So far from constituting a decisive breaking point between east and west, the Council in Trullo confirmed most of the canons which were shared in both halves of Christendom.'[169] Moreover, even after Justinian offered the papacy the chance to edit the council and strike out those elements that he found offensive (at least for application in Rome), which should have removed any problem with the canons, the popes did not at first accept the council.[170]

If it was not what was said and done, to what then did the papacy object? Ohme's compelling answer is twofold and based principally on close analysis of the signature list.[171] Firstly, the sees of East

[167] See Ohme, 'Die sogenannten "antirömischen" Kanones', and Ohme, 'Sources', 82–3.

[168] E.g. C.3 mostly adjudicated in favour of the Roman position on clergy who had married twice.

[169] Herrin, 'The Quinisext Council', 163–4.

[170] The papacy's reaction is recorded in *Liber Pontificalis*, ed. L. Duchesne, 3 vols (Paris, 1886–1957), Lives 86:6, 88:4, 90:3–6.

[171] See in particular Ohme, 'Causes of conflict'.

Illyricum, officially under the jurisdiction of Rome, were at Trullo placed under Constantinople.[172] This appears to have been an early attempt at the measures later enacted by the Isaurians to align the jurisdiction of the patriarch of Constantinople more closely to the actual reach of imperial administration, which would create lasting resentment between Old and New Rome.[173] Moreover, that the Isaurians returned to the issue implies that Justinian's attempt was not successful and that part of the agreement with Pope Constantine I was recognition of Rome's jurisdiction over East Illyricum.

Most significantly, however, Trullo advanced a conciliar theory that was at odds with the stance of the papacy.[174] For Rome increasingly defined itself as the Champion of Orthodoxy.[175] For the papacy, the *sine qua non* of ecumenicity was not just papal participation, but acceptance of the papal line. At Trullo the old pentarchy was similarly sidelined, but this time in favour of the emperor. Thus, in C.1 it is the role of emperors in calling and enforcing ecumenical councils that is emphasized, with clergy and theologians almost invisible. In contrast, the only pope mentioned is listed as a heretic.[176] Moreover, the focus on the Second Ecumenical Council, to the extent that it was quoted almost verbatim in the culmination of the *Logos*, further emphasized the centrality of the emperor, for that council had similarly lacked papal representation.[177] Together these attempted to redefine ecumenical as a council summoned by the emperor to legislate for the whole Christian world, which was of course coterminous with the Christian empire.[178]

The greatest symbol of this imperial dominance is that Justinian II added his own signature to those of the bishops.[179] Only one previous emperor, his father Constantine IV at the Sixth Council, had ever done so before, a fact deliberately highlighted in C.1: 'which council's authority is all the greater because the pious Emperor affixed his seal

[172] Ohme, 'Sources', 79.

[173] For the disputed Isaurian attempt, see C. Zuckerman, 'Learning from the enemy and more: studies in "Dark Centuries" Byzantium', *Millennium* 2 (2005), 79–135, 89–92. Cf. Brubaker and Haldon, *History*, 174–5.

[174] Ohme, 'Sources', 83.

[175] For the growing autonomy of the papacy in this period, see T. Noble, *The Republic of St Peter: The Birth of the Papal State, 680–825* (Philadelphia, 1984), 15–23.

[176] Further, this is in marked contrast to the huge role given to Pope Agatho in 680/81.

[177] Ohme, 'Causes of conflict', 32–3.

[178] Ohme, 'Causes of conflict', 39–43.

[179] Ohme, *Bischofsliste*, 345–8.

to its tome, for its perpetual security.'[180] Furthermore, the verbatim citation of the Second Council is interpolated only the once, to make the original request for general confirmation include the specific requirement of 'your pious signature', *eusebōn keraiōn.*[181] Moreover, while Constantine had signed after all the bishops, Justinian signed first, before the space left blank for the pope. Thus, the signature list was written testimony to the imperial claim to pastoral authority over the Church and the power to confirm canons, reinforcing the message of the *Logos* that Justinian was the leader and shepherd appointed by God for the entire Christian flock, both clerical and lay.

CONCLUSIONS: JUSTINIAN II AND THE END OF ANTIQUITY

The Council in Trullo marks a watershed moment in numerous ways. In the narrow discourse of canon law, it represented, in Ohme's words, 'the final stage in the development of canon law of the early Church'.[182] More broadly, its repeated assertion of traditionalism and conservatism belies a significant degree of change, adaption, and outright innovation, as simultaneously the doctrinal and canonical corpus were declared closed, while the political, economic, social, and cultural underpinnings of late antiquity that had generated it came apart. In short, Trullo represents the end not only of early canon law, but also of ancient Christianity. Indeed, its novelties and rhetoric position Trullo more on the 'medieval' end of that transformation, but it itself firmly evinces that it is ushering in a return, not creating something new.

This transitional, Janus-faced nature is even more pronounced in its political ideology. For Justinian II was implicitly imitating his great namesake, producing a code for canon law to match Justinian I's great civil law programme. Indeed, like his forebear, Justinian was imposing imperial authority on a discourse of legal power that had retained a significant degree of autonomy, and then using this purified and centrally controlled tool for imperial restoration. Thus, Trullo was intended to provide the canonical counterpart to the *Corpus*, together

[180] *Trullo Revisited*, 61:19–62:1. [181] *Trullo Revisited*, 54:20–55:1.

[182] Ohme, 'Sources', 79. For Trullo as codification, see Ohme, *Konzil Quinisextum*, 32–4.

elucidating a conception of empire and the imperial office defined by Justinianic law. Furthermore, Justinian II is deliberately placed in the line of emperors since Constantine I who had called ecumenical councils, sharing in their prestige. His imperial authority to convoke such councils, and to intervene to regulate the Church in general, was based on their past precedent, and in particular the reforms and ideals of Justinian I. Moreover, everything was aimed at rejuvenating and reconquering the old empire. Finally, Justinian broadcast his essential 'Roman-ness' by signing the acts as *basileus Rhōmaiōn*, emperor of the Romans.[183] Therefore, he was fundamentally looking to the past.

Yet these aspirations were filtered and expressed through a contemporary rhetoric and conceptual foundation that has more in common with the coming world of eighth-century Byzantium than even sixth-century New Rome. Indeed, in the body of the text, the qualifier 'Roman' is only used to describe the see of Rome.[184] Instead, the empire is the Christian empire, Justinian the pious and Christ-loving emperor. Further, Justinian II is only the third emperor ever to be called in their own legislation 'Christ-loving', *philochristos*, after Justinian I in his Edict on the True Faith, and Constantine IV in the edict confirming the Sixth Council.[185] The people were Christians organized socially into religious functions of clergy, monks, and laity. The imperial past was subsumed into the Christian story, previous emperors presented as convenors of subsequent stages in the unfolding of the Truth. Everything was elided into the grand salvation narrative. Scripture had become the ultimate referent, the authority to which one appealed and the repository of rhetoric through which thought and action were expressed.

Two figures dominated Trullo. The first was Christ. It was Christ who gave truth and salvation, who illuminated the world with the light of true knowledge. It was Christ who created the path to heaven, who was the beginning and end of time. It was he who had established the Fathers and the emperor. It was his name that identified and defined the people and the empire. It was the Eucharist that sanctified the people and was the central ritual of Christian life. Even the Scripture utilized throughout was dominated by the New Testament, and its thoughts of what it meant to be Christian, that peculiar people defined by belief in Christ and identified through participation in the Eucharist administered by his church.

[183] Ohme, 'Bischofsliste', 145.
[184] *Trullo Revisited*, 70:9.
[185] Rösch, *Onoma Basileias*, 103.

The second was Justinian II. It was on his authority that the council was called. As C.3 informs us, he addressed it and read out a statement calling for the reformation of the clergy.[186] Indeed, considering its highly structured nature, precise number of canons, and repeated praise of the emperor, most of the canons—and almost certainly the entirety of the introductory corpus—were constructed by the emperor and his advisors, and simply presented to the bishops for confirmation. It was the emperor, not the corporate Church, nor bishops, nor the patriarchs, who was the shepherd of the Christian flock. He was not just a new Justinian, but a second Phinehas. Indeed, the critical model for Justinian was Christ himself, with whom he is constantly linked. Justinian I may have indubitably been a Christian emperor, and invoked the Almighty, especially in his novels, and Constantine IV might have declared that he co-ruled with the Almighty, but here those themes are taken to new heights and proclaimed with an unparalleled intensity. Justinian II could, therefore, be legitimately described as the first Christocentric monarch.

A further measure of distance between Justinian I and II, indeed between Justinian II and Heraclius, the founder of the dynasty, was the decision to use canon law as the preferred tool for legislation and reformation. Justinian I had felt more than able to legislate on the minutiae of ecclesiastical affairs, to use edicts to proclaim the faith and novels to exhort the people and crush sin. That Justinian II chose instead to employ canons is due not just to the virtual mummification of civil law. Rather, canons fitted the ideology and rhetoric espoused by Justinian II. Reformation was the stated aim, and the healing and ascetic connotations of Christian canons presented a more useful tool than Roman law in assuring Christ's support. This in turn flowed from the great ructions of the seventh century and the diagnosis of sin as the cause of imperial decline. That Islam was also a faith that called for stringent morality to be practised not just by spiritual elites but by all believers, combined with pre-existing ascetic trends and a loss of confidence in an establishment that had lost control, must have helped in the creation of a spiritual crisis in the late seventh century that focused on popular morality and correct practice.[187] The choice of genre further underlined the identification of people and ruler as

[186] *Trullo Revisited*, 69:17–70:8.

[187] For a general sketch of the period as one of spiritual crisis, see Brubaker and Haldon, *History*, 18–22.

Christian above all else, whose travails had religious origins that called for divine law to remedy. Trullo's canons were meant not to replace civil law, but to act as the basis of a moral rejuvenation that would restore the conditions permitting civil law to be revived from suspended animation.

In conclusion, at Trullo Justinian furthered and intensified the programme begun under Constantine IV, combining the doctrinal orthodoxy of the Sixth Ecumenical Council with a programme of moral reformation that it was hoped all Christians could unite behind, and which would enable imperial revival through the winning of heavenly support. All of this was couched in a rhetoric and proclaimed an ideology rich in elements from the past, recent and ancient, but an ideology also caught in profound flux. In this it reflected the times. For the Christian, Roman Empire, with the emphasis now overwhelmingly on the former, was on the point of a final decisive round of warfare with the Islamic Caliphate, newly revived under the Marwanid Caliphs and for the first time proclaiming a differentiated, public, Muslim message.[188] The battle of Sebastopolis in 692/3, and even more significantly the loss of North Africa in 697/8 and with it any chance of parity in resources with the Caliphate, ended any pretensions to reconquest.[189] This loss of superpower status, and the Byzantines' eventual realization of it, would have long-reaching effects, as shrunken Byzantium became, in Whittow's words, a 'satellite culture' of the vastly larger, richer, and more powerful Islamic world.[190] However, by removing any possibility of a revival of the old Justinianic Empire, it eliminated the necessity for those conceptual contortions and frictions that had kept imperial discourse anchored in the late antique world, while increasingly employing a language and discussing issues that looked forward to the medieval. Out of the wreckage arose a new symbolic and ideological universe that once again can be traced most fully in the discourse of law.

[188] See R. Hoyland, 'New documentary texts and the early Islamic state', *Bulletin of the School of Oriental and African Studies* 69 (2006), 395–416; C. Robinson, *'Abd al-Malik* (Oxford, 2005); Donner, *Muhammad and the Believers*, 194–224; Howard-Johnston, *Witnesses to a World Crisis*, 501–7.

[189] Howard-Johnston, *Witnesses to a World Crisis*, 499–501.

[190] Whittow, *Making of Byzantium*, 161.

2

The *Ecloga*

> On account of the frequent assumptions of imperial power and the prevalence of usurpation, the affairs of the empire and of the City were being neglected and declined; furthermore, education was being destroyed and military organization crumbled. As a result, the enemy were able to overrun the Roman state with impunity causing much slaughter, abduction, and the capture of cities. For this reason also the Saracens advanced on the Imperial City itself.[1]

The picture painted by the chronicler Nicephorus of the late seventh and early eighth centuries is one of utter collapse. Indeed, the half-century that separates Trullo and the promulgation of the *Ecloga* in 741, the next great imperial legal undertaking, was one of huge turbulence.[2] Seven emperors seized the throne between 695 and 717 in a bewildering succession of coups, plots, and infighting. Meanwhile Africa was lost and Arab forces made ever deeper inroads into Anatolia. By 717 the Arabs had reached the gates of Constantinople, and the very survival of the Empire was in peril.

Patently the package so carefully crafted and proclaimed by Justinian II had failed. Successive regimes scrabbled to find a replacement formula to propitiate a wrathful God, and unite and motivate a defeated and demoralized people. For instance, Philippicus Bardanes reintroduced monotheletism, but conspicuously failed to stem the tide, and so both he and the discredited doctrine were overthrown.[3] The increasingly desperate search for divine help went beyond court and capital, as the following gruesome passage about the siege of Pergamon in 716 indicates:

1 Nicephorus, 52; trans. Mango, 121.
2 See the excellent recent summary of Auzépy, 'State of emergency'.
3 Theophanes, 382.

> Now Masalmas [the Arab general] came to Pergamon, which he besieged and, by God's dispensation, captured because of the Devil's machinations. For, at the instigation of a magician, the inhabitants of the city produced a pregnant woman who was about to give birth and cut her up. And after removing her infant and cooking it in a pot, all those who were intending to fight dipped the sleeve of their right arm in this detestable sacrifice, and for this reason they were delivered to the enemy.[4]

Factually accurate or not, this gives a chilling vista onto a dramatic loss of faith in the established structures of faith and society. In the event, the empire would survive the Arab siege of Constantinople in 717–18.[5] However, although temporarily rebuffed, raids major and minor continually struck the empire, with the Asia Minor border only stabilizing in the 730s. Insecurity worsened the economic retardation that had begun in the mid-sixth century, reaching a nadir by the mid-eighth century.[6] Cities, and the elites who dwelled in them, were in crisis.[7] Impoverished, battered, and besieged, the imperial edifice required fundamental renovation.

Yet the degree of structural damage should not be overemphasized.[8] Constantinople, and the emperor, court, and administration situated there, endured. The fiscal system altered, but taxes were still collected and distributed by imperial officials, and coins were still struck.[9] An imperial army and navy, perhaps differently recruited and supplied, not only weathered the crisis but were increasingly able to contain the empire's many foes.[10] The empire was smaller and poorer, but even diminished, it remained comparatively sophisticated and organized. Perhaps, then, even more pressing than

[4] Theophanes, 390–1; trans. Mango and Scott, 541.

[5] For the importance of this moment, and the leadership of the Isaurians, see M. Angold, 'The Byzantine political process at crisis point', in P. Stephenson (ed.), *The Byzantine World* (London, 2010), 5–21.

[6] A. Laiou and C. Morrisson, *The Byzantine Economy* (Cambridge, 2007), esp. 38–42; M. McCormick, *The Origins of the European Economy: Communications and Commerce A.D. 300–900* (Cambridge, 2001), esp. 115–19, 433–41.

[7] Haldon, *Seventh Century*, 92–124.

[8] A good overview of the continuities that allowed the empire to survive can be found in Whittow, *Making of Byzantium*, 96–133. For the narrower paradigm of the economy see Whittow, 'The middle Byzantine economy (600–1204)', in Shepard (ed.), *Cambridge History of the Byzantine Empire*, 465–92, esp. 467–72, 482–6.

[9] Brubaker and Haldon, *History*, 470–88, 665–722.

[10] Brubaker and Haldon, *History*, 723–71. For the navy in particular, see also H. Ahrweiler, *Byzance et la mer: la marine de guerre, la politique et les institutions maritimes de Byzance aux VIIe–XVe siècles* (Paris, 1966), 17–44.

practical changes to the way the empire and society was run were ideological changes to how it thought about itself in the light of defeat and a decline so severe that it could not be ignored.

At this pivotal moment, a remarkable dynasty emerged whose energetic leadership and reforms rightly receive fulsome credit for the survival and stabilization of the empire.[11] Leo III (r.717–41) and his Isaurian successors stridently reworked both the organs of state and its image and conceptual outlook within a deliberately retrenched schema. It must, however, be noted that Leo's policies did not emerge fully formed, but rather evolved over the course of his reign. Gaining the throne chiefly due to his credentials as a general, Leo successfully led the defence of Constantinople in 717–18. During this, he seems to have begun his dynasty's association with the Cross, the ultimate symbol of imperial Christianity and rejection of Islam, by parading around the city carrying a cross, before striking the sea with it to dispel the invaders, in imitation of Moses leading the Israelites out of Egypt.[12] Vindicated by victory, Leo sought to further his militant Christian credentials by attempting to convert the Jews in 721/2.[13] Magdalino plausibly suggests that this was the context in which Leo set up, at the Chalke Gate (the principal entrance to the palace and a key part of the topography of Constantinople), a picture of the Cross surrounded by Apostles and Prophets holding texts supporting veneration of the Cross.[14] Certainly it reinforced Leo's promotion of the Cross, also seen on his coinage, seals, and in a supposed dialogue between the emperor and Caliph 'Umar II recorded by the Armenian historian Ghewond.[15]

[11] One of the most forthright positive overviews of the Isaurians, and in particular of Leo III, can be found in J. B. Bury, *A History of the Later Roman Empire: From Arcadius to Irene (395 A.D. to 800 A.D.)*, 2 vols (London, 1889), vol. 2, 408–24. Indeed at 410, Bury declared that Leo III's life's work 'was no less than the regeneration of the Roman Empire'.

[12] Gero, *Leo III*, 36–43, 135–6.

[13] Theophanes, 401.

[14] Germanus, *Letter to Thomas of Klaudioupolis*, Mansi XIII, 108 A7–128 A12. See P. Magdalino, 'The other image at the palace gate and the visual propaganda of Leo III', in D. Sullivan, E. Fisher, and S. Papaioannou (eds), *Byzantine Religious Culture* (Leiden, 2012), 139–53.

[15] In general see J. Moorhead, 'Iconoclasm, the Cross and the imperial image', *Byzantion* 55 (1985), 165–79. For the coins and seals, see Conclusion, 258–61. For the dialogue, see A. Jeffery, 'Ghevond's text of the correspondence between 'Umar II and Leo III', *The Harvard Theological Review* 37 (1944), 269–332, esp. 321–2.

However, this brief upturn in imperial fortunes was cut short by the return of serious Arab raids in the 720s. More spectacularly, in 726 there was a massive volcanic eruption at Thera, an unavoidable manifestation of divine wrath.[16] Then, in 727, an Arab army reached Nicaea, deep in the western heart of Anatolia and the site of the first Ecumenical Council.[17] Evidently the Empire was in need of far greater reform, moral and practical, than Leo III had originally thought. Responding to the challenge of those reforms would be wide-ranging and fundamental. However, the full gamut of those reforms is beyond our remit. Our task is rather to examine one thread, namely the legal programme. Yet the contention here is that both the structural and ideological changes of the eighth century found their fullest expression in the Isaurian legal programme, and most obviously in its foundational document, the *Ecloga*.[18]

THE *ECLOGA*: ITS COMPILATION, SOURCES, AND FORMAT

The *Ecloga* might have emerged out of the ideological and administrative retrenchment and reorganization of the 720s, but it was completed and promulgated only in 741, in the final months of Leo III's reign.[19] It therefore encapsulates the Isaurians' practical and ideological programme as it overcame the crises threatening to overwhelm the empire, and the Isaurians' regime. Further, it appeared at that potentially fatal point for any dynasty, the transition of power to the second generation. It therefore had to solidify the succession. That such a vital function was entrusted to a legal work is itself significant testimony to the importance attached to law.

Furthermore, one must note the significance of this revival of imperial utilization of civil law after the suspension of the seventh century charted above. From it, one can infer a rejection by the

[16] Theophanes, 404–5; Nicephorus, 59.

[17] Theophanes, 405–6; Nicephorus, 60.

[18] *Ecloga*, ed. L. Burgmann, *Ecloga: Das Gesetzbuch Leons III. und Konstantinos V.* (Frankfurt, 1983).

[19] For the difficulty of dating, the preference for 741, and other relevant literature see Burgmann, *Ecloga*, 10–12, 100–4.

Isaurians of Justinian II's policies, or more particularly their form, for as we shall see, many of the purificatory and moral themes expounded at Trullo were continued in the *Ecloga*, and indeed all the law of the era. However, the Isaurians chose not to employ canons as a tool of imperial reform. Perhaps canons had become too indelibly linked to Justinian II and thus tarred by association. More significantly, the massive diminution of imperial power and the realization of it made the restoration of the sixth-century world impossible and, as importantly, unimaginable. Therefore, eighth-century Byzantines could now mentally unpack their antique inheritance, of which civil law was a prominent component, selecting from it what was contemporaneously relevant, and then set it within a vastly altered and diminished world.

However, due to the scantiness of the evidence, the condition and shape of that legal heritage is difficult to uncover.[20] Generally, modern legal historians have been highly pessimistic, seeing progressive decline from the heights of Justinian to a virtual caesura in Roman law, corresponding to the bleak image on all education as conveyed above by Nicephorus. The *Ecloga* is then judged against that decline, portrayed variously as a moderate revival foreshadowing the later Macedonian reforms,[21] a transition point to a Christianized law,[22] or evidence as to how far law had slumped under the vulgarizing pressure of custom and the Orient.[23] Certainly, as we have seen, the stream of novels had dried up in the seventh century. The general disruption and dislocation of the seventh century must have negatively affected jurisprudence and legal education.[24] The decline of cities, both materially and in their institutional control over their hinterlands, surely impacted on the capability of the initial ranks of the judicial administration, the courts of the *defensores* and provincial

[20] See Pieler, 'Byzantinische Rechtsliteratur', 429–44; Van der Wal and Lokin, *Historiae*, 38–51, 71–7; Troianos, *Pēges*, 63–80.

[21] Van der Wal and Lokin, *Historiae*, 71–7.

[22] Zacharia von Lingenthal, *Geschichte*, 15–21, 57–62; See also Bury, *A History of the Later Roman Empire*, vol. 2, 410–18; and Bury, 'Graeco-Roman law', Appendix 11 in E. Gibbon, *The History of the Decline and Fall of the Roman Empire*, ed. J. B. Bury with an Introduction by W. E. H. Lecky, 12 vols (New York, 1906), vol. 8, 261–5. This was followed by E. Freshfield, *Roman Law in the Later Roman Empire: The Isaurian Period* (Cambridge, 1932); and in the introduction to his translation of the *Ecloga*, E. Freshfield, *A Manual of Roman Law, The Ecloga* (Cambridge, 1926).

[23] Pieler, 'Byzantinische Rechtsliteratur', 429–44.

[24] Haldon, *Seventh Century*, 264–76.

magistrates, based in them.[25] Further, the deconstruction, economically and intellectually, of the old Roman elite, whose members provided the legal personnel and whose interests and outlook were intimately entwined with Roman law, probably further disrupted the legal system.[26] This bleak picture finds some colourful support in the *Ecloga*'s *prooimion*, which virulently complains about venal and incompetent judges with a widespread and deep lack of understanding of what was the law.[27]

Yet those who characterize the seventh and indeed the eighth centuries as a legal 'dark age' overemphasize and overdramatize decline.[28] Law was still studied and taught prominently enough in the capital for the Trullan canons to criticize civil law students.[29] Indeed, Trullo itself testifies to the continued ability to legislate and codify on a large scale, if within canon law. Further, the commission empowered to create the *Ecloga* reveals a sophisticated and hierarchical legal administration little altered from the sixth century.[30] The chief legal officer and presumably head of that commission was the *Quaestor*, still occupying his late antique role as judge and preparer of imperial legislation.[31] He was aided by the *antigrapheis* (s. *antigrapheus*), the heads of various secretariat assigned to him.[32] However, before both the *Quaestor* and the *antigrapheis* are listed the otherwise

[25] For general overview see G. Dagron, 'The urban economy, seventh–twelfth centuries', in *EHB*, 393–461. Cf. Haldon, *Seventh Century*, 92–124; and Brubaker and Haldon, *History*, 531–72.

[26] J. Haldon, 'The fate of the late Roman senatorial elite: extinction or transformation?', in J. Haldon and L. Conrad (eds), *Elites Old and New in the Byzantine and Early Islamic Near East* (Princeton, 2004). For the *defensores*, see Jones, *Later Roman Empire*, vol. I, 479–80.

[27] E.pr.36–40, 69–72.

[28] This is the title of the chapter dedicated to the era in Pieler, 'Byzantinische Rechtsliteratur', 429–44.

[29] Trullo C.71.

[30] E.pr.40–43; discussed in Burgmann, *Ecloga*, 3–4.

[31] E.pr.41. See Bury, *Administrative System*, 73–5; Oikonomidès, *Listes de Préséance*, 321. Here the *Quaestor* has the dignities of patrician and *endoxotatos*, 'most glorious'.

[32] E.pr.42, 104. See Bury, *Administrative System*, 75–6; Oikonomidès, *Listes de Préséance*, 321–2. It should be noted that before the appearance of the *antigrapheis* are *endoxotatoi hypatoi*, 'most glorious consuls'. Although the Greek is not clear, these are probably titles held by the *antigrapheis*; see Burgmann, *Ecloga*, 3 n. 3. This linkage might explain the use in a tenth-century text of *hypatos* as an official with judicial functions; see Oikonomidès, *Listes de Préséance*, 325.

unspecified *endoxotatoi patrikioi*, 'most glorious patricians'.[33] Who these officials were and what (if any) competence they had to sit on the commission is unknown.[34] However, if the ninth-century *Taktikon Uspenskij* can be taken as a guide, all the principal military, administrative, and judicial officials held the rank of *patrikios*, implying a wide input from across Leo III's court.[35] Finally and most sweepingly, the commission included *loipous ton tou Theou phobon echontas*, 'those who fear God'.[36] Suggestively, in a later derivative revision of the *Ecloga*, the *Ecloga Privata Aucta Sinaiticus*, this phrase is replaced with the office of *scholastikoi*, legal advocates.[37] This might plausibly have been the original reference of the *Ecloga*, but it is still suggestive that membership of the commission was nowhere defined as due to legal expertise, despite the reality of the personnel, but through piety. The compilers of the *Ecloga* were, therefore, drawn from and testament to an extant legal administration, but their function was expressed through a dominating religious prism.

If we turn to the rest of the *Ecloga*, we find more members of the legal order. Firstly, the *Ecloga* repeatedly references *taboularioi* (s. *taboularios*), notaries, who drew up legally correct forms and contracts.[38] Even the old office of *defensor*/*ekdikos* is mentioned once, although reduced to a role analogous to a notary.[39] We also hear of a *dikastērion*, 'court', where cases were proved and witnesses heard.[40] Turning to judges, four kinds are mentioned. The first, the classical and biblical *kritēs*, we can immediately discount as they appear only once, and then as part of a biblical quotation.[41] Far more important are the *archontes* (s. *archōn*), magistrates who in time-honoured Roman fashion held judicial functions by virtue of their office.[42] Also mentioned are *dikastai* (s. *dikastēs*), literally 'judges', and

[33] E.pr.40–41. [34] Burgmann, *Ecloga*, 3.

[35] *Taktikon Uspenskij*, ed. Oikonomidès, *Listes de Préséance*, 47–63; see 47–51.

[36] E.pr.42.

[37] *Ecloga Privata Aucta Sinaitica*, ed. D. Simon and S. Troianos, *FM* III (Frankfurt, 1979), 168–77. For discussion and references, see Burgmann, *Ecloga*, 3.

[38] E.10.1.2; 14.8; 14.9.

[39] E.10.1.2. This seems to have been an early phenomenon, as *defensores* have a similar role in the sixth-century Lombard code the *Edictum Theoderici*, ed. G. Pertz et al., *Monumenta Germaniae Historiae: Leges V* (Hanover, 1875–89), 145–79, chs.52–53. See S. Lafferty, 'Law and society in Ostrogothic Italy: evidence from the *Edictum Theoderici*', *Journal of Late Antiquity* 3 (2010), 337–64, esp. 351–2.

[40] E.4.4.345; 14.7.658. [41] E.pr.74.

[42] For an introduction, see A. Kazhdan, 'Archon', in *ODB*, vol. 1, 160.

akroatai (s. *akroatēs*), 'hearers'. The relationship between these three we shall consider later, but one thing is clear: the milieu described by the *Ecloga* was no judicial void. An array of judges, courts, and legal officials are described, all evoking an established, operating legal system, with distinct continuities with late antiquity.

Moreover, if we consider the limited evidence for provincial legal administration not contained in the *Ecloga*, one can plausibly suggest an increasing specialization of judicial officers from the seventh century onwards, emerging from the dismemberment of the generalist praetorian prefecture. For as Brubaker and Haldon have argued, the *anthypatoi*, 'proconsuls'—senior governors that had largely replaced the old *vicarii*, the intermediary level between the praetorian prefects and the governors in late antiquity—had by the eighth century been shorn of their financial role, and therefore formed a purely judicial office.[43] If this is so, and if the governors subordinate to them also had by the accession of Leo III become chiefly, even solely judicial officers, then that would imply a marked provincial *strengthening* of the judicial administration. It is even possible, albeit impossible to prove, that these *anthypatoi* were part of the commission that compiled the *Ecloga*, hidden among either the *patrikioi* or 'those who fear God'. If they were, they would have provided useful knowledge on the state of the legal order in the provinces and from the offset would give the impression that the *Ecloga* was intended for implementation across the Empire. Furthermore, Leo's administrative reforms *c*.730–1 probably reinforced this specialization of the imperial administration into military, fiscal, and judicial arms, which marks a major difference from the Roman model of the multipurpose, generalist magistrate.[44] Indeed, it is probable that the *Ecloga* project itself sprang initially from those reforms. Therefore, the *Ecloga* emerged from a legal administration more marked by continuity and, probably, expertise than rupture and incompetence.

The situation as to what the law actually constituted, rather than who administered it, is even murkier.[45] The *Ecloga*'s *prooimion* notes that 'the laws enacted by the previous Emperors have been written in

[43] Brubaker and Haldon, *History*, 671–9. Supporting this notion is the fact that some manuscripts give the names of two officials who could represent the two dioceses of Asiana and Pontus left to the empire; see Burgmann, *Ecloga*, 162.

[44] See Conclusion, 261–5.

[45] Considering the complete absence of contemporary documentation, the law that was actually enforced, if different from written, is virtually impossible to discern.

many books'.[46] As remarked upon in the Introduction, this diffusion of law into multiple texts was a natural consequence of the Justinianic programme.[47] Firstly, as the title of the *Ecloga* highlights (on which more below), Justinian's own output consisted of three discrete works, the *Institutes*, *Code*, and *Digest*, and the *Novels*, which were never formally catalogued or reduced to one volume.[48] To explicate this difficult and mostly Latin corpus, a large mass of Greek commentaries, paraphrases, and translations were created in the sixth century by the *antecessores*.[49] Primarily designed as teaching aids, these frequently simplified and provided examples to ease explanation. Due to this central didactic role and utilitarian outlook, combined with the lack of a linguistic barrier, these texts increasingly became the 'living law'—that is, the law that was actually applied, rather than the distant, difficult, and vast Justinianic corpus. This natural process of virtual exegesis from a central text was strengthened as time rendered elements of Justinianic law irrelevant, a process hastened by the governmental and societal transformations of the seventh and eighth centuries.[50] With the cessation of imperial legislation by novel under Heraclius inevitable alteration was left to the *antecessores* and the decisions of individual judges. Indeed, it should be noted that the rulings of judges had always been an element in the evolution of Roman law, in particular in the application of punishments, an area where Roman practice granted considerable leeway to judges, resulting in a notable increase in the severity of punishments over the course of late antiquity.[51] Therefore, the *Ecloga* had inherited a complex and diverse legal world, where the Justinianic *Corpus* was the bedrock, almost sacred text, but which was known primarily through multiple commentaries that had rephrased, reorganized, and generally simplified. This was then applied and understood differently by judges also influenced by ever-changing and growing

[46] E.pr.36–7. [47] See Introduction, 25. [48] E.pr.1–8.

[49] For this development, see Scheltema, 'Byzantine law', 55–77; Burgmann, *Ecloga*, 4–7, and Burgmann, 'Die Gegenwart', 591–3; Van der Wal and Lokin, *Historiae*, 38–51.

[50] Indeed, E.pr.46–47 states that the *Ecloga* would repeat contract law and criminal law, *synallagmatōn tas kriseis kai tas katallēlous tōn egklēmatōn*, while saying nothing about the administrative or religious law of the *Corpus*, namely those elements most probable to have been rendered anachronistic.

[51] In particular see R. MacMullen, 'Judicial savagery in the Roman Empire', *Chiron* 16 (1988), 147–66.

precedent, and moreover by external forces such as canon law and other Christian discourses.

Disentangling these strands and plotting a precise path from Justinianic law to the chapters of the *Ecloga* is rendered nigh on impossible by the paucity and fragmentary survival of works by the *antecessores*.[52] As such, it is extremely difficult to establish the extent to which the *Ecloga* merely repeated pre-existing raw material. Therefore, when change is evident, the question becomes whether it was created by the compilers of the *Ecloga*, preceding imperial legislation, or at some point in the previous two centuries of juristic change. This ambiguity has not stopped legal historians from fixating on the question of whether the law of the *Ecloga* is primarily Justinianic or not, and to question the extent of change that can be ascribed to the Isaurians.[53] Below we shall examine closely four key topics with these questions in mind; however, some general points should be made now.

Firstly, it is suggestive that the *Ecloga*'s editor, Ludwig Burgmann, could positively establish just one definite link between the text of the *Ecloga* and a work of an *antecessor*.[54] From this, Burgmann concluded reasonably that whenever one dates certain legal changes, and however much one can conclude that the substance of civil law remained the same, the compilers of the *Ecloga* did substantially rewrite and rework the material they inherited. Indeed, as we shall examine below, the *prooimion* proclaims that part of its purpose was to restate the substance of established law, but in an avowedly more succinct and utilitarian form, implying a distinct degree of editing and recasting.[55] Moreover, the language in which the *Ecloga* is written follows this pattern. It is simple syntactically and grammatically.[56] It is rarely convoluted, with occasional extended rhetorical

[52] Most of what has survived was gathered together in the *scholia* of the ninth-century *Basilika*, ed. H. Scheltema et al., *Basilicorum libri LX*, Series A (Text), 8 vols, Series B (Scholia), 9 vols (Groningen, 1953–88). This is at least evidence that the texts endured throughout the Iconoclast era.

[53] For example, this is the dominant interest to the point of almost exclusivity of Bury, 'Graeco-Roman law'; Bury, *Later Roman Empire*, 410–18; and Freshfield, *Ecloga*. It is also naturally the case for all the synoptic legal histories, beginning with Zacharia von Lingenthal, *Geschichte*, which by their very nature sought to delineate legal changes and continuity across the Byzantine period.

[54] E.17.41 cf. D.9.2.30.3 and Dorotheus at B.S.60.3.30. See Burgmann, *Ecloga*, 5.

[55] E.pr.47–48.

[56] Burgmann, *Ecloga*, 13–18.

interludes demarking highly significant sections.[57] The vocabulary is not demotic, and does contain several technical terms, but it is not leaden legalese either.[58] In short, it is written in a style to be easily understood, perhaps by the general public, most probably by legal administrators.

In a similar manner, the *Ecloga* is not beholden to any of the preceding Justinianic texts for its arrangement, as Table 1 demonstrates:[59]

Table 1. The contents of the *Ecloga* compared to their correspondents in the *Corpus*

Ecloga	D	I	C	N
1 Betrothal			5.1	
2 Marriage and divorce	23.2	1.10	5.4–5	22; 74; 97; 117
3 Dowry law			5.15; 8.17	97; 100
4 Gifts		2.7	8.55–6	87
5 Wills	28.1; 29.1	2.10–13	6.23	1; 18; 115
6 Intestacy and legacies		2.23	6.30, 37, 42	115; 118; 127
7 Orphans and guardians		1.13, 23	1.4.30	131
8 Freedom and slavery	25.3; 40.7	1.5	1.13; 7.6; 8.50	5; 22; 123
9 Sale and deposit	21.1	3.23	4.21, 44	
10 Loans and security	13.7	3.25	4.24	134
11 Deposits	16.3		4.34	
12 *Emphyteusis*	6.3		4.66	7; 120
13 Leases			4.65	120
14 Witnesses			4.20	18; 90
15 Contract			2.4	73
16 *Peculium*		2.12	1.3; 3.28; 6.22, 61	18
17 Crime	9.1, 2; 13.6; 47.7, 9, 12, 14; 48.4, 5, 8, 13, 15, 19; 49.16	4.1, 8, 18	1.12; 3.35; 4.1; 5.5; 6.1; 8.4; 9.2, 7–9, 13–14, 16, 18, 20, 24	6; 12; 77; 123, 134; 141
18 War booty				

In part this disparity was caused by the *Ecloga* combining elements from across the *Corpus*, of which some topics are not covered by each

57 Outside the *prooimion*, they occur at E.2.5, 2.9, and 18.

58 Burgmann, *Ecloga*, 14–16.

59 This table only lists the most direct correspondents between the text of the *Ecloga* and the *Corpus*, i.e. those that seem to have constituted the ultimate source for the *Ecloga*. There are other more general matches, but they do not alter the general picture of the *Ecloga* having an independent organization. For further information, and the precise chapters of the *Corpus* not given here for want of space, see Burgmann, *Ecloga*, 168–244.

text, and by the addition of a completely novel title on the division of war booty. There is a surface similarity in that private law issues come before crime and punishment, yet even compared by general topic the arrangement is not close; when compared chapter by chapter, the correlation is even looser. Instead, the *Ecloga* is organized by the principle of association, to wit that topics are grouped together by shared interests, in a manner reminiscent of the Trullan canons.[60] Thus the first section, E.1–3, systematically proceeds from betrothal to marriage and divorce, and to the law of dowry. Dowries introduce the issue of property transfer, logically leading to the topic of gifts (E.4) and then inheritance (E.5–7). Title 7 also concerns the legal power of one person over another, from which E.8 on manumission and slavery naturally follows. That in turn touches on the law of contract, which E.9–16 systematically examines. Having established private law, or as the *prooimion* phrases it, contract law in its broadest sense, E.17 turns to criminal law. The completely novel E.18 is placed at the end, although it does follow on from the final stipulation of E.17 concerning deserters. This is an organization based on utility. Moreover, as Burgmann forthrightly claims, the *Ecloga* established a new format for a legal handbook, designed to encompass concisely the vast majority of cases heard; it is a practical text created for actual jurisprudence.[61] Indeed, this format was to prove so successful that it spawned a series of imitators. Therefore, in form and style, the *Ecloga* represents an original representation of law.

Furthermore, the text repeatedly described itself as new. Its *pinax*, contents list, an apparently original feature of the text and one that incidentally furthers the impression of intended utility by making the text more easy to reference, announces the contents as *nearas nomothesias*, 'new legislation'.[62] The *prooimion* refers to *hēmōn nearōs thespisthentōn*, 'our new enactments', against which previous imperial legislation should be compared.[63] In the text proper, E.2.3 and 2.9 explicitly mention new Isaurian legislation.[64] Most importantly, the *Ecloga*'s title claims it is correcting the Justinianic corpus, not just restating it.[65] These examples tell us that at least some of

[60] Burgmann, *Ecloga*, 8. The pattern is also shared in the arrangement of chapters, thereby frequently differing from the arrangement of their sources.

[61] L. Burgmann, 'Ecloga', in *ODB*, vol. 1, 672–3.

[62] E.pinax.2.

[63] E.pr.45.

[64] E.2.3.155–6; E.2.9.1.281.

[65] E.pr.1–6.

the changes detailed were directly the work of previous Isaurian legislation, and imply a wide remit for the compilers to revise existing law. Moreover, as the Trullan codification testifies, compilation and innovation were easily joined in the same work, and the authorities of the period were perfectly able to legislate as well as repeat existing legislation. As shall be explored in respect to the subjects of judicial process, marriage, criminal law, and martial matters, much of the law does adhere to Justinianic ordinances, but it was altered in significant and telling ways along with being rephrased and reorganized. However, perhaps the most important aspect of the *Ecloga* was how it reimagined what the law was, the society in which it operated, and the role of the emperor towards both. For a significant conceptual refashioning had occurred since the time of Trullo, let alone from the rhetoric and ideology of Justinian I, even when there was significant substantive continuity. For the best evidence of this fundamental transformation, we must now study the rhetoric of the *prooimion*.

THE *ECLOGA*'S TITLE AND *PROOIMION*: THE SCRIPTURAL TURN IN CIVIL LAW AND THE PREDOMINANCE OF THE OLD TESTAMENT

> A selection of the Laws compiled in a concise form by Leo and Constantine, the wise and pious-loving emperors, taken from the Institutes, Digest, Code, and the Novels of the Great Justinian and corrected towards greater humanity.[66]

In its very title, the *Ecloga* declares several significant themes. Most prominently, it delineates its source material as the legal corpus of the 'Great Justinian'. The veracity of that claim has been the prime topic of debate among legal historians and shall be explored later, but the very fact of it is significant. It affirmed the *Ecloga*'s loyalty to the established and by then virtually hallowed legal programme, and to the revered emperor who instigated it.[67] Thus, from the outset the

[66] E.pr.1–6.

[67] For the enduring image of Justinian, especially as a lawgiver, see Prinzing, 'Das Bild Justinians I.', 54–67.

Ecloga legitimized itself through reference to Justinian I, clear indication of the continued force of his image—at least in the legal sphere. Furthermore, it positioned Leo III and Constantine V as Justinian's heirs, and their legal reforms as imitating Justinian's magnum opus.

That project, however, was not one of simple repetition. Rather, it was an *Eklogē*, 'a selection'. This did not, as Justinian's great programme had, abrogate that which was not included. Indeed, the Justinianic *Corpus* would never be truly abrogated in Byzantine law. What selection does imply is contemporaneity—that is, what was included was thought to be the most, although not necessarily the only, relevant and useful sections of Justinianic law for the eighth-century context. What was selected, and what was not, are therefore good indications of what the emperors and/or eighth-century Byzantine law considered important. Furthermore, that selection was to be 'gathered in a concise form'. The *Ecloga* thereby proclaimed itself as a condensation of disparate texts into one, positively trumpeting its brevity. Hence the *Ecloga* was claiming practicality and utility as a guiding goal in its very title.

That aspiration was not aimless, but given a defining direction. For this legal florilegium was to be *epidiorthōsis eis to philanthrōpoteron*, 'corrected towards greater humanity'.[68] The ideal of correcting law was itself a Justinianic trope, but its application makes clear the Isaurian intention to change the law, even as established by the Roman legislator par excellence, rather than merely repeat it.[69] That aim speaks volumes about the ambitions and world view of the Isaurians. They had the ability, and implicitly the duty, to reform the law, presumably flowing on from being such 'wise and pious-loving emperors'. Indeed, wisdom and piety were intrinsically linked in the *prooimion* with justice and the very nature of God, thereby associating the Isaurians with the divine.[70] Through these attributes, the law, that quintessentially Roman genre, was not primarily to be restored or cleansed, in the well-worn Roman manner, but reformulated within the explicitly moral paradigm of *philanthropia*.

Philanthropia was a key concept in Byzantine thought, seen especially as a desired imperial attribute.[71] The central facet of the

[68] E.pr.6. [69] Hunger, *Prooimion*, 103–9. [70] E.pr.3.

[71] See P. Magdalino, 'Philanthropy', in *ODB*, vol.3, 1649–50 for introduction and bibliography. The best survey work remains D. Constantelos, *Byzantine Philanthropy and Social Welfare* (New Brunswick NJ, 1968).

nebulous ideas encompassing the concept was the *philanthropia*, the love of man, by God, witnessed principally in the Incarnation. Man was called to follow this divine example, and the emperor, as the leader of men and vicegerent of God, was beholden to imitate God, *mimēsis*, above all in *philanthropia*. These ideas had long antecedents in Greek thought, but had been remoulded in the fourth century. There was also an increased prominence given to the concept in the theological works of the seventh and eighth centuries, with *philanthropia* conspicuously appearing in the works of men such as Maximus the Confessor, John Climacus, and John of Damascus.[72] Thus the emperors of the period were operating within a thought-world that was placing mounting emphasis on *philanthropia* concurrent with their own attempts to strengthen and simplify the connection of the emperor with God and the closeness of *mimēsis*. It is not, then, surprising that both Justinian II's and Leo III's prime legislative acts were framed as attempts to reform and purify mankind, thus permitting salvation as well as garnering divine aid in the here-and-now. Furthermore, in this they were following the Justinianic archetype, for it was the 'Great Justinian' who had first used the term *philanthropia* conjoined with laws, as well as being remembered for his foundation of several charitable institutions.[73] Leo III not only took up this idea but made it a foundation of his law code. Thus civil law was fitted within a Christian framework as a tool emanating from and sanctioned by God, entrusted to the emperors for a moral purpose. One final aspect is the convergence of the concept of *philanthropia* with Justice in the person of God, for it was held that both (potentially contradictory) ideas were perfectly combined in Him. Therefore, due to mimesis, both should be combined in the emperor, and the *Ecloga* was a central component in the attempted realization of that ideal.

Bridging the Title and the *prooimion* is the Trinitarian invocation: 'In the name of the Father, and of the Son and of the Holy Ghost: Leo and Constantine, Faithful Emperors.'[74] This serves to proclaim the Isaurians' orthodox credentials, with the imperial office radically aligned solely to the quality *pistos*. The emperors' closeness to heaven was underlined through textual adjacency, a technique enlarged in

72 Constantelos, *Byzantine Philanthropy*, 20ff.

73 Constantelos, *Byzantine Philanthropy*, 48. For example, see N.81, 89, 129, 147. See also Hunger, *Prooimion*, 143–54.

74 E.pr.9–10.

the first two sections of the *prooimion* proper. Indeed, the *prooimion* literally begins with God:

> Our God, the Lord and Maker of all things, who made man and bestowed on him free will, who, according to what the Prophets said, 'gave the Law to help' him (Is. 8:20), and through it made known to him everything that should be done and what should be refrained from, so that he might choose the one as it brings Salvation, and spurn the other as the cause of chastisement; and no-one who keeps or—away with them!—rejects His commandments shall be denied the appropriate repayment of their deeds.[75]

God was, therefore, the original and greatest legislator. Moreover, the law was the same as that described in the Old Testament, and was designed for moral guidance necessary for salvation. Immediately, the legal discourse has been subsumed into a greater narrative. The law of Justinian invoked in the Title is transplanted from Roman legal history to the biblical past of God's covenant with the Chosen People. It continues:

> For it is God who promised both these things before, the power of whose words is immutable and which measures the worthiness of each man by his deeds, and which, according to the Evangelist, 'shall not pass away' (Mt. 24:35).[76]

To gainsay the law, which was imbued with eternity through the word of God, was to flout divine authority, and so by definition to sin. Law is thereby proclaimed as the fundamental contract between God and his creation.

The *prooimion* then posits the emperor's response to God's institution of the law.[77] As God had created man and given him law, so he had entrusted the empire to the Isaurians.[78] Moreover, 'according to Peter, the supreme Head of the Apostles, He ordered us "to be shepherds of" the most faithful "flock" (1 Pet. 5:2).'[79] This is only the second time in the legal genre, after Trullo, explored above, that the emperor had been associated with the image of a shepherd, and the first occasion in civil law.[80] This in itself evinces the increasing sacralization of both the imperial office and its representation in law.[81] That this claim is advanced through the words of St Peter, the

[75] E.pr.11–17. [76] E.pr.17–20. [77] E.pr.21–31. [78] E.pr.21.
[79] E.pr.22–24. [80] Hunger, *Prooimion*, 100–2.
[81] See in general Dagron, *Emperor and Priest*.

highest apostolic authority, is highly significant. The emperors are positioned as the successors to the Apostles, the inheritors of the early Church. Further, the passage drawn upon is a wider injunction on the leaders of Christian communities to tend their flocks so that they might receive salvation from Christ the Chief Shepherd. The emperors are, therefore, presented as sharing not just the authority of the apostles, but their calling to guide and guard the Christian people, for the sake of their own souls.

The manner of that tending is then made manifest:

> we can think of nothing more important or greater in return than steering 'in judgement and righteousness' (Is. 9:7; III Kings 10:9) those entrusted to us by Him, so that thereby 'the bonds of all injustice shall be broken, and the knots of violent covenants dissolved' (Is. 58:6), and the assaults of sinners beaten back, and thus with victories over our enemies by His almighty hand we shall be crowned with the encircling diadem, both more precious and worthy, and the Empire established in peace for us, and the State made steadfast.[82]

The emperors were to imitate the divine judge through righteous application of the law, protecting the weak and punishing the wicked. Given power by God, they should rule righteously to secure divine pleasure, and thereby victory over enemies and the peace of their realm. This long-established notion would have been given added urgency considering that Leo III's reign witnessed constant invasion and multiple rebellions.[83] The posited key to imperial survival and success was to rule in 'judgement and righteousness'. This is a recurrent theme in the Old Testament.[84] Yet more suggestively, it is also the description given to Solomon by the Queen of Sheba as the concluding compliment on his just and wise rule.[85] Thus, the nature of good government was defined on explicitly Old Testament lines, and more specifically on the correct application of God's law following the pattern of Solomon, the paragon of royal judgement.

Having established the law and emperor within a specifically biblical discourse and past, the *prooimion*'s third section narrates the current problem.[86] It starts with the Justinianic motif of the emperor busied with the cares of his people, 'watching with sleepless mind

[82] E.pr.25–31. [83] See Theophanes, 391–414.

[84] For instance, in Isaiah 9 it is one of the attributes of the prophesied Messiah.

[85] III Kings 10:9. [86] E.pr.32–51.

[*akoimēton ton noun*] for the discovery of those things which please God, and are conducive to the public interest'.[87] Again the emperors were portrayed as working in the conjoined effort of obedience to God and reformation of their subjects, with justice the stated goal:

> preferring Justice to all things terrestrial as being the promise of heavenly things, and which is, by the power of Him honoured in her [Justice], sharper than any sword against enemies . . .[88]

Here, the intrinsic link between justice and heaven was further emphasized as something that anticipated the celestial realm and whose terrestrial application honoured God. Also restipulated is the martial dividend from God-pleasing justice.

The problem was then relatively briefly defined.[89] Essentially, it was twofold. Firstly, the laws of previous emperors—and indeed imperial legislation is the only sort envisaged as possible—were scattered among multiple books, inhibiting physical accessibility. Secondly and relatedly, the texts were frequently misunderstood or unintelligible, especially to those outside Constantinople. Thus in the formation of the problem, practical and provincial access to Justice was a central concern. This bipartite problem was to be solved in the first instance by the creation of the *Ecloga*. A commission was empowered to collect the diverse texts, combined with the Isaurians' own legislation, and bring them before the emperors. Then:

> having examined them all with careful scrutiny for the useful content in both these books and in our own new decrees, we deemed it fitting that those frequent matters, decisions on contracts, and appropriate penalties for crimes should be repeated in this present book more clearly and minutely.[90]

Thus the *Ecloga* was presented as the personal project of the emperors. When combined with the repeated association of law with the emperors, this positioned the emperors as the sole terrestrial wellspring of law, fulfilling the mould created by Justinian. This physical condensation and literary simplification was designed:

> for the purpose of easily comprehensible knowledge [*eusunoptos eidēsis*] of the meaning of such pious laws, for the facilitation of the correct decision of cases, for the just punishment of offenders, and for restraint and correction of those favourably disposed towards sin.[91]

87 E.pr.33.
88 E.pr.33–35.
89 E.pr.36–40.
90 E.pr.43–48.
91 E.pr.48–51.

Eusunoptos is the key term, the quality of being able to take in everything at once. Hence, the practical accessibility of the new text had a didactic role, educating the people and above all the judges in the law. That education and the utility of the text for court cases were meant to ease the administration of justice, so the *Ecloga* was always intended to be a used and useful text. Finally, its highest function was moral, ensuring the punishment of sinners and the prevention of sin through deterrence and correction.

The fourth and concluding section of the *prooimion* is an extended admonition of those who administered justice.[92] Given its length, at 57 lines more than half the length of the whole preface, this was evidently a vital function of the *prooimion* and by extension the entire *Ecloga*. The first half is highly indebted to the ideas and imagery of Basil of Caesarea, in particular adopting much of the language of his homily *In Principium Proverbiorum*.[93] It begins:

> And we exhort and at the same time command those who have been appointed to the practice of law to abstain from all human passions and by a sound understanding give judgements of true Justice, neither disdaining a poor man nor letting a powerful man who has done wrong go unpunished, nor in pretence or word admire justice and equality, but in practice prefer injustice and greed as profitable.[94]

This introduces the Basilian concept, which in turn was based on Aristotelian precepts, that the law and 'true justice' were rational and should be administered through reason free from passion.[95] The law and the rational judge were impartial and blind to social rank. Indeed, there is almost a call towards a form of social justice, protecting the weak from the encroachments of the powerful. Certainly the only imaginary case given follows this precept:

> but when two men have a case before them, the one having taken advantage of the other who now has less, to bring equality between them and take away from the seizer the same amount he took, and give this to the impoverished man who was wronged.[96]

[92] E.pr.52–109.
[93] E.pr.52–86, cf. Basil of Caesarea, *In Principium Proverbiorum*, PG 31:385–424, 400C5, 401B8–C6. See Burgmann, *Ecloga*, 107.
[94] E.pr.52–57.
[95] Aristotle, *Politics*, III.1287a 29–33; trans. S. Everson, *Aristotle: The Politics and the Constitution of Athens* (Cambridge, 1996).
[96] E.pr.57–60.

This admonition had both judicial incompetence and corruption in its sights. This fitted the Hellenistic focus on the rational judge, as reason requires both knowledge and impartiality, and also the Christian, patristic emphasis on the protection of the poor and powerless. Yet it also had marked Old Testament overtones, rendered explicit in the extended and multiple quotations that underpin the remainder of the text. For instance, Psalm 58:1–2 is quoted:

> Do you truly speak righteousness, do you judge rightly, you sons of men? For in your hearts you practise lawlessness on the earth, your hands weave injustices.[97]

The Psalm is an admonition to the fair application of justice, in particular against the powerful, as a proof of the benevolence of God. This is followed by:

> And just as the wise Solomon, intimating in parables concerning the dispute over unfair measures, said, 'a weight great or small is abominable to the Lord' (Prov. 20:10, 23).[98]

Here the figure of Solomon is explicitly invoked for the first time as a font of wisdom, that attribute shared with the emperors and Christ, and which formed the basis of sound understanding and just administration of the law. These and further exegetical encouragements to judicial virtue culminated in the command:

> Let those who possess intellect, sense and a clear knowledge of true justice see rightly in their judgements and dispassionately dispense to each according to their worth. For thus our Lord Jesus Christ, the power and wisdom of God, grants to them even more abundantly the knowledge of Justice and uncovers those things that are hard to discover; and he also made Solomon truly wise when he sought out Justice and granted him the ability to accomplish rightly and correctly the dispute between the women concerning the child.[99]

The triangle of knowledge, justice, and God was reinforced, with Christ, the 'wisdom of God', giving knowledge of justice. Again, it was Solomon who provided the historical exemplar of the just ruler, given the essential wisdom by God to adjudicate in a seemingly insoluble case. The admonition is then pointed directly at contemporary judges:

[97] E.pr.64–66. [98] E.pr.66–68. [99] E.pr.75–82.

> Let those who have been appointed by our piety to judge cases and entrusted with the just weighing of our pious laws consider and understand these things, and conduct themselves accordingly.[100]

Notably, again the law was unequivocally imperial, and only to be administered by those appointed by the emperor. What followed was a repeated refrain on the nature and purpose of the imperial office:

> For by these things we endeavour to serve God who entrusted us with the sceptre of the Empire; with these weapons, by His power, we wish to firmly resist our enemies; by these things we trust to increase in goodness and prosper the flock signified by Christ, subjected by his authority to our clemency; and with these we hope for the restoration of the ancient jurisdiction of the state by us.[101]

The Isaurians were heaven's appointees, who through justice and divine approval would defeat foes and morally reform Christians. Importantly, the identity of the emperors' subjects was triply affirmed as Christian: they were a flock, imprinted with Christ's seal, *christosēmeiōtos*, ruled by those chosen by God.[102] Indeed, the only identifier throughout the *Ecloga* of those subjected to the law and the authority of the emperors is Christian. A law code for Christians necessarily had a moral and salvific purpose, as alluded to in the reference to *philanthropia* in the title and explicitly set out in the above passage. The slightly enigmatic reference to the restoration of the ancient jurisdiction of the state probably alludes to the hallowed judicial past of Solomon and Justinian, reaffirmed and reapplied by the Isaurians.

The thickest knot of exegesis opens the *prooimion*'s final paragraph, with five quotations in five lines of text, the last four producing one extended statement:

> Our Lord and Saviour Jesus Christ said, 'Do not judge by appearances, but judge with righteous judgement' (John 7:24), judgement that abstains from all give-and-take. For it is written, 'Woe to them who justify the ungodly for rewards (Is. 5:23), and pervert the way of the humble (Amos 2:7), and take away Justice from the righteous; their root shall be as chaff, and their flower shall go up as dust, for they were not willing to fulfil the law of the almighty Lord (Is. 5:24). For gifts and presents blind the eyes of the wise (Deut. 16:19).'[103]

[100] E.pr.86–89. [101] E.pr.87–95.
[102] E.pr.92. [103] E.pr.96–101.

The significance of the statement is flagged by the prominent ascription to Christ that opens the paragraph, heightened by the emphasis on Christ's role as saviour, thereby implying the injunction given was necessary for man's salvation.

This exegetical barrage repeatedly hits the same mark: the necessity for judges to ignore personal reward. The rhetoric has an immediate purpose in justifying one of the most important practical changes in the whole Isaurian legal programme:

> Wherefore, being eager to utterly check such sordid love of gain, we have ordained that the most glorious Quaestor, the *antigrapheis* and all those who serve in the legal system shall be granted salaries from our pious purse, so that they should not take anything at all from whatever person is tried before them.[104]

This provision of imperial stipends for everyone involved in the administration of justice, and the prohibition of any payment, whether by gift or fee, from those involved in a case was a radical departure from standard Roman practice stretching back to the Republic.[105] Roman magistrates had combined fiscal, military, and judicial roles, while their legal advisors, along with advocates, were remunerated primarily through fees.[106] Centralized salaries for all officials involved would naturally have reinforced central control over the justice system, and should be related to the emerging specialization of administration that occurred over the seventh and into the eighth centuries. The precise role of the Isaurians in the creation of a specialized judiciary and legal administration is difficult to discern, yet the creation of salaries must have greatly reinforced the process. The strengthening of the imperial grip on the judicial system, and through it their subjects, especially those beyond the capital, was not the stated purpose, however. Rather it was that:

> the words spoken by the prophet may not be fulfilled in regard to us, 'they sold Justice for money' (Amos 2:6), and that thereby we might not incur the wrath of God as transgressors of His commandments.[107]

The *prooimion* thus ends where it began, with the law of God transmitted through the prophets, which needed to be obeyed to

[104] E.pr.102–106.

[105] For the importance of this change, see Simon, 'Legislation as both a world order and legal order', 14.

[106] Jones, *Later Roman Empire*, vol. I, 494–516.

[107] E.pr.107–109.

avoid divine wrath. Judicial probity, achieved through admonition and salaries, was as essential to that project as the creation of a practical, concise code for use by that administration.

In all the above, there are clear lines of continuity with Trullo, most conspicuously and significantly in the prominent use of Scripture. Indeed, just as Trullo was the first canon law text to make extensive use of biblical quotations and language, the *Ecloga* is the first civil law code to do so. In contrast, although Justinian's legislation makes frequent references to God and the divine support for imperial undertaking, they had been general expressions; indeed the only quotation in the confirmation of the *Digest* is from Homer![108] The *Ecloga*'s *prooimion*, like Trullo's *Logos*, is virtually an extended exegetical homily. There are no fewer than 15 direct quotations, combined with one long paraphrase, and various biblical references, imagery, and cadences. Together they constitute nigh on a third of the text. The only other direct inspiration and repository of phrases is a patristic exegetical homily. In short, the Bible has a monopoly on rhetoric in the *prooimion*.

Yet, even compared with Trullo, the *prooimion*'s ideology and imagery is utterly dominated by the Bible. Even old Hellenic but thoroughly Christianized concepts receive remarkably little attention here.[109] The Aristotelian idea of reason free from passion as the ideal law was, as explored above, garnered from patristics and expressed so forcefully through exegesis that it is posited as a scriptural injunction. Indeed, the sheer number of direct quotes combined with the repeated expressions 'as it is written' and 'as Christ/the prophet/the apostle said' firmly set up the Bible as the repository of authority. Thus, whereas at Trullo Scripture dominated the rhetorical expression of well-worn imperial themes and on occasion acted as direct inspiration, by the time of the *Ecloga*, the very images and concepts of rulership were directly drawn from the Bible. Moreover, the *Ecloga* elided imperial law with the law of the prophets, thereby granting the

108 *Digest*, *Const. Tanta*, 11.

109 For instance, the metaphor of the ship of state, found in Plato, *The Republic*, trans. D. Lee (2nd rev. edn., London, 1974), 1:341c, repeated in a Christian context by Agapetus, *Ekthesis*, 2:10, and employed in an extended metaphor at Trullo, 49:19–50:2, 51:1–12, is almost entirely missing in the *Ecloga*. The only passing reference is the use of the term *kubernēsis*, 'steering', at E.pr.25 as a stock expression for government. For the general image and references to Plato and Agapetus, see Bell, *Three Political Voices*, 100 n. 7.

Bible the status as a quasi-legal text, both as a source of written law and judicial principle.

Furthermore, unlike Trullo's exaltation of the New Testament, the *Ecloga* is dominated by the Old Testament, in particular the rich and interconnected veins of the pious lawgiver and righteous judge. Twelve of the 15 quotations cited above, and all the additional references, are from the Old Testament. Only one of the three New Testament quotations is more than a phrase. Most revealingly, that extended quotation is John 7:24 introducing the concluding paragraph explored above. That passage comes from a section where Christ was explicitly declaring his obedience to the Law of Moses. It thereby connects the conclusion of the *prooimion* with its introduction's focus on God the lawgiver, attested to by the Old Testament prophets.

In another notable change from the New Testament-dominated Trullo, the model of providing healing and guiding regulation is overshadowed by the emphasis on good judgment. It is in this vein that Solomon is repeatedly invoked. The pious monarch's prime scriptural model is less the production of legislation than the righteous and just application of law. Finally, there is a notable shift away from the Christocentric schema so stridently expounded at Trullo, towards a more theocentric, Mosaic, and Solomonic ideal. Emperors were still shepherds, implicitly imitating Christ, but the model is left implicit. Instead, the wisdom of Christ is emphasized, a wisdom that also inspired Solomon.

Of course, this does not mean that the Isaurians were not strident Christian emperors—for they clearly were—any more than Trullo meant Justinian II rejected the Old Testament, or models such as David. Both Justinian and Leo were militant Christian emperors, seeking the moral reformation of the New Israelites. But the emphasis has definitely shifted. Not only does the Old Testament take on a far larger profile, but it is treated in a far more literal way. The sins of the Old Israelites were the same as those of the New, requiring restatement of the law, although crucially corrected through the grace of *philanthropia*. At the same time, the Isaurians were repudiating Justinian II's direct, figural representation of Christ, and instead promoting the symbols of the Cross and Communion.[110] Thus, while

[110] For the significance of Communion to the Isaurians, see M. Anastos, 'The ethical theory of images formulated by the iconoclasts in 754 and 815', *DOP* 8 (1954), 151–60.

accepting much of the ideological schema of Trullo, the *Ecloga* reflects a marked altering and reshaping of that inheritance worthy of the description of a paradigm shift.

To sum up, the *prooimion* elucidates a world in which the emperors are Moses and Solomon reborn, morally reforming their peoples through corrected law and its just administration. The people are still above all Christian, but conceived primarily as the successors to Israel as the new elect, governed by a law ultimately descended from God, the same law as recorded by the prophets, although now corrected through the Christian grace of *philanthropia*. Through this model, future salvation and present security were achieved. Indeed, there is a persistent martial tone, again reminiscent of Trullo, yet impending reconquest has transformed into besieged emperors continually resisting the advances of heathens, with divine aid the *sine qua non* of imperial defence. This siege mentality resulted from the hostile conditions of the early eighth century, when Byzantium was locked in a struggle for survival, and found its ideal analogue in the trials of the constantly tested and surrounded Israelites. This was a full-scale reconception of Roman law, to the extent that it was no longer identified as Roman, as a central component of a broader ideological survival mechanism. Having traced how the law was ideologically elided with the Old Testament, it remains to explore the extent to which that altered the actual legal content. Before that, however, we must assess how the *Ecloga* envisaged cases would be heard, and who would hear them.

JUDICIAL PROCESS AND THE LEGAL ORDER OF THE *ECLOGA*

Naturally flowing on from the *prooimion*'s focus on the correct and impartial administration of justice was a repeated concern for judicial process. Most prominently, the *Ecloga* included significant alterations to the rules of testimony, in particular in the number of witnesses required for various contracts and proceedings. Firstly, E.2.3 declared that a written marriage contract must 'be contracted through a written dowry contract, before three trustworthy witnesses, in accordance with our recent pious decrees'.[111] As noted already, this is one of the few cases in the *Ecloga* where a change is explicitly linked to previous Isaurian legislation. This was an element of a broader reform on the number of witnesses required. Previously, seven witnesses had been the stipulated number, although it was relaxed in late antiquity to five. Throughout the *Ecloga*, however, there is a repeated insistence on five or three witnesses.[112] This is only loosened in the case of wills made *in extremis* and at the point of death, where just two witnesses were permissible.[113] This followed an established principle of Roman law, but for the first time inserted a requirement for a precise number of witnesses.

Perhaps the more suggestive fact than this slight technical tweak is the constant insistence on a prescribed number of witnesses, while the source material from the *Corpus* hardly ever stipulates witnesses, let alone a number. Moreover, an entire Title, the relatively long E.14, is solely dedicated to the topic. Indeed, the word *martus* is almost the most frequent in the *Ecloga*, appearing no fewer than 33 times in a text only 958 lines long.[114] No previous Roman law work had ever devoted so much attention to witness law. Evidently, the Isaurians were attempting to strengthen the rules of testimony and establish more uniform judicial proceedings.

To ensure credible testimony, E.14.1 states that those who held a dignity or served the state, and the well-off, were competent witnesses, while exhorting the judges to test contentious witnesses to ascertain the truth. The procedure for gathering evidence was outlined in E.14.4, with judges examining witnesses multiple times to adduce whether they had relevant information, and who would then be put on oath. Indeed, oaths seem to have been a favoured tool of the Isaurians, and here it is clear that they were central to all judicial proceedings.[115] This centrality is acknowledged in E.6.4.3, where an

[111] E.2.3.154–56.

[112] This form appears at E.4.1, 5.4, 5.8, 8.1.1. Only three witnesses are stipulated in E.15.1.

[113] E.5.8. Cf. D.29.1.1.

[114] Burgmann, *Ecloga*, 272. In addition the word *martureō*, 'to bear witness', occurs five times, and *marturia*, 'testimony', thrice.

[115] For the general Isaurian use of oaths, see, M. Nichanian, 'Iconoclasme et prestation de serment à Byzance?: du contrôle social à la Nouvelle alliance', in M.-F. Auzépy and G. Saint-Guillain (eds), *Oralité et lien social au Moyen Âge: Occident, Byzance, Islam: parole donnée, foi jurée, serment* (Paris, 2008), 81–102.

heir was to absolve himself of personal liability of any debts unknowingly accrued to an inheritance through an oath before witnesses, and E.14.7, where testimony of a deceased witness can be transferred to an appellant court through a sworn declaration. The significance of oaths in the judicial process is further evinced in the harsh penalty of tongue amputation for perjury after swearing on the Gospel in court.[116]

Finally, there was a marked preference for the written over the oral. In classical Roman law, oral contracts were as acceptable as written ones, and indeed for much of the *Ecloga* they were treated similarly. Oral wills, gifts, contracts, and loans all received no preference over the written.[117] However, on the critical issue of marriage, the written form is clearly preferred. Betrothals could only be contracted through a written contract or the giving of an engagement gift; simple oral agreements were not stipulated.[118] E.2.6 only permitted oral marriages for the poor and misfortunate. Together, the preference for the written, oaths, and proper testimony demonstrate the frequent and central concern of the *Ecloga* for correct and just process, to ensure the application of corrected law throughout the empire.

Of course, the most important factor in the application of correct justice was the judiciary. As noted previously, three types of judge are recorded in the body of the *Ecloga*: *archontes*, 'magistrates', *dikastai*, 'judges', and *akroatai*, 'hearers'. Who were these officials, and what was the relationship between them? Considering these in turn, the first appearance of the *archontes* in the *Ecloga* is at E.8.1.6, where a freedman who had unjustly fallen back into slavery should appeal for restoration to liberty to the Church and 'to the appropriate magistrates', *tois prosphorois archousi*.[119] Then, in E.8.3, freedmen could be reduced back to slavery if proven guilty of ingratitude before either an *archōn* or a *dikastēs*. Further, E.12.6 states that neither 'civil or military officials', *archontes politikoi ē stratiōtikoi*, could be party to contracts of *emphyteusis* or hire.[120] Finally, E.17.5 and 21 both refer to action being taken 'by the magistrate of the place', *hupo tou kata ton topon archontos*, in the former instance thrashing someone who took the law into their own hands in settling a dispute, and in the latter seizing a slave whose master had had sex with them

[116] E.17.2. [117] Respectively E.5, 4, 9, 10. [118] E.1.1.
[119] E.8.1.6.490–91. [120] E.12.6.617–18.

and selling her beyond the province, with the proceeds going to the fisc.[121]

This is a rather wide set of competences, embracing both civil and criminal law. Moreover, it highlights the potential ambiguity and multiple usages of the term *archōn*, a term used in both military and civilian settings. Furthermore, if there were 'appropriate magistrates', there must be 'inappropriate' ones. There is no clue as to who they were or why they were inappropriate, but it does indicate there was still a range of courts, each with differing competences, and that the differences were recognized.[122] Similarly, that the *Ecloga* was addressing articles to magistrates of a particular place implies that the application of the *Ecloga* in the provinces was a priority to its compilers. Precisely what level of jurisdiction imagined is uncertain, although as E.17.21 refers to the ability of the *archōn* to sell a slave beyond the confines of a 'province', *eparchia*, that might mean that in this case a provincial governor was indicated.[123]

The recorded role of the *dikastai* by contrast is rather limited. As noted already, in E.8.3 a freedman could be reduced to slavery again if ingratitude was proved to an *archōn* or a *dikastēs*.[124] In E.15.2, minors could appeal to *dikastai* to release them from unfavourable contracts that had taken advantage of their lack of years. All their other appearances are found in E.14 concerning witnesses. So in E.14.1, *dikastai* are to question, under torture, witnesses who are unknown and whose testimony is contested. As noted already, E.14.4 states that *dikastai* receive testimony first not under oath, and if it is demonstrated that the testimony is relevant, the witness is then put on oath. E.14.7 details how witnesses called 'before ordinary judges', *para koinois . . . dikastais*[125]—presumably meaning judges in the first instance—could be brought again on appeal to the 'final judges', *eschatoi dikastai*.[126] Finally, E.14.10 ordains that in criminal proceedings, unlike civil ones, witnesses had to appear 'before the judge hearing the case', *para tō akroōmenō tēs hupotheseōs dikastē*.[127] So *dikastai* had competence to judge at least some criminal cases, but overall are more linked with civil cases and are overwhelmingly associated with the hearing of testimony.

[121] E.17.5.786–87; 17.21.827.
[122] Noted by Haldon, *Seventh Century*, 273 n. 63.
[123] E.17.21.828. [124] E.8.3.503–504. [125] E.14.7.656.
[126] E.14.7.661. [127] E.14.10.674–75.

The most prominent judges in the *Ecloga*, however, are the mysterious *akroatai*, a slightly obscure Greek word literally meaning 'hearers'. They first appear at E.5.5, which demanded that the *akroatai* investigate wills that disenfranchised children, to enquire whether they were valid. Then E.5.8 regulated the number of witnesses needed *in extremis* for *akroatai* to validate wills. E.8.2 records that when ransomed prisoners of war agreed to reimburse their ransomers by acting as servants, both parties had to register the agreed amount paid back every year before the *akroatai*. These were also the authority who decided, in disputes over unreturned loans or lost deposits, whether there was a case.[128] In E.15.3, the *akroatai* are the authority for adults to appeal to for release of contract made 'through fear of power or some kind of fraud', *dia phobon exousias cheiri ē kai dolō tō oiōdēpote*.[129] Moreover, their role was not confined to civil law. For in E.17.27, they were required to investigate into the beginnings of an adultery and interrogate the accusers, to ensure that either the adulterers or slanderers were appropriately punished. In E.17.41, it is an *akroatēs* who must *periergazesthai*, 'investigate thoroughly', whether a farmer was negligent or malicious in intent when starting a fire in his field.[130] Indeed, this is one of the few deliberate interpolations in an otherwise highly faithful translation of the original *Digest*. Finally, E.17.47 requires the *akroatai* to adjudicate liability in fights that resulted in death. This highly diverse range of duties are only those specifically mentioned in the *Ecloga*, and can be assumed to have been wider. Indeed, in the *Farmer's Law*, that range is explicitly expanded, as we shall explore in Chapter 5.

What then was the relationship between the three? Part of the problem in reconstructing this is the ambivalence of three terms. In the non-legal sources we find the term *archōn* linked to various palatine bureaux; multiple regions and places, from themes, to provinces, to cities; and standing on its own without any qualifier, geographic or administrative.[131] Some of these were clearly the surviving provincial governors, but not all. The term might also bleed into that of *dikastai*, just as in Justinianic legislation, governors are often

[128] E.10.1.1, E.11. This responsibility is clearly linked to an *akroatēs*' duty to oversee loans concerning land documented in NG.67; see Chapter 5, 221–2.

[129] Minors go to the *dikastai*; see E.15.2.

[130] E.17.41.904. This is a subject closely linked to NG.56–58; see Chapter 5, 215–17.

[131] Oikonomidès, *Listes de Préséance*, 343–3, 352–4.

referred to as *iudices* in Latin, and *dikastai* in Greek, highlighting that the governors were normally the court of first instance and also indicating the predominant importance of their judicial roles.[132] In Justinianic law, *dikastai* could be either *archontes* or not *archontes*—that is, they were judges either because of their role as magistrates or they were judges delegated by magistrates. For instance, N.90.1.1, the source for E.14.1, stipulated that *dikastai* who were also *archontes* could apply torture themselves, but if they were not also *archontes*, they had to appeal to particular magistrates to do so on their behalf. The situation in the *Ecloga* is either the result of a truncation, and the old divide was maintained in practice, or the *dikastai* mentioned were in this case also *archontes*, or by the eighth century *dikastai* who were not *archontes* could torture certain dubitable witnesses. It is impossible to know which option is correct. It is also possible that some of the *dikastai* of the *Ecloga* might refer to the panel of 12 *theioi dikastai* established by Justinian in N.82 as a pool of professional judges sitting continuously in Constantinople.[133] However, whether they still existed in the eighth century is unknown. The picture is made murkier still when considering the *akroatai*, a word meaning 'hearers' which could easily apply to any judge, magistrate or not, hearing a case. Indeed, as noted above, E.14.10 refers to a *dikastē*, 'hearing', *akroaomai*, 'a case'.[134] More suggestively, in N.25.3 the newly reformed *praetor* of Lyaconia is called an *akroatēs* when exhorted to investigate and adjudicate cases brought to him.[135] *Akroatai* can also be found in Justinianic law acting as arbitrators.[136] Evidently, then, none of these terms can be safely delineated into neat, administrative limits.

Looking beyond the legal material sheds some—but only some—light on the matter. For whereas *archontes* in all their forms are found on numerous seals, there is not a trace of either *dikastai* or *akroatai*. In the *PMBZ*, some four *dikastai* appear, yet one is a seventh-century

[132] Jones, *Later Roman Empire*, vol. I, 481; Haldon, *Seventh Century*, 269.

[133] For the *theioi dikastai* see Jones, *Later Roman Empire*, vol. I, 501–2. For the possibility that they are the same as the *dikastai* and indeed the *akroatai* of the *Ecloga*, see Zacharia von Lingenthal, *Geschichte*, 358–61, esp. 359 n. 1265; cf. A. Christophilopulos, '*Akroatēs*', *BZ* 44 (1951), 86–8.

[134] E.14.10.673.

[135] N.25.3, 199.2.

[136] N.113.1., 532.5. For more uses of *akroatēs* and the verb *akroaomai*, and the argument that they represent the Greek versions of Latin *auditor* and *audire*, see Christophilopulos, '*Akroatēs*'.

inscription recording a *theios dikastēs* (which at least suggests the office lasted into the seventh century),[137] while the other three are all from literary sources clearly using the term *dikastēs* as a description rather than as an office.[138] The account for *akroatēs* is more meagre still, with just the one entry in the *PMBZ*, and then used to mean a spy.[139] Of course, if the *dikastai* and *akroatai* were provincial or sub-provincial judicial officials, that might explain this low profile, given the biases in both the literary and sigillographic sources towards the capital. Furthermore, the cases listed above for both *dikastai* and *akroatai* would have produced little documentation with attendant seals that was worth preserving. Still, if they were defined offices, one would have expected more of an impact. Perhaps the *dikastai* and in particular the *akroatai* are mere phantoms of the *Ecloga*? Are they in fact equivalent terms, devoid of any technical meaning, simply referring to generic judges?[140]

In response and returning to the *Ecloga*, we should note the following. Firstly, E.8.3 had deliberately distinguished between *archontes* and *dikastai*. Clearly there was a distinction, and there is no reason to suppose that it wasn't exactly that of Late Antiquity, in that *archontes* were magistrates and *dikastai* were their delegated judges, who specialized in petty and civil cases. However, there is no similar distinction between *archontes* and the *akroatai*.[141] Secondly, the *akroatai* hold magisterial powers, able to adjudicate and punish crimes as serious as adultery, arson, and homicide. These are considerably more serious issues than those associated with the *dikastai*. In this E.15.2–3 is informative, for in E.15.2 the *dikastai* deal with proving that a minor was taken advantage of into making a disadvantageous contract, whereas in E.15.3 the *akroatai* investigate the more important case of adults being forced or defrauded into making a contract.[142] Thirdly, in E.8.2 the *akroatai* are treated as an office;

[137] *PMBZ* 8248.

[138] *PMBZ* 10997, 11266, 11671. For instance, *PMBZ* 11671's office is clearly *Eparch* of Constantinople.

[139] *PMBZ* 10470.

[140] This is the argument of Christophilopulos, '*Akroatēs*'.

[141] Jones, *Later Roman Empire*, vol. I, 479, 501–2.

[142] In both cases this involved the remedy of *restitutio in integrum*, namely the return of property ceded in inequitable circumstances; see D.4.1–4, 6. However, fraud (Lat. *dolus*) and duress (Lat. *metus*) were more serious, the former bringing *infamia*, 'infamy', if proved (D.3.2.13.8), and the later leading to quadruple damages if the

they are not hearing a case but registering the amount calculated each year that was owed by a prisoner of war to his ransomer.[143] Finally, the *akroatai* are by far the most prominent authority, associated with a much wider range of cases than either *archontes* or *dikastai*. Evidently the *Ecloga* is deliberately focusing on the role of the *akroatai*, for they always could have used the other two terms if they were interchangeable.

Considering all this, perhaps the most probable solution to the puzzle is that the *akroatai* were *archontes*, or rather that the existing magistrates were being rebranded as 'hearers'. This would explain the lack of seals. It might also explain who those *archontes* without any qualifier were: sub-provincial magistrates focused on hearing cases.[144] It would also explain why, in some later versions of E.17.27, the *akroatai* of the original have morphed into an *archōn*.[145]

The significance of such a rebranding can be inferred from the derivation of the word *akroatai*. As we have noted, in Justinianic law magistrates had already been called *akroatai* in the context of hearing and investigating cases. Using the word in the eighth century could then be taken as reimposing a Justinianic institution in the pursuit of justice. However, almost certainly more important was the word's biblical connotations.[146] Romans 2:13 declares: 'For it is not the hearers (*hoi akroatai*) of the law who are righteous in God's sight but those who obeyed the law who will be declared righteous.' The theme is elaborated by James 1:22: 'Do not merely be hearers of the word, and so deceive yourself. Do what it says.' Thus the *akroatai* were associated with law, righteousness, and obedience, all aligned towards the eternal goal of salvation, a theme found throughout the Isaurians' works. Moreover, if (as has been suggested) the old provincial administration had, by the eighth century, become primarily

property was not immediately restored (D.4.2.14.1). That E.15.3 ends on the injunction that *after* cancelling the contract the *akroatai* were to 'investigate the case from the beginning', *ex huparchēs to kat' auton zēteisthai kephalaion*, strongly implies that prosecution was then brought for fraud or duress. Therefore, *pace* Christophilopulos, '*Akroatēs*', 88, I do not believe that E.15.2–3 demonstrate an equivalence between *dikastai* and *akroatai*, but a difference.

143 A similar registering of a contract before an *akroatēs* is found in NG.67.

144 For seals of *archontes* without any qualifier see, for example, *ZV* 679, 694, 865 A, 1053, 1659, 1844, 2562, 2962, 3201.

145 See Burgmann, *Ecloga*, 234.

146 Isaiah 3:3, Ecclesiasticus 3:29, Romans 2:13, James 1:22–5. See G. Abbott-Smith, *A Manual Greek Lexicon of the New Testament* (Edinburgh, 1999), 18.

and even solely a judicial operation, then this rebranding neatly encapsulated the changed focus. The job of magistrates was to be hearers of cases and dispensers of justice, paid centrally, and following biblical injunctions. All told then, the changes to judicial process and the reworking of the judiciary evince time and again the Isaurians' desire that the law of the *Ecloga* be more than an ideological construct, and actually be competently and justly applied throughout the empire. What, then, was the law that these rebranded, exhorted, and salaried judges were supposed to enforce?

MARRIAGE LAW

Marriage was always a fundamental issue to Roman law and society in general.[147] It uniquely combined those subjects most dear to the Roman heart: property, family, and morality. Every major Roman legislator had focused on the issue, from Augustus to Justinian.[148] It is therefore hardly surprising that some of the most significant of the Isaurian legal reforms centred on marriage. Indeed, the importance of the subject is conveyed by opening the text with the issue, with three titles comprising around a quarter of the whole dedicated to it.[149]

The *Ecloga*'s treatment of the subject also encompasses the entire range of usage of the Justinianic material, ranging from almost repetition (if compressed) to rephrasing, and finally to significant alteration. Concerning the law of betrothal, the *Ecloga* is generally very close to Justinian's precepts. For instance, E.1.1 maintained the rule of C.5.1.5 that a woman in her majority who breaks a betrothal must pay back both the engagement gift and the same amount again as punishment. Similarly E.1.3 complies with the principle of C.5.1.2 that if a marriage is not contracted within two years, the betrothal is nullified and the woman may legally and honourably marry another. On the manifold issues of property transferred before and during

[147] One should also note the preoccupation of legal historians with marriage, as Kazhdan declared, 'Of all the Byzantine institutions marriage is, probably, the favourite child of the historians of law.' Kazhdan, 'A new history of Byzantine law?', 13.

[148] See, for instance, C.5.1–20, 9.9; D.23–24, 48.5; I.1.10; N.22, 97, 117. See also Introduction, 13, n. 53.

[149] E.1–3 comprises 205 lines (110–315) from 848 lines of the text proper, i.e. not including the 109 lines of the *Prooimion*.

marriage, and the claims of a spouse on a deceased partner's estate, the *Ecloga* again mostly follows Justinianic law, although there are some tweaks.[150] For example, N.97.1 ordered that prenuptial dotal contracts between husband and wife should be of equal value, so that a dowry should equate to the husband's prenuptial gift to his wife that was designed to support her beyond her husband's death. Yet E.2.3 prohibited any demand for a prenuptial gift to equal the wife's dowry. Again, E.2.4 mostly adheres to N.22.20 but slightly lessens a husband's claim on a deceased wife's estate while affirming hers on his. However, Zacharia von Lingenthal's notion of a new regime of joint matrimonial property has been shown to be a chimera, with Burgmann convincingly arguing that substantively the property relations between spouses remained essentially Justinianic.[151]

More importantly, several passages are fundamentally re-expressed beyond simple compression and resultant simplification. For instance, while E.2.5.1 is legally very similar to N.22.23, with a wife controlling all her deceased husband's property on behalf of her children while she remained unmarried, it also contains a brief homiletic saying that:

> Her children shall not have the power to oppose her or demand from her their father's property, but rather must show her all honour and obedience as their mother, according to the commandment of God. And naturally the mother is bound, as is fitting for a parent, to educate her children, and provide for their marriages and give them dowries, as she thinks best.[152]

Hence, the order and cohesion of the family was made the fundamental aim of the legislation, to fulfil the ordinances of heaven. This tendency is even more pronounced in E.2.5.2, where the legal difference was negligible but the law is expressed through extended exegesis. Children were to show their father:

> all honour and obedience as is fitting to a parent, for as is written: 'Honour your father and mother in word and deed, so that a blessing may come upon you from them. For the blessing of the father establishes the houses of children, but the curse of the mother roots out the

[150] See in particular Zacharia von Lingenthal, *Geschichte*, 89–92; and L. Burgmann, 'Reformation oder Restauration? Zum Ehegüterrecht der Ecloga', in D. Simon (ed.), *Eherecht und Familiengut in Antike und Mittelalter* (Munich, 1992), 29–42.

[151] Burgmann, 'Reformation oder Restauration?'.

[152] E.2.5.1.

> foundations. For you were begotten of them, and how can you repay them for what they have done for you?' (Eccles. 3:8–9; 7:28). And the apostle Paul confirms this when he says, 'Children obey your parents in the Lord, for this is right; and Parents do not provoke your children, but bring them up in the training and instruction of the Lord' (Eph. 6:1, 4).[153]

Again, Justinianic law was symbolically aligned with the commandments of Scripture. The earthly issue of parental control over property was thereby presented as obeying the moral injunction for the correct ordering of the family. The pattern is replicated in E.2.5.3 forbidding a widowed husband or wife to be freed from the charge of minors, as they should:

> take care and provide for them, for as the apostle says, 'a widow who has children or grandchildren should first learn to live piously in their own home; for this is pleasing to God' (I Tim. 5:4).[154]

E.2.5 therefore represents Justinianic law being both continued and reimagined. Indeed, considering the relative lack of rhetoric in the rest of the *Ecloga* outside the *prooimion*, combined with the prominence of Scripture, it is evident that moral exhortation was seen as a central facet of the marriage legislation.

Furthermore, there was a fundamental reconception of marriage as a quintessentially Christian institution, rather than the classical Roman idea of a private contract.[155] Most patently, E.1 and 2 both begin by describing betrothal and marriage as being explicitly and exclusively 'of Christians'.[156] Considering that this comes immediately after the *prooimion*'s focus on the emperors' provision of justice for Christians, this strongly implies that a foremost duty for the pious Christian emperors was the protection of marriage as a divinely ordained institution. This impression was reinforced by the repeated employment of Scripture.

This conceptual repositioning led to several substantive legal changes. Firstly, the bounds on prohibited marriages were considerably tightened. This issue had long been a prime concern of Roman law.[157] In essence, close blood relations were forbidden to marry, up

153 E.2.5.2. 154 E.2.5.3.

155 Zacharia von Lingenthal, *Geschichte*, 57; Bury, *Later Roman Empire*, 416–17; Bury, 'Graeco-Roman law', 262–3; Freshfield, *Ecloga*, 21–8.

156 E.1.1 begins: *Synistatai mnēsteia christianōn*; E.2.1: *Sunistatai gamos christianōn.*

157 Cf. I.10.1–9.

to first cousins. Similarly banned were relations by marriage—for instance, stepparents with stepchildren or a brother to a sister-in-law. The precise boundaries of incest had shifted over antiquity, with Christian emperors from Constantine I onwards slightly extending them, but mostly these represented long-established regulations.[158] However, canon law, which had mostly accepted these boundaries, had at Trullo markedly expanded them, indicating a contemporary concern to ensure the purity of marriage.[159] In particular, Trullo C.53 had posited the spiritual relationship of godparent to godchild as equal, or indeed higher, than blood and marriage, and therefore prohibited a godfather from marriage to the mother of the godchild. E.2.2 incorporated these recent canon law changes into civil law, including the primacy of the spiritual relationship over that of blood, a demonstration of the novelty of at least this element of the *Ecloga*, and the interpenetration of canon and civil law. Moreover, E.2.2 considerably augmented the prohibitions by including the sons of godparents from marrying godchildren and their mothers, and expanded the previous civil law regulations to include even second cousins. Thus the *Ecloga* not only aligned civil law with canon law, but even amplified the prohibitions to ensure pious marriage. That it did so in only nine lines when the *Institutes* took nine chapters is testament to the *Ecloga*'s pithiness, and, when combined with its Christian inspiration, explains why this segment of the text was one of the most copied in the manuscript tradition.[160]

However, the most significant alterations occur in divorce law. In classical Roman law, marriage, as a simple private contract based on affection, could be easily dissolved unilaterally or conjointly. Throughout late antiquity, influenced primarily by Christianity, emperors had limited this, so that divorce by mutual assent was forbidden, and a strict set of conditions were given for unilateral divorce. However, E.2.9 represents stringency beyond precedent, and indeed is seldom repeated by later Byzantine emperors. Only adultery by the wife, impotence of the husband, or a spouse either plotting against the other or becoming a leper were considered

158 For the extent of the Constantinian changes, see J. Evans-Grubbs, *Law and Family in Late Antiquity* (Oxford, 1999).

159 For instance, Basil Cs.27, 68, 75–6, 78–9, 87 present virtually identical limitations to those of I.1.10.1–9.

160 Some six MSS of the 30 containing excerpts, but not the whole *Ecloga*, contain E.2.2 (*RHBR*.3, 87, 135, 255, 276 and 278).

legitimate grounds for divorce. This conservatism was explained and justified through another of the *Ecloga*'s rare extended pieces of rhetoric, yet again anchored by exegesis:

> The wisdom of God, the Maker and Creator of all things, teaches that marriage is an indissoluble union of those living together in the Lord. For He who brought mankind from nothingness into being, did not form man and woman in the same fashion, although able to, but created her from the man, so that he might ordain through the wise uniting of 'one flesh' in two persons the inseparability of the union. Hence he did not separate them when the woman by the suggestion of the serpent lead the man to the bitter taste, nor besides did he break the marriage when the man worked with the woman to transgress God's commandment, but punished the sin and did not break the union. Moreover this active law was confirmed anew by the Creator and through the Word, when the Pharisees asked Him, 'if a man may divorce his wife for any reason', and he answered that those who have been joined by God shall in no way be parted by man, 'except for adultery'.[161] And we who follow and obey shall not ordain anything more beyond this. But since the majority of mankind has become naturalized to the state of vice, and hence are not affectionately disposed towards one another, and on many grounds, although they are not such as these [i.e. not the valid grounds given below], cause the dissolution of their life together, we have decided it is necessary to expressly place in the present legislation the grounds by which marriage can be dissolved.[162]

Echoing the *prooimion*, the wisdom of the creator educates mankind on a seminal issue, here the indissolubility of marriage. This distinctly un-Roman statement is justified through reference to both God the Father in the Old Testament, and Jesus Christ in the New, with the Isaurians and their law code fulfilling and following the heavenly legislators. Indeed, the language confirms the continuity of the subject, from Father to Son, and then to the emperors. For God the Creator ordained, *nomotheteō*,[163] one flesh in two persons, which 'active law was confirmed anew', *energei nomothesia authis . . . kurōtheisē*,[164] by Christ, which the Isaurians followed in the 'present legislation', *parousē nomothesia*.[165] The Isaurians were once more imitating heaven and being obedient to its commands, actively reshaping the law so as to obey divine precepts. It then proceeds to

[161] Cf. Mt. 19:3–6. [162] E.2.9.1. [163] E.2.9.1.268.
[164] E.2.9.1.272–73. [165] E.2.9.1.281.

delineate the only grounds permitted to break the sacrament of marriage, permission couched as a form of economy given *in extremis*. Having done so, E.2.9.4 concludes that even insanity was not legitimate grounds for divorce and that:

> Except on these known grounds it is not possible to dissolve a marriage, for as it is written, 'whom God has joined let not man put asunder' (Mt. 19:6).[166]

Hence the word of God was cited to complete this radical tightening of divorce law, vividly conveying the mindsets of the Isaurians. It was Scripture and its commandments that dominated utterly their rhetoric and motivated change. Overall then, the marriage law of the *Ecloga* evinces both considerable continuity with Justinianic law and important alterations. However, the fundamental shift is rhetorical and conceptual, the transforming of marriage into a Christian sacrament ordained by God, and therefore protected by the pious emperors.

CRIME AND PUNISHMENT

The *prooimion* declared the necessity to repeat the laws of contract and the penalties for crimes.[167] This already gave criminal law a far higher profile than traditional Roman law.[168] Indeed, E.17 is by far the longest title, and in multitudinous ways it forms the heart of the *Ecloga*.[169] However, like marriage law, much in the *Ecloga*'s treatment represents continuity more than change. Naturally, universal crimes such as murder and theft reappear, but so do the more peculiarly Roman ones, such as the linkage of poisoners and magicians.[170] Further, E.17.41's stipulation of death, by burning for urban arsonists and by beheading for the rural variety, is virtually a verbatim quotation from D.9.2.30.3, and is the sole identified example of the *Ecloga*'s compilers employing a translation of an *antecessor*.[171]

[166] E.2.9.4.291–3. [167] E.pr.46–47.

[168] For the *Ecloga*'s penal law, see B. Singowitz, *Studien zum Strafrecht der Ekloge* (Athens, 1956). For individual crimes, see S. Troianos, *Ho Poinalios tou Eklogadiou* (Frankfurt, 1980).

[169] E.17 comprises 180 lines (E.17.762–942). [170] E.17.43, cf. C.9.18.

[171] Burgmann, *Ecloga*, 5.

Moreover, legal principles that stretched back to the Republic were maintained. For instance, murderers were still punished through execution by the avenging sword of the *Lex Cornelia*.[172] Adultery was still defined, according to the *Lex Julia*, as illicit intercourse with a married woman, discounting married men with unmarried women. Moreover, it was still treated as a public crime as it threatened marriage, and punished a cognizant, cuckolded husband who condoned it.[173] The *Lex Aquilia* continued to provide the basis for restitution for the loss of property through another's negligence, i.e. delict law.[174] The guilty were to replace the damaged property or make fiscal restitution. Delicts that involved force, forethought, or other aggravating factors were punished by restoring some multiple (normally double) of the value of the thing destroyed as restitution and punishment. Thus, E.17.8 ordained double restitution for anyone who forcibly impounded the cattle of another that were subsequently damaged. The only change was the positing of delict law under the title of criminal punishments, yet as delict had always represented a form of quasi-crime, this is hardly revolutionary.[175] A similar case concerning property is found in E.17.7, where someone who hires a horse and takes it beyond the agreed terms is liable to indemnify the owner for any damage or death.[176] Simple theft is treated, in a peculiarity of Roman law, as a form of delict.[177] As E.17.11 states:

> Anyone who steals in another part of the State shall, in the first instance, if he is free and has the means, besides restitution of the thing stolen hand over twice the value of the thing stolen; but if he is poor shall be beaten and exiled. On the second occasion, his hand shall be cut off.[178]

The difference between punishment of the man who could afford to pay restitution and those who could not had long been recognized in Roman jurisprudence.[179] Indeed, Roman magistrates had increasingly substituted an array of physical punishments in lieu of restoration.[180] The precise significance of those punishments we shall consider below, yet when considering the continuity of the *Ecloga*,

[172] E.17.45, cf. I.4.18.5. [173] E.17.27, cf. C.9.9.29.

[174] E.17.7–9, cf. D.9.2; C.3.35.

[175] See J. Harries, *Law and Crime in the Roman World* (Cambridge, 2007), 45.

[176] Cf. D.13.6.5.7. Of course, this is not strictly delict, but an action rising from the misuse of a loan.

[177] Harries, *Law and Crime*, 44–5. [178] E.17.11. [179] D.48.19.1.3.

[180] Harries, *Law and Crime*, 31.

one should note that both the punishment and the principles underpinning them find precedence.[181] Similarly, E.17.12 upholds the liability of the master whose slave steals either to indemnify the wronged or to transfer ownership of the slave, while E.17.13 maintains the category of cattle stealing as a special and more serious form of theft.[182] Both law and penalty are maintained, in strikingly similar language, when E.17.15 ordained that thieves who stole from the sanctuary be blinded, while those stealing from any other part of the church were to be flogged, tonsured, and exiled.[183] Its inclusion, along with E.17.4 punishing anyone who dared to beat a priest in a church or during the liturgy, marks the Isaurians' interest in protecting the clergy and church property from sacrilegious despoliation.

However, change, major and minor, was significant. Again there was simple compression and simplification, as in the case of E.17.18 where all currency forgers were punished by having their hand cut off, replacing the complex Justinianic system of graded punishment.[184] There were also several novel crimes and altered penalties. E.17.6 banished any prisoner of war who renounced his faith from church and country, if ever they returned, underlining the Christian ideological foundations of the state. Similarly, deserters were punished with decapitation, a penalty with precedent but not found in Justinianic legislation; its inclusion here is a measure of the *Ecloga*'s comprehensiveness and the concerns of a realm in a state of constant war.[185]

The greatest novelties, however, concern sexual crimes. Indeed, the whole of E.17 is unprecedentedly skewed towards the subject, comprising E.17.19–39. Of these, eight chapters were entirely new.[186] For the first time explicitly in Roman law, an unmarried man fornicating was punished with six lashes (E.17.20), half the rate of a married man who was guilty of illicit sex, *porneia*, rather than adultery, *moicheia* (E.17.19).[187] Following on from E.2.2's extension of the boundaries of

[181] For instance, N.134.13 *mitigated* the established penalty of amputation of both hands, by ordaining that one hand would be sufficient.

[182] D.47.14.

[183] E.17.15. This is the same penalty as D.48.13.11.

[184] Cf. D.48.10.8–9 and C.9.24.

[185] E.17.53.

[186] Or at least have no simple correspondent in the *Corpus*. These were E.17.19, 20, 25, 26, 29, 34, 37, 39.

[187] The difference was an aspect of Roman law, but it had never stipulated any precise punishment. See Harries, *Law and Crime*, 95–105.

prohibited marriages, E.17.25 condemns anyone who intends to marry their godparent or has sex with them, with both being explicitly punished in the manner of adulterers—having their noses slit. Those who had married their godparent were to be severely beaten and have their noses cut off.[188] The less serious and newly introduced crime of cousins and second cousins illegally marrying was only punished with separation and a flogging.[189] Bigamy, beyond being outlawed, was given a precise penalty of a flogging for the man, and the banishment of the second wife and any children.[190] E.17.34 stipulated nose amputation for anyone who knowingly had carnal intercourse with a mother and daughter. The culminating sin of bestiality was criminalized and penalized with castration.[191]

Adultery, unsurprisingly, boasts the longest and most elaborate chapter of the title.[192] Both man and woman were to have their noses slit. The adulteress' marriage would be dissolved following E.2.9, which is linked through the citation of the injunction from Scripture that marriage makes 'one flesh'.[193] The man, however, was not to be separated from his wife, as adultery was not grounds for divorcing a husband. The judges, *akroatai*, were exhorted to investigate carefully, underlining the public and serious nature of the crime, with relatives classed as better witnesses than strangers, again revealing the Isaurian desire for due process and correct judgement, especially when concerning such a morally charged offence. To help ensure a correct conviction and deter maliciousness, slanderers were to suffer the same penalty as that threatened to those they had accused, an established aspect of Roman law repeated in a generalized context at E.17.51.[194]

It is evident that the real grievance underlying these chapters was less breach of marriage than immoral sex. Only E.17.35 on bigamy and E.17.37 on cousins' marrying do not directly concern sex, which were punished through relatively lenient separation and flogging. The remainder of E.19–39 provided penalties scaled to the severity of the impiety. Thus, sex with one's own slave was only punished through the forced selling of the slave with the proceeds forfeited to the treasury,[195] while fornication with another man's slave, debauching both his marriage and another's property, incurred a fine of 36 *nomismata*, or, if the guilty were poor, a whipping and payment

188 E.17.26. 189 E.17.37. 190 E.17.35. 191 E.17.39.
192 E.17.27. 193 E.17.27.850. 194 Cf. C.9.16.7. 195 E.17.21.

of as much of the fine as possible.[196] Anyone who copulated with a nun had committed adultery, as the nun was wedded to the Church of God.[197] Rape of nuns or virgins was similarly punished by nose amputation, with abettors exiled.[198] Corruption of someone betrothed to another was also punished as adultery.[199] Sex with a minor, namely under 13, again resulted in a nose slitting but also the forfeiting of half his property to the seduced girl.[200] However, the greatest sexual crimes were those that broke natural law. Thus E.17.33 ordained decapitation for incest, but only nose amputation for intercourse between kin by marriage. As noted, bestiality carried the penalty of castration. Homosexuality was punished with death.[201]

Together, these chapters represent the most sustained assault on sexual immorality in either civil or canon law yet seen in Roman history, dwarfing the comparable canons in Trullo. Indeed, the model drawn upon is not Roman but biblical—for the catalogue of sin, with its overwhelming focus on immoral sexual acts, bears striking resemblance to Leviticus 18–20. It is Leviticus 18:23 that outlawed bestiality, and Leviticus 18:22–23 that provided the concluding couplet of homosexuality and bestiality as the ultimate sins. Further, the motivating factor is here revealed, for immediately following that commandment is the general divine order to the Israelites to keep themselves morally pure or the land 'will vomit you out as it vomited out the nations that were before you'.[202] The only difference was that the Byzantines had already been evicted from much of their land, and therefore their new realm had to be founded the more surely on God's commands, with sexual purity at the forefront of the new covenant. Thus, once again the law of the *Ecloga* was subsumed within the dictates of heaven, and Leo was imagined as a second Moses.

As strikingly, and more commented upon, as the changes noted above is the shift in the nature of punishment. The classical Roman system of punishment as reported in the *Digest* consisted of capital punishment (including decapitation, being thrown to the wild beasts, being sentenced to the mines, or deported to an island), confiscation of property, and fines.[203] Moreover, across late antiquity, the number

[196] E.17.22. [197] E.17.23. [198] E.17.24.
[199] E.17.32. [200] E.17.31.
[201] E.17.38. For the *Ecloga's* place in the development of Byzantine attitudes to homosexuality, see M. Hubel, 'Die Haltung zur Homosexualität im byzantinischen Reich', *Das Altertum* 49 (2004), 291–310.
[202] Leviticus 18:28. [203] D.48.19.

of offences in primary law carrying a capital punishment increased dramatically.[204] However, several of the classical penalties fell into disuse. More significantly, great leniency had been granted to magistrates, particularly in the provinces, with regard to punishments, especially concerning criminal law. This resulted in a trend towards greater severity and variety in punishment, and a rise in corporal chastisement, which had previously been alien to Roman law. Physical punishment was relatively easy to administer and was seen as a public deterrent, seamlessly integrated with the magistrate's duty to maintain order. Furthermore, when dealing with the poor, for whom Roman law with its focus on property and status had little time, and who could not afford to pay fines or restore a thing damaged, chastisement was the simplest means of retribution.[205] Indeed, one of the prime legal differences between the high-status *honestiores* and low-status *humiliores* is that the former were protected from corporal punishments.[206] This punishment, then, began to seep into primary legislation, reflected in N.134.13, which abolished the amputation of both hands or both feet, as one was sufficient. The relative lack of documentation concerning criminal cases, which unlike civil affairs did not generate the incentive (to at least the winning side) of keeping the paperwork to affirm their legal case, hides the prevalence of corporal punishment in late antiquity. Yet the increasingly grisly toll of mutilations of political prisoners in the seventh century recorded in the chronicles, who would have nearly all been *honestiores*, implies that the trend only strengthened.[207]

Therefore, the widespread use of corporal punishment in the *Ecloga* was no great novelty. Instead, its significance lies in the *Ecloga*'s desire to ordain precise punishments, and thereby to assert imperial control over criminal proceedings. Moreover, the replacement of crimes that had carried a capital punishment with a corporal penalty does

[204] See MacMullen, 'Judicial savagery'; P. Garnsey, 'Why penal laws became harsher: the Roman case', *Natural Law Forum* 13 (1968), 141–62. Cf. Harries, *Law and Empire*, 135–52.

[205] For Roman law's attitude to the poor, see C. Humfress, 'Poverty and Roman law', in M. Atkins and R. Osborne (eds), *Poverty in the Roman World* (Cambridge, 2006), 183–203.

[206] See P. Garnsey, *Social Status and Legal Privilege in the Roman Empire* (Oxford, 1970); and P. Garnsey and R. Saller, *The Roman Empire: Economy, Society and Culture* (London, 1987), 107–25.

[207] Perhaps the most famous case was the mutilation of the troublesome cleric Maximus the Confessor who had his tongue amputated.

represent significant change. Indeed, only 13 of the 53 chapters carry the death penalty.[208] Likewise, confiscations, fines, and exile were included, but rarely. In contrast, 16 chapters ordain beating,[209] eight amputation of the hands,[210] 11 amputation of the nose,[211] and one each the removal of the tongue,[212] castration,[213] and blinding.[214] It is thought that this substitution of corporal for capital punishment is what the title's insistence on a correction towards *philanthropia* is referring to.[215] Indeed, it has been plausibly argued that this prominence emanated from a strict interpretation of Mt. 5:28–30: 'if your right hand causes you to sin, cut it off and throw it away. It is better for you to lose one part of your body than your whole body to go to hell.' This passage is steeped in Jewish ideas of external pollution creating a barrier with God, ideas which had increasingly come to dominate intellectual discourse in the seventh century across the Mediterranean, as we saw in relation to Trullo, and was probably in response to the rise of rigorist and pietist Islam.[216] These ideas are manifested in the marked correspondence between crime and punishment, normally the removal of the polluted limb. Thus thieves lost their hands, perjurers their tongues, and zooerasts were castrated. Similarly, adulterers' noses were amputated as a form of symbolic castration.[217] Moreover, it was a law that envisaged no social demarcation; the old *honestiores/humiliores* divide was forgotten, and the only differentiation in penalty was based on the practical ability to pay the fine. Therefore, the penalties in the *Ecloga* could be construed as not only impartial and equal justice for crimes, or penalties for deterrence, but also as actually part of a process of purification and healing

[208] Respectively, E.17.3, 33, 38, 41, 42, 43, 45, 46, 49, 50, 51, 52, 53. They concern respectively: treason, incest, homosexuality, arson, intentional homicide, brigandage, certain heresies, and desertion.

[209] E.17.1, 4, 5, 10 [for theft of arms from camp], 11 [first offence], 13 [first offence], 15 [theft from church but not sanctuary], 19, 20, 22, 28 [for husband who condones wife's adultery], 29, 35, 36, 37, 47 [death from fight with lighter weapons].

[210] E.17.10 [for theft of horse from camp], 11 [second offence], 13 [third offence], 14, 16, 18, 46 [non-lethal wound by sword], 47 [death from a fight not including swords].

[211] E.17.23, 24, 25, 26, 27, 28 [for adulterers], 30, 31, 32, 33 [sex with non-blood relations], 34.

[212] E.17.2.

[213] E.17.39.

[214] E.17.15 [theft from sanctuary].

[215] Burgmann, 'Ecloga'.

[216] See Haldon, 'The works of Anastasius of Sinai', 143.

[217] See J. Frembergen, 'Honour, shame, and bodily mutilation. Cutting off the nose among tribal societies in Pakistan', *Journal of the Royal Asiatic Society* 16 (2006), 243–60.

intended to propitiate God's wrath, both for the state and the sinner. In this, the diagnosis and intended result were the same as at Trullo, but the prescribed remedy of punishment is utterly different, emanating from an altered legal ideology that posited the application of Mosaic Law as the ultimate cure for the sins of the New Israelites.

MILITARY LAW

The final set of notable changes in the *Ecloga* concern issues touching on martial matters. Examining these in the order they appear, the first pertinent laws are found in E.8 concerning slavery and freedom. E.8.2 ordained that if ransomed prisoners of war did not have the means to pay back their ransomer, they were to become hired servants and thereby to work off their ransom, thus offering an incentive for people to provide ransoms for captives. E.8.4.1 offered immediate emancipation for slaves who resisted the enemy and escaped, while those who did nothing, bar managing to escape, were to remain slaves for five years. E.8.4.2 extended this by punishing slaves who willingly deserted by removing any chance of emancipation. The effect was to encourage resistance and to discourage either passivity or active support by slaves towards enemy raiders. All three regulations have no civil law precedent and convey a society constantly beset by invasions needing to prevent any emergence of a fifth column, while encouraging such an occurrence among their enemies.

Additionally, soldiers and property are repeat concerns. E.12.6 barred soldiers from any participation in leases based on *emphyteusis*, or hire, or being employed in other people's businesses, or serving in others' households, 'for their sole occupation is to fight for the State against the enemies'.[218] These instructions had clear Justinianic precedent and were enacted for the same purpose: to prevent soldiers from abusing their positions of power, keeping them focused on protecting the state and not lining their own pockets at the expense of those they were supposed to protect.[219] In a more militarized society, with soldiers almost certainly physically closer to the taxpayer, such regulations were probably even more important than under Justinian I.

[218] E.12.6.621–2. [219] Cf. C.4.65.31; C.12.35.15–16.

On the positive side, E.16 stipulated soldiers' rights regarding property. E.16.1 repeated the established right of soldiers to make wills even when still under parental power. Incidentally, this confirms that that distinct oddity of Roman law—paternal control over descendants' property during the parent's lifetime—was retained, even if other aspects of *patria potestas* had declined.[220] E.16.2 is more peculiar to the circumstances of the eighth century, regulating the parental inheritance between brothers when one is a soldier and any others are not.[221] There is a clear sense here in the unity of the family, and also the normality of having a brother serving while others attend to the family property. Moreover, there is a distinct idea, supported in E.16.4, that the soldier was supported, at least partially, by a state salary. However, E.16.2 also represented an encroachment on the guarded right of *peculium castrense*, the right of soldiers to control property gained by them through military service, as it grants his brothers rights, which gradually degrade over time, probably correlated to issuing of pay, to this property as a form of compensation for the family's outlay in outfitting the soldier. This would suggest an element of the soldiery supported, at least in part, by family lands, with the emperors engaged in a careful balancing act of encouraging families and individuals to provide recruits, while protecting the individual rights of soldiers.

The final section concerns issues of soldiers in camp and on campaign. E.17.10 established flogging for stealing in camp or on the march, and amputation of the hand for the theft of a horse, a harsher sentence than contained in the *Digest*.[222] E.17.53 stipulated death for desertion. However, by far the most original is E.18 on the division of war spoils. The very existence of such a title, and that it is placed at the culmination of the work, is highly suggestive of the militarized nature of Byzantine society. The Title established the

[220] For an introduction to *patria potestas*, see J. Crook, *Law and Life of Rome* (London, 1967), 107–11; for developments in late antiquity, see A. Arjava, 'Paternal power in late antiquity', *JRS* 88 (1998), 147–65; for argued changes in the *Ecloga*, see Zacharia von Lingenthal, *Geschichte*, 109–11.

[221] For a more detailed study on these stipulations, see N. Oikonomidès, 'Middle Byzantine provincial recruits: salary and armaments', in J. Duffy and J. Peradotto (eds), *Gonimos: Neoplatonic and Byzantine Studies* (Buffalo, 1988), 121–36, esp. 130–4; R.-J. Lilie, 'Die zweihundertjährige reform: zu den Anfängen der Themenorganisation im 7. und 8. Jahrhundert', *Byzantinoslavica* 45 (1984), 27–39, 190–201, esp. 194–6; and J. Haldon, 'Military service, military lands, and the status of soldiers: current problems and interpretations', *DOP* 47 (1993), 1–67, esp. 21–3.

[222] Cf. D.49.16.3.14.

principle that five-sixths of the spoils should 'be divided amongst all the men equally, both great and small', deliberately not preferring the officer corps, 'for the additional payment of their salaries is sufficient for the officers'.[223] This suggests that the Isaurians were deliberately incentivizing the soldiery with the prospect of booty, and also that officers' pay, whether in kind or cash, was intended to cover their wants, and that they at least were a professional salaried force.

Overall, several points arise from these regulations on soldiers and martial matters. Above all, the Isaurians were posing as protectors of the army's welfare. Considering the army was always the pre-eminent force in the Roman state, essential to maintaining imperial power both externally and internally, this is hardly a novel Isaurian concern. Yet as Leo III had seized power through a military coup and the continuation of his regime was ultimately based on his success in the field, both in the stemming of Arab attacks and the concomitant prestige and justification for his rule that it provided, it is unsurprising that he should wish to be seen as upholding soldiers' rights. More than that, E.18 suggests a deliberate attempt to motivate resistance by the army, while E.8.2 and 8.4 offer a brief snapshot of Isaurian attempts to motivate wider Byzantine society against the invaders.

But perhaps the most telling element of E.18 is the rhetoric it employs and the Isaurian ideology it reveals. The introduction weaves the subject of war with Christian piety and wisdom. Proverbs 24:6 is paraphrased: 'for the "help" of God is given "to the hearts of councillors".'[224] I Maccabees 3:19 is then invoked: 'victory in war does not come from might in numbers, but by the power of God.'[225] This phrase could be the summation of the *Ecloga*, and indeed all Isaurian ideology. The various laws contained in the *Ecloga* were all aimed at this goal, gaining the approval and therefore the strength of God, so to ensure victory on the battlefield. Indeed, the Maccabees provided a strong biblical model for the Isaurians, warlords, and priests who simultaneously fought a heathen empire and restored the purity of their subjects, thus renewing the covenant with God. The reference to the Maccabees, however, is telling, for they were not conquerors but liberators, fighting a recognizably stronger foe not only for the moral reformation and refounding of Israel, but also for survival. The gulf between them and Phinehas is exactly that between Justinian II at Trullo and the Isaurians in the *Ecloga*.

[223] E.18.953. [224] E.18.948–9. [225] E.18.949–50.

CONCLUSIONS

Edwin Freshfield described the *Ecloga* as 'the first Christian lawbook' building on the ideas of Zacharia von Lingenthal, popularized in English by Bury's assertion that '[the *Ecloga*] is a deliberate attempt to change the legal system of the Empire by an application of Christian principles'.[226] Certainly, the *Ecloga* did introduce several substantive changes, particularly with regard to marriage and punishments, which have clear Christian overtones. Yet it is also evident that several key principles of Roman law were maintained, and that the majority of Titles hardly differ from Justinianic law. There is a balance pronounced from the beginning between selection and improvement, and probably the bulk of the *Ecloga* lies in the former. However, the *Ecloga* is a Christian document in more important ways than the content of its laws. It posited Roman law as not just ultimately emanating from God, but in fact a continuation of the same law given through the prophets. Similarly, emperors were not part of a separate narrative, but the heirs to the apostles and prophets, Moses and Solomon. Thus both law and emperors were subsumed into the paradigm of providential and salvation history. The *Ecloga* expresses both this thought-world and the deliberate situating of the Isaurians within it. It was the emperor who was the nexus of this matrix, the point where God and people, law and righteousness, justice and its administration, the biblical and imperial past, converged. By fulfilling that claimed role, the Isaurians were justifying their position as the inheritors of this common past, and aimed to win and retain divine support. In doing so, they fundamentally reshaped the image of the imperial office and the nature of law, refashioned after and aligned with the Old Testament. In this, they were espousing an ideology befitting a shrunken and besieged realm.

Married to this ideological and symbolic text lies a practical work that throughout evinced concern for the just administration of law. The *Ecloga* was designed to be used in support of a reformed judiciary, with new rules of testimony to ensure that the law, now aligned with God's Word, was applied across the empire, thus securing it and the ruling dynasty. Further, all the extant evidence suggests that the *Ecloga* was highly successful in achieving its aim. There are some

[226] Freshfield, *Ecloga*, xi; Bury, 'Graeco-Roman law', 261.

21 surviving manuscripts of the entire (or almost entire) text, and a further 30 that contain some extract.[227] Although the eldest of these manuscripts is only from the eleventh century—that is, 300 years after the publication of the *Ecloga*—it strongly implies that the text had been distributed across the empire, as its own ideology presumed it would. Furthermore, the *Ecloga* would spawn a host of derivatives, official and private, and was translated into Slavic, Arabic, and Armenian, entering canon law among the Armenians, Copts, and even the Latin Crusader Kingdoms—all testimony to its enduring appeal.[228] Even the Macedonian criticisms of the (by now deemed heretical) Isaurians and their work testify to how successful the *Ecloga* had been as a work of law and a vehicle for ideology; it was successful enough to force a response that could not break the mould set by its predecessor. Even after multiple derivatives had appeared and the Isaurians had been condemned to a virulent *damnatio memoriae*, the *Ecloga* remained recognized and used—if one can judge from repeated copying—for the rest of Byzantine history and beyond. Indeed, the *Ecloga* only finally ceased being legally operative in Romania in 1928![229]

Perhaps just as important was the state remuneration of judges and all involved in the justice system. This could only promote a growing legal specialization in the administration of justice.[230] Moreover, it plausibly encouraged further interest in the collection and collation of Justinianic law, following the model of the *Ecloga*. Indeed, there is no indication that the commission that compiled the *Ecloga* stopped work. Rather, the *Ecloga* was the foundation of a whole legal programme. It is those legal works that arose from the *Ecloga*'s foundation that we shall consider next.

[227] See Appendix, Table 9, for full manuscripts. Description is given in Burgmann, *Ecloga*, 29–45.

[228] For these translations, see Burgmann, *Ecloga*, 24–7, 80–2; see also L. Burgmann, 'Law in Slavic countries, Byzantine', in *ODB*, vol. 2, 1195; and L. Burgmann, 'Law in the East, Byzantine', in *ODB*, vol. 2, 1195–6. See also D. Obolensky, *The Byzantine Commonwealth: Eastern Europe 500–1453* (London, 1971), 317–21. The Arabic version is edited by S. Leder, *Die arabische Ecloga* (Frankfurt, 1985). For the *Ecloga's* influence on the canon law of the kingdom of Jerusalem, see B. Kedar, 'On the origins of the earliest laws of Frankish Jerusalem: the canons of the Council of Nablus, 1120', *Speculum* 74 (1999), 310–35.

[229] See Freshfield, *Roman Law*, 32.

[230] I use the word specialization rather than professionalism as that might imply a specified, required education and training for the post, and there is little evidence of that.

3

The Appendices to the *Ecloga*

The *Ecloga* was not an isolated text. In the manuscript tradition it is always accompanied by other works. In part, this reflects its brevity, at 958 lines in its current edition and in the manuscript tradition most frequently occupying around 12 folios, therefore being far too short to warrant its own codex.[1] Incidentally, this is perhaps indicative of the original published format, with 12 folios divided into three quires constituting a sort of pamphlet, one which could be easily produced, disseminated, and carried by all the judges of the empire, although considering the difficulty of the manuscript evidence, this is impossible to prove. What can be plausibly suggested is that the regularity of association in the manuscripts between the *Ecloga* and a few texts betrays a far closer relationship than mere codicological chance. In particular, the works known as the *Krisis peri gambrōn stratiōtōn*,[2] the so-called *Appendix Eclogae* (AE),[3] the *Nomos Mosaikos* (NM),[4] and the most famous and oft-interrelated by legal scholars, the *Nomos Stratiotikos* (NS),[5] *Nomos Nautikos* (NN),[6] and *Nomos Georgikos* (NG)[7]

[1] See Burgmann, *Ecloga*, 29–45.

[2] *Krisis peri gambrōn stratiōtōn*, ed. D. Simon, 'Byzantinische Hausgemeinschaftsverträge', in *Beiträge zur europäischen Rechtsgeschichte und zum geltenden Zivilrecht: Festgabe für J. Sontis* (Munich, 1977), 91–128, 94, analysis 95–100.

[3] *Appendix Eclogae*, ed. L. Burgmann and S. Troianos, *FM* III (Frankfurt, 1979), 24–125.

[4] *Nomos Mosaikos*, ed. L. Burgmann and S. Troianos, *FM* III (Frankfurt, 1979), 126–67.

[5] *Nomos Stratiotikos*, ed. W. Ashburner, 'The Byzantine mutiny law', *JHS* 46 (1926), 85–109.

[6] *Nomos Rhodion Nautikos*, ed. W. Ashburner, *The Rhodian Sea-Law* (Oxford, 1909).

[7] *Nomos Georgikos*, ed. I. Medvedev et al., *Vizantiĭskiĭ zemledel'cheskiĭ zakon* (Leningrad, 1984).

are frequent textual bedfellows, while also sharing notable similarities in substance, language, and form.[8] This interrelationship was recognized by the Byzantines themselves through the inclusion of the *Ecloga* and these associated legal texts in the *Ecloga ad Prochiron mutata*, a twelfth-century private collection.[9]

This led the great nineteenth-century legal scholar Zacharia von Lingenthal to claim official authorship for Leo III and Constantine V of the NS, NN, and NG, seeing them as published alongside (or perhaps immediately after) the *Ecloga*.[10] For a long time the majority of Byzantinists accepted this association mostly unquestioned, encouraged by succeeding editions that supported the connection, such as that of Momferratos based on *RHBR*.9, which included the *Ecloga*, the AE, NM, and NS.[11] This position came to dominate Anglophone Byzantine studies through its wholesale acceptance in the early twentieth century by J. B. Bury, who declared that the Isaurians deliberately issued all these texts along with the *Ecloga* as a comprehensive corpus of law that reflected the new world of the eighth century.[12] This in turn was reinforced by the translations and studies of Edwin Freshfield in the 1920s, in particular his 1926 translation of Momferratos' edition of the *Ecloga* and AE.I–IX, XI, which remains the gateway for most English-language study of the *Ecloga* and AE. In this schema, the Isaurians were great legal reformers, refashioning Roman law under the influence of Christianity and custom during the Byzantine 'Dark Ages'. This corpus was then supplanted by the Macedonian reforms beginning in the late ninth century, which deliberately reconnected with the Justinianic past and purged some of the intervening, 'vulgar' accretions.

A succession of early twentieth-century scholars questioned aspects of this paradigm, but did not repudiate it. For instance, Ostrogorsky criticized the presumed role of the Isaurians, preferring seventh-century emperors, in particular Justinian II, and the pressure

[8] See Appendix, Table 9.

[9] *Ecloga ad Prochiron mutata*, ed. K. Zacharia von Lingenthal, *IGR* IV, 49–170 = Zepos, *IGR* VI, 217–318.

[10] Zacharia von Lingenthal, *Geschichte*, 17. Cf. Mortreuil, *Histoire du Droit Byzantin*, vol. I, 387–407 that listed the NN, NG, and NS as private laws produced sometime between 610 and 867.

[11] A. Momferratos' edition, *Ecloga Leonis et Constantini cum appendice* (Athens, 1889).

[12] Bury, *Later Roman Empire*, 410–21; and Bury, 'Graeco-Roman law', 261–5.

of 'orientalizing' custom as the motors of change.[13] More radically, Dölger posited texts such as the NG as purely private works, products of the transformations of the seventh century, but principally representing Justinianic law as preserved through the intermediary of the *antecessores*.[14] Russian scholarship, which was fixated on the NG and the world of the peasantry, and beset by bitter internal politics, oscillated between wholesale agreement with Zacharia von Lingenthal and complete rejection.[15] In the English-speaking world, Walter Ashburner created new critical editions of the NS, NN, and NG, which argued for the possibility of Isaurian authorship of the NG, but also highlighted serious legal problems with that relationship. Rather, Ashburner argued for a wide date range, specifically *c*.600–800 for the NN, and for a diffusion of source material and motivation.[16] However, all agreed, based on more limited knowledge of the manuscripts than we now enjoy, that there was some connection between the *Ecloga* and these attendant texts. They only denied the Isaurians credit, instead generally positing these texts as preceding, rather than conjoint or succeeding the *Ecloga*. A further common thread was the constant focus on the three '*nomoi*', the NS, NN, and NG, in ascending order of interest to the eclipse of all else.[17] Further, the dominant research interest was in measuring the distance these 'vulgar' laws had strayed from the Justinianic standard, rather than studying the texts for what they might say about the society that produced them.[18] The end result was a paradigm not far removed

[13] G. Ostrogorsky, 'Über die vermentliche Reformtätigkeit der Isaurier', *BZ* 30 (1929–30), 394–400; and G. Ostrogorsky, *History of the Byzantine State*, 90–1 esp. n. 7, and 135–7.

[14] F. Dölger, 'Ist der Nomos Georgikos ein Gesetz des Kaisers Justinians II?', in *Festschrift für Leopold Wenger Vol. II* (Munich, 1945), 18–48.

[15] D. Górecki, 'The Slavic theory in Russian pre-revolutionary historiography', *Byzantion* 56 (1986), 77–107; and D. Górecki, 'The Slavic theory of the Byzantine rural community in Soviet and post-Soviet historiography', *Byzantinoslavica* 67 (2009), 337–64.

[16] W. Ashburner, *The Rhodian Sea-Law* (Oxford, 1909); W. Ashburner, 'The farmer's law', *JHS* 30 (1910), 85–108 (Edition) and 'The farmer's law II', *JHS* 32 (1912), 68–95 (commentary); and W. Ashburner, 'The Byzantine mutiny act'.

[17] The *Krisis* was only given attention with Simon's edition and the ensuing discussion on its relevance to the heated subject of the Theme system. The AE and NM similarly remain curios seldom studied beyond their critical editions.

[18] The great exception to this is of course the NG, which has been extensively exploited, indeed vastly overexploited, in the attempt to derive a picture of agriculture in this period. See Chapter 5.

from Zacharia von Lingenthal's; namely that by the mid-eighth century, and probably earlier, a basic corpus of law, consisting of the *Ecloga* and attendant texts, had come into being as a recognizable stepping stone from Justinian to the Macedonians.

In the latter half of the twentieth century, with the emergence of a specialized school of Byzantine law, interest by non-specialists in anything bar the NG and occasionally the *Ecloga* slowly faded. However, a succession of new critical editions did appear, mostly under the aegis of the Frankfurt series *Forschungen zur byzantinischen Rechtsgeschichte*, based on a far wider and more systematic analysis of the manuscript evidence.[19] Generally, this reappraisal complicated and strained the assumed relationship between the *Ecloga* and its supposed associated works. Furthermore, it highlighted the grave methodological hindrance caused by manuscripts only surviving from the tenth century—that is, at least two centuries after the presumed publication of the texts in question—and then only in significant numbers from the twelfth. Furthermore, in stark contrast to the works studied previously in this book, all these texts are undated, and perhaps un-datable, with no explicit attribution of author or issuing authority. Moreover, Burgmann has recently stressed that far from being an interchangeable and undifferentiated mass, the NN, NS, and NG actually represent considerable diversity, in subject, form, and length.[20] The new *communis opinio*, also elucidated by Burgmann, is that the 'appendices' to the *Ecloga* were only gradually intertwined in the manuscript tradition, so that by *c.*800, together they 'constituted a corpus of secular law unrivalled until the end of the 9th C[entury]'.[21]

A broad, if unconvincing, challenge to this revised schema has been issued by Andreas Schminck. Again focusing on the *nomoi* (though including in their number the normally ignored NM), Schminck argues that the NM, NN, and NG were composed by the patriarch Photius in association with his work on the *Eisagoge*, while the NS represents an even later work of Leo VI.[22] Detailed refutation will be

[19] For the importance of the Frankfurt school, see Stolte, 'Balancing Byzantine law', 63–4.

[20] L. Burgmann, 'Die Nomoi Stratiotikos, Georgikos und Nautikos', *Recueil Zbornik Radova Vizantološkog Instituta* XLVI (2009), 53–64.

[21] Burgmann, 'Ecloga'.

[22] A. Schminck, 'Probleme des sog. *Nomos Rhodiōn Nautikos*', in E. Chrysos et al. (eds), *Griechenland und das Meer* (Mannheim, 1999), 171–8; and A. Schminck, 'Bermerkungen zum sog. "Nomos Mosaikos"', in *FM* XI (Frankfurt, 2005), 249–68.

offered below, yet it is worth noticing at this point that Schminck proffers a strikingly similar model to Zacharia von Lingenthal's: one prime authority was responsible for the bulk of work as part of a grander project to reinvigorate Roman law; for Leo III, simply read Photius.

The following three chapters will broadly agree with—though seek to refine—the paradigm of Burgmann et al. It shall also attempt to demonstrate that those texts which Zacharia von Lingenthal originally associated with the *Ecloga* were indeed most plausibly components of an Isaurian legal programme, but one stretching across the half-century after 741. Moreover, within that, it is possible to detect waves of work, rather than one coherent appendix. Further, it will be argued that there is notable difference between the *Krisis*, the majority of the AE, and the NS on the one hand (which can be seen as deliberate extensions and appendages of the *Ecloga*), and the NM, NN, and NG on the other, which represent separate, if associated, works. The latter shall be discussed in Chapter 4 and 5, while the former provide the present focus. Finally, if one accepts the (necessarily tentative) dating proposed, then it should be possible to utilize these texts, which, save the NG, are mostly unknown to broader scholarship, as signifiers of the society that produced them.

THE *KRISIS PERI GAMBRŌN STRATIŌTŌN*

In all likelihood, the earliest addition to the *Ecloga* was a seldom studied and short text, the *Krisis peri gambrōn stratiōtōn*. This was an imperial, juridical decision, the emperors plausibly identified by Simon as Leo III and Constantine V.[23] Indeed, this text is a rare testament to what was probably a major locomotive of legal change: adjudication from established legislation and legal principles to novelties of a specific case, which, when issued by the emperor, had general validity.[24] It therefore reminds us of the emperor's role as both legislator and highest judge, and how those functions were entwined.

[23] Simon, 'Byzantinische Hausgemeinschaftsverträge'.

[24] Little is known of the emperors as judges in this period. However, see Millar, *The Emperor in the Roman World*, 228–40 for the early empire.

It portrays emperors not just as ideologically the basis of legal system, but as actually present and acting at the centre of juridical affairs.

Naturally, the text also served to reinforce the symbolic importance of the emperors. Explicitly it was they who decided the issue. Moreover, the pious nature of that decision was emphasized, as it was a *eusebeis nomous*, which reflected the fact that the emperors were 'pious and justice loving', *oi eusebeis kai philodikaia hēmōn basileis.*[25] Thus, piety and love of justice were presented as the foremost imperial attributes in continuation of the *Ecloga*'s message. The imperial plural is, furthermore, one of the keys to dating the text, for the manuscript evidence unequivocally ties the *Krisis* to the *Ecloga*, as demonstrated in Table 2:

Table 2. The manuscripts of the *Krisis peri gambrōn stratiōtōn* in the *RHBR*

RHBR	Contents of manuscript
6	.4 (E) .5 (K)
53	.8 (EP) .9 (K)
55	.46 (E) .47[–53] (AE) .51 (K)
109	.8 (E) .9 (K)
127	.7 (EP).8 (K)
141	.3 (E) .4 (K)
151	.5 (E) .6 (K)
241	.6 (E) .7 (K)
244	.54 (EP) .55 (K)
263	.21[–38] (*Epitome Marciana*) .33 (K)
289	.1[–22] (*Epitome Marciana*) .17 (K)
319	.1 (P). . . .5–6 (Novels of Irene) .7 (NS) .8 (NN) .9 (NG). . . .12[–15] (AE) .14 (K)
321	.1 (EP) .2 (PD) .3 (E.17–18) .4 (K). . . .6 (AE)

In nine of its 13 extant manuscripts, the *Krisis* immediately follows the *Ecloga* or a derivative; in two others it is combined within the AE, and in the final two it is an element of the *Epitome Marciana* along with the *Ecloga*.[26] Indeed, the *Krisis* is frequently described in the manuscripts as Title 19 of the *Ecloga*, enjoying a similar situation in the later compilation of the *Ecloga ad Prochiron Mutata* as Title 33.2, following E.18.[27] Given this unambiguous connection, and the specific imperial attribution, the text was patently intended to be an

[25] K.3–4.

[26] *Epitome*, ed. K. Zacharia von Lingenthal, *IGR* II, 277–431, and VII, 1–199 = Zepos, *IGR* IV, 276–585; see A. Schminck, 'Epitome Legum', in *ODB*, vol. 1, 724.

[27] Burgmann, *Ecloga*, 135.

adjunct to the *Ecloga*, a quasi-E.19. Therefore, the emperors mentioned were almost certainly Leo III and Constantine V, especially as one would expect any others to have been named, whereas that would be unnecessary when directly appended to an already promulgated text by the same emperors. This interpretation is supported by the hiatus between the death of Leo III in June 741 and the co-crowning of Leo IV in 751, when there was only one emperor, Constantine V. It is unlikely that after a decade-long gap, during which there is the high probability that at the least some components of the AE were created, the *Krisis* would be so strongly associated as a direct appendage to the *Ecloga*. Further, there is little reason to suppose that the *Krisis* predated the *Ecloga* as otherwise a text that was manifestly deemed worthy of attachment and which, as we shall explore shortly, closely relates to a legal novelty in the *Ecloga*, would have been included in the *Ecloga*. Therefore, the most plausible date for the issuing of the *Krisis* would be between the promulgation of the *Ecloga* in March 741 and the death of Leo on 18 June of that year.

The position of the *Krisis* also reflects its subject matter, which dovetails with the issues raised in E.16.2 concerning a soldier's *peculium castrense* in the altered military and social conditions of the eighth century.[28] The *Krisis* relates the situation of a soldier who enters the household of his father-in-law, but later seeks to leave it. Explicitly the soldier had complete rights over all the property he had brought into the household, whether this consisted of imperial gratuities, his salary, or booty. However, the father-in-law had rights to any military equipment he had provided. Just as in the situation in E.16.2, the soldier is clearly being supported, at least in the provision of martial equipment, by a household which thereby had a claim to compensation; however, the graded compensation of E.16.2 is unnecessary here, as the son-in-law had no claim to the estate. Both laws therefore elucidate a common form of military recruitment and subsequent need to clarify (and indeed restrict) the ancient *peculium castrense* to provide compensation, and thereby to incentivize households to produce an equipped soldiery.

[28] See Chapter 2, 126. As for E.16.2, the *Krisis* is discussed, with the focus on its significance for the nature of the army in the eighth century, by Oikonomidès, 'Middle Byzantine provincial recruits', esp. 134; Lilie, 'Die zweihundertjährige reform', esp. 196–7; and Haldon, 'Military service, military lands, and the status of soldiers', esp. 21–3.

The social and military implications of this lie beyond this study, and have been fruitfully examined elsewhere.[29] What is important to note for our purposes is the legal activism of the Isaurian emperors in legislating and adjudicating on the issue. Patently and naturally, as it concerned the soldiery, who constituted their prime power base and who were engaged in incessant warfare, the Isaurians considered the subject significant and desired to regulate it through the mediums of legislation and judicial decision. Moreover, if the above dating is correct, it suggests a rapid reception and impact for the *Ecloga*; for it would seem plausible that the legal changes posited by E.16.2 generated either a real case or a legal question that was then resolved by imperial decision in the *Krisis*, all within the space of three months. If so, this is impressive testimony to the legal machine that had created both the *Ecloga* and the *Krisis*. Finally, it would signify willingness by the centre to clarify and expand the *Ecloga*, an attitude repeatedly demonstrated across the following texts.

THE *APPENDIX ECLOGAE*

Since the nineteenth century, a nebulous set of texts have been graced with the seemingly official appellation of the *Appendix Eclogae* (AE).[30] Certainly, the *Ecloga* is more often than not surrounded by a set of texts ultimately derived from the *Corpus* that are comparable in style and format.[31] Further, the titles of the AE are not provided with any indication of independent authorship or authority. Instead their rubrics consist of a reference to a source usually combined with the typical construction *peri*. . . , 'concerning . . .'. Hence they read as direct continuations of the legal handbook with which they are associated in any particular manuscript. Indeed, the vast majority of the AE's titles only ever appear with the *Ecloga*, its Macedonian successors, or a derivative of either, the former being the most popular with 11 manuscripts extant that have a significant

[29] Oikonomidès, 'Middle Byzantine provincial recruits', esp. 134; Lilie, 'Die zweihundertjährige reform', esp. 196–7; and Haldon, 'Military service, military lands, and the status of soldiers', esp. 21–3.

[30] Mortreuil, *Histoire du Droit Byzantin*, vol. I, 375–86. For further literature, see Burgmann/Troianos, *Appendix Eclogae*, 24–8.

[31] See Appendix, Table 9.

textual link.[32] Thus it is only reasonable to concur with the *communis opinio* that the AE was composed and connected with the *Ecloga*, at some point after the latter's promulgation and before the Macedonian reforms of the late ninth century, probably close to the former.[33] Moreover, given the weight of association with the *Ecloga*, and the fact that the only known commission tasked with collecting, editing, and abbreviating Justinianic law was the one that created the *Ecloga*, and for which there is no evidence that it ceased operation with that work, it seems probable that at least part of the AE was issued soon after 741. However, given the civil war of the early 740s, it is likely that the late 740s and 750s would prove a more fruitful time.[34] If this plausible (if unprovable) hypothesis is accurate, then the AE would fulfil a propagandistic role for Constantine V, acting as the continuator of his father's legal programme, which of course was also promulgated in Constantine's own name.

Yet several thorny problems remain. Firstly, the title *Appendix Eclogae* is a misnomer. There is no such text. As its editors Burgmann and Troianos admit, it is far better to speak of *Appendices* to the *Ecloga*.[35] Their edition of 14 titles exists in no surviving manuscript.[36] Furthermore, no manuscript follows the precise ordering they describe. Moreover, although individual titles are mostly stable, there can be significant variation; for instance, AE.II has multiple forms and AE.V is similarly disturbed.[37] Burgmann and Troianos plausibly argue from the manuscript evidence for a central appendix of AE.I–X combined with the *Nomos Stratiotikos* (NS), with AE.XI–XIV and a collation of diverse works frequently found with the AE acting as a sort of wider and less stable appendage.[38]

However, this hypothesis can be refined by systematic analysis of the textual groupings, in particular when found in conjunction with the *Ecloga*.[39] For, as with all the texts studied in this book, the

[32] See Tables 3 and 4, and Appendix, Tables 9 and 10. *RHBR*.151 and 272 are discounted as they have no significant textual association with the *Ecloga*.

[33] Burgmann, 'Ecloga'.

[34] For this civil war see P. Speck, *Artabasdos, der rechtgläubige Vorkämpfer der göttlichen Lehren: Untersuchungen zur Revolte des Artabasdos und ihrer Darstellung in der byzantinischen Historiographie* (Bonn, 1981).

[35] Burgmann/Troianos, *Appendix Eclogae*, 29.

[36] Burgmann/Troianos, *Appendix Eclogae*, 32–40, lists the MSS.

[37] Burgmann/Troianos, *Appendix Eclogae*, text 98–100, commentary 41–4.

[38] Burgmann/Troianos, *Appendix Eclogae*, 68–73.

[39] Cf. Burgmann/Troianos, *Appendix Eclogae*, 40–95.

surviving manuscripts of the AE only exist from the tenth century onwards, hence obscuring the original process of publication. By default, one is forced to rely on copying centuries after the fact into codices that, normally, have a plethora of other works and their own (usually unknown) agendas. Hence any conclusions drawn from such uncertain evidence can only be tentative and subject to counter-argument and potential revision from future evidence. Yet it is a reasonable proposition to suppose that the manuscripts that contain the *Ecloga*—which is the agreed original reference text for the AE—should retain a more accurate echo of the original form of publication. The 11 manuscripts with a significant textual association between the *Ecloga* and AE are given in Table 3 as follows:[40]

Table 3. The manuscripts of the AE with the *Ecloga* as recorded in the *RHBR*

RHBR	Contents of manuscript
9	.10 (XI) .11 (NM)....13 (E) .14[–15] (AE.I–II, NS, AE.III–IX)
21	.69 (IX) .70 (NM) .71 (II) .72 (E)
25	.3 (E) .4[–7] (NS, AE.III–VI, X, C.8.10.12, AE.I, N.119.7, AE.II)
29	.41 (NM) .42 (AE.II) .43 (E) [Here on from *RHBR*.219] .44 (NN) .45 (AE selection)
55	.45 (XI) .46 (E) .47[–53] (Irene's novels, AE.I–II, NM, AE.III–VIII, X, K, N.119.7, AE.XII–XIII, NS)....58 (NN.III)....61 (NN.II) .62 (C.8.10.12)
61	.59 (NM) .60 (AE.II) .61 (E) .62[–66] [Here on from *RHBR*.103] (NS, III–VI, X, NN [Here on from *RHBR*.61], C.8.10.12, AE.I, N.119.7, AE.II, IX)
134	.9 (NM) .10 (II) .11 (E)....13 (NN)
197	.4 (E) .5[–6] (NS, AE.III, V–VI, X, I–II)....9 (NG)
274	.40 (E) .41[–2] (AE.IX–X, I, XII, II, NS, AE.III–VIII)
310	.29 (E)... 31.[–2] (AE.XIII, XI, I, XIV, N.12, AE.II, IX–X, IV, XII, V, III) .33 (NN) .34 (NS)
327	.12 (NS) .13 (NN) .14 (NG) .15 (AE.II, I) .16 (Novel of Leo V)... 20 (E) .21 (AE.III–VI)....26 (AE.XI)

Patently there is a marked degree of divergence, both in regards to the presence and ordering of titles. Thus, while ten manuscripts contain AE.II and eight AE.III, only three have AE.XII, two AE. XIII, and one AE.XIV. AE.II comes before the *Ecloga* four times, six after; similarly AE.IX and XI appear both before and after the *Ecloga*. However, there are some constant groupings within the variety. Most

[40] On how to read this and other tables in this work, please see Note on Language and Tables. To aid the reader, a brief explanation specific to this table shall be given here. The numbers are those given in the *RHBR* and indicate the numerical order of texts within a given MS. So in *RHBR*.9 AE.XI is the tenth text to appear, NM the eleventh, the *Ecloga* the thirteenth, and so on.

strikingly, AE.III–VI forms a very stable assemblage that appears in seven MSS, one *sans* AE.IV. On three of those occasions, AE.III–VI is expanded with the insertion of AE.VII–VIII, which when with the *Ecloga* only appear here. In four of those seven manuscripts, AE.X immediately follows the group, compared to only once with AE. IX. Interestingly, in three of these AE.X follows AE.III–VI, and only once AE.III–VIII, strengthening the impression that AE.III–VI was the original form. The final component in this unit is the NS. This appears in six of the 11 MSS, four times immediately preceding AE. III–VI[VII–VII]-X, while in *RHBR*.55 its 'normal' position was displaced by the NM, and in *RHBR*.327 it is joined with the NN and NG. Therefore, there are three MSS (*RHBR*.25, 61, 197) that contain the unit NS-AE.III–VI-X, forming a coherent appendix to the *Ecloga*.

A second text-group is AE.I–II. This occurs in six MSS, once interpolated with N.119.7 and once reversed as AE.II–I. We can safely ignore this latter formation as it has little direct link with the *Ecloga* and is conjoined with the NS-NN-NG combination. Hence, of the remaining five MSS, AE.I–II immediately follows the *Ecloga* twice, while it appears thrice after NS-III–VI-X. On the two occasions where it comes before that grouping, *RHBR*.55 is a sixteenth-century codex that manifestly has an abnormal ordering and is interpolated by the late eighth-century/early ninth-century novels of Irene. Similarly, *RHBR*.9, the basis of Momferratos edition of the *Ecloga*, although a more stable and typical manuscript, does contain the oddity of following AE.XI with NM, and AE.III–VIII with IX, the only instance of such in the entire textual tradition.[41] However, the three times it does not immediately follow the *Ecloga* are also those MSS with the unit NS-AE.III–VI-X. Moreover, in two of those manuscripts, AE.I–II is found with C.8.10.12 and N.119.7, together forming a logical cluster concerning issues of property.[42]

[41] AE.IX does follow AE.III–VIII in two MSS of the *Ecloga Privata*, but is immediately followed by AE.X. This is the only occasion known to me where AE.IX completes the unit AE.III–VIII, let alone AE.III–VI. AE.XI and NM only appear in one other MS (*RHBR*.188) together, and then in a long and jumbled appendix *following* the *Prochiron*, ed. K. Zacharia von Lingenthal, *Ho Procheiros Nomos* (Heidelberg, 1837); and *Ecloga Privata Aucta*, ed. K. Zacharia von Lingenthal, *IGR* IV, 7–48 = Zepos, *IGR* VI, 12–47.

[42] C.8.10.12 concerns buildings, and N.119.7 the alienation of property in bad faith.

A third common set is NM-AE.II preceding the *Ecloga*, found in four manuscripts. This formation is further attested in manuscripts containing other handbooks and as an independent arrangement, and is frequently combined with AE.IX in the grouping AE.IX-NM-II. The significance of the NM will be discussed in the following chapter, but it is important to note here its link with the *Ecloga* and AE, nearly always as a form of introduction to the former. However, the clear majority of manuscripts with the unit [IX-]NM-AE.II are from canon law codices, while it is a rarity in the secular tradition. This would imply that the unit was a later creation by canonists of a selection of Isaurian texts considered most relevant to the Church, and in particular monasteries. This would explain the otherwise peculiar conjoining of texts concerning consanguinity, biblical commandments, and property boundaries, for the Church and monastic communities had a clear moral interest in the first two, and, as great landlords, an economic one in the last.

The manuscript evidence proffers a few more insights into the other titles. Firstly, it is patent that AE.XII–XIV, although having some connection with the *Ecloga*, are peripheral to the main AE. However, AE.XI, although demonstrating a weaker association than AE.I–VIII, X, does have a significant link with the *Ecloga* in four of its seven manuscripts, appearing twice before and twice after the *Ecloga*. As it consists of a selection of statements from the introductions to the *Digest* and *Institutes* concerning the nature and origins of justice and law, it is likely that AE.XI was designed as an ideological frontispiece for the *Ecloga*, a secular equivalent to the NM. Yet considering the variation, relatively small numbers, and that none of its manuscripts overlaps with the posited 'original' unit of NS-AE.III–VI-X, this would imply a later creation, which, although designed as a frontispiece, could be interpolated elsewhere in the greater appendix. Finally, AE.IX, although the most prolific title across all manuscripts, displays a surprisingly weak link with the *Ecloga*, appearing only five times and in a multitude of different positions. This relative separation, conjoined with AE.IX's occasional position as the closing title of the texts appending the *Ecloga*, plausibly suggests that it emanated after NS-AE.III–VI-X, although not necessarily long after.

Collectively, the manuscript evidence suggests the following pattern of publication. Firstly the group NS-AE.III–VI-X was issued, and at some later point interpolated with AE.VII–VIII. AE.I–II, probably conjoined with N.119.7 and C.8.10.12, were either published

Table 4. The manuscripts of the AE with other legal handbooks in the *RHBR*

RHBR	Contents of manuscript
79	.18 (EP)....20 (AE.IX)
124	.8[-11] (Pr.) .9 (AE.I–II)
127	.4 (NM)....7 (EP) .8 (K) .9–10 (Novels of Irene) .11 (AE.I, XIV, II)....13 (NS) .14 (PD) .15 (NG) .16 *Epitome* selection .17 (AE.III–IV, XII, V–X)
148	.43 (Pr.) .44[-5] (AE.II, I, N.119.7, AE.XII–XIII, X, III, V.1–2, IV, VI–VII, V.6–7, 4–5, 3, VIII, NN, AE.XI) .46 (NS)
188	.1 (Pr.) .2 (EPA) .3[-4] (AE.IX–X, IV, XII–XIII, VIII, N.119.7–8,... AE.I, NS, AE. V, III, XI) .5 (NN) .6 (NM)....9 (NG)
193	.20 (EP) .21[-4] (AE.I–II, NS, Novels of Irene, AE.III–X) .25 (E.17.42–43) .26 (NG)
221	.1 (Eis.) .2 (AE.II, IV–V)
263[43]	.1 (Eis.) .2 (NN) .3[-4] (II, I, NS, III–VIII, X) .5 (EP.4, 2, 3)
280	.1 (EPAs) .2 (Pr.)....5 (NN) .6 (NS) .7 (NM) .8 (AE selection)
298	.1 (Eis.) .2 (NN) .3[-4] (II, I, NS, III–VIII, X) .5 (EP.4, 2, 3)
319	.1 (Pr.)....5–6 (Novels of Irene) .7 (NS) .8 (NN) .9 (NG)....11 (Novel of Leo V) .12[-15] (AE.XIII, N.119.7, K,... AE.IX, XI,)....18[-19] (AE.I–II, NS.55–56, III–VIII, X)
321	.1 (EP) .2 (PD) .3 (E.17–18) .4 (K)....6 (AE.II, I, N.119.7, AE.XII–XIII, V, VIII)

simultaneously or soon after, but following rather than preceding NS-AE.III–VI-X. AE.IX and XI were probably issued in a second wave, perhaps contemporaneously with AE.VII–VIII; certainly all four titles betray a closeness to their respective original texts and a relative lack of reworking that set them apart from AE.I–VI, X. AE.XII–XIV constituted a third and final wave. These basic formations are also found in the manuscripts shared with the other legal handbooks—as given in Table 4—though with a greater propensity for variation and interpolation, especially from the novels of Irene and Leo V, as one would expect with the passage of time. It is notable that it is here that AE.I–II are repositioned at the start of the appendix, while AE.IX is found before X, giving the classical arrangement of texts found in the editions of Momferratos and Burgmann/Troianos.

Examining the source material from which the AE was drawn, several significant aspects emerge. Firstly, the overwhelming bulk of the AE originated, directly or indirectly, with Justinianic legislation; only AE.II.5 and III.20 have no certain correspondence in the *Corpus*.[44]

[43] Copy of *RHBR*.298.

[44] The first is a pithy summary of AE.II.1–4, to wit that no one should remove landmarks, and the rubric indicates that it was taken from some source now unknown. The second claims to be a canon.

Moreover, the vast majority of chapters adhere closely to their Justinianic forebears, if undergoing the process of truncation, translation, and simplification familiar from the creation of the *Ecloga*. However, there are two important differences. First, the degree of significant legal change is exceedingly small in the AE, far smaller than in the *Ecloga*, with the truly novel entirely absent. Secondly, the AE is studious in referencing its source material, normally accurately, where the *Ecloga* only referred to the Justinianic *Corpus* in its title.

Thanks in part to those references, it is possible to detect the intermediary texts from which the AE was composed. These were the very same works of the sixth-century *antecessores* whose numerous and diverse translations and commentaries had provided the raw material for the *Ecloga*. For instance, the rubrics to AE.V.3 and 4 cite the works of Athanasius Scholasticus and John Kobidas, respectively, and AE.XIII.6 and 7 refer to a Stephen, with Stephen and John explicitly called *antecessores*.[45] AE.VII declares itself 'from the *paratitla* of the Codex title 18, chapter 3'.[46] AE.IX is a paraphrase of I.3.6. pr.–6, 9, which, although not from the relatively well-known paraphrase of the *Institutes* by Theophilus, was, as Burgmann and Troianos plausibly posit, from a contemporary sixth-century work.[47]

By far the most frequent source, however, is the sixth-century canon law work, the *Collectio Tripartita*, which had translated and collected Justinianic law pertinent to the Church.[48] For instance, 18 of AE.III's 20 chapters are from *Coll. Trip.*I.5–7, 9, 11, consisting of virtually verbatim quotations, although on six occasions truncated, and the whole significantly rearranged to suit a more thematic order.[49] For example, AE.III.1 repeats *Coll. Trip.*I.5.2 while I.5.1 is relegated to AE.III.4, as I.5.2 contains a generic definition of heresy. AE.III also expands on the *Coll. Trip.*, with AE.III.16 adding from the original source, C.1. Meanwhile, the rubric of AE.III.20 claims to be drawn from the Council of Nicaea, presumably C.19, when in truth it originated in the second ecumenical council of 381, C.7, and more immediately from its repetition and expansion in Trullo C.95. Here,

[45] AE.V.3.15, AE.V.4.22.

[46] Burgmann/Troianos, *Appendix Eclogae*, 111.1.

[47] Burgmann/Troianos, *Appendix Eclogae*, 59.

[48] See Van der Wal and Stolte, *Collectio Tripartita: Justinian on Religious and Ecclesiastical Affairs*.

[49] AE.III.3, 5, 9, 10, 11, 17 are truncated, to various degrees, of *Coll. Trip.* I.5.4, 9. Paratitla.1, 5.17, 5.20, 5.5, and 11.10, respectively.

then, is a classic example of the interpenetration of canon and civil law in Byzantium: a text composed of Justinianic civil legislation, created by canonists as an appendage to canon law, reworked in a civil law context, extended with a canon, and then appended to an imperial code that declared itself the continuation of biblical law!

AE.III, then, might consist of extant raw materials, but it was no mere work of copy and paste. In contrast, AE.VI is a straight replica, down to its order and rubrics, of *Coll. Trip.*II.87–96, although the Latin technical terms are rendered into Greek equivalents. Indeed, in their zeal the rubricators have created some unfortunate distortions. For AE.VI.6 gives *tropos palin*, 'again in the same manner/fashion', as its translation of *Coll. Trip.*II.92's *Mod. Idem*. Evidently *Mod.* was thought to mean *modus*, the Latin equivalent to *tropos*. Yet in fact it refers to the jurist Modestinus! Similarly, it appears that the jurist Ulpian has become in AE.VI.1–3 and 5 *diakrisis*, 'a decision'.[50] Patently, the creators of AE.VI were far from perfect, and lacking in a degree of understanding of the texts they were dealing with. Yet this also reveals the underlying motivation to present their legal inheritance in Greek and in a way that made sense. Likewise, AE.VIII on the prohibition of Jews and heretics owning Christian slaves is a comprehensive duplication of *Coll. Trip.*I.10, even including its title, with the only alteration the addition of *Coll. Trip.*I.13.Paratitla.1 as AE. VIII.6 to produce a more complete title, as it stipulates freedom for any slave who wished to convert to Christianity if owned by a Jew, Samaritan, or heathen.

Without a fuller picture of the work of the *antecessores*, it is impossible to determine precisely how much of the AE is merely repeating extant texts; yet it is safe to describe the AE as far more derivative than the *Ecloga*. Indeed, in this respect it can be more accurately called a selection of Justinianic law than the *Ecloga* itself. Cumulatively, three important points can be inferred. Firstly, the pattern of construction of the AE's titles generally (if not perfectly) fits the threefold division deduced from the manuscript evidence. For there is a considerable difference between AE.I–V, X–XI, which are normally drawn from multiple sources and witness a degree of rearranging and editing, and AE.VI–IX, which are extremely derivative. AE.XII and XIV consist of only one chapter, while AE.XIII is

[50] See Burgmann/Troianos, 54, and Van der Waal and Stolte, *Collectio Tripartita*, xxxi.

drawn solely from C.6–8, probably taken primarily from the work of one jurist.[51] In this, the first grouping is by far the closest to the model of the *Ecloga*.

Secondly, although varying between titles, the construction of the AE must have been a relatively easy exercise. With minimal legal change, minor editing, and a marked propensity for copying, the AE represents a far lesser intellectual achievement than the *Ecloga*. While AE.I–V, X–XI required a degree of editorial exertion, similar in practice and purpose to the commission's task in creating the *Ecloga*, AE.VI–IX may well denote pre-existing works that were merely inserted whole. There is, therefore, little reason to doubt a speedy process of construction and appending to the *Ecloga*.

Thirdly, the authority underpinning all the AE's titles, apart from their textual adhesion to the *Ecloga*, was their original Justinianic promulgation. The frequent (and normally accurate) references to the *Corpus* in their rubrics, and the closeness in legal content and language, underline the continuing efficacy of Justinianic legislation in the eighth century. Repetition reaffirmed the position of Justinian as the ultimate legitimating referent in Byzantine law, with the AE serving to buttress the *Ecloga*'s claims, ideological and practical, to be collating, and therefore both following and easing access to, Justinianic law.

Regarding the subject matter of the individual titles, these results are reinforced. For instance, AE.III–VI is one long section entitled *Poinalios kata hairetikōn, manichaiōn kai tōn loipōn haireseōn kai kata epaoidōn kai pharmakōn*, 'Penalties against heretics, Manicheans and the remaining heresies, and against sorcerers and poisoners'.[52] In this it mirrors the titles of E.17 and the NS, which immediately preceded it.[53] Like them, this was a collection from across the *Corpus* of punishments arranged under a general heading. Moreover, it is evident that this title does not refer to AE.III alone, for it contains nothing about sorcerers or poisoners. Rather, those subjects are found in AE.V–VI, along with the expansion of AE.VII, grouped under the rubric of *peri phoneōn kai goētōn*, 'concerning murderers and sorcerers'.[54] Furthermore, this title comes after, rather

[51] Cf. Burgmann/Troianos, *Appendix Eclogae*, 63–6.

[52] Burgmann/Troianos, *Appendix Eclogae*, 101.1–2.

[53] Burgmann/Troianos, 91.

[54] Burgmann/Troianos, *Appendix Eclogae*, 107.2. Indeed, in Momferratos' edition, AE.V–VIII are treated as one long title.

than before, a rubric giving the reference to the original section of the *Corpus* that the material was drawn from, as with AE.IV, but in marked contrast to AE.I–II, VIII–XI, which can all be treated as independent titles. The peculiarity of this section is AE.IV, which covers neither heretics nor murderers nor magic, but valid and invalid marriage and immoral sex.[55] Similarly, AE.V.2–3, 5 concern adultery. Although ill-fitting with the title, these were fundamental interests of the *Ecloga* and especially E.17, and could be combined with the more relevant material of AE.III, V.1, 4, 6–7 and VI under a shared focus into particularly immoral crimes that broke God's law. Or perhaps, like its corresponding penalty collections of E.17 and NS, AE.III–VI contained a wide collection of punishments only loosely bound to its title. Thus, AE.III–VI might be considered a collection of penalties concerning civilians that were not covered, or that were under-explored, in E.17.

AE.VII on magicians makes a natural continuance of AE.III–VI. Likewise, AE.VIII explores the related but separate topic, and indeed it is separated by a new title, of Jews and heretics owning Christian slaves.[56] AE.IX, however, is dedicated to explaining the degrees of kinship, appended with a consanguinity table. There is here a connection with AE.X on the status of legitimate and illegitimate children, which might explain the pairing of the two in manuscripts not with the *Ecloga*. Meanwhile, the unit AE.I–II combined with N.119.7 and C.8.10.12 create a coherent group concerning property law. AE.XI's focus on the nature of law and justice sets it apart from the other titles, as does AE.XII on witnesses, AE.XIII on heirs and inheritance, and AE.XIV concerning imperial *coloni*.

All, apart from the rare AE.XIV, find correspondences (to lesser and greater degrees) in the *Ecloga*. Thus, E.17.52 ordered execution for Manichaeans and Montanists, a subject massively expanded by AE.III. Likewise, AE.V–VII expanded E.17.42–44's stipulations against poisoners and magicians. AE.IX has a clear correspondent in E.2.2's delimitation of legitimate marriage, as does AE.IV.1–3. AE. X and XIII develop E.5–6 on inheritances, while AE.XII adds to E.14 on witnesses. AE.I–II share E.9–13's focus on property and contract, while AE.XI echoes the opening of the *Ecloga*'s *Prooimion*.

[55] Burgmann/Troianos, *Appendix Eclogae*, 106–7.
[56] Burgmann/Troianos, 112.1–2.

What is notable here is the relative lack of repetition between the *Ecloga* and AE. For instance, AE.IV.1 developed E.2.2 with the inclusion of the prohibition on senators marrying low-status women, while AE.IV.2 clarified the explicit ban of E.2.2 on marrying your brother's wife. Further, AE.IV.3 ordains that even an imperial dispensation could not make valid a marriage with either a brother's wife or a sister's daughter. Finally, AE.4.4 ordained that any woman who had sex with their own slave should be decapitated, any children of the union barred from inheritance, and the slave himself burnt to death. This chimes with E.17.21–22 concerning a man who copulated with a slave, but fleshes out the subject by including the proportionally much harsher penalties for the woman's crimes, which were considered far worse.[57]

There is only one case of apparent contradiction between the *Ecloga* and the AE, namely that AE.V.2 repeats N.134.10.pr.'s stipulation that adulterers, and any intermediaries or abettors, should be punished capitally. On the one hand, this is an extension of E.17.27–28, which had ordained amputation of the nose for adultery, but had not mentioned any punishment for those who aided the crime. However, the penalty, prima facie, does clash. The matter might be resolved by recognizing that capital punishment did not necessarily equate in Roman law to death, and indeed in N.134.10.1, the adulteress is punished corporeally and confined to a monastery, and that amputation of the nose did symbolically subject the guilty to a form of internal exile. Indeed, the Greek *kephalikē hupoballontai timōria*, 'they shall be subject to capital punishment', could be conceived as reading 'head punishment', which nose amputation certainly was—but this is pure speculation.[58] Or it is always possible that the compilers simply copied and pasted without noticing the difference. AE.V.5, also on adultery, more easily dovetails with the *Ecloga*, clarifying that a man is not classified as an adulterer if he has intercourse with a married woman who has prostituted herself to many others, as he is not responsible for her debauchery.

Therefore, overall the AE demonstrates less shared interest with the *Ecloga* than a careful and systematic extension of that code's legislation. Thus there was evidently a perceived need to continue the work of the *Ecloga*, and augment it with more Justinianic material.

[57] Cf. C.9.11.1.

[58] Burgmann/Troianos, *Appendix Eclogae*, 108.14.

Given the shared principles of construction, avoidance of repetition and contradiction, and the stability of the formation NS-AE.III–VI-X, I–II, these titles were most probably created and issued by an official body, perhaps by the same (or similar) commission that produced the *Ecloga*, or indeed by the *Quaestor*. The impetus for this work was probably threefold: the natural intellectual side effect of the creation of the *Ecloga* and a salaried legal profession tasked with cataloguing Justinianic law as it existed in its fragmentary forms; the practical administration of justice bringing forth cases that were not easily settled by the *Ecloga* and hence generating a need for further legal guidance; and finally the prestige and propaganda value that accrued to Constantine V for continuing his father's legal programme.

The precise balance between these factors is difficult to judge, yet the actual content of the AE is suggestive. Firstly, the overriding concern of AE.II–VIII is punishment.[59] Indeed, these titles evince the same ideological agenda as E.17, with the provision of a simplified schedule of penalties for various classes of crimes, with the purpose of providing a uniform and just legal system. Furthermore, there is a manifest moral and theological programme, from AE.III's attack on heresies, and AE.V.4 ordering invokers of devils to be thrown to wild beasts, to AE.V.6–7's penalties for abortion and makers of potions that produced abortion, and AE.VI.10's condemnation of astrologers. Again, this deepened the moralistic aspects of the *Ecloga* as a force for correction and deterrence for the sake of heavenly reward, for both state and sinner.

This long-term dynastic strategy in positioning the Isaurians as orthodox and pious moral crusaders was given short-term impetus in the 740s, with the polemic generated by the civil war of *c.*742–3, the soul-searching caused by the plague of 746–7, and finally the divisions in the run-up to the Iconoclast Council of Hiereia in 754 all sapping Isaurian legitimacy, requiring forthright countering.[60] In particular, Constantine V's orthodoxy and piety came under sustained attack in this period. This, then, would prove fertile ground for the issuing of the first wave of the AE, and in particular AE.III

[59] Burgmann/Troianos, *Appendix Eclogae*, 90–1.

[60] For the general period, see Brubaker and Haldon, *History*, 156–89. For the psychological impact of the plague in particular, see D. Turner, 'The politics of despair: the plague of 746–47 and iconoclasm in the Byzantine Empire', *The Annual of the British School at Athens* 85 (1990), 419–34.

with its cataloguing and punishing of heresy helping to position Constantine as the lawful and orthodox prince, upholding tradition against heterodoxy, and implicitly the pre-eminent role of the emperor in the regulation of the Christian faith.

Indeed, it is precisely at this moment that we know that Constantine was actively and personally leading the charge for moral reformation. Theophanes records for 752/3:

> In this year the impious Constantine, puffed up in his spirit and making many plans against the church and the orthodox faith, held audiences every day and treacherously urged the people to follow his designs.[61]

This was part of a process of persuasion that Constantine V engaged in to prove his orthodoxy and prepare the ground for the next stage of the iconoclast drama. Constantine prepared a series of arguments, the *Peuseis*, which rejected the creation of icons of Christ on Christological grounds, and promoted instead the Eucharist as the true image of Christ.[62] In this, Constantine repeatedly associated himself with orthodox tradition, stressing the rule of established authority. Here one can easily see the utility of AE.III, whose contents ultimately originated with Justinian I, *the* lawgiver, drawn from a text, the *Collectio Tripartita*, that was an established part of canon law, and whose contents brought the full weight of the legal order against heretics. Not only did this underline Constantine V's attack on heresy, but it restipulated all the legal penalties against heretics, who after Hiereia would include iconophiles. Furthermore, the prominent penalties against pagans and Jews also served contemporary ends. The central plank of the iconoclast critique of icons was that they were idols, the things that pagans, not good Christians, senselessly worship.[63] Repeating the punishments against pagans thereby underscored the Isaurian push against 'pagan' practices, such as icon worship. Meanwhile, the constant response of the iconophiles was that the iconoclasts were behaving like Jews. Therefore, reiteration of the legal liabilities of the Jews served to put clear, ideological water between them and the Isaurian regime.

[61] Theophanes, 427; trans. Mango and Scott, 591.

[62] For the *Peuseis*, see Gero, *Constantine V*, 37–52; Brubaker and Haldon, *History*, 179–83. For the importance of the Eucharist, see Anastos, 'The ethical theory of images'.

[63] Haldon and Brubaker, *History*, 135–40.

Nor was iconoclasm the only aspect of the late 740s/early 750s that finds resonance in the AE. Even AE.X, with its repeated stress on the assured rights of inheritance of children (legitimate and illegitimate), fits the politics of the era, with Constantine V challenged for the throne by his father-in-law and seeking to establish the rights of his son Leo IV, as part of the general dynastic stress in Isaurian propaganda.[64] The third theme in that primary wave of legislation, property rights and (most strikingly) AE.II's penalties for the destruction of boundaries and the infringement of other people's land, also befit an era when the imperial centre was reimposing and reorganizing its tax structures across a polity hit by economic and political upheaval.[65] Therefore, although falling within a natural trajectory from the *Ecloga* and some of the chapters perhaps being generated by practical legal need, this first tranche evinces a state reasserting practical and ideological control, through the medium of Justinianic law.

The second wave, comprising AE.VII–VIII, IX, XI, maintains several of these features. Magic and heresy were further condemned, and the concern over legitimate marriage reinforced. However, these titles are more scholarly and technically focused. AE.XI is manifestly abstract and philosophical, its collation testament to an increased interest in the nature of law, and especially Justinianic legislation which needed cataloguing and reissuing. Further, AE.VIII is unlikely to have had great practical application given the probable rarity of non-Christians owning Christian slaves in eighth-century Byzantium. Rather, this second wave conveys a process that continued to collect Justinianic law, but one driven more by internal momentum and professional interest than immediate political or broader ideological concerns.

The final wave of AE.XII–XIV has no obvious political or symbolic value, but comprises highly technical subjects mostly concerning property law, from AE.XIII.2–3 on legacies to AE.XIV on imperial *coloni*. These issues have only faint resonances with either the previous sections of the AE or the *Ecloga*. Instead, they convey a more sophisticated legal and economic world, with issues of property more complex and prominent; in short, the world of the ninth century, after the revival of both the legal profession, Justinianic law, and the broader economy.[66] The evolution of the AE would, therefore,

[64] See Conclusion, 258–61. [65] See Conclusion, 261–5.

[66] For the revived fortunes of the Byzantine empire, see W. Treadgold, *The Byzantine Revival, 780–842* (Stanford, 1988).

represent the transition of law from political tool to academic and professional interest, laying the foundation for the grander reworking of Justinianic law under the Macedonians.[67]

To conclude, several significant points can be drawn from the creation of the AE. Firstly, the AE buttressed the idea of the supreme importance of the Justinianic *Corpus* as the repository of Roman law. It was that law which was perceived as the font of answers for legal questions; the Isaurians were not asked to issue new law, but to restate and improve access to Justinianic decisions. This implied a perceived continuity with the Justinianic past, while at the same time an awareness of a severe disconnect which necessitated this new abridgment, works that did not abrogate the previous law but rendered it more accessible. Furthermore, the selection chosen is indicative of the peculiar concerns of the age. Evidently, Christian morality was an elemental and essential focus. The non-Orthodox had to be punished and contact with them regulated, while 'pagan' practices like magic and divination had to be purged. The overwhelming message, then, of the AE coincides virtually identically with the *Ecloga*—namely the use of the law by emperors to support and regulate, and to be seen to support and regulate, the lives, and particularly the morals, of their subjects.

THE *NOMOS STRATIOTIKOS*

As noted frequently above, the text usually referred to as the *Nomos Stratiotikos* (NS) is repeatedly found as part of the AE, with the manuscripts of the *Ecloga* in particular suggesting an original codicological position immediately after the *Ecloga* and before AE.III–VI.[68] Despite this, the NS is usually treated alongside the NN and NG. Together, they are normally posited *c*.600–800, with any accreditation to the Isaurians denied.[69] Recently, Schminck has attempted to redate all three to the Macedonian period, consigning the NS to either a production of Leo VI (r.886–912) or a contemporary.[70] Schminck,

[67] For which see Chapter 6, 244–8.
[68] See Table 3, 000, and Appendix, Tables 9–11.
[69] See L. Burgmann and E. McGeer, 'Nomos Stratiotikos', in *ODB*, vol. 3, 1492.
[70] Schminck, '*Nomos Rhodiōn Nautikos*', 176.

however, does not challenge the close proximity in the timing of production of all the *nomoi.*

Burgmann has cogently countered Schminck by arguing for a lack of stylistic or substantive overlap between the three.[71] Furthermore, the manuscript evidence is not conclusive. Discounting the *c.*70 of the *Ecloga ad Prochiron mutata* and the *Hexabiblos,* later collections which incorporated the *nomoi,* there are 74 MSS that contain one of the three codes, testament to their great influence and popularity.[72] Of these, only 18 contain all three as a group, in multiple arrangements, and a further 18 contain two of the three, again in various permutations.[73] Thus, under half of the manuscripts contain more than one code, and there is no definite ordering to suggest an official collection. Undeniably, many thought, from the date of these manuscripts, emanating from the eleventh century onwards, that there was some link, but it is not enough in itself to establish proximity in composition. Likewise, all three were incorporated into the twelfth-century *EPrM,* although not as a contiguous block.[74]

Having cast doubt on any original connection, Burgmann also posits that not only can the NS not be a product of Leo VI, but also that it cannot date later than the middle of the seventh century.[75] The crux of his argument stems from a highly convincing, per se, critique of the critical edition prepared by Ashburner.[76] Ashburner only used six, from *c.*50, MSS in his edition, although they include the oldest and most important. Strangely, however, he ordered his edition according to *RHBR.*148 (Oxford, *Bodleian Library* Laud 39), which he thought to be the oldest extant manuscript.[77] This manuscript's arrangement, however, is on almost every chapter in contrast to his other MSS, as can be seen in Table 5. Meanwhile, *RHBR.*274 (Rome, *Biblioteca Vallicelliana* F 47) is as venerable, contains every chapter in an order far more closely supported by the other manuscripts, more closely follows the original ordering of its sources, and generally

[71] Burgmann, 'Die Nomoi'.

[72] Burgmann, 'Die Nomoi', 56. Constantine Harmenopoulos, *Hexabiblos,* ed. G. Heimbach, *Constantini Harmenopuli: Manuale legum sive Hexabiblos* (Leipzig, 1851).

[73] Burgmann, 'Die Nomoi', 57–9, for full details of the manuscripts.

[74] The NG was incorporated in *EPrM.*25–6, the NS as 34, the NN as 40.

[75] Burgmann, 'Die Nomoi', 60.

[76] Ashburner, 'The Byzantine mutiny act'.

[77] Ashburner, 'The Byzantine mutiny act', 80.

Table 5. The chapters of the NS in the manuscripts detailed by Ashburner

V=*RHBR*.274	L=148	F=61	B=249	M=302	m=289
1	41	I:1	1	1	1
2	42+43	I:2	2	2	2
3	44	I:3	3	3	3
4	45	I:4	4	4	4
5	46	Not	5	5	5
6	47	I:5	6	6	6
7	48	I:6	7	7	7
8	49	I:7	8	8	8
9	13	I:8	9	9	9
10	50	I:9	10	10	10
11	8	I:10	11	11	11
12	9	I:11	12	12	12
13	10	I:12	13	13	13
14	12	I:13	14	14	14
15	11	I:14	15	15	15
16	35	II:27	16	16	16
17	14	II:8	17	17	17
18	36	II:28	18	18	18
19	29	II:29	19	19	19
20	17	II:30	20	20	20
21	37	II:31	21	21	21
22	51	II:32	22	22	22
23	38	II:33	23	23	23
24	6+39	Not+II:34	32+Not	32+Not	32+Not
25	40+28	II:35+II:21	24	24	25
26	1	II:1	25	25	24
27	52	II:37	Not	Not	Not
28	54+53	II:38	27+28	27+28	27+28
29	16	II:10	28	28	28
30	55	III:1	Not	Not	Not
31	56	III:2	29	29	29
32	2	II:2	41	41	41
33	3	II:3	Not	Not	Not
34	4	II:5	30	30	30
35	5	II:4	31	31	31
36	6+7	II:6–7	32+Not	32+Not	32+Not
37	15	II:9	33	33	33
38	18	II:11	Not	Not	Not
39	19	II:12	Not	Not	Not
40	20	II:13	34+35	34+35	34+35
41	21	II:14	Not	Not	Not
42	22	II:15	36	36	36
43	23	II:16	37	37	37
44	24	II:17	Not	Not	Not
45	25	II:18	26	26	26
46	26	II:19	26	26	26
47	27	II:20	Not	Not	Not
48	30	II:22	38	38	38
49	31	II:23	39	39	39
50	32	II:24	Not	Not	Not
51	33	II:25	40	40	40
52	34	II:26	41	41	41
53	1+2	II:36	Not+41	Not+41	Not+41

follows a more intelligible pattern.[78] It is therefore reasonable to conclude that *RHBR*.274 represents the oldest extant version of the NS.[79]

This manuscript is divided into four sections.[80] After the title, *peri stratiōtikōn epitimiōn ek tou rophou kai tōn taktikōn*, 'concerning penalties for soldiers from Rufus and the Tacticians', come 15 numbered chapters,[81] taken virtually verbatim from the *Strategikon*,[82] a late sixth-century work attributed to the emperor Maurice.[83] Then follows a heading *poinalios stratiōtikos*, 'martial penalties',[84] with 14 unnumbered articles, which are normally prefixed with references to the passage of the *Digest* or *Code* from which they are derived.[85] Next there is the title *peri stratiōtikēs katastaseōs*, 'concerning the status of soldiers',[86] with two unnumbered chapters, again tagged with the relevant reference.[87] Then comes the Latin word *Feliciter*, 'luckily/ happily'. Finally, there is the heading *eti peri stratiōtikōn katastaseōn ek tou 49 biblou tōn digestōn titlou 16*, 'further concerning the status of soldiers from the 49th book of the *Digest*, title 16',[88] which contains 22 unnumbered and unreferenced chapters.[89]

Burgmann convincingly argues that this structure is evidence of multiple recensions.[90] Certainly section one, excerpting the penal

[78] See Tables 5 and 6, and Appendix, Table 11.

[79] According to Ashburner, 'The Byzantine mutiny act', 82, *RHBR*.188 closely follows the arrangement in *RHBR*.274. In truth, all the conclusions of this section are inherently tied to the inadequate edition of Ashburner, and a new edition could potentially change many of the conclusions.

[80] Ashburner, 'The Byzantine mutiny act', 81–2 for a description. Burgmann, 'Die Nomoi', 59–60 also gives a slightly different description. On the first section of 15 chapters we are in agreement. However, Burgmann combines my sections 2 and 3 into one, ignoring a heading. Burgmann also counts 18 excerpts, whereas in Ashburner there are 16. It appears Burgmann placed one chapter in the wrong section, and double-counted what in this MS was actually one chapter. Burgmann's misplaced chapter should appear in the final fourth section, so instead of Burgmann's 21 chapters there are in fact 22.

[81] Ashburner, 'The Byzantine mutiny act', 81.

[82] *Strategikon*, ed. G. Dennis and E. Gamillscheg, *Das Strategikon des Maurikios* (Vienna, 1981).

[83] In Ashburner's edition: 41, 42+43, 44, 45, 46, 47, 48, 49, 13, 50, 8, 9, 10, 12, 11.

[84] Ashburner, 'The Byzantine mutiny act', 81.

[85] Ashburner: 35, 14, 36, 29, 17, 37, 51, 38, 6+39, 40+28, 1, 52, 54+53, 16.

[86] Ashburner, 'The Byzantine mutiny act', 82.

[87] Ashburner: 55, 56.

[88] Ashburner, 'The Byzantine mutiny act', 82.

[89] Ashburner: 2, 3, 4, 5, 6+7, 15, 18, 19, 20, 21, 22, 23, 24, 25, 26, 27, 30, 31, 32, 33, 34, 1+2.

[90] Burgmann, 'Die Nomoi', 60.

articles of the *Strategikon*, is plausibly a work emanating from soon after the publication of the *Strategikon*, and it is clear that it is this which is referred to as 'from Rufus and the Tacticians', although the identity of Rufus is unknown.[91] Essentially this section reworks the *Strategikon* to remove any repetitions and set forth the articles in a more logical way, thus: NS:1–4 concerning insubordination, 5–6 breaking leave, 7–10 crimes outside battle, 11–15 disorder in battle. Interestingly, the only chapter not repeated is *Strat.*1.6.11, which concerned the allowance for soldiers to purchase their own weapons, suggesting that this section was created after that allowance had been removed by Heraclius in 616.[92]

However, Burgmann also argues that essentially the rest, all taken from the *Corpus*, represents either a single unit, or that the third is so close to the second that it must also have been produced soon after, and that the use of the Latin *Feliciter* in a Greek text means that this recension could, at the latest, date to the mid-seventh century.[93] Yet Latin terms were long maintained within the Byzantine Empire, especially when touching law or the army. For instance, the word *poinalios* is a direct Greek transliteration of *poenalis*, interestingly first securely attested in Greek in the *Ecloga*.[94] Most importantly, however, it appears at a formal and stylistic break in the text which, *pace* Burgmann, would strongly suggest a third recension. The final section of the text lacks any prefixed references, bar the title itself. Unlike the second section, but similar to the first, the final 22 chapters are almost all from one source and generally follow the original order, as seen in Table 6 at the end of this chapter.[95]

Moreover, the use of *eti*, 'further', in the title implies the deliberate appending of this section to the end of an extant work. This notion is reinforced by the use of the word *katastasis*, 'status', which suits the minor third section with its two chapters banning the employment of

[91] Several theories have been pronounced. C. Brand, *Roman Military Law* (Austin, 1968), 132–6 discusses the problem, and the NS in general, but his own speculation that Rufus was a pre-Justinianic tactician from whom both the *Strategikon* and the NS ultimately derive has no basis in the evidence.

[92] See W. Treadgold, *Byzantium and its Army* (Stanford, 1995), 20.

[93] Burgmann, 'Die Nomoi', 60.

[94] *LBG*, vol.6, 1328; Burgmann/Troianos, *Appendix Eclogae*, 92.

[95] NS.38–39 are from D.49.16.3, NS.40–43 from D.49.16.4, and NS.44–46 from D.49.16.6, and all follow the order of the *Digest*. Only three of the 22 chapters are not from D.49.16. See Table 6.

Table 6. The NS as described in *RHBR*.274 (Rome, *Biblioteca Vallicelliana* F 47)

NS	Subject	Source	Ashburner
	Peri stratiōtikōn epitimiōn ek tou rophou kai tōn taktikōn		
1	Mutiny	Strat.I.6.5	41
2	Insubordination to officers	Strat.I.6.1–2 (7.12)	42+43
3	Insubordination due to ignorance	Strat.I.6.8	44
4	Unjust treatment of soldiers	Strat.I.6.3	45
5	Breaking leave	Strat.I.6.4	46
6	More leave	Strat.I.7.14	47
7	Planning desertion to the enemy	Strat.I.6.7	48
8	Injury and compensation between soldiers and civilians	Strat.I.6.10+7.13	49
9	Desertion of a fort or town	Strat.I.6.6+7.15	13
10	Failure to report finding stray animals	Strat.I.6.9	50
11	Desertion/breaking ranks in battle	Strat.I.8.16	8
12	Regiment routing	Strat.I.8.17	9
13	Loss of a standard	Strat.I.8.18	10
14	Rout and not returning to the fort	Strat.I.8.19	12
15	Throwing away arms in battle	Strat.I.8.20	11
	Poinalios stratiōtikos		
16	Extortion of landowners	N.130.4	35
17	Leaders of mutiny/sedition	D.48.19.38.2	14
18	Mutiny	D.49.16.3.19–21	36
19	Soldier striking an officer	D.49.16.13.4	29
20	Soldier abandoning an officer	D.49.16.6.8	17
21	Palace guards abandoning their post	D.49.16.10	37
22	Desertion or dealing with enemy embassies	C.4.41.2	51
23	Exciting the enemy/betraying Romans	D.48.4.3	38
24	Attempted desertion by any inhabitants	D.49.16.3.11 +48.8.3.6	6+39
25	Scouts revealing secrets/any disturbance of the peace	D.49.16.6.4 +49.16.16.1	40+28
26	Insubordination in wartime	D.49.16.3.15	1
27	Wounding a soldier	D.49.16.6–7	52
28	Soldiers stealing/those who commit a public crime cannot enlist		54+53
29	Dismissal from the service makes ineligible for honours of office	C.12.36.3	16
	Peri stratiōtikēs katastaseōs		
30	Soldiers not to be employed as administrators or labourers	C.4.65.35	55
31	Soldiers not to be farmers, traders or any civic duty	C.12.35.15–16	56
	eti peri stratiōtikōn katastaseōn ek tou 49 biblou tōn digestōn titlou 16		
32	Soldiers who desert, absent themselves, flee in camp or battle, lose/sell their arms	D.49.16.3.4, 6.3, 3.13	2
33	Feign illness	D.49.16.6.5	3

(*continued*)

Table 6. Continued

NS	Subject	Source	Ashburner
34	Desert palisade	D.49.16.3.17–18	4
35	Treason	C.9.8.6.2	5
36	Intend to desert/neglect their post	D.49.16.3.11, 3.5	6+7
37	Deserters who return	D.49.16.3.10 + D.48.19.38.1	15
38	Stealing arms	D.49.16.3.14	18
39	Mutiny	D.49.16.3.19–21	19
40	Ineligible to enlist due to deportation	D.49.16.4.2–4	20
41	Ineligible to enlist due to adultery/public crime	D.49.16.4.7	21
42	Avoiding call-up	D.49.16.4.9	22
43	Fathers preventing sons from the call-up	D.49.16.4.11	23
44	Raising hand against officer	D.49.16.6.1	24
45	Wounding a fellow soldier	D.49.16.6.6	25
46	Attempted suicide	D.49.16.6.7	26
47	Recap: desertion in battle, scouts betraying secrets, wounding fellow soldiers	D.49.16.6.3–4, 6	27
48	Flight from prison	D.49.16.13.5	30
49	Offences due to drink	D.49.16.6.7	31
50	Breaking ranks	D.49.16.3.16	32
51	Prison guards who let charges escape	D.48.3.14.2	33
52	Soldiers who create an adultery agreement	D.48.5.11	34
53	Recap: insubordination in war, desertion, flight, selling/losing arms	D.49.16.3.15, 3.4, 6.3, 3.13	1+2

soldiers in non-martial roles, thus defining their precise social position relative to civilians.[96] However, the range of topics covered in the final section, touching on what were almost entirely essentially internal military problems, does not neatly fit such a title. Rather, the last section was a later appendage organized primarily around verbatim excerpts from the *Digest*, in this instance D.49.16, 'On Military matters', joined with a smattering of other regulations, in a manner highly reminiscent of the AE, which was then tagged on to an existing work. Incidentally, *katastasis* augurs against any association with Leo VI, as by the tenth century the word was firmly associated with ceremony, which would be totally incongruous here.[97]

All this would imply that the second and third sections, viz. NS.16–31, started by a transliterated Latin word and ended by a

[96] For *Katastasis* as 'personal status', see I. Avotins, *On the Greek of the Code of Justinian* (Hildesheim, 1989), 80; and I. Avotins, *On the Greek of the Novels of Justinian* (Hildesheim, 1992), 121.

[97] *LBG*, vol. 4, 796.

Latin word, represent a single recension, a kind of anthology of military law selected and abridged from the *Corpus*, while NS.32–53 was added as a third recension. Moreover, there is no reason to believe that the recensions were produced in close temporal proximity. Indeed, it is clear that those chapters in the final section are not preserved as widely as the others. There are some nine chapters that are only in *RHBR*.148 and 274, of which seven are from the closing section.[98] The title of the final section is also only rarely preserved, while *poinalios* became a standard feature.[99] If, as Burgmann argues, the two sections were composed contemporaneously, there is no reason why this should be, but a later recension would solve the problem.

Dating these recensions is manifestly difficult and imprecise. Certainly, they must date after their sources, the *Strategikon* and the *Corpus*, while later recensions including chapters from the *Ecloga* and the *Basilika*, and a reworking associated with Leo VI's *Taktika*, give a *terminus ante quem* of the tenth century, as does the word *katastasis*.[100] This would at the least imply that the legal change was well established by the late eighth century.

Furthermore, it can be reasonably assumed that a work concerning military discipline and law pertaining to soldiers, and their relationship with civilians, would have emanated from a period of military and/or legal reform. There is no trace in the text of any antiquarian interest that could imply authorship by an 'armchair' general. Rather, the text is a composite of the received wisdom and legal rulings governing topics from desertion to extortion of landowners. Thus, this should be considered an official amalgamation designed to uphold military discipline. That would suggest a date either in the mid-to-late seventh century during the murky changes associated with the development of the Theme system, or the eighth century when the Isaurian soldier-emperors attempted to reassert military

[98] NS.33, 36, 39, 41, 44, 47, 50. NS.40 and 45–6 also see marked reordering. The only others are 27 and 30.

[99] F=*RHBR*.61 does have the title *katastasis* before NS.30–31, although then repositioned at the end of the text, as it is in L=*RHBR*.148. This would suggest that this version represents a halfway house between V=274 and L=148.

[100] For later versions of the NS, see E. Korzenszky, *Leges poenales militares e codice Laurentiano* LXXV, 6 (Budapest, 1931); and V. Kuchma, '*Nomos Stratiōtikos*', *Vizantiiskii Vremennik* 32 (1971), 276–84. See also Leo VI, *Taktika*, ed. G. Dennis, *The Taktika of Leo VI* (Washington DC, 2010), esp. 146–53.

discipline, and their own control over the army, conjoined with several military reforms.[101]

The *Ecloga* and the *Krisis* both demonstrate the Isaurian interest in military law, and indeed are associated with the NS in the *EPrM*, with E.18 and Krisis forming *EPrM*.33 and the NS *EPrM*.34. Furthermore, Constantine V engaged in a series of military reforms, such as the creation of a mobile field army under direct imperial control, the *tagmata*, and the subdivision of the potentially over-powerful *Opsikion* Theme, especially after the civil war of 742–3 demonstrated their threat to the Isaurian regime.[102] If this was also the time of the composition and promulgation of much of the AE, which arranged verbatim citations of Justinianic law to buttress and complete the *Ecloga*, the third recension and republishing of the NS would reflect this renaissance of law, especially Justinianic law, under the Isaurians. The connection with the AE is further highlighted by the actual title given in the early manuscripts, *peri stratiōtikōn epitimiōn*.[103] It is categorically not a *nomos*, a separate law code. It reads as both another title of the *Ecloga* and the AE, a companion *poinalios* to E.17 and AE.III–VI, which two, as noted, it frequently intervenes between in the manuscript tradition. This would, therefore, suggest a dating of the third recension to the compilation of this part of the AE, namely soon after the *Ecloga* during the reign of Constantine V.

Two further pieces of evidence support this dating. Firstly, even if the NS frequently abbreviated previous law, it only substantively changed it on two occasions. NS.32, repeated at NS.53, is a compilation of D.49.16.3.4/6.3/3.13 listing various offences—desertion, flight, a soldier selling his arms—which were punishable by death.[104] Likewise, NS.21 followed D.49.16.10 where the palace guards who abandon their watch were executed.[105] However, both add the qualification that if humanity, *philanthropia*, prevails, the miscreants can be flogged and dismissed.[106] As we have seen, *philanthropia* was a key concept in the *Ecloga*. Yet NS.21 falls in the middle of the section that, following Burgmann, it has been suggested earlier emanates from the seventh century. Moreover, this is an isolated

[101] For changes in the seventh century, see Haldon, *Seventh Century*, 208–53. For changes in the eighth century, see Brubaker and Haldon, *History*, 723–71.

[102] See J. Haldon, *Byzantine Praetorians* (Bonn, 1984), 205–9.

[103] Ashburner, 'The Byzantine mutiny act', 85.

[104] Ashburner: 2. [105] Ashburner: 37.

[106] Ashburner, 'The Byzantine mutiny act', 89, 2:6, and 103, 37:3, respectively.

example in a unit that freely employs capital punishment and there is no indication why this particular offence should be worthy of amelioration.

Its use in NS.32 and 53,[107] however, is of a completely different order. Here, *philanthropia* bookends and underpins the entire section. Furthermore, whereas NS.21 is a specific case, NS.32 reports a litany of offences, which could now be moderated through *philanthropia*. This comprehensiveness is reinforced in NS.53 where the chapter is combined with the regulation from D.49.16.3.15 stating that anyone who in wartime does something which is forbidden, or fails to fulfil orders, is to be capitally punished. This is almost the universal rule for all civilians and soldiers, the latter not being specified, in wartime.[108] When combined with the particular offences of soldiers, which would not be covered by the broad remit of the above regulation, NS.53 represents virtually the totality of military law, i.e. the law that pertained always to soldiers, and the law relevant to all during war. Considering that eighth-century Byzantium was almost constantly at war, this law was of huge import, and deliberately founded upon the concept of *philanthropia*. Thus this third recension was ideologically extremely close to the *Ecloga*, a fact reflected in the fact that this deliberate repetition brought the number of chapters to 53, the same as E.17. The NS was, therefore, deliberately designed to be the military law companion to the penal code of the *Ecloga*, and surely dates, along with the primary wave of the AE, to the immediate aftermath of the *Ecloga*'s promulgation.

The NS also shares common concerns with the *Ecloga*. E.17.53 had punished all deserters with death. This stipulation is, not unexpectedly, greatly expanded in the NS, with NS.7, 9, 11–12, 14, 21–22, 32, 34, 36–7, 47, and 53 all dealing with varying aspects and situations concerning desertion.[109] E.17.3 condemned those who plotted against the emperor, repeated in NS.35.[110] The *Ecloga* pronounced the need for soldiers not to be engaged in any other occupation or involved in private enterprise.[111] NS.30–1 repeated that prohibition, while

[107] Ashburner: 1+2.

[108] Ashburner: 1, following D.49.16.3.15, is deliberately non-specific, while *RHBR*.274's version of Ashburner: 2 removes mention of a soldier, *stratiōtēs*; see Ashburner, 'The Byzantine mutiny act', 89.

[109] Ashburner: 48, 13, 8–9, 12, 37, 51, 2, 4, 6+7, 15, 27, 1+2.

[110] Ashburner: 5.

[111] E.12.6.

NS.16 condemned soldiers who extorted money from the land to pay back twofold.[112] There is a recurring concern in this legislation to maintain soldiers as a separate social order, under imperial and not private control, unencumbered and uncompromised by other economic activities. Another shared anxiety is adultery: NS.41 highlights adultery as a public crime that made one ineligible for enlistment.[113] Further, NS.52 declared that any soldier who condoned a man committing adultery with his wife was to be dismissed.[114] Both make clear the determination to keep the army clean from this sin. Interestingly, both are found in the final section of the NS, which, as I have argued, was composed under the Isaurians.

In a similar fashion to the AE, the chapters of the NS, although sharing considerable common ground with the *Ecloga*, in substance rarely repeated its ordinances, but rather expanded and clarified. For instance, E.17.10 condemned anyone who stole arms while in camp or on the march to be flogged, and, if they stole a horse, to have their hand amputated. Prima facie, this would be in conflict with NS.28, which stipulated that soldiers who stole anything should pay back twofold, and be dismissed, and NS.38, which ordered a soldier who stole arms of another to be demoted.[115] Yet, on further inspection, it is evident that although both concern stealing, especially of war materials, E.17.10 is clearly a sanction aimed at civilians, followed by other kinds of stealing in E.17.11. NS.28 is also part of the broader unit of NS.27–29, which ended the second recension of the NS, that listed the various grounds for dismissal and the consequences from the loss of privileges. The broader point is not just the discipline and lawfulness of the troops, but the maintenance of a morally and legally pure soldiery.

As a whole, the NS focuses on exactly the issues which one would expect of a code of military law: desertion, insubordination, enlistment, indiscipline, relations with non-soldiers, and crimes committed by soldiers. The recurrent concern is to maintain military discipline and morale, the distinction with civilians, and good relations between the two groups. It also makes clear that the privileges of being a soldier were considered significant, as their withdrawal was used as a threat. More surprising is the number of chapters that evidently

[112] Ashburner: 55–6, 35. [113] Ashburner: 21.
[114] Ashburner: 34. [115] Ashburner: 54, 18.

refer to both civilians and soldiers. NS.22 stipulated that anyone who goes over to the barbarians, or sells any war materials to them under the pretence of an embassy, would be executed.[116] Similarly, NS.23 punished capitally anyone who betrayed the Romans to the enemy or excited enemies against the empire.[117] NS.24 combined two separate laws in the *Digest* into execution for anyone living in Roman territory who planned to desert to the barbarians, and criminal immunity for any subject who killed them.[118] Together, these three were an assertion of state control over its subjects in an effort to stop any aid being given to the enemy.

A more nuanced picture emerges if we consider each recension in turn. The absolute attention of the first recension is the discipline of the army, in peace and war. It is a concise condensation of best practice, suited to a reassertion of discipline, befitting the early seventh century and the reforms of the emperor Heraclius in the face of the Persian advance. The second recension is far more variegated, with discipline and insubordination still important, but the cynosure being the broader mobilization and control of Byzantine society in a situation of constant warfare, while ensuring that the soldiers did not engage in any economic activity. Again, this would fit the mid-to-late seventh century, with its incessant warfare and shifting local loyalties.[119] Moreover, with the payment of soldiers most probably shifting more towards being in kind, combined with more decentralized administration and recruitment, the soldiery was more integrated with rural society than ever before, necessitating a reaffirmation of the legal barriers prohibiting soldiers from engaging in occupations that might both distract them from military operations and provide an alternate income, thus lessening imperial control.

The third recension, while keeping the regulations and doubtless the interests of the previous two, introduces new concerns, including enlistment. Fathers who removed their sons from the army during wartime, for whatever reason, were exiled and lost a portion of their property, while any father who deliberately disabled his son(s) to avoid their enlistment would also be exiled.[120] More sweepingly and tellingly, NS.42 declared:

[116] Ashburner: 51. [117] Ashburner: 38. [118] Ashburner: 6+39.
[119] See inter alia, Treadgold, *Byzantium and its Army*, 22–4.
[120] NS.43 = Ashburner 23.

> Whoever flees from the army is subject to military punishment. For it is a grave sin to avoid the duties of military service. For those who are summoned to serve and flee are enslaved as betrayers of their liberty.[121]

Now although this is a fairly close translation of D.49.16.4.9–10, it alters Justinianic law by leaving out several key phrases. In the original, the punishment of enslavement was described as the old law, now no longer used as volunteers had largely replaced the levy. Presumably the penalty was reinstituted due to the increased importance of the levy from the seventh century onwards, and was made to seem an established tradition through clever editing.[122] Evidently the Isaurians were concerned with maintaining the manpower of their armies. Yet this was definitely not the only, or even the prime, interest of the compilers, for two chapters restated multiple barriers to enlistment, including that particular Isaurian bugbear, adultery.[123] The whole of society might be liable for the war effort, but recruits were to be morally upright, in order to avoid God's displeasure. Similarly, any soldier who attempted the sin of suicide should be dishonourably discharged if he had a valid excuse, but if he had none, he would be executed.[124] This combination of piety, law, and martial strength was an Isaurian leitmotif.

Various breaches of discipline—harming your fellows due to drink,[125] falling out of line,[126] leaving your post,[127] laying hands on an officer,[128] wounding a fellow soldier,[129] heedlessness, or complicity in the escape of prisoners[130]—were punished. Desertion or flight, planned or enacted, were punished with death.[131] Another appreciable concern is imperial control over the army. For NS.35 restipulates that traitors to the emperor would be executed, their property confiscated and their memory damned, while NS.39 condemns anyone who rouses the soldiery to disorder. All of this fits exactly the period of the late 740s when, after the civil war with Artabasdus, Constantine V sought to

[121] NS.42 = Ashburner 22.

[122] Cf. BS.38.1.6.11.

[123] NS.41 = Ashburner 21; see also NS.40 = Ashburner 20 that punished people who had been sentenced to various degrees of exile, who then tried to enlist in the army.

[124] NS.46 = Ashburner 26.

[125] NS.49 = Ashburner 31.

[126] NS.50 = Ashburner 32.

[127] NS.34 = Ashburner 4.

[128] NS.44 = Ashburner 24.

[129] NS.45 = Ashburner 25.

[130] NS.51 = Ashburner 33.

[131] NS.33 = Ashburner 3; NS.36 = Ashburner 6+7; NS.37 = Ashburner 15; NS.47 = Ashburner 27; NS.48 = Ashburner 30.

undermine the overweening power of some of the Themes, and to prepare an army loyal to him and his family, one which would contain the Arabs and repeatedly beat the Bulgars.[132] By compiling a new selection of military punishments, appending it to an established text, and issuing it as part of the grander legal programme, Constantine was seeking to re-establish discipline and moral correctness in the present through application of an authoritative past, aimed squarely at the essential power base of the regime, the army.

To conclude, the NS is in fact no *nomos*, but a Title produced in the same style, at the same time, and for the same aims as the first wave of the AE. Its purpose was to expand and clarify issues in the *Ecloga* through relevant, predominantly Justinianic, law, which also continued the intent of the *Ecloga* in abridging in a relevant, contemporaneous code the great bulk of Roman law, as both a tool in itself and channelling the authority of that law and its great compiler Justinian. The NS is best preserved in its original form in *RHBR*.274, which offers manifest evidence of three recensions. The first consisted of a refashioning of the penal articles of the *Strategikon*, probably dating to the early seventh century. The second, adding NS.16–31, was a mixture of different sections of the *Corpus* covering diverse matters, but generally reflected a more war-focused society, most probably emanating from the mid/late seventh century. Finally, the third recension dates from the aftermath of the *Ecloga* as part of the process that created the AE. This final recension reinforced the importance of Justinianic law by being anchored on an extended citation from D.49.16, and the supreme importance of *philanthropia* as a foundation of Isaurian ideology, especially in relation to their legal activities. Thus, the NS sought to affirm imperial control of the army, military discipline, and piety, in the creation of a loyal and godly army to protect the Chosen People of Byzantium.

CONCLUSIONS

The above texts demonstrate an impressive outpouring of work after the *Ecloga*. The nature of that work, however, was noticeably

[132] Brubaker and Haldon, *History*, 156–67, 739–43.

conservative. These were works of collection, and then editing, ranging from limited rewriting and major reordering, to no substantive alteration to the original whatsoever. One could almost characterize this as an encyclopaedic endeavour, similar to the movements in the contemporary Caliphate and Carolingian kingdom.[133] Indeed, one major spur for the creation of these works was probably the broader improvement in the socio-economic conditions of the Byzantine Empire from the mid-eighth century, which underpinned a better-known intellectual revival, evidenced by the re-emergence of historical writing and the increasing sophistication of the iconoclast dispute.[134]

More particularly, the central payment of the legal order instituted by the *Ecloga*, and the momentum imparted by the creation of that work, must have spilled over into these appended works. A good historical comparison would be the trajectory of the Justinianic *Corpus*, which saw work beget work, especially with Tribonian at the helm. The likelihood that the *Ecloga* did not have a similar effect, if proportionally reduced, is small. Indeed, the evidence of the *Krisis* is that the imperial centre was highly reactive and, in all probability, proactive in further legal work. Further, much of the above, in particular AE.III and the NS, have patent ideological import that would resonate especially in the reign of Constantine V. Of course, this does not necessarily mean that the emperor personally commissioned these works—though that is impossible to rule out—but it seems reasonable to suggest that they enjoyed at least an implicit imperial imprimatur. As such, the consistent focus on the collection of the past had a distinct symbolic purpose, namely the situating of the Isaurian regime within two narratives: the Old Testament and the Justinianic Roman-Christian.

Moreover, this does not exclude a practical purpose for the reproduction of much of the above, which, given the voluminous manuscript evidence, must have been significant. Indeed, much of the content of these appendices is distinctly practical and day-to-day in nature. Manifestly, the law was seen not just as a tool for propaganda

[133] See for general movement H. Kennedy, *The Court of the Caliphs: The Rise and Fall of Islam's Greatest Dynasty* (London, 2004); and R. McKitterick (ed.), *Carolingian Culture: Emulation and Innovation* (Cambridge, 1994).

[134] For a good introduction, see C. Mango 'The revival of learning', in C. Mango (ed.), *The Oxford History of Byzantium* (Oxford, 2002), 214–29.

and symbolism, but as a significant facet and tool of government. Furthermore, the predominant focus is criminal law, with the listing of crimes and punishment constituting the bulk of chapters. These appendices were more than engaging in an academic exercise; they were generating practical texts that were intended to punish miscreants, and therefore provide terrestrial justice and reform. Moreover, these appendices repeatedly evince three overarching concerns: firstly, the discipline, well-being, and status of the army; secondly, property law in general, but more specifically agricultural issues; and finally, general morality, with a special interest in sex and marriage. In this, the pattern of the *Ecloga* was followed and expanded. By continuing that work, Leo III's successors were tending to those twin pillars of Byzantine society, the army and the peasantry that paid for it, all the while seeking to reform the spiritual life of their subjects, to ensure divine support.

4

The Associated Codes of the *Ecloga* I

The *Nomos Mosaikos* and the *Nomos Rhodion Nautikos*

Alongside those texts that essentially extend the *Ecloga* stand three others: the *Nomos Mosaikos* (NM) or Mosaic Law, the *Nomos Rhodion Nautikos* (NN) or Rhodian Sea Law, and the *Nomos Georgikos* (NG) or Farmer's Law. These three frequently appear in manuscripts of the *Ecloga* and its derivatives, yet unlike the wrongly but similarly named NS, they rarely do so as components of the AE. Indeed, the NM commonly precedes the *Ecloga*, while the NN and NG have a more varied and distant textual relationship.[1] Yet their frequency in the manuscript tradition, combined with significant affinities in language and subject-matter with the *Ecloga*, has led to a long, and oft-contested, association between them and the Isaurian work.[2]

However, misapprehension of the nature of the NS, combined with a tendency to dismiss the NM, has meant that analysis has always focused on the grouping of NS-NN-NG.[3] In truth, this did become a recognizable combination in Byzantine law, representing a collection of concise, pragmatic texts as a sort of miniature corpus of contemporary law.[4] However, it is evident from the manuscript evidence that such a tight relationship only emerged in conjunction with the tenth-century *Eisagoge Aucta*.[5] Indeed, as argued above, the NS in truth

[1] See Appendix, Tables 9, 12–14. [2] See Chapter 3.
[3] Burgmann, 'Die Nomoi'. [4] Burgmann, 'Ecloga'.
[5] *Eisagoge Aucta*, ed. K. Zacharia von Lingenthal, *IGR* IV 180–370 = Zepos, *IGR* VI 57–216. For relationship with NS, NN, and NG see Appendix, Tables 11, 13–14. For introduction to EA see, A. Schminck, 'Epanagoge Aucta', in *ODB*, vol. 1, 704.

originated as a title within the AE, only later, probably in the tenth century, transmuting into a 'nomos'. There are, in fact, several important similarities between the NS and the NN and NG, but these should be considered as part of a trajectory of development from the former, rather than part of a preconceived plan for these three famous works.

Instead, the NN and NG shall here be studied with the NM, primarily for their shared and distinct form. For, unlike those texts examined in the previous chapter, those here employed formats that declared themselves independent works. The conventional shorthand of *nomos*, while conveniently conveying the idea of separate texts dealing with a specific subject, such as sailors and farmers, obscures as much as it illumines, while their actual titles are far more revealing:

NM: *Eklogē tou para Theou dia tou Mōuseōs dothentos nomou tois Israēlitais*[6]	NN.Part 3: *Nomos rhodiōn nautikos kat' eklogēn ek tou 14 bibliou tōn digestōn*[7]	NG: *Nomos geōrgikos kat' eklogēn ek tōn Iustinianou bibliōn*[8]
A Selection of the Law given by God through Moses to the Israelites.	The Rhodian Sea Law selected from the 14th book of the Digest.	The Farmer's Law selected from the books of Justinian.
Pinax: *Kephalaia kat' eklogēn tou mōsaikou paraggelmatos*[9]	Pinax: *Kephalaia nomou rhodiōn kat' eklogēn peri nautikōn*[10]	Pinax: *Kephalaia nomou geōrgikou kat' eklogēn ek tōn Iustinianou biblōn*[11]
Chapters from the selection of Mosaic commandments.	Chapters selected from the Rhodian Law concerning seafaring.	Chapters of the Farmer's Law selected from the books of Justinian.

Manifestly, the titles of the NN and NG are mirrors of each other, and share important aspects with the NM. All three declare themselves excerpts of some authoritative source. In this they clearly echo the *Ecloga*. There is a significant difference, however. *Eklogē* is the subject of the titles of both the *Ecloga* and the NM, while the NN and NG

6 Burgmann/Troianos, *Nomos Mosaikos*, 140, l.1–2.

7 Ashburner, *Rhodian Sea-Law*, 10. There are in fact a large variety of titles for the NN, discussed in Ashburner, lxvii–ix. This variant, however, is the most frequent in the manuscript tradition including, in the twelfth century, *RHBR*.61 (J in Ashburner's edition), where the NN is found following the *Ecloga* as part of the AE, although here it gives the eleventh rather than fourteenth book of the *Digest*.

8 NG, ed. Medvedev, 96 for selection of titles.

9 Burgmann/Troianos, *Nomos Mosaikos*, 138.

10 Ashburner, *Rhodian Sea-Law*, 5.

11 NG, ed. Medvedev, 93. The only known *pinax* is found in *RHBR*.327.

describe themselves as *nomos,* literally 'law', selected from another source. Yet importantly, the titles of the NM, NN, and NG described themselves as independent law codes, while deliberately mirroring the language and form of the *Ecloga*. Indeed, one could describe these 'nomoi' as consciously miniature *Eclogae*, an association that goes far beyond mere similarity in title.

THE *NOMOS MOSAIKOS*

As the NM's title indicates, this text stands apart from those previously studied as consisting not of excerpts of Justinianic but of Mosaic Law.[12] The text is composed from 70 or 71 extracts from the *Septuagint*, dependent on version, arranged under 50 thematic titles.[13] It exists in two versions, christened A and B by its editors, that are identical in substance save that B contains one extra extract, NM.8.1, and is significantly reordered.[14] Both versions contain a *pinax*, in language reminiscent of the *Ecloga*, implying a degree of organization and visualization of the text as a relatively consistent whole.[15] Indeed, the NM represents a far more stable work than any in the AE, perhaps in part due to the relative fixity of its source-text, the *Septuagint*, compared to the fluidity of transmission ascribed to the legal material. However, that stability, combined with a notable internal coherence, plausibly suggests one authoritative author, whose creation was then reworked once.

Its editors convincingly posit the NM following the *Ecloga*, in the same era as the AE.[16] Primarily this is based on the manuscript evidence; Burgmann and Troianos list 38 MSS, of which eight have a significant link to the *Ecloga*, three others to a derivative,

[12] See A. Kazhdan, 'Mosaic law', in *ODB*, vol. 2, 1413–14, for a brief introduction and bibliography.

[13] Burgmann/Troianos, *Nomos Mosaikos,* 130.

[14] Burgmann/Troianos, *Nomos Mosaikos*, 126–7, 130–2; 131 provides a concordance table of the versions.

[15] Burgmann/Troianos, *Nomos Mosaikos*, 138–9; Cf Burgmann, *Ecloga*, 153–9; Ashburner, *Rhodian Sea-Law*, 5–9.

[16] Burgmann/Troianos, *Nomos Mosaikos*, 132–4.

and 17 to the AE.[17] This affiliation is even stronger if one considers only the secular rather than canon law manuscripts, for in the former the NM is virtually always attached to the *Ecloga* and its appendices, while in the latter it has a much greater independent transmission.[18] Thus, modern consensus had virtually subsumed the NM as part of the AE produced simultaneously, for a similar purpose, which at some point during the late eighth and ninth centuries was associated with the *Ecloga*.[19]

This connection has been challenged by Schminck.[20] He has argued, combined with his controversial redating of the NG, that the NM was actually composed on the orders of the patriarch Photius. He even provides a date of 866–7, thus positioning the text at the very start of the Macedonian reforms.[21] Schminck also argues that version B, previously considered the later, was in fact the original.[22] Indeed, his argument needs this as he asserts that NM.8.1, the one addition to A, along with a few other examples, is stylistically linked to Photius' works.[23] He expands his argument by citing Photius' documented interest in Moses, and apparent similarities with Hincmar of Rheims' *Lex Dei*, which Photius may have had access to after the former travelled to Constantinople as an envoy.[24] Finally, Schminck expounds the idea that the purpose of the NM was to parallel the late antique *Collatio legum Mosaicum et Romanum*, with Photius using the NM as a deliberate refutation of the *Ecloga* by contrasting it to the law of God, to be used for the conversion of the Slavs, and eventually employing it to buttress his work of the *Eisagoge*.[25]

Although shining some overdue light on this fascinating text, Schminck's theory is highly speculative and unconvincing. His own

[17] Burgmann/Troianos, *Nomos Mosaikos*, 127–9. See Appendix, Table 12, which also adds *RHBR*.282 and 347; *RHBR*.124 is not included as it only contains NM.8.2.

[18] Burgmann/Troianos, *Nomos Mosaikos*, 135.

[19] Indicative of this overlap of both the texts and the scholarly perception of them is that the NM is edited by Burgmann and Troianos immediately after, almost as an appendix, to their edition of the AE. On the latter they lavished 71 pages of analysis, while the NM warrants a mere 11.

[20] Schminck, 'Nomos Mosaikos'.

[21] Schminck, 'Nomos Mosaikos', 262.

[22] Schminck, 'Nomos Mosaikos', 250–1.

[23] Schminck, 'Nomos Mosaikos', 259–60.

[24] Schminck, 'Nomos Mosaikos', 257–8.

[25] Schminck, 'Nomos Mosaikos', 252–3, 266. *Collatio legum Mosaicum et Romanum*, ed. M. Hyamson (London, 1913). On this text see R. Frakes, *Compiling the Collatio Legum Mosaicum et Romanum in Late Antiquity* (Oxford, 2011).

work illuminates the NM's numerous links with the *Ecloga*, arguing persuasively that the rubrics of the NM's titles were not drawn from its source-text, the *Septuagint*, but correspond to the *Ecloga*.[26] Furthermore, the manuscript evidence, while furnishing multiple codices that link the NM with the *Ecloga* and AE, barely registers any with the *Prochiron*, and offers a correlation weak to the point of non-existence between the NM and the *Eisagoge*.[27] Thus, one can isolate the association of the NM within the legal tradition almost entirely to the *Ecloga* and its aftermath.

Further, Schminck's argument that version B was the original is implausible. Firstly, the manuscript evidence, Schminck's central data, is hardly conclusive. He argues that the earliest manuscripts are more often B than A, although the original dating in Burgmann and Troianos is exactly the reverse.[28] The dating of manuscripts purely on palaeographical grounds is notoriously difficult, and all that can be said with a degree of confidence is that both versions existed by their writing down in the eleventh century. However, that date is at least 150 years after Schminck's proposed date, and 250 years after the *Ecloga*, an agreed *terminus post quem*. In short, the manuscript evidence cannot prove which version came first. However, it most certainly shows which was the most popular, for version A appears in 28 MSS and B in only seven.[29] Given that the content is virtually the same, the reasons for this marked popularity would stem from A either being the original and/or the more authoritative. Another insight from the manuscript evidence is the distance between the *Ecloga* and B, for none of its manuscripts contains the *Ecloga* or the AE.[30] Further, all seven are not juristic texts but canonistic. In total contrast, 19 out of 28 manuscripts of the A tradition have some manuscript link with the *Ecloga* or the AE.[31]

This distance is replicated in the concordance of the language of the rubric and the *Ecloga*. Table 7 lists the correspondences as noted by Schminck:[32]

[26] Schminck, 'Nomos Mosaikos', 254–5 n. 35 gives a collation of those links.

[27] See Appendix, Table 12.

[28] Schminck, 'Nomos Mosaikos', 250 n. 15.

[29] See Appendix, Table 12. [30] See Appendix, Table 12.

[31] See Appendix, Table 12. Six manuscripts contain the *Ecloga* and AE, two just the *Ecloga*, and 11 just the AE, normally AE.II.

[32] Schminck, 'Nomos Mosaikos', 254–5, esp. ns. 35, 39, and 41.

Table 7. The rubrics of the NM compared with the *Ecloga*

NMA	Ecloga	NMB
NM.1 *Peri krimatos kai dikaiosunēs*	E.pr.24–25 *en krimati kai dikaiosunē*	1
NM.9 *Peri metrōn kai stathmiōn dikaiōn*	E.pr.89 *dikaia stathmia*	9
NM.10 *Peri klēronomōn*	E.6.5.pinax *Peri klēronomōn*	11
NM.11 *Peri daneiou . . . kai enechurisamou*	E.10.pinax *Peri daneiou kai enechurōn*	3
NM.12 *Peri pasēs parathēkēs . . .*	E.11 *Peri pasēs parathēkēs*	5
NM.15 *Peri kleptōn*	E.17.10–13 *Peri kleptōn*	15
NM.16–17: *eleuthera kleptontōn sōmata kai pipraskontōn . . . agorazontos eleutheron sōma*	E.17.16: *sōma eleutheron kleptōn kai pipraskōn*	20
NM.20 *Peri tōn emprēsmous poiountōn*	E.17.41 *Hoi . . . emprēsmon . . . poiountes*	13
NM.25: *Peri phthoreōn*	E.17.29.pinax: *Peri phthoreōn*	27
NM.26 *Peri moichōn*	E.17.26–28 *Peri moichōn*	26
NM.27 *Peri gunaikos amblōsēs . . .*	E.17.36.pinax. *Peri gunaikos . . . amblōsēs*	24
NM.29 *Peri gunaikos alogeuomenēs*	E.17.39 *Hoi alogeuomenoi*	41
NM.30 *Peri haimomiktou*	E.17.33.pinax *Peri haimomiktōn*	28
NM.42 *Peri ktēnobatōn*	E.17.39.pinax *Peri ktēnobatōn*	42
NM.43 *Peri aselgōn*	E.17.38.rubric *Peri aselgōn*	43
NM.44 *Peri tou phoneuontos . . . ton idion oiketēn*	E.17.49 *Ei tis ton idion oiketēn . . . tupsē apothanē*	44
NM.45 *Peri tou en machē tuptontos ton plēsion*	E.17.48 *Ho en machē . . . tuptōn kai phoneuōn*	45
NM.46 *Peri phonōn ekousiōn*	E.17.45.pinax *Peri phonōn ekousiōn*	46
NM.49 *Peri marturōn kai pseudomarturōn*	E.14.pinax *Peri marturōn pistōn kai apistōn*	49
NM.50 *Peri pharmakōn, eggastrimuthōn kai epaoidōn*	E.17.43.pinax *Peri goētōn kai pharmakōn*	50

Patently there is a high degree of concordance. Furthermore, the vocabulary of NM's rubrics is sometimes highly distinctive from the *Septuagint*. For instance, *phthoreus* for corrupters (in this case, of women), used in the rubric of NM.25, is not found in the main text, but does correspond to E.17.29.pinax, and the text of E.17.28–30. Most significantly, the word *haimomiktēs* used in the rubric of NM.30 to describe incest, the topic for NM.30–41, is first attested in the *Ecloga*, E.17.33, and is entirely unknown in the *Septuagint*.[33] Thus Schminck is right to argue that the rubricator of the NM was drawing upon the *Ecloga* for his vocabulary.[34] However, as Table 7 demonstrates,

[33] Schminck, 'Nomos Mosaikos', 254–5. *LBG*, vol. 1, 34.

[34] Schminck, 'Nomos Mosaikos', 255.

it is the ordering of A not B which more closely resembles that of the *Ecloga*, although the match is not perfect. Indeed, the most glaring irregularity in the NM, the listing of bestiality before homosexuality (NM.42, 43), in contrast to their source in Leviticus, the *Ecloga*, and all other later codes, is in fact shared in A and B. Evidently, the NM does not slavishly follow the order or language of the *Ecloga*, in either A or B, yet it is undeniable that the linguistic associations suggest a secure link.

That concomitance is made more explicit when the *Ecloga* and *NM* are compared by subject, shown in Table 8:

Table 8. The subjects of the NM compared with the *Ecloga*

NMA	Ecloga	NMB
1–6: Justice, righteousness and honouring parents	*Prooimion*: Justice	1–2 (=1–2 NMA): Justice
7–8: Treating justly labourers, widows, and orphans	1–3: Marriage	3 (=11): Loans and interest
9: Just weights and measures	4–7: Property and wills	4 (=7): Treating justly wage labour
10: Inheritance	8: Freedmen and slavery	5 (=12): Deposits
11–12: Loans, interest, and deposit	9–11: Contracts, loans, and deposits	6–7 (=13–14): Cattle
13–15: Cattle	12–13: Tenure and leasing	8.1: Oaths
16–17: Freedmen	14: Witnesses	8.2 (=8): Widows and orphans
18–21: Agriculture	15: Dissolution of contract	9 (=9): Just weights and measures
22–43: Marriage and sexual immorality	16: Soldiers' property	10 (=3): Blasphemy
44–9: Homicide and witnesses	17: Crime and punishment	11 (=10): Inheritance
50: Sorcerers and pagan practice	18: War spoils	12–16 (=18, 20, 19, 15, 21): Agriculture
		17–19 (=4–6): Honouring parents
		20–1 (=16–17): Freedmen
		22–43 (=22–23, 27, 24, 26, 25, 30–41, 28, 29, 42–3): Marriage and sexual immorality
		44–9 (=44–9): Homicide and witnesses
		50: Sorcerers and pagan practice

Even this general schematic reveals a commonality of subject, with a focus on property, agricultural relations, marriage law, sexual immorality, and contract law. Moreover, it is clear that A is again closer to the *Ecloga* than B, and that A has a more coherent and consistent structure than B. Furthermore, the overwhelming majority of the NM finds some, and often very close, parallel in the subject matter of the *Ecloga*, in particular E.17; this is unsurprising given, as we have explored, the *Ecloga*'s repeated use of the Old Testament for inspiration and supporting citation. This is perhaps best highlighted in NM.25 concerning rape, where the three scriptural quotations from Deuteronomy (NM.25.2–4) break the order set by their actual source, and instead follow the order of the *Ecloga*.[35] True, the NM does not replicate entirely or precisely the *Ecloga*'s subject matter and arrangement. It is still an independent text with its own internal purpose, and derived from a specific source. However, when combined with the manuscript evidence and the language of the rubrics, it is evident that there is an exceedingly close relationship between the NM and the *Ecloga*, that A is closer to the order of the *Ecloga* than B, and that, considering its overwhelming relative popularity and dominance in the juristic rather than canonistic manuscripts, it is far more plausible that A was indeed the original version.

The final proof of this hypothesis is also illuminating, for, whereas version A contains 70 quotations from the Pentateuch, arranged into 50 titles, B has 71.[36] The addition, NM.8.1, is a lengthy extract concerning vows and obedience to parents.[37] It bears no scriptural or subject relationship with NM.8.2, which is an exaltation to treat widows and orphans well. The addition appears as an artificial appendage, and might well be linked to work of Photius, as Schminck suggests.[38] Yet the fundamental point is that this artificial addition spoils the perfect numerology evinced by version A. Seventy is a vital number in the Old Testament, representing ten times seven, seven

[35] Text Burgmann/Troianos, *Nomos Mosaikos*, 154–5. NM.25.1 cf. E.17.29 on consensual sex with a virgin; NM.25.2 cf. E.17.30 on rape; NM25.3–4 cf. E.17.32 on sex with another's fiancée. If the NM were following the order of its source, it should instead run NM.25.1, 4, 2, 3.

[36] Burgmann/Troianos, *Nomos Mosaikos*, 129.

[37] Burgmann/Troianos, *Nomos Mosaikos*, 144.

[38] Schminck, 'Nomos Mosaikos', 259–60.

being God's number.[39] It is also a number directly linked to Moses, who had 70 elders, the forerunner of the Sanhedrin.[40] There were also 70 nations in Genesis descended from the sons of Noah,[41] while Jesus despatched 70 disciples to the nations in order to prepare his way.[42] Seventy also acknowledged the NM's source, the *Septuagint*. Seventy, therefore, stood as a symbol for the totality of the world and the old law, given by God through Moses, the basis for the old covenant between the Israelites and God. The numerology continues, as 50 was also a fundamental number.[43] There are 50 days of Pentecost, the foundation feast of the Church, and traditionally linked with Moses. Fifty also was the number associated with law. The *Digest* had 50 books. John Scholasticus arranged his compendium of canon law after the same fashion with his *Synagoga in L Titulorum*. Thus 50 symbolized law (civil and canon), Moses, and the Church. The combination of the two texts into one tells much about the sophistication of this text and its purpose. Here was a symbol and a digest of the old law.

The prime problem, however, with the hypothesis of the NM as a rebuttal to the *Ecloga* is that it in no way provides this. The only possible contention could be the far more recurrent use of the death penalty, which the *Ecloga* minimized, but this could be seen as part of the *Ecloga*'s philanthropic aim of improving the old law, especially considering that the *Ecloga* conceived itself as an inheritor to a legal tradition that included not only Roman law, but the law given by God through the prophets, of whom Moses was indubitably the chief. This comparison was underscored in the title to the *pinax* in *RHBR*.61 and 141, which describes the NM as the *palaias nomothesias*, 'the old law',[44] in deliberate contrast to the *Ecloga*, which is found, respectively, immediately after and before in these same manuscripts, whose *pinax* declares it *nearas nomothesias*, 'new law'.[45] Indeed, so compatible were the injunctions of the NM with Byzantine law that one

[39] See V. Hopper, *Medieval Number Symbolism: Its Sources, Meanings and Influence on Thought and Expression* (New York, 1938), 25.

[40] Num. 11:16. [41] Gen. 10. [42] Lk. 10.

[43] Schminck, 'Nomos Mosaikos', 263.

[44] Burgmann/Troianos, *Nomos Mosaikos*, 138. The MSS are, respectively, A and F in Burgmann/Troianos critical apparatus.

[45] E.pinax.2. *RHBR*.61 [=E in Burgmann's critical apparatus of the *Ecloga*] includes the *pinax* of the *Ecloga*, but *RHBR*.141 [=Q in Burgmann's critical apparatus of the *Ecloga*] does not.

manuscript contains the marginal note, 'mark how all this corresponds with our legislation.'[46] Such a comment was exactly the effect the creator of the NM was aiming for.

Moreover, there is every reason to suppose that the Isaurians had as much interest (and probably more) in Moses, in particular his role as lawgiver, as did Photius. The *Ecloga* deliberately positioned itself as the successor to biblical law, and its promulgators as New Moseses. Furthermore, the Isaurians were criticized for blindly following the Old Testament in their iconoclast policies, in particular the Second Commandment's injunction against graven images, which was included as NM.2.[47] Therefore, if Photius did re-edit the NM—which is far from proven—it was because this was another text that had proven highly successful and now needed to be disentangled from the heretical Isaurians.

Considering the repeated allusions to the *Ecloga*, the simplest and most plausible explanation for this text is that it was meant as an accompaniment. One can also postulate, from the manuscripts it shares with the *Ecloga* and AE, that the NM became associated with the AE during the second wave of publication, evincing a comparable pattern with AE.XI.[48] Indeed, both are legitimizing texts rather than collections of practical law. However, it is evident that the NM was by far the more important and popular, a further reflection of the comparative significance to the Isaurians of the biblical versus the Roman past. Therefore, the NM would most plausibly be a creation of the mid-to-late eighth century, by a polity straining to justify and imagine itself through an Old Testament lens. Consequently, it is best considered as a deliberate adjunct, ideologically supporting the *Ecloga*, deliberately mirroring the 'new law' in language and form. The continuity of Byzantine law from that of the prophets, proclaimed in the *Ecloga*, was proved, while continuing to justify its correction 'towards greater humanity'.[49] Above all, the NM highlighted the *Ecloga* and Byzantine law in general as the new covenant between the new Israelites and their God, a law designed to reform

[46] Burgmann/Troianos, *Nomos Mosaikos*, 140; *RHBR*.151 [=E in Burgmann/Troianos critical apparatus]: *sēmeiōsai pōs sumballousi tauta panta tois eis hēmas nenomothetēmenois.*

[47] For this sensible argument, see also the comments of Magdalino and Nelson, 'Introduction', 21.

[48] See Chapter 1, 42–3.

[49] See Chapter 2, 93–5.

the people and crush sin, and thereby ensure divine protection of the Chosen People.

THE *NOMOS RHODION NAUTIKOS*

The NN, or Rhodian Sea-law as it is commonly called, is a very different text from the NM, despite a similarity in title and format.[50] While the former is resoundingly symbolic, almost propagandistic, the latter is resolutely pragmatic. It was, however, one of the most popular works ever of Byzantine law. All or parts of it are found in more than 50 manuscripts produced across the centuries and the Mediterranean.[51] Clearly, the NN was a remarkably successful work, repeatedly invoked for centuries. Yet it remains a mysterious and peculiar text. The important and interrelated questions of its authorship, date of composition, relation between its three parts, the possibility of multiple recensions, its association to the *Basilika* where it appears in Bk. 53, and its actual use, both for the Byzantines themselves and as a source for historians, are all debated, and will certainly remain so until the publication of a new edition to replace Ashburner's scholarly and still useful, but dated effort.[52] These questions can only be touched upon below, as our main interest is the extent to

[50] *Nomos Rhodion Nautikos*, ed. W. Ashburner, *The Rhodian Sea-Law* (Oxford, 1909).

[51] See Appendix, Table 13, which excludes six MSS listed in the *RHBR* as containing only selected chapters of the NN.

[52] Ashburner, *Rhodian Sea-Law*, provides a long and useful introduction, xiii–ccxciii in particular discussing these problems, but at extremely varied lengths. The NN has been remarkably little studied since, but see D. Letsios, *Nomos Rhodiōn Nautikos—Das Seegesetz der Rhodier. Untersuchung zu Seerecht und Handelsschiffahrt in Byzanz* (Rhodes, 1996); and D. Letsios, 'Sea trade as illustrated in the "Rhodian Sea Law" with special reference to the reception of its norms in the Arabic Ecloga', *Graeco-Arabica* 6 (1995), 209–25. An interesting comparative approach, comparing the NN with contemporary Arabic texts, can be found in V. Christides, 'Raid and trade in the eastern Mediterranean', *Graeco-Arabica* 5 (1993), 63–102; and H. Khalileh, *Admiralty and Maritime Laws in the Mediterranean Sea (c. 800–1050)* (Leiden, 2006). For the need for a new edition, see Burgmann/Troianos, *Appendix Eclogae*, 30 n. 27. A specific example of re-editing the Ashburner text can be found in I. Spatharakis, 'The text of chapter 30 of the Lex Rhodia Nautica', *Hellenika* 26 (1973), 207–15. An edition based on the NN's incorporation in the *Basilika* has appeared; see G. Rhodolakes, *Apo to Nomo Rhodiōn sto 53o Biblio tōn Basilikōn: sumbolē stē meletē tou Buzantinou nautikou dikaiou* (Athens, 2007).

which the NN was an 'official' code, or reflects the legal and political universe of the Isaurians.

For Zacharia von Lingenthal, the NN was an official work initiated either by Leo III or Constantine V in deliberate association with the *Ecloga*, along with the Farmer's Law and the NS.[53] Von Lingenthal based his view upon the fact that several manuscripts of the *Ecloga* contained these works, and upon supposed legal commonality between them. Ashburner fundamentally disagreed, and in this particular case stated that the NN was a private work, composed *c*.600–800.[54] He denied any convincing legal continuity between the NN and the *Ecloga*, demonstrating that the vast majority of Zacharia von Lingenthal's points evinced little difference between the NN and Justinianic legislation, rather than anything peculiar in the *Ecloga*.[55] Ashburner also concluded that the NN must have been created before 800, due to variations that had emerged in the earliest MSS of the tenth and eleventh centuries, which originated from separate manuscript traditions, with these deviations representing organic development.[56] Generally, this schema has been accepted by scholars.[57]

ROMAN LAW, THE NN, AND THE *ECLOGA*

Certainly, there is very little in the NN that is legally inconsistent with Justinianic legislation. Yet, as we have seen, the *Ecloga* itself rarely contradicted those principles, and indeed was deliberately designed to uphold them, or at least uphold what the eighth century thought they were. Furthermore, it can be deduced that the NN fits the world post-*Ecloga* better than any other period. Indeed, the NN presumes an existing legal system. Its imagination was not confined to the world of the ship, but envisaged courts, with evidence taken, disputes adjudicated, and punishments enforced. For instance, there is a repeated concern for legitimate contracts to be ensured by three credible witnesses, and a preference for the written over the oral, also found

[53] Zacharia von Lingenthal, *Geschichte*, 313–19.

[54] Ashburner, *Rhodian Sea-Law*, cxii–xiv.

[55] Ashburner, *Rhodian Sea-Law*, lxxvii–xcvii.

[56] Ashburner, *Rhodian Sea-Law*, lxvi.

[57] See Burgmann, 'Die nomoi', 53–5 for overview of the literature and general consensus.

in the *Ecloga*.[58] Indeed, many chapters either assume that the contract was written or stipulate that it had to be.[59] Concurrently, the threat of perjury is raised in NN.3.14 which in at least one manuscript is punished with amputation of the tongue, instituted by E.17.2.[60] This insistent and repeated focus on veracity, although a frequent object of many legal codes, chimes especially closely with the ideals of the *Ecloga*.

Furthermore, elements of the NN, at least prima facie, are not in accordance with classical Roman law, but are broadly in line with how it had evolved by the eighth century. For instance, NN.3.14 is, as Ashburner notes, inconsistent with strict Roman law as it demands a twofold restitution for a denied deposit for both necessary and ordinary deposits, whereas in Roman law it should only be given to the former.[61] It was, however, perfectly consistent with, and linguistically similar to, E.11. Moreover, the prominent concern with criminal law and its punishment, forming as it does the first chapters of NN.3, also echoes the *Ecloga*, as do some of the penalties, such as NN.3.1–3, which concern stealing, and ordain flogging and repayment of twice the amount stolen, although corporal mutilation is not a feature of the NN.[62]

More significant than commonality in interests and specific ordinances is that the NN not only presupposes an existing legal universe remarkably similar to the *Ecloga*, but also seems to assume the existence of the *Ecloga* as a text. For example, NN.3.1 ordained flogging and repayment of twice the damage for anyone who robbed a ship's anchors; NN.3.2 stipulated punishment for sailors from one ship stealing the anchor of another's at the captain's behest; NN.3.3 documented the different liabilities and penalties arising from a sailor robbing a merchant or passenger on his own accord or the captain's; and NN.3.38 had an aside on stealing during salvage. Evidently theft was considered an important and frequent enough offence to warrant multiple chapters at the very beginning of the work, with the listed punishments in accordance with the practice of the *Ecloga*. Yet

[58] See, for example, NN 3.12 (where deposits should be made in front of three witnesses); NN 3.22 (where merchants should protest in front of three witnesses if the captain is overloading a ship); and NN 3.27 (where those denying partnerships require three witnesses to ensure a conviction). Cf. E.2.4, 4.1–4, 5.4,8, 8.1, 15.1. See Ashburner, *Rhodian Sea-Law*, lxxxix–xc.

[59] E.g. NN.3.22, 23, 25, 30, 32, 39. Cf. Ashburner, *Rhodian Sea-Law*, xc–xcii.

[60] *RHBR*.230. See Ashburner, *Rhodian Sea-Law*, lxxxvi–vii.

[61] D.3.1.1. Cf. Ashburner, *Rhodian Sea-Law*, lxxxix.

[62] See Chapter 2, 118–25.

nowhere is there any chapter on sailors stealing from other sailors or the captain—a surprising oversight given the villainy imagined in other cases! Of course, one could argue that such a chapter was not needed, as it would be covered by recourse to the common delict of theft. Yet the point here is not that this option was not open to sailors, or indeed that it wasn't as obvious to the writers of the NN as it is to modern scholars, but that they deliberately chose not to put it in this text, despite patent interest in the subject.

Another set of curious lacunae concern homicide. NN.3.6 proffers the well-established principle of Roman law that self-defence acquitted a man from charges of murder—here specifically the unintentional killing of a fellow sailor after the other had started the fight.[63] NN.3.7 notes that if a man who kicked someone else on board, and that person later died from the injury, then the man was liable for trial for homicide, *enochos estai ho krousas tēs dikēs tou thanatou.*[64] Yet there is no chapter that envisages intentional murder or assault with a sword.[65] Why these curious lapses? Manifestly, the NN was concerned with these issues, or it would not have mentioned the subjects of theft or homicide in the first place. Moreover, by the same reasoning, the authors of the NN evidently believed themselves competent to list criminal as well as civil law.

Nor can one blame the original source material. The only agreed and certain source of the NN was Justinianic law, as moderated through custom and the written transmission of the period—both opaque processes, as we have often noted. Further, as mentioned above, one early, plausibly original, title for NN Part 3 described it as excerpts from D.14, the first two titles of which do indeed concern maritime law.[66] However, the NN by no means slavishly follows the *Digest* or indeed any constituent of the *Corpus*. To some extent, this reflects the relative lack of interest in maritime law displayed by Roman lawyers and emperors. A complex system of public law had regulated the supply of Rome and Constantinople, but after the cessation of the public grain dole in 618, this fell into abeyance.[67] Essentially this left private law, which on maritime issues was heavily

[63] Cf. D.9.16.2–3. [64] Ashburner, *Rhodian Sea-Law*, 15.

[65] Cf. E.17.46, C.9.16.6.

[66] See Ashburner, *Rhodian Sea-Law*, lxvii–ix.

[67] See B. Sirks, *Food for Rome: The Legal Structure of the Transportation and Processing of Supplies for the Imperial Distributions in Rome and Constantinople* (Amsterdam, 1991).

influenced by Hellenic precedent and custom. This is evidenced by the continued respect given to the 'Law of the Rhodians', which is more a shorthand for Mediterranean maritime custom, in particular concerning jettison, than any specific legislation.[68] Mostly, sailors and sea commerce were subjected to the same legal principles that governed the land, and no specifically maritime courts ever materialized.[69] Three peculiar aspects of maritime law did emerge, however, namely: maritime loans,[70] which attracted a higher level of interest due to their inherent riskiness; the action against a shipowner who had a range of liability for the conduct of affairs of the vessel he owned in particular concerning the rights of passengers and merchants;[71] and the so-called 'Rhodian law of Jettison'.[72] These indeed comprise the bulk of the NN, or at least NN.3, but the NN was manifestly not closely bound by the language, arrangement, or content of the *Digest*. Indeed it represented a markedly original collection, one which deliberately chose to include the subjects of theft and homicide, while choosing not to iterate the basic forms of those laws.

The answer to this riddle can only be that the authors of the NN thought it superfluous. In this they were entirely correct, for the *Ecloga* precisely fills these deficiencies. Thus, E.17.11 ordains that simple theft was punished by restitution by those who could afford it, flogging for those who could not, and amputation of the hand for a repeat offence, while E.17.10, 12–17 elucidated variations on the central theme. However, nowhere did it envisage the specific problems involved in maritime theft, such as the stealing of anchors that endangered the life and property of multiple others, and the issue of responsibility when acting under orders. NN.3.1–3 and 38, therefore, act as an extension of the *Ecloga* in regard to a peculiar context. Similarly, E.17.45 condemned murder with capital punishment, E.17.46 punished injury inflicted by a sword as a form of attempted homicide, while E.17.47–8 listed the penalties for involuntary homicide from fighting ranked on the nature of the weapon used. What NN.3.6 added was the justification of self-defence with a particular interest in the nature of weaponry reminiscent of E.17.47.[73] This is

[68] Christides, 'Raid and trade', 85; Ashburner, *Rhodian Sea-Law*, lxviii.

[69] Khalilieh, *Admiralty and Maritime Laws*, 10.

[70] D.22.2. [71] D.14.1. [72] D.14.2.

[73] E.17.47.928: *dia xulōn teleiōn ē lithōn megalōn ē lakteōn*, 'by means of a stick, or a big stone, or by kicking', cf. NN.3.6, l.4–5: '*ē lithō ē xulō ē sidērō*, 'with a stone, stick, or axe'. Ashburner, *Rhodian Sea-Law*, 84 adds that the *sidēron*, in his translation a

not to say that there was no such idea in 741, but an integral component of the *Ecloga* project and extensions was to enumerate concrete, legal scenarios and list the respective penalty. The NN was here continuing that process.

Further, E.17.48 ordained that 'In a fistfight the man who strikes and kills shall be flogged and exiled as guilty of involuntary homicide'.[74] Meanwhile, NN.3.7 declared that in a fistfight, if a man blinds another, he should pay the doctor's bill and 12 gold pieces. It further added that if a man kicks another and causes a hernia, he should give ten gold pieces, but if the kicked man dies, the first man is liable for trial for homicide.[75] It says nothing about what happened if a man died in a fistfight, covered by E.17.48, nor does it stipulate the penalty for death resulting from a kick, which was given at E.17.47. What NN.3.7 added was a method of recompense for physical injury, in the specific context of someone aboard a ship attacking someone else, an area of law not specifically touched upon in the *Ecloga*. Justinianic jurisprudence had treated physical injury as a form of delict, laying down the principle that the guilty party was liable for medical expenses and loss of earnings, as indeed is prescribed in NN.3.5.[76] The stipulation of a precise monetary value for physical loss, however, is not found in the *Digest*, yet it appears as a common element of the so-called 'barbarian' law codes of the post-Roman west, and might indeed have precedent in practice.[77] One can easily envisage the mutation of a principle into a fixed sum as a matter of convenience. Further, in this case there is a logical reason for the difference between NN.3.5 and 3.7, namely that the fight was specifically delimited to between sailors in the former, strongly implying ship-mates, who would naturally share a physical residence (the ship), allowing the guilty party to pay accurately for lost wages; in NN.3.7, however, it is between anyone on ship and someone else, the implication being that it did not concern a fracas between individuals on board one ship, or that the parties involved only had a transitory relationship, meaning

carpenter's axe, was deliberately added to suit the peculiar context of a ship. It could also just be rendered as 'iron'.

[74] E.17.48, trans. Freshfield, *Ecloga*, 113, altered.

[75] *Ei de ho to lax kroustheis apothanē*: Ashburner, *Rhodian Sea-Law*, 15, l.1–2.

[76] Cf.D.9.1.3, 9.2.7.pr. See Ashburner, *Rhodian Sea-law*, lxxxiv–v.

[77] Ashburner, *Rhodian Sea-Law*, lxxxv. On the post-Roman western legal developments more generally, see P. Barnwell, 'Emperors, jurists and kings: law and custom in the late Roman and early medieval west', *Past and Present* 168 (2000), 6–29.

that a fixed penalty was more convenient. Moreover, such specificity of penalty falls neatly within the *Ecloga*'s tradition of explicit enumeration of punishments.

Furthermore, while these chapters neatly expand the provisions of the *Ecloga* without repeating its central points, by the time of the late ninth-century law-books the *Prochiron* and the *Eisagoge*, these principles had been incorporated into the body of the main text, thus rendering the chapters of the NN superfluous.[78] What this would suggest is that the NN, or more precisely NN.3, was created after the *Ecloga*, with that text deliberately in mind, and before the Macedonian texts. Overall, then, the NN best suits the situation after the *Ecloga*.[79]

THE NN AND OTHER LEGAL TEXTS

Schminck, however, believes that NN.3 was initiated by Photius as a counterpart to the NG, also composed by him.[80] Meanwhile, NN.2 was created later on in Leo VI's reign, which also saw the composition of NS.[81] Schminck's argument for this radical redating is as follows: the NN was clearly a private work, bearing no mention of an emperor, and that a private work of law could not have been composed in the 'Dark Ages'.[82] Furthermore, it could not be an Isaurian work, for the deliberate intention of the *Basilika*, in which Schminck plausibly argues the NN was from the start incorporated in Bk.53, was to purge the law of its iconoclastic taint.[83] Schminck proceeds to claim a direct link between the NN and NG as extremely regular companions in the manuscript tradition.[84] Moreover, they apparently represent the Platonic elements of earth and water, with biblical undertones, a point deliberately brought out in the rubric introducing the NN in B.53.1.1: *ta nautika ēgoun ta kata thalassan tō rhodiō nomō krinetai*, 'the affairs of sailors, or rather of the Sea are decided by the Rhodian Law'.[85] Finally, as the NG was a work by Photius, as

[78] For references see Ashburner, *Rhodian Sea-Law*, lxxxvi.

[79] Letsios, *Nomos Rhodiōn Nautikos*, 238, also concludes this, if for different reasons.

[80] Schminck, *Nomos Rhodiōn Nautikos*, 178 provides a ten-point summation of the article.

[81] Schminck, *Nomos Rhodiōn Nautikos*, 174, 176–8.

[82] Schminck, *Nomos Rhodiōn Nautikos*, 173.

[83] Schminck, *Nomos Rhodiōn Nautikos*, 173.

[84] Schminck, *Nomos Rhodiōn Nautikos*, 174.

[85] Schminck, *Nomos Rhodiōn Nautikos*, 173.

demonstrated by the similarity in style between it and the *Eisagoge*, and the NN is associated with the NG, it too must be a text composed by the prolific patriarch.[86]

The first rejoinder to this esoteric approach is the remarkable assumption that the eighth century was incapable of producing private law, and that therefore all these *nomoi* must belong to the (presumably more enlightened) late ninth. This seems untenable in the face of the legal and ideological sophistication of the *Ecloga*, and the (mostly successful) aim of the AE to appropriate contemporaneously useful sections of Justinianic law. We have also seen how the NS and NM most plausibly belong to that world as well. Patently the eighth century was not so 'dark' as to make a legal flowering wither. That the Macedonians would not include an Isaurian work is a more logical point. However, both the *Eisagoge* and *Prochiron* have clear stylistic, format, and legal foundation in the *Ecloga*.[87] Thus, despite their denunciations, the Macedonians seem to have felt more than able to adopt much of the Isaurian legacy. Moreover, there is little overtly propagandistic in the NN to imprint the Isaurians on the text indelibly, and therefore it could be relatively easily appropriated.

Attempts to link the NN to Photius are even more tenuous. If it was a private work, why would the patriarch patronize a text concerning seafarers? Schminck does not provide any stylistic or legal continuity between the NN and the *Eisagoge*, Photius' authorship of which is itself contested.[88] Indeed, he does not discuss the content at all, nor any possible link with the legal thought of the *Ecloga*. The only ideological association adduced is the line in the rubric of the *Basilika* mentioning the sea, thus making the NN a platonic counterpart to the NG. Even if such an interpretation were proved, it would not justify the identification with Photius; others could imagine such a simple construct of earth and water! More pertinently, the rubric patently echoes D.14.2.9, where Antoninus Pius is recorded as saying:

> I am master of the world, but the law of the sea must be judged by the sea law of the Rhodians where our own law does not conflict with it.[89]

[86] Schminck, *Nomos Rhodiōn Nautikos*, 175–6.

[87] See Chapter 6.

[88] For the dispute over the *Eisagoge*'s date and authorship, including the role of Photius, see A. Schminck, *Studien zu mittelbyzantinischen Rechtsbüchern* (Frankfurt, 1986); cf. T. Van Bochove, *To Date and Not to Date: On the Date and Status of Byzantine Law Books* (Groningen, 1996).

[89] D.14.2.9, trans. Watson, *Digest*.

This would be a far more direct model for the *Basilika*'s authors than Plato. Moreover, there is no indication in the NN that it was meant as referring to the general sea, while seafarers are always mentioned. Thus, the association would be a creation of the rubric writer, again a role not proven to have been influenced by Photius whatsoever. Furthermore, the more natural reading of the rubric would not be ideological. Rather, it neatly describes the peculiar amalgam of regulation contained in the NN, including things that do not have much to do with maritime law. For example, although NN.3.12 refers to deposits on a ship and in a house, it is plausible that the original meaning was concerned exclusively with deposits made on land.[90] Similarly, NN.3.14 has no specific maritime context.[91] Indeed, the best description of the NN is a collection of laws, regulations, and customs that could affect sailors, merchants, shipowners, or anyone who had to deal with affairs at sea. This is similar to the NS's regulations, which on several occasions do not, prima facie, concern soldiers, or just soldiers, but cover the broader area of society and law that had dealings with anything of a military nature.[92] Thus the *Basilika*'s rubric would capture this subtlety nicely, without any need to refer to a higher ideological construct. Finally, Schminck's argument relies not on the NN, but on the NG being a Photian text—a deeply problematical assertion, as we shall see.

However, Schminck is correct in highlighting the significant manuscript association between the NG and NN.[93] But as Burgmann makes clear, the manuscript evidence is complicated and proffers no overwhelming pattern.[94] There is no dominant ordering pattern of the codes, nor a constant context in which they appear, although the abundance of manuscripts with some relationship makes it patent that the three were considered somehow conjoined. The problem also holds true for any association with the *Ecloga*, which includes nine manuscripts significantly proximate to the NN, fewer than a fifth of all the NN's manuscripts, although on the other hand almost half of the *Ecloga*'s.

However, if the NN, or indeed NS and NG, did originate in the late ninth century, there would be little reason to have conjoined them with the *Ecloga* at all. Moreover, there is manifestly an association

[90] See Ashburner, *Rhodian Sea-Law*, lxxvi, 93.
[91] Ashburner, *Rhodian Sea-Law*, lxxvi.
[92] See Chapter 3, 156–60.
[93] Schminck, *Nomos Rhodiōn Nautikos*, 174.
[94] Burgmann, 'Die nomoi', 56–9.

between the NN and the various manuals of Byzantine law produced in the eighth to tenth centuries, with the NN nearly always appearing with one or more of these. The strongest grouping is with the *Eisagoge Aucta*, with six manuscripts reproducing exactly the same order of *Eisagoge Aucta-Rhopai*-NG-NS-NN.3.[95] Still, all this would prove is that in the early tenth century, the date of composition of the *Eisagoge Aucta*, these three *nomoi* created a corpus of law which, along with the successor of the *Ecloga*, represented a basis for jurisprudence. This association between manual and *nomoi* would, most probably, predate this grouping. Indeed, the NN is commonly found with various titles of the AE, with a strong association found in 14 manuscripts.[96] Only twice, however, is the NN surrounded by the AE, thus in effect subsuming it within a greater Appendix, although these are two of the oldest and most important manuscripts, and one is also after the *Ecloga*.[97] Rather, if one examines the six manuscripts that contain the *Ecloga*, AE, and NN, the latter is normally found on the periphery of the AE. What this implies is that, unlike the NS, the NN was largely considered a separate work from the AE, but was either from the beginning or very soon after publication associated with the *Ecloga*, its successors, and their derivatives.[98]

THE DIFFERENT PARTS OF THE NN

The manuscripts also illuminate to some extent the relationship between the several parts of the NN. NN.3 is found in all the manuscripts, frequently accompanied by a *pinax*.[99] NN.2 is fairly common and always appears with NN.3.[100] NN.1, the short introduction giving a fantastical fable of the NN's creation by various

[95] See Appendix, Tables 9, 13, 14. The *Rhopai*, ed. F. Sitzia, *Le Rhopai* (Naples, 1984), is a treatise on the division of time.

[96] See Appendix, Tables 10 and 13.

[97] *RHBR*.61[=J in Ashburner] and 148 [=L in Ashburner].

[98] The NN also became incorporated into the very text of the Arabic version of the *Ecloga*, further implying the perception that the NN was an extension of the *Ecloga*. See Letsios, 'Sea trade as illustrated in the "Rhodian Sea Law"'; Leder, *Die arabische Ecloga*, 19, 115–19.

[99] Ashburner, *Rhodian Sea-Law*, lxiii–lx.

[100] Ashburner, *Rhodian Sea-Law*, lxx–i.

emperors, is exceedingly rare and almost universally accepted as a creation of the eleventh or twelfth centuries.[101] Therefore, in Ashburner's edition NN.1 is relegated to an appendix, while the actual NN is NN.2-Pinax-NN.3. Ashburner, however, gave brief consideration to the relationship of the stylistically highly distinct sections.[102] NN.2 contains 19 mostly very short chapters, the majority of which can hardly be described as law.[103] NN.2.1–7 stipulate the varying shares of the different crew members in the profits of the ship. More mundane regulations include agreed space for passengers' luggage (NN.2.9, 13), and a measure on how to value the ship (NN.2.16). These are more regulations, guidelines, or customs than law. The nearest the section comes to law is NN.2.17–19, concerning loans, which, although garbled, seems to refer to the legal difference between ordinary and maritime loans in Roman law. Here there is also reference to the 'Rhodian law' as the authority for their statements, which most probably served as a common referent, shorthand for accepted and established custom, rather than an actual text.

NN.3 is utterly different. Its 47 chapters are longer and better constructed.[104] Ashburner also discerned a clear unity of structure, even if certain chapters are rather forced into an unnatural order.[105] Most of NN.3's chapters comprise scenarios either on ship, concerning ships, or any maritime activity, which in some respect involve the law. Chapters try to establish legal liability in case of theft or damage (NN.3.10–11), deposits (NN.3.12–14), or contribution after loss (NN.3.26–44). Suggestively, all the evidence that Zacharia von Lingenthal adduced for a connection with the *Ecloga*, and which Ashburner thought better represented the continuance of Justinianic law, are from NN.3.[106] In this NN.3 bears comparison with the NS in creating a code that brought established law together in one text as it affected a particular section of society, in this case sailors, merchants, or anyone engaged in maritime activities.

The difference between the parts is clear, but the relationship is not. Ashburner, in his remarkably brief comments on the matter, thought

[101] Ashburner, *Rhodian Sea-Law*, lxxi–lxxiv.

[102] Ashburner, *Rhodian Sea-Law*, lxx–lxxi.

[103] Ashburner, *Rhodian Sea-Law*, xiii–iv, cf. Letsios, *Nomos Rhodiōn Nautikos*, 43.

[104] Ashburner, *Rhodian Sea-Law*, xiv, lxiii–iv.

[105] Ashburner, *Rhodian Sea-Law*, xiv–v. Cf. Letsios, *Nomos Rhodiōn Nautikos*, 43–4.

[106] Zacharia von Lingenthal, *Geschichte*, 316, cf. Ashburner, *Rhodian Sea-Law*, lxxviii–xcviii.

that NN.2 was created when NN.3 was incorporated into the *Basilika*.[107] Indeed, he argued that the work as it exists now was an edition made to fit B.53, due to how well the subject matter filled the holes of the rest of the book.[108] In this theory, NN.2 was excerpted as either repetitious or unworthy of inclusion.[109] Certainly, much in NN.2 was of scant interest to lawyers and parts would be repetitious—for example, NN.2.14–15 are combined in better language as NN.3.13.[110] However, the theory seems implausible. Considering the stark contrast in language and content between the sections, it is hard to imagine them as ever being part of one continuous text. Moreover, the neatness of NN.3 in relation to B.53 could easily be the product of the authors of B.53 moulding their text around an accepted and pre-existing one, rather than vice versa. This would help explain why Ashburner's faint traces of his original edition, the one produced *c*.600–800, barely exist, in that the text as we have it is substantially the original one, undergoing little or no editing for B.53.[111] As it stands this is impossible to prove, but so is Ashburner's idea, and this sequence would be the simpler.

Schminck also believes that NN.2 was a later construct, although he places it in the reign of Leo VI.[112] Again this appears implausible. Why would anyone in the early tenth century wish to append to a well-constructed and ordered text a collection of short, poorly worded, and legally and ideologically unimportant regulations, which included repeating one regulation in worse language and confusingly splitting it into two sections? Burgmann concurs that there is clear evidence for a two-phase development of the text, although he does not state any preference for which came first.[113] Such an evolution, however, would again compare that of the NS with a short section drawn from a non-legal source appended with a much longer one focused on various legal scenarios.[114] It would, therefore, fit the limited evidence and provide the simplest explanation if NN.2 was in fact the older part, to which someone later added a

[107] Ashburner, *Rhodian Sea-Law*, lxx–lxxi.
[108] Ashburner, *Rhodian Sea-Law*, cxii.
[109] Ashburner, *Rhodian Sea-Law*, cxiii.
[110] Ashburner, *Rhodian Sea-Law*, lxxvii.
[111] Ashburner, *Rhodian Sea-Law*, lxxvi–vii.
[112] Schminck, *Nomos Rhodiōn Nautikos*, 174.
[113] Burgmann, 'Die Nomoi', 62.
[114] See Chapter 3, 155–65.

longer and more directly legal section, which in turn was then added to the *Basilika*.

THE NN: CONCLUSIONS

This similarity with the NS implies a degree of contemporaneity, while the evolution of the form of *nomoi*, and the NN's appearance on the edges of the *Ecloga*'s manuscript tradition, suggest publication after the NS, probably around the time of the NM in the second half of the eighth century, which would also tally with Ashburner's hypothesis that the NN could not date after *c*.800. A few extraneous processes strengthen this dating. Firstly, after a nadir in the early eighth century, shipping and sea commerce were growing from *c*.750.[115] Intensifying movement and trade would, *ceteris paribus*, also produce a small increase in cases involving seafarers, prompting renewed interest in maritime law. Secondly, the Byzantine fleet underwent a degree of reorganization, whose precise evolution is difficult to trace.[116] Thirdly, it is evident that significant administrative reforms took place in the reign of Constantine V (r.741–75), including the emergence of an independent department of the *dromos*, the imperial transport system, under its own *logothete*, which affected the working of the *basilika kommerkia*, who were more narrowly focused on the Byzantine littoral.[117] Finally, a new tax on commercial transactions, the *kommerkion*, had been imposed, first mentioned in 795.[118] Considering that the tax and judicial systems had always been intertwined, a new fiscal imposition would be a natural bedfellow with the renewed emphasis, and perhaps enhanced application, of maritime law. One can, therefore, be

[115] McCormick, *Origins*, esp. 115–19, 433–41.

[116] See Ahrweiler, *Byzance et la mer*, 17–44; cf. Brubaker and Haldon, *History*, 729–30, 739–40.

[117] Brubaker and Haldon, *History*, 707–9; for more general changes in the fiscal administration, see 665–722; cf. W. Brandes, *Finanzverwaltung in Krisenzeiten. Untersuchung zur byzantinischen Administration im 6.–9. Jahrhundert* (Frankfurt, 2002); and Hendy, *Studies in the Byzantine Monetary Economy*, 409–24, 619–62.

[118] Theophanes, 469–70. For the *kommerkion*, see N. Oikonomidès, 'The role of the Byzantine state in the economy', in *EHB*, 973–1058, esp. 986.

reasonably confident in positioning the NN in the wake of the *Ecloga*, and probably in the third quarter of the eighth century.

Was it, therefore, an 'official' or a 'private' work? In many aspects this is a thoroughly sterile debate, for it is evident that even if the NN—or indeed any of the texts examined in this work—began as a 'private' effort, it very quickly became part of the standard corpus of legal texts that had indubitable 'official' status. Further, it was conceived as a collation of established law, in this case from the 'Rhodian law' and Justinian. Whether it actually contained Justinianic material, let alone 'Rhodian', is irrelevant; that was the way it was imagined and portrayed. Therefore, the chapters were already 'official', their authority unquestioned because they were thought unquestionable. Moreover, it does seem most probable that the articles of NN.3 were collected from Justinianic law concerning maritime affairs, as practised or transmitted in the eighth century. There is little that is private about a text composed from established law that became itself established. Furthermore, there is no indication that NN.3 was ever intended as an unofficial work—that is, one that was not used by lawyers or officials. It has nothing in it of academic interest, no distracting verbiage or extended analysis, historical, legal, or moral; in short, nothing that a non-practising lawyer, or someone not a party in a lawsuit, would find interesting or useful. Rather, NN.3 reads as a set of common legal scenarios, perhaps derived from actual cases, and the appropriate sentencing guidelines. It is aimed at an authority who could adjudicate the cases described, who was interested in correct legal procedure, and could inflict a degree of punishment; that is, it was a text designed for judges. Such a work could conceivably have been created by a lawyer or judge on his own volition, and then spread organically. Yet it did become an inherent part of the established corpus, so at the least it was tacitly approved by some central authority. However, given its popularity, links to the *Ecloga* and its appendices, and relative internal stability, the NN most plausibly was from its origins an 'official' work. That does not mean (although it does not preclude) initiation or even awareness by the emperor. Rather, the text drew sufficient authority from its collation of already legitimized ordinances, and from its publication and distribution as an adjunct to an imperially sanctioned text, by the central legal administration, for use by officially appointed judges.

If so, the NN reveals three aspects of the Isaurian world. Firstly, even in a text as apolitical and practically minded as the NN, Old

Testament language and thought crept in. For NN.3.5 echoes Exodus 21:18–19, which was included as NM.45, both linguistically and substantively.[119] Evidently, this was a society and a legal discourse indelibly imprinted in Scriptural ideas and rhetoric. Secondly, this same chapter's invocation that 'If sailors set to fighting, let them fight with words and let no man strike another' is indicative of NN.3's principal concern, the maintenance of law and order.[120] Crime and punishment, the peaceful resolution of disputes, and in particular the operation of delict law dominate the text. Finally, this was a legal discourse that continued to collect and represent, in a practical form, relevant law expressively legitimized by reference to past authority. In summary, the NN was continuing the work of the *Ecloga* and its appendices, but in a new format of a *nomos* dedicated to a specific subject.

[119] Ashburner, *Rhodian Sea-Law*, lxxxv, 84.
[120] Ashburner, *Rhodian Sea-Law*, 83; Greek at NN.3.5, 13.1–2.

5

The Associated Codes of the *Ecloga* II

The *Nomos Georgikos*

The farmer who is working his own field must be just . . .[1]
The soil, the basis of the economy, is also the base of the state.[2]

Perhaps no other legal document has received so much scholarly attention, and generated so much disagreement, as the *Nomos Georgikos* (NG) or *Farmer's Law*.[3] It has been described as an official work composed by Justinian II,[4] Leo III,[5] or Photius,[6] or a private document.[7] It has been variously dated from pre-Justinianic to the late ninth century. Its contents have been described as primarily Justinianic, pre-Justinianic, or customary.[8] Its provenance has been given as Southern Italy, the Balkans, Constantinople, or inner Anatolia.[9] Its

[1] NG.1; trans. Ashburner, 'The Farmer's Law II', 87.
[2] P. Lemerle, *The Agrarian History of Byzantium* (Galway, 1979), 1.
[3] For good introductions to the compendious historiography, see A. Kazhdan, 'Farmer's Law', in *ODB*, vol. 2, 778; J. Karayannopulos, 'Entstehung und Bedeutung des Nomos Georgikos', *BZ* 51 (1958), 357–73. For Russian historiography in particular, see the excellent Górecki, 'The Slavic theory in Russian pre-revolutionary historiography', and Górecki, 'The Slavic theory of the Byzantine rural community in Soviet and post-Soviet historiography'.
[4] G. Vernadsky, 'Sur les origines de la loi agraire byzantine', *Byzantion* 2 (1925), 169–80; Ostrogorsky, 'Reformtätigkeit der Isaurier'; and Ostrogorsky, *History of the Byzantine State*, 90–2, 135–7.
[5] Zacharia von Lingenthal, *Geschichte*, 249–57.
[6] Schminck, '*Nomos Rhodiōn Nautikos*'; and Schminck, 'Nomos Mosaikos'.
[7] F. Dölger, 'Ist der Nomos Georgikos ein Gesetz des Kaisers Justinians II?'; Lemerle, *Agrarian History*, 34–5.
[8] N. Svoronos, 'Notes sur l'Origine et la Date du code Rural', *Travaux et mémoires* 8 (1981), 487–500. Cf. L. Burgmann, 'Ist der Nomos Georgikos vorjustinianisch?', *Rechtshistorisches Journal* 1 (1982), 36–9.
[9] Haldon and Brubaker, *Sources*, 290; Kazhdan 'Famer's Law'.

inspiration has been described as Slavic custom, biblical precedent, or Hellenic or eastern precepts. It has been tied into far-reaching debates on the Byzantine economy and administration, particularly the rise of the Theme system, and the existence (or not) of collective property.[10] It has been subjected to multiple conflicting theories based more on contemporary intellectual debates than anything contained in the text, from nineteenth-century Russian debates between Slavophiles and Westernizers, to Marxist discussion on communal property and the rise/existence of feudalism.[11] Within this historiographical minefield, the detail of the text is frequently ignored, and the insights it offers into law, politics, and ideology downplayed. Debate has revolved around three interlocking questions: when was the NG produced? What was the character and origins of the law therein? And who produced it, or, more accurately, was it an official or private document?[12] Here we shall firstly sketch a brief historiographical outline of conflicting views on the subject. Then we shall explore the text to offer some conclusions about those questions, before considering questions of the text's intended purpose.

THE HISTORIOGRAPHY OF THE NG

Modern study of the NG began, along with most Graeco-Roman law, with Zacharia von Lingenthal. Having originally thought the NG to be a private work, his final, and most influential, pronouncement was that the NG was an official Isaurian production, enacted *c.*740, either with or closely following the *Ecloga*.[13] In it he saw the Isaurians

[10] See, inter alia, K. Setton, 'On the importance of land tenure and agrarian taxation in the Byzantine Empire, from the fourth century to the Fourth Crusade', *The American Journal of Philology* 74 (1953), 225–59; J. Teall, 'The Byzantine agricultural tradition', *DOP* 25 (1971), 33–59; A. Kazhdan, 'State, feudal, and private economy in Byzantium', *DOP* 47 (1993), 83–100. For dangers of overusing the NG to describe agrarian conditions in the period, see Whittow, *Making of Byzantium*, 115–17.

[11] See especially the work of Górecki, 'Slavic theory in Russian pre-revolutionary historiography' and 'Rural community in Soviet and post-Soviet historiography'.

[12] See Karayannopulos, 'Nomos Georgikos', 357.

[13] His first view was stated in K. Zacharia von Lingenthal, *Historiae Juris Graeco-Romani Delineatio* (Heidelberg, 1839), 32. For his final view, see K. Zacharia von Lingenthal, *Geschichte*, 249–57.

reforming Byzantine society through legislation, in this case either ushering in or solidifying a revolution in the countryside that had created a free peasantry out of the late-antique colonate.[14] Moreover, Zacharia von Lingenthal posited the Slav migrations from the sixth century onwards as the great factor in the transformation of the Byzantine agrarian economy, and it was in reaction to this that the NG was composed as primarily a collection of customary, Slavic law, aimed firstly at these new settlers in the empire, which then spread far and wide. These ideas filtered through to the western scholars, such as in the influential works of Bury,[15] and in the more cautious critical edition of Ashburner, who accepted the idea that the NG was an official Isaurian work, but downplayed any link with the *Ecloga*, emphasizing its continuities with Justinianic law.[16]

However, the more immediate and detailed response to Zacharia von Lingenthal's ideas came in Russia. As Danuta Górecki has vividly narrated, pioneering Russian scholars on the NG either were caught in an ideological mesh which sought to show the universality and antiquity of Slavic institutions (especially that of the collective village) as the bedrock of Russian society, or were violently reacting to such romantic and nationalist ideas.[17] Thus, while scholars like Uspenskii[18] and Pavlov[19] mainly nuanced Zacharia von Lingenthal's theories, Panchenko completely undermined them, and his study remains fundamental, if often unread due to linguistic barriers.[20] Panchenko denied that the *chōrion*, 'village', of the NG, or the actual Byzantine

[14] For discussion and literature on this debate, see works of Górecki, and Haldon, *Byzantium in the Seventh Century*, 132–41. For the colonate—a term of many potential meanings but often used to mean tied peasants—and its development in the legal sources of late antiquity, see B. Sirks, 'The colonate in Justinian's reign', *JRS* 98 (2008), 120–43.

[15] Bury, *Later Roman Empire*, 418–21.

[16] Ashburner, 'Farmer's Law II', 71–83.

[17] Górecki, 'Slavic theory in Russian pre-revolutionary historiography' and 'Rural community in Soviet and post-Soviet historiography'.

[18] F. Uspenskii, 'K' istoriikrest'ianskogo zemlevladeniia v Vizantii', *Zhurnal ministerstva narodnogoprosveshchenia* 225 (1883), 30–87. See Górecki, 'Rural community in Soviet and post-Soviet historiography', 344.

[19] A. Pavlov, 'Vizantiiskiia 'Knigi zakonnyia' v drevne-russkom perevode', *Sbornik Otdeleniia russkogo iazyka i slovesnosti Imperatorskoi akademii nauk* 38 (1885), 1–92. See Górecki, 'Rural community in Soviet and post-Soviet historiography', 344.

[20] B. Panchenko, *Krest'ianskaia sobstvennost' v Vizantii. Zemledel'cheskii zakon i monastyrskie dokumenty* (Sofia, 1903). See Górecki, 'Rural community in Soviet and post-Soviet historiography', 346–8.

world, was a unit either of collective ownership of the land or of collective production. Rather, he cogently argued that the NG presents a world of individual ownership and production, with the family household the vital unit of socio-economic organization.[21] Despite later misunderstanding, Panchenko did accept the existence of common land, to which members of the community had rights and which was administered by the collective group, although he was sceptical over the extent to which any universal institution existed that corresponded to the *hē tou chōriou koinotēs*, 'the commonality of the village', found in NG.81, classifying it as a 'juristic person'.[22] More importantly, Panchenko saw the overriding importance of the tax system, with the *chōrion* collectively responsible for the taxes of individual taxpayers, thus leading to the usufruct of abandoned land being given to neighbours in order to meet fiscal liabilities (NG.18).[23] For Panchenko, this was a continuation of the Roman world of private property, combined with an evolution in the reality of agricultural relations, which needed no Slav mass migration as a prompt.[24] Furthermore, Panchenko saw no official hand behind the NG, lacking as it does introduction, date, or division into thematic chapters.[25] Thus, for Panchenko, the NG was a private document of customary (but not Slavic) law, produced sometime in the seventh or eighth centuries.

Russian ideas reached western scholarship through Vernadsky, who adopted the Slavic theory but also posited Justinian II as the author.[26] Ostrogorsky, although rejecting the Slavic theory, accepted Justinian II's authorship, based on the presumption that the NG primarily contained new rather than old Justinianic law, and on the title given in Ashburner's edition: *nomos geōrgikos kat' eklogēn ek tōn Iustinianou bibliou*, 'the Farmer's Law selected from the book of Justinian'.[27] Ostrogorsky argued that the Justinian referred to could not be Justinian I, as the correct title would have had *books* of

[21] Górecki, 'Slavic theory in Russian pre-Revolutionary historiography', 91.

[22] Górecki, 'Rural community in Soviet and post-Soviet historiography', 346. For the Greek, see 206 n. 72.

[23] Górecki, 'Rural community in Soviet and post-Soviet historiography', 347.

[24] Górecki, 'Rural community in Soviet and post-Soviet historiography', 347.

[25] Górecki, 'Slavic theory in Russian pre-Revolutionary historiography', 91.

[26] Vernadsky, 'Sur les origins'.

[27] Ostrogorsky, 'Reformtätigkeit der Isaurier'; and Ostrogorsky, *History of the Byzantine State*, 90–2, 135–7. Ashburner, 'Farmer's Law I', 97.

Justinian. Moreover, he considered this agrarian reform the counterpart to Heraclius' foundation of the Theme system, which created two fundamental pillars of Byzantine society—the free peasant villages and the soldier-peasant—thereby ensuring the survival of the empire.[28]

Franz Dölger fundamentally disagreed, arguing (surely correctly) that the use of the name Justinian could only refer to Justinian I, who was celebrated as the imperial legislator par excellence.[29] Further, Dölger thought that the NG was composed of Justinianic material, and especially from the *Digest*, in particular D.9.2 on the *Lex Aquilia*.[30] To Dölger this is the book referred to in the title, but the NG, instead of restating the principles (which in any case were exceedingly complex in the original), set forth multiple cases which realized and embellished those principles.[31] Differences naturally occurred due to the evolution of practice on the ground, combined with the fact that the compilers of the NG were not using the Latin original of the *Digest* or other Justinianic works, but the various Greek commentaries which had become the real, living law instead of the original.[32] These, through processes of simplification, truncation, provision of examples, and multiple juristic views had naturally evolved from the original, and, when combined with the inevitable evolution of legal practice on the ground, created the apparent differences between the NG and Justinianic legislation.[33] Further, Dölger denied any official authorship, arguing that the NG was too repetitious and unsystematic for an official work, and that it mentioned no emperor apart from the clearly historical and almost mythical Justinian.[34] For Dölger, then, the NG was a private work created by provincial judges, from Justinianic law as it existed between his dates of the last quarter of the seventh century and the reigns of Leo III and Constantine V.[35]

Paul Lemerle agreed that the NG referred to Justinian I, but found Dölger's links between the *Corpus* and NG unpersuasive.[36] Instead he

[28] Ostrogorsky, *History of the Byzantine State*, 95–8.
[29] Dölger, 'Ist der Nomos Georgikos ein Gesetz des Kaisers Justinians II?', esp. 31.
[30] Dölger, 'Ist der Nomos Georgikos ein Gesetz des Kaisers Justinians II?', 35–8.
[31] Dölger, 'Ist der Nomos Georgikos ein Gesetz des Kaisers Justinians II?', 39.
[32] Dölger, 'Ist der Nomos Georgikos ein Gesetz des Kaisers Justinians II?', 39.
[33] Dölger, 'Ist der Nomos Georgikos ein Gesetz des Kaisers Justinians II?', 39.
[34] Dölger, 'Ist der Nomos Georgikos ein Gesetz des Kaisers Justinians II?', 45–8.
[35] Dölger, 'Ist der Nomos Georgikos ein Gesetz des Kaisers Justinians II?', 47–8.
[36] Lemerle, *Agrarian History*, 34.

thought the NG was a private compilation of customary and practical law, 'an aide-mémoire of rural administration, a practical guide for the benefit of the country judge'.[37] Moreover, he saw even less organization to the NG than Dölger, commenting, 'There is then untidiness and repetition, but no contradiction.'[38] Lemerle further brought forth the salience of the tax system underpinning the NG, which, although clearly not a document for tax inspectors, did demonstrate that the fundamental concern of the state vis-à-vis farmers was the maintenance of tax revenues, with the *chōrion* foremost a fiscal unit, and, flowing from that, an administrative and juridical unit.[39]

Subsequent debate has focused on attempts to redate the NG from the broad *communis opinio* of the seventh or eighth centuries, and whether such a difficult legal document can be safely used to study actual agrarian conditions. Svoronos tried unconvincingly to position the NG as a pre-Justinianic text, arguing that it bears similarity to laws in the Theodosian Code.[40] Moreover, he demonstrated the marked degree of biblical influence on the phraseology of the NG, linking it to the NM.[41] Yet Burgmann has shown that the NG is closer to Justinianic law, and that the link with the NM, which the Burgmann and Troianos edition dated to the late eighth or ninth centuries, was evidence of the NG's post-Justinianic nature.[42] The modern Russian critical edition of the NG by Medvedev et al. agreed that it was primarily Justinianic law, composed sometime between 533 and 572, although possibly it received official recognition at the time of the *Ecloga*.[43] However, Schminck adapted Svoronos's ideas, although he placed the NG in the opposite direction, as an initiative of Photius in 867, positing a direct link with the NM, which Schminck also believes was a Photian text.[44] As noted already, Burgmann has criticized Schminck's—and wider scholarship's—uncritical assumption of the contemporaneity of the NG, NS, and NN, pointing out the linguistic, format, and manuscript differences between the texts, seeing all as private works, emanating sometime between the seventh

[37] Lemerle, *Agrarian History*, 36. [38] Lemerle, *Agrarian History*, 36.
[39] Lemerle, *Agrarian History*, 65.
[40] Svoronos, 'Notes sur l'Origine et la Date du code Rural'.
[41] Svoronos, 'Notes sur l'Origine et la Date du code Rural', 493–4.
[42] L. Burgmann, 'Ist der Nomos Georgikos vorjustinianisch?'
[43] Medvedev et al., *Vizantiĭskiĭ zemledel'cheskiĭ zakon*, 138–41.
[44] Schminck, 'Nomos Mosaikos'.

century and the Macedonian reforms of the later ninth, and eventually brought into a wider appendix to the *Ecloga*.[45]

THE MANUSCRIPTS OF THE NG

One reason for this glut of opinions is the common realization that the NG is self-evidently informative and important, combined with the almost complete absence of other textual information on the contemporary Byzantine countryside.[46] Indeed, if numbers of manuscripts can measure significance, the NG was perhaps the most important legal text ever produced in Byzantium, appearing in some 106 MSS in the *RHBR*, from the eleventh to the sixteenth centuries.[47] It is found exceedingly frequently in conjunction with the great official legal handbooks of the eighth and ninth centuries, the *Ecloga* and *Prochiron*, and their derivatives. Later it became part of the important tenth- and eleventh-century works the *Epitome Legum* and *Ecloga ad Prochiron mutata*.[48] In the fourteenth century, it was revised by Constantine Harmenopoulos and attached to his *Hexabiblos*, under which the Greek population of the Ottoman Empire would be ruled for centuries after the fall of Byzantium.[49] The NG was also translated into Slavic languages, becoming a major influence on Slavic, and in particular Russian, law.[50]

The manuscript tradition allows several interesting observations on the NG, beyond its obvious popularity. Firstly, its ubiquity is testament to the importance accredited to the NG. There is little in it of literary or prima facie ideological merit, so its popularity is testament to its utility and applicability. Whether originally a private

45 Burgmann, 'Die nomoi'. 46 Lemerle, *Agrarian History*, 27.

47 Appendix, Table 14 lists only those manuscripts containing the NG not with the Hexabiblos.

48 *Epitome*, ed. K. Zacharia von Lingenthal, *IGR* II, 277–431, and VII, 1–199 = Zepos, *IGR* IV, 276–585; see A. Schminck, 'Epitome Legum', in *ODB*, vol. 1, 724.

49 For the relationship between the NG and *Hexabiblos*, see J. de Malafosse, 'Les lois agraires à l'époque byzantine; tradition et exégèse', *Recueil de l'Académie de Législation* 19 (1949), 1–75. Cf. F. Dölger, *Harmenopulos und der Nomos Georgikos* (Thessalonica, 1951).

50 Kazhdan, 'Farmer's Law'; Burgmann, 'Law in Slavic countries, Byzantine'; Obolensky, *Byzantine Commonwealth*, 317–21.

or a public initiative, it clearly obtained the status of authoritative and legitimate law. This reflected its contents, which can be seen as Justinianic, customary, or an amalgam, but which were self-evidently accepted as the actual law of the land, and also tells us that this selection became accepted as the de facto official anthology of law concerning farmers.

This impression is reinforced by the fact that the NG became associated as a kind of appendix to those Byzantine handbooks produced in the eighth and ninth centuries. Indeed, of the 59 MSS listed in the *RHBR* that are not part of the *Hexabiblos*, the NG is associated with a legal handbook in 54.[51] Further, the oldest incontestably dated text with which the NG is associated is the *Ecloga*, featuring in 11 MSS with it, nine times closely—a significant if not overwhelming relationship.[52] The figures are similar for the more voluminous *Prochiron*, which shares 16 MSS significantly.[53] Their derivatives demonstrate an even closer association. Collectively, these codes highly imply a relationship between the NG and indubitably official texts, a relationship which, if anything, was considered closer as time progressed. Further, the NG is hardly ever found alone with any of these central texts, but either with the AE, or above all with the NS (34 MSS) and NN (40 MSS).[54] Like the NN, this relationship is closest with the tenth-century *Eisagoge Aucta*, which clearly was issued with a deliberate appendix of *Rhopai*-NS-NG-NN, suggesting that the private jurists of the tenth century thought there was a binding relationship between the codes and that this grouping somehow represented a corpus of law.[55] However, there is an indubitable, although less fixed, relationship with the *Ecloga*, but only faintly with it and the AE, where the NG is always found on the periphery.[56] Given this, it would seem that the most plausible (though admittedly not concrete) reconstruction from the manuscript evidence would posit the NG sometime around the production of the *Ecloga*, although unlike the NS, not as a direct part of the AE but a separate document which became associated with the *Ecloga*.

[51] See Appendix, Table 14.
[52] See Appendix, Tables 9 and 14.
[53] See Appendix, Table 14.
[54] See Appendix, Tables 11, 13, and 14.
[55] See Chapter 5, 188.
[56] Only three MSS, *RHBR*.25, 197, and 327, contain the *Ecloga* and AE.

THE ARRANGEMENT AND CONTENTS OF THE NG

The contents of the oldest recension of the NG we possess, as constructed by Ashburner and confirmed by Medvedev, consist of 85 chapters under a title that varies in specifics but which is most commonly 'the farmer's law taken from a selection of the book(s) of Justinian'.[57] Only one manuscript, *RHBR.*327, has a *pinax.* One subheading occurs in some manuscripts, including some of the oldest, where before NG.23 there is written *peri agelariōn*, 'concerning herdsmen'.[58] The arrangement of the chapters is by the now familiar principle of association, adhering to the schema laid out below:[59]

1–22: Issues of land ownership and general cultivation:
    1–2: Respect of property rights
    3–5: Exchange of land
    6–8: Controversies over ownership
    9–10: Tenancy by *mortē* contract
    11–17: Subletting land
    18–19: Taxation and right of neighbours to usufruct of uncultivated land
    20–1: Disputes over land use
    22: Theft of agricultural implements
23–9: Concerning herdsmen
30: Theft of cattle bells
31–3: Trees:
    31–2: Delicts concerning trees
    33: Theft of fruit
34–35: Theft of sheep's milk or fodder
36–55: Delict or theft concerning cattle:
    36–37: Hiring of oxen
    38–40: Destruction of another's cattle
    41–42: Stealing oxen
    43: Accidental destruction of another's cattle
    44–5: Destruction of stray cattle in woods
    45–7: Unlawful dealings of slaves with cattle
    48–53: Trespass of cattle
    54–5: Deliberate destruction of animals
56–66: Destruction of non-animal property:
    56–8: Fire

57 See Chapter 5, 170.
58 NG, ed. Medvedev, 105.
59 Cf. Ashburner, 'Farmer's Law II', 69–70.

- 59–61: Stealing of crops
- 62–3: Destruction of implements
- 64–6: Destruction of buildings

67: Lending at interest and land
68–70: Stealing and injustice:

- 68–9: Stealing from storage
- 70: Unjust measures

71–7: Delicts concerning animals
78–9: Disputes over early harvest
80–4: Disputes over land, especially over mills
85: Delict concerning damage to trespassing cattle

The first point to note is the reasonable level of organization. Generally, similar cases are grouped together, moving from disputes arising from ownership and rights to usufruct of land, to disputes about animals, primarily cattle, and then non-animal property. The organizational principle may not be thematic—i.e. arrangement by legal ideas—but then the NG was not designed to catalogue legal principles. Nor was it meant to create new legislation or a general law. Rather, it was a collection of established law, and in particular those delicts, negligent or intentional acts giving rise to claims by one person on another even without a contract, which most commonly occurred in village life.[60] The NG, therefore, adopts the most utilitarian arrangement for its purpose, an association of similar cases.

This associative principle helps to explain some prima facie peculiar placements. For instance, NG.22 concerning the theft of agricultural implements is not found under a general category of theft, but after a collection of issues concerning ownership and use of land. Similarly, NG.30 concerns the theft of cattle bells after a list of delicts concerning cattle and herdsmen, and NG.33, dealing with theft of fruit, is positioned after issues concerning trees. Moreover, this associative principle is frequently used in moments of transition between general topics. Thus, NG.33 leads to discussion of stealing of sheep's milk and fodder as a prelude to the long section, NG.35–55, on animals. Most chapters flow naturally on from the previous. The clarity of organization declines after NG.70, and this section indeed contains the most repetitious chapters.[61] However, the general

[60] For brief introduction, see L. Burgmann, 'Delict', in *ODB*, vol. 1, 601. The seminal survey is R. Zimmerman, *The Law of Obligations* (Oxford, 1990).

[61] Lemerle, *Agrarian History*, 30, 35; cf. Ashburner, 'Farmer's Law II', 70.

associative principle still holds. Moreover, if we compare this to the NS and NN.3, there is a similar organization by association and a collection of articles at the end, of less organized and more repetitious nature. This might be explained by later recensions adding extraneous material to the end of the text rather than interpolating it, or editors compiling from multiple sources and placing long extracts next to each other rather than combining them to make one text, or a mixture of both.[62] However, the desire for greater and more systematic order seems more a wish of modern scholars than these text's contemporaries, for considering the huge popularity of the NG, NS, and NN, they must have been found to be useful. Indeed, when combined with their comparative brevity and simple language, this principle of arrangement by association makes it relatively easy to discover the appropriate rules or punishments for specific cases, which must have increased these texts' utility to their users.

This utilitarian work had a dominant concern: the property relations between villagers and in particular the *geōrgoi*.[63] In the NG, this term has no specific, technical meaning, and is employed to cover a range of occupations and status.[64] For instance, NG.1, 18, and 19 all referred to a *geōrgos* cultivating *idion agron*, 'his own land', and one can reasonably presume that small peasant freeholders comprised the largest section, both numerically and in terms of percentage of land held, of Byzantine agriculture in the seventh and eighth centuries.[65] However, the term *geōrgos* was also used when farmers were cultivating another's fields, whether on the *mortē* or *hēmiseia* contracts examined below, and was also differentiated from the *kurios tou agrou*, normally translated as landowner but who Sarris convincingly argues could signify someone who possessed a usufruct of the land.[66] Thus, there is little in the NG to suggest that there were no large estates or significant numbers of tenant farmers, or, as in cases in late antiquity, whole villages that were owned by one landlord.[67]

[62] Ashburner, 'Farmer's Law II', 70.

[63] See J. Howard-Johnston, 'Social change in early medieval Byzantium', in R. Evans (ed.), *Lordship and Learning* (Woodbridge, 2004), 39–50, esp. 44.

[64] Howard-Johnston, 'Social change in early medieval Byzantium', 47.

[65] Howard-Johnston, 'Social change in early medieval Byzantium', 47–50.

[66] NG.2, 15, 16, 17, 20, 21. See P. Sarris, 'Economics, trade, and "feudalism"', in L. James (ed.) *A Companion to Byzantium* (Chichester, 2010), 25–42, esp. 28–9. Cf. Howard-Johnston, 'Social change in early medieval Byzantium', 48.

[67] For the continuing existence of great estates in this period, see Lemerle, *Agrarian History*, 51–8. For their growth and organization in late antiquity, and increasing domination over villages, see Sarris, *Economy and Society*, esp. 177–99.

Further, a whole range of agricultural professions are found in the NG, from herdsmen and shepherds, to tenders of trees and slaves.[68] What is presented is not an idealized collective, but a diversified and sophisticated agricultural community of rich and poor farmers, tenants, and landowners, a specialized and divided labour force of wage-earning proletariat, slaves, and family production, within a variegated landscape of both common land and private property.[69] Moreover, a range of potential outsiders are mentioned, from the *chōrodotēs*, 'the grantor of land',[70] to the judges who enforced and adjudicated at least some of the cases listed, the *akroatai*.[71] Further, one case (NG.7) concerns disputes between *chōria*, while others concern the infringement upon common land, with NG.81 contrasting the individual who built a mill on common land with the *hē tou chōriou koinotēs*, 'the commonalty of the village'.[72] What is interesting, however, is how infrequently the *chōrion* appears, and then chiefly as the administrative, fiscal, or judicial setting for a case.[73] This is no law for *chōria*; the overwhelming focus is on individuals. The only appearance of the village collective is surely, as Panchenko argued, the commonalty appearing as a judicial personage, a litigant in a case. There is no internal evidence in the NG as to whether this was a defined institution, or merely an ad hoc collection. The vast majority of cases concern delicts against private property, with individuals both the transgressors and the transgressed. The NG was not, therefore, designed for some sharply delimited section of Byzantine society, but covered those frequent disputes and legal questions that occurred at the village level, concerning a range of actors and situations, although primarily between individuals within the *chōrion*.

The legal topics covered by the NG fall into three broad groupings: land law and contract; delict law concerning damage to property and persons; and criminal law. These generally follow the principle of

[68] E.g. NG.23–9, 33, 34, 45–7.

[69] For good descriptions of the world painted by the NG, see Lemerle, *Agrarian History*, 36–58; Haldon, *Seventh Century*, 132–41.

[70] NG.9–10.

[71] NG.7, 37, 67.

[72] NG.81, ed. Ashburner, 108. In Medvedev's edition, 126, the phrase is rendered *hoi tou chōriou koinē*, 'the men of the common weal of the village', which is very similar to Ashburner, yet since Medvedev et al.'s own critical apparatus cites more than four times as many manuscripts supporting the Ashburner reading than their own, I see no reason to abandon the traditional phrase.

[73] For the juridical character of the *chōrion*, see Haldon, *Seventh Century*, 137–9.

association laid out above, so that all cases of land law and contract are found in NG.1–21, except for NG.67, concerning lending at interest. This is less of an anomaly on closer inspection, for the Isaurians were clearly wary of interest, not mentioning it in the *Ecloga* and including biblical censures against it in the NM.[74] Therefore, placing loans between sections on destruction and theft of property, leading to the biblical attack on unjust measures in NG.70, was a stark ideological point. Delicts and crimes are mixed and arranged by subject, with some 40 chapters on delicts and 23 on crimes. Moreover, considering that the delicts are all about damage to property, and that the crimes listed are principally theft and arson, it is plain that the overriding interest of the NG is in property. Indeed, every single article is concerned with it in some form. In all this, as multiple scholars have noted, the NG closely resembles the 'barbarian' law codes of the early medieval west. This does not imply any causative relationship, however, simply that the norms and conditions of village life were similar.[75] Indeed, the sorts of cases catalogued in the NG would remain consistent and recurrent in agricultural life well into the modern era, and are to a reasonable degree applicable across time and space, which is one reason for the NG's popularity.

ROMAN LAW, THE NG, AND THE *ECLOGA*

However, although issues of property would indubitably have provided the great bulk of disputes in agricultural societies, the NG as it stands is not a comprehensive legal code. Not only does it not cover several pertinent issues that would have occurred, but it does not cover all the subjects touched upon by its sources pertaining to the land and cultivators, whether from the Justinianic *Corpus* or what we

[74] E.10; NM.11. See A. Laiou, 'A note on the Farmer's Law, chapter 67', *Byzantion* 41 (1971), 197–204.

[75] Ashburner, 'Farmer's Law II', 87 neatly summarizes as follows: 'The same circumstances occurring in different ages raise the same difficulties and are met by the same solutions. Pigs have always trespassed and will always trespass in search of acorns. There is no more delicate problem for legislators or jurists than to adjust the equities between owner of pig and owner of acorns. Because in different laws these problems are resolved on a similar principle, that is no evidence that one law is borrowed from the other or that both have a common origin.'

know from the *Ecloga* to have been the law in 741.[76] For instance, Lemerle expressed surprise that there is no mention in the NG of the removal of boundary stones, a recurrent agricultural problem.[77] There is no mention of crimes not concerning property, such as homicide or rape, apart from NG.28 including the penalty for perjury. Contract law is barely scratched. More advanced types of lease are not mentioned, even though E.12 documented *emphyteusis*, which seems to have been a common form of tenure in the eighth century, in particular associated with Church land.[78] Even well-explored issues such as theft have strange absences; for there is no injunction against theft per se, or a specific case of theft of something non-agricultural or domestic in nature. Similarly, there is mention of fights among dogs but not humans.[79]

No law is a vacuum. It requires legal structures, ideas, and normally other legislation to be enforced and understood. Standing alone, the NG does not make sense. Nor, indeed, was the NG isolated. It declares itself a selection of Justinianic law, thereby drawing its authority from it. Further, as we have seen, it shares many manuscripts and features with the NS and NN, which also declare their fundamental reliance on an original authority. However, these similarly lack the fundamental framework of law and jurisprudence to work in reality. That is why these codes are nearly always paired in the manuscripts with at least one central, underpinning law code, beginning with the *Ecloga*. Moreover, as we have explored, the NS and NN are both consistent with the legal and ideological world of the *Ecloga* and the broader policies and beliefs of the Isaurians. The NG has a similarly close correspondence, noted since Zacharia von Lingenthal, and debated since Ashburner.[80] To begin with Lemerle's observation, a truly independent text on agrarian relations would surely have had some regulation concerning boundary markers. However, the NG did not need one, for AE.II.1–5 had recited Justinianic law on the subject.[81] This would imply either that the NG was produced

[76] Cf. Howard-Johnston, 'Social change in early medieval Byzantium', 48–9.

[77] Lemerle, *Agrarian History*, 36 n. 2.

[78] Haldon, *Seventh Century*, 134; A. Cappel, 'Emphyteusis', in *ODB*, vol. 1, 693–4.

[79] NG.76–7.

[80] Zacharia von Lingenthal, *Geschichte*, 250. Cf. Ashburner, 'Farmer's Law II', 71–6.

[81] Indeed, six out of the eight manuscripts with a significant link between the NG and AE contain AE.II. See Appendix, Table 14.

contemporaneously or soon after AE.II—which we saw was in all likelihood published soon after the *Ecloga*—or that the Justinianic law contained therein was already so widely known beforehand that the authors of the NG did not feel the requirement to include it.[82]

A second example of this dovetailing of topics between the *Ecloga* and NG, rather than repetition or overlap of general interest, concerns cattle-stealing, *apelasia*.[83] This had a very precise definition in Roman law, given at D.47.14, where the theft of a single ox was treated as ordinary theft, while repeated or mass theft was classed as cattle-rustling, and punished capitally. In E.17.13, *apelasia* is punished for a first offence by a flogging, for a second offence, banishment, for a third, hand amputation, and for each offence the culprit had to make restitution to the owner. Thus, the *Ecloga* was here fulfilling its aim of making the law more humane by downgrading capital punishment.[84] Prima facie, as Ashburner argued, the NG is closer to the Justinianic law than the *Ecloga*, but on closer inspection the differences disappear.[85] NG.41 recognized the theft of a single ox or ass as simple theft, punished with whipping and replacement of twice the value. NG.42 stipulated that anyone trying to steal an ox from the herd—i.e. attempting a simple theft—who ended up putting the whole herd to flight, which was consequently lost, should be blinded. This is not, nor is called, *apelasia*, but rather an aggravated class of theft, and so punished more harshly.[86] Strictly, the only mention of *apelasia* in the NG is in NG.46–7 concerning slaves cattle-rustling, with a stipulated punishment of hanging. Moreover, these are aggravated forms of *apelasia*, as in NG.46 the slave, while attempting to cattle-rustle, drives the entire herd to destruction, and in NG.47 the slave is repeatedly cattle-rustling, and also is interested in the liability of the master to replace the lost cattle. Under strict Roman law any cattle-rustler, slave, or freeman after one offence would have been punished capitally. Here, only slaves who commit *apelasia* regularly or who cause additional damage are hanged. Indeed, what is striking is that the general rule on *apelasia* is not

[82] See Chapter 3, 138–52.

[83] For *apelasia* see Troianos, *Poinalios*, 26–9. The Latin equivalent is *abigeatus*.

[84] See Chapter 2, 124.

[85] Ashburner, 'Farmer's Law II', 76.

[86] Ashburner in his commentary, 'Farmer's Law II', 76, refers to *apelasia*, even when *apelastheisa* is the word used in his edition, 'Farmer's Law I', 103, and in Medvedev's, NG.42, 112, and in Ashburner's translation, he correctly translates it not as cattle-rustling but as 'put to flight', 'Farmer's Law II', 91.

given in the NG. Therefore the NG is not only compatible with E.17.13, but severely incomplete without it. Moreover, the NG significantly nuances E.17.13 by giving concrete cases establishing the difference between simple theft and cattle-stealing (NG.41), the problem of simple theft causing additional destruction (NG.42), and the cases of slaves cattle-rustling regularly (NG.46–47)—precisely the sort of real-life rural problems that the principle in the *Ecloga* did not cover. Cumulatively, these form a neat unit which followed a principle of Roman law and shared a common concern with it, but whose punishment had been significantly changed to limit the extent of capital punishment.

A further correspondence is in the respect for due process. Roman law had attempted to establish the principle that correct, legal proceedings were the legitimate and lawful way to settle disputes. Therefore, if anyone forcibly seized property before a judicial decision was made, even if he had a just claim, he lost any title to the land; if his original claim was baseless, he had to pay the equivalent value of the land as well, i.e. he was treated as a thief.[87] E.17.5, from this, extolled the general principle that anyone who had any dispute with another person, and did not appeal to the magistrate but forcibly seized the disputed object, lost both the object and his just claim; if his claim were baseless he was flogged as well, again given the standard punishment for theft in the *Ecloga*, forced to make restitution, and censured for becoming an outlaw. The NG does not state this key principle, but several articles impinge upon it. Most obviously, NG.6 says that if a farmer, who has a claim on a field, reaps against the sower's will, he forfeits the crop, while if his claim were baseless, and so in effect he was stealing, he must hand over twice the amount harvested. The difference between the *Ecloga* and NG is only one of punishment: flogging and simple restitution in the former, and twofold restitution in the latter. Both punishments regularly appear throughout both codes, and in Justinianic law. Indeed, originally corporal punishment had been an option instead of twofold restitution, and clearly was largely at the discretion of the magistrate. Here we can see the preference for the easier punishment, although it is based on the same concerns and principles, most probably as it was a more suitable punishment for a question of seizure of produce during

[87] C.8.4.7, 11.

a dispute of ownership, rather than seizure of the land itself. When someone in a dispute caused deliberate damage to the property in question, as in NG.66 and 80, which person is conspicuously described as *anarchos*, 'lawless',[88] like E.17.5's *ekdikos*, 'outlaw', the punishment was amputation of the hand.[89] There is here no contradiction, for the NG was documenting more serious cases of flouting judicial process than imagined in E.17.5, for which suitably harsher punishment was invoked. Moreover, the difference between E.17.5 and NG.6 is that between a general and a specific prescription, with the specific qualifying and not repudiating the general. Further, it is clear that in this case both the *Ecloga* and NG were maintaining essentially unaltered Justinianic law.

A more significant shift occurred in a related principle of Roman law, that of *superficies solo cedit*, that anything constructed on the land is the property of the owner of the land.[90] This is followed in NG.1–2, where those who sow or plough another's lands cannot gain from them. In NG.21, however, if a farmer builds a house or plants a vineyard on another's land, the owner cannot simply pull down the house, but must accept an equivalent in land. Only if this is not forthcoming can they legally remove the house or vines. NG.66 expands this by saying that anyone who dared to pull down another's building or fence without legal consent would lose their hand. Further, NG.31 stated that if a tree overhung another's garden, the owner of the garden could trim it, following D.43.27.[91] However, NG.31 limits this only to cases of overshadowing gardens, i.e. when inhibiting the productivity of the patch, whereas the original Roman conception had no restrictions. Finally, NG.81 states that if someone living in the district built a mill on common land and the other villagers complained, they could appropriate the mill, but only if they paid the costs of construction and shared the usufruct with the builder, when under Roman law they could simply appropriate or dismantle the building. NG.82, however, stipulates that if the builder built on his own land, the other villagers had no say whatsoever. Clearly, the NG was not abrogating this central principle, any more than it rejected private property, for NG.1–2 did follow it. The rationale behind the modifications is purely utilitarian, permitting the infringement of private property only when it interfered with the

[88] NG.66, 80; Medvedev, 120, 126. [89] E.17.5.788.
[90] D.43.17.3.7; I.2.1.30. [91] NG.31.

rights of neighbours, and trying to protect profitable investment. A tree was a useful source of income, which could only be pruned if it impinged on the productivity of a specific, high-yield investment. Here the NG conspicuously protected the (probably considerable) outlay by an individual while balancing the legal claims of the community. The pragmatic result chimes with the greater picture portrayed by the NG of a sophisticated agrarian world, and specific legal protections on investment in order to increase its utility, and ultimately the tax yield. In all this, there is no overlap with the *Ecloga*, for it did not greatly consider property ownership. However, in no way are the precepts or regulations of the *Ecloga* contradictory to these articles, and again one could say that the NG was expounding upon an area unexplored by the *Ecloga*, and, therefore, considering its obvious importance, in need of exploration.

Moving to tenure law, the *Ecloga* set forth two different kinds, *emphyteusis* and simple leases limited to a maximum of 29 years.[92] Both go into considerable detail into who could and could not engage in these different forms, especially circumscribing state officials and soldiers from contracts of *emphyteusis*, and the variant rights of tenants. E.13 describes imperial and religious lands being leased, including mention of villages (*chōrion*) and fields (*agros*).[93] Evidently, these kinds of contract existed and were being regularly used in the eighth century, and external evidence proves the contemporary existence of estates and landlords.[94] Yet there is no mention of these forms of tenure in the NG. Instead there is a form of subletting between neighbours, where one farmer worked the land, usually of an *aporēsas geōrgos*, 'a poor farmer',[95] with produce being split equally, *hēmiseia* (NG.12–15).[96] NG.9–10 describes a form of rent that plausibly could have been paid to an external landowner, the *chōrodotēs*, by the cultivator, *mortitēs*.[97] These set down that the share should be nine-tenths to the *mortitēs*, which probably meant that the *mortitēs* bore

[92] Respectively E.12 and 13.

[93] E.13.1.628. Here *chōrion* could refer to estates rather than villages. Both terms are also found in E.17.41.900 concerning arson, where *chōrion* is very probably referring to villages.

[94] Lemerle, *Agrarian History*, 52–8.

[95] NG.11, 13, 14, ed. Medvedev, 100–2. The phrase could also mean a farmer without the means to cultivate, which could imply absolute poverty, temporary inability, or choice.

[96] Lemerle, *Agrarian History*, 38–9.

[97] Lemerle, *Agrarian History*, 38.

other liabilities, in particular the tax burden for the land.[98] To ensure correct apportionment, the *mortitēs* could not reap without the *chōrodotēs*' assent, on risk of forfeiture of the entire crop.[99] Interestingly, the only penalty for a different division of produce was divine censure: 'he who divides outside these limits is accursed.'[100] Evidently the *mortitēs* had little legal recourse if the *chōrodotēs* charged more rent.[101] Thus the legislator, although reserving the polemic for the greedy landlord, only legally punished the fraudulent tenant.

Such articles are in no way incompatible with the contracts of the *Ecloga*. Indeed, as those contracts do not stipulate levels of rent, the contract of *mortē* could be seen as expanding upon the *Ecloga* with a customary arrangement. Moreover, in contrast to the relatively well fleshed-out *hēmiseia* contract, that of *mortē* assumes the legal requirements were already known. Surely, then, this is a regulation on the payment and level of rent levied within established Roman contract law. Otherwise, the *Ecloga* would be detailing contracts of no relevance, or the NG did not have jurisdiction over contracts of *emphyteusis* or leases, when there is no reason why it should not. Similarly, nowhere in the NG is there mention of a right of sale. Yet it is clear that the land was private property, coexisting with unallocated common land.[102] The right and existence of land sale and purchase must have existed, but if one were to draw an agricultural world solely from the NG, it is not present, despite proprietors being able to do practically anything else with it as long as they did not infringe on the rights of their neighbours and paid their taxes. The answer to this quandary is, of course, that the NG did not operate in a legal vacuum, but was part of Roman jurisprudence, and so did not need to stipulate general contract law here, for it had already been laid down.

Concerning delict law, Dölger demonstrated that the NG is in many respects an elaboration through concrete case-law of the *Lex Aquilia* as contained in D.9.2, which also underpins several chapters in the *Ecloga*.[103] Indeed, neither the *Ecloga* nor the NG specifies this key principle, and so both are reliant on previous jurisprudence, which both declare in their titles was the law of Justinian. Further,

[98] Lemerle, *Agrarian History*, 38. Cf. Ashburner, 'Farmer's Law II', 83.
[99] NG.9. [100] NG.10; trans. Ashburner, 'Farmer's Law II', 88.
[101] Lemerle, *Agrarian History*, 38.
[102] Górecki, 'Slavic theory in Russian pre-revolutionary historiography', 91.
[103] Dölger, 'Ist der Nomos Georgikos ein Gesetz des Kaisers Justinians II?', 35–8.

both apply the principle predominantly to one class of case: damage to or caused by animals. E.17.7 states that anyone who hires a horse and sends it beyond the stipulated distance is liable to indemnify the owner for injury or death, restipulating D.13.6.5.7 and the general principle of D.47.2.40, 77, that something taken beyond the terms of contract is deemed theft. These ideas are found in NG.37 where a man hires an ox and it dies: if it died in the agreed work he has no liability, but if it died while doing non-agreed work he must give the value of the ox. Apart from horses becoming oxen, this is the same law based on the same Justinianic ordinance. E.17.8 declares that if anyone impounds another's cattle and they die, he must make two-fold restitution. Again this is almost a verbatim translation of C.3.35.5. NG.54 follows the principle precisely, but replaces cattle with a pig or a dog. E.17.9, which is a simple translation of D.9.1.11, states that if rams or bulls fight one another and the aggressor is killed, there is no case; however, if the other is killed, the owner of the dead beast can be indemnified either by being given the murdering beast, a noxal exchange, or paid the value of his lost animal.[104] In the NG, the only fights between animals mentioned are those between dogs. NG.76 ordains that if two dogs are fighting, and the master of one should kill or maim the other's dog by striking him with a sword, stick, or stone, he must pay the dog's value.[105] There is here no direct parallel in Roman law, but NG.76 is hardly incompatible with it. NG.77 states that a man who deliberately aggravated his dog to attack others, resulting in one being maimed or killed, must make restoration and receive 12 lashes, which follows the principle (if not the punishment) of D.9.2.11.5. Interestingly, as Ashburner highlighted, despite these and other frequent cases of animal damage and damage caused by slaves in the NG, there is no mention of noxal actions, which the *Ecloga* allows.[106] However, this is a sleight of hand, for NG.76–77 only mention reparation, but do not require it in monetary form. Moreover, the damage done in NG.76 was done by the man solely, and in NG.77 it was the direct result of the man's actions, so a

[104] Cf. D.9.1.4. See L. Burgmann, 'Noxal actions', in *ODB*, vol. 3, 1500.

[105] Medvedev's edition, 125, does not mention a further penalty of 12 lashes as Ashburner's does, despite being a frequent addition in many manuscripts, although most do not stipulate a number, some 12, and one states 100.

[106] E.17.9 and 12. See Ashburner, 'Farmer's Law II', 76.

noxal exchange—that is, the bodily handover of the culprit, animal, or slave—was not appropriate.

The important point is not that the *Ecloga* and the NG share a common interest in legal questions concerning animals, for as we have seen, these chiefly have a source in their shared Justinianic inheritance. Indeed, the *Corpus* is replete with legislation on animals, as is that other common repository of ideas, the Bible, as seen vividly in several sections of the NM.[107] Considering that in pre-modern economies, with overwhelmingly rural societies, animals were a prime constituent in agriculture, industry, and travel, none of this is surprising. The striking thing is not that the *Ecloga* and NG repeat the same detailed regulations, but that they do not. For instance, why does the NG not deal with rams or bulls fighting each other without any human interference? It is absurd to presume that this most common of disputes did not happen in the world of the NG—or are we to presume that in the idealized world of the village commune imagined by some scholars, dogs were somehow more vicious than the cattle that abound in the text? Did village life exist without the hiring of horses? Perhaps. Without the impounding of cattle? Surely not. If one only had the NG, cattle would wander fields regularly causing damage, but only pigs and sheep would be impounded by aggrieved farmers. Once more, the NG and *Ecloga* not only perfectly coincide, but without the latter, the former is incomplete to the point of incredulity.

Furthermore, the NG never repeats the legislation of the *Ecloga*, but builds upon it. The NG only comes close to repeating the *Ecloga* twice, with NG.56–57 on arson exceedingly close to E.17.40–41. E.17.40 states that anyone who burnt another's forest or cut down their trees *out of that* forest was liable to double restitution, thus restating C.3.35.1.[108] NG.57 expands this by declaring that anyone who burnt another's hillside or cut down *any* tree belonging to another was liable to restore double.[109] This is a fine distinction, and one completely compatible with both Justinianic law and the *Ecloga*. Yet while the *Ecloga* confines itself to repeating the Justinianic

[107] NM.13–15, 18–19, 21.

[108] E.17.40: *Ho pur embalōn en allotria hulē ē koptōn ex autēs dendra eis to diplasion katadikazetai.*

[109] NG.57: *Ho kaiōn oros allotrion ē koptōn dendra allotria eis to diplasion katadikazetai.*

regulation, the NG adds what must have been an existing expansion of living law. Moreover, if we just had NG.57, it would be technically legal to burn someone else's forest, so long as it was not on a hillside!

E.17.41, or more specifically the latter half, is one of the closest translations of Justinianic law, in this case D.9.2.30.3, and one of the few we can directly trace through an intermediary Greek translation.[110] It also combines D.47.9.9, 12 and D.48.19.28.12 to provide one article enumerating that malicious arson in town was punished with burning, outside the town with execution, and if someone caused accidental damage by creating a fire in his own field, if he was negligent—in that he took no precautions or did it on a windy day when fire could be expected to spread—was condemned, but if he was not negligent, he was not liable. NG.56 hugely simplifies this, stating that those who set fire in their own forest or field are only condemned if they did it in a strong wind. This is a significant simplification that essentially transforms an example of negligence into the legal definition of it in this particular case, an alteration that fits with the general desire in the Isaurian legal works to set down precise punishments for specified crimes in an attempt to aid and control judicial action. NG.58 further expands with the ordinance that he who burns the fence of someone's vineyard should be beaten, branded, and pay twice the damage. Is this contradictory to E.17.41?[111] If so, then E.17.40 and the respective existing legislation are as well. The difference seems to be if the act was intentional—that is, the difference between arson (*emprēsmos*,[112] *ballontes pur*)[113] and accident. The principle is the same as NG.57, but given the greater value of vineyards, a stiffer penalty was imposed. The same principle, with the original lower penalty of E.17.40, is extended to burning another's cart in NG.63. Deliberate arson of threshing-floors or corn stacks was punished by burning, presumably as these were classed as public property, most probably in the centre of the village and so classed as the eighth-century equivalent of in-town.[114] However, arson of places of storage for fodder (presumably individual, private property) was punished by the cutting off of a hand only.[115] Yet again, on close inspection, this does not contradict E.17.41, as this penalized deliberate arson of

[110] Dorotheus, BS.60.3.30; See Burgmann, *Ecloga*, 5 n. 1.

[111] Ashburner thought so—see his 'Farmer's Law II', 75–6.

[112] E.17.41.899, 912. [113] NG.64–65, ed. Medvedev, 120.

[114] NG.64. [115] NG.65.

'fields or farmhouses'[116] with execution—incidentally specifics otherwise uncovered in the NG—and not places of storage for fodder, which could be classified as a less vital property than home and livelihood. Therefore, once again, the NG both expands and depends upon the *Ecloga*.

The final topic in the NG is theft. This had been dealt with briefly in the *Ecloga*, with E.17.10 decreeing that anyone who stole arms while in camp or on the march was to be flogged; while if they stole a horse, their hand was to be amputated. E.17.11 stipulated that in all other cases of theft, for the first offence, a rich freeman was to pay back twice the value, while a poor man was flogged and exiled; for a second offence, all had a hand amputated. The NG, as it was wont to do, provided not this general principle, with its martial exceptions, but a series of cases that modify or extend the ideal as appropriate to actual cases. So, NG.22 required those who stole tools at the time of their use to pay the equivalent of their daily hire of 12 *folles*, as in effect they had stolen the tool's usufruct. We are not told in the NG what would be the punishment if they could not pay this cost, nor if they did these things repeatedly, because this was covered by E.17.11. This principle of monetary penalty is extended to stealing of ploughs in NG.62. In NG.33 the *hopōrophulax*, 'guardian of fruit', lost his wages and was severely beaten if he stole the fruit he was supposed to guard—hardly a great deviation from the spirit of Roman law.[117] The same idea was applied to shepherds in NG.34, while in NG.35 a man stealing another's straw is made to restore twice the amount; again we are not told what would happen if he could not do so. The most peculiar chapter is NG.61, where people could freely enter other's vineyards or figyards to eat, but if they came to steal they were flogged, a principle almost certainly taken from the Old Testament, as we shall explore below.[118] The greatest deviation comes in NG.68, where if a man is found stealing from a granary, for a first offence he is flogged 100 times and must pay back what he stole, for a second offence he must pay back double, and on the third offence he is blinded. NG.69 expands the same punishments to include stealing wine from storage. This is manifestly a harsher punishment than ordained in the *Ecloga*, given for specific infringements that were

[116] E.17.41.900–1: *agrous ē oikias agrōn.*

[117] NG.33, ed. Medvedev, 110.

[118] Ashburner, 'Farmer's Law II', 92 n. 32.

considered worse crimes than ordinary theft. This is, therefore, a case of the specific expounding and altering, in minor ways, the general rule. Such things happen in all legal systems, as the complexities and nuances of life, reflected in the generation of case-law, complicate and deviate from the universal principles neatly set forth in general handbooks. Clearly, people in the eighth century did not feel there was any great contradiction. Thus, yet again we can say the *Ecloga* and NG not only share common laws and precepts, but that the latter extends and needs the former. For without the *Ecloga*, the NG does not actually condemn any form of theft that does not include agriculture.

Further, the NG and *Ecloga* share a penchant for corporal punishment.[119] Some 21 articles stipulate penalties of whipping or loss of limb.[120] This compares to only two uses of fines[121] and three of capital punishment.[122] As discussed in relation to the *Ecloga*, corporal chastisement was hardly unknown in Roman law, and there had been a growing use of it in late antiquity.[123] However, its prominence, particularly over capital or fiscal penalties, is a peculiarity of the world of the *Ecloga*, and would suggest a measure of contemporaneity. Similar is the high profile of oaths to ensure truthful testimony.[124] In particular these were oaths before God, and perjury was thereby punished, as it was in E.17.2, by cutting out the tongue.[125] Again this regulation (first securely attested in the *Ecloga*) and the use of oaths do not prove a relationship, but do imply temporal proximity.

THE *AKROATAI* AND THE LANGUAGE OF THE NG

This is reinforced by similitude in phraseology between the NG and *Ecloga*, and with the NS, NN, and NM. The best example of shared terms and phrases also answers the questions of for whom the NG was primarily made and who enforced it. For both NG.7 and 37 employ the phrase *tēreitōsan hoi akroatai*, 'let the judges consider',

[119] Zacharia von Lingenthal, *Geschichte*, 250–1; Cf. Ashburner, 'Farmer's Law II', 73–5.

[120] Burgmann, 'Die Nomoi', 61.

[121] NG.21 and 62.

[122] NG.46, 47, 64.

[123] See Chapter 2, 122–3.

[124] NG.26–28, 73.

[125] NG.28.

with NG.67 using a slight variation,[126] which precise phrase is found in E.5.5, 10.1.1, 11, and slight alteration in 17.27 and 17.47, and rarely elsewhere in Byzantine legal history.[127] The *akroatai*, as discussed in Chapter 2, were the most prominent kind of judge mentioned in the *Ecloga*, and probably represent rebranded *archontes*, 'magistrates', at both the provincial and sub-provincial levels, who possessed a wide range of civil and criminal competences. In the NG they are the only judicial authority mentioned, called upon to adjudicate a land dispute between *chōria* (NG.7), to decide whether a hired ox had died doing the stipulated work, and therefore whether the hirer was liable under the *Lex Aquilia* (NG.37). They were also called upon to take account of when someone who had a secured loan against land had had the contract for seven years, before which half the usufruct of the land was set against the principal, and after which the whole could be (NG.67). These are diverse problems of civil law, implying the *akroatai* had wide-ranging jurisdiction, including cases involving multiple *chōria*.

Considering the *akroatai*'s broad operational remit recorded in both the *Ecloga* and the NG, it is highly probable that the whole of the NG was addressed to them, whether as Lemerle's aide-memoire or like the *Ecloga* an official, codified selection of relevant cases.[128] In either case, it would imply an organized judiciary, being provided with clear and precise documents to aid them, and acting at the lowest level of society. What is unknown is how the *akroatai*—incidentally most often mentioned in the plural, perhaps suggesting a panel of judges—operated in practice.[129] Given the NG's expectation that they were the correct judges for rural cases, it is likely that some of them at least were sub-provincial officials. Obviously, it is implausible that every village would have had its own *akroatēs*, let alone multiple ones, and as NG.7 tells us that they could adjudicate land disputes between *chōria*, the likelihood must be they were resident at a higher level. Perhaps every city or every province had a panel of *akroatai* instead of a *defensor*, but too little is known of either Byzantine administration

[126] *Psēphisatō ho akroatēs*, 'let the judge take account'.

[127] See NG, ed. Medvedev, 147.

[128] As such I agree with Lemerle, *Agrarian History*, 36 n. 1, that the argument of A. Christophilopulos, '*Akroatēs*', *BZ* 44 (1951), 86–8, stating that the title has no technical value, is incorrect.

[129] A single *akroatēs* appears only in NG.67 and E.17.41. Cf. the *dikastai* who are mentioned five times in the *Ecloga* (E.8.3, 14.1,4,10, 15.2) and twice are in the singular.

or cities in the eighth century to confirm this.[130] E.14 makes it clear both that there were central, public courts to which witnesses were called, and also that if witnesses lived far away, people were dispatched to gather their testimony. However, considering that E.14 also only speaks of *dikastai*, perhaps this was only the provincial court, with some level of organizational division with the *akroatai*, just as Justinian had stipulated that all cases under 300 *solidi* should be tried by the *defensor*, with the governor acting as the court of appeal and responsible for more major cases.[131]

Clearly, the *akroatai* were not merely the *defensores* under a new title, for the *akroatai* are more linked to rural cases, and E.17.41 and 47 suggest they could try to punish serious cases like arson and homicide, and E.17.27 issues as sensitive and important to the Isaurians as adultery. Moreover, E.10.1.2 actually mentions an *ekdikos*, the Greek form of *defensor* as the official with whom public valuation of a debtor's property should be registered.[132] However, there are obvious similarities: local judges appointed in the interests of the people, providing quick, accessible, and cheap justice, being the point of register and validation of documents, such as contracts and wills, and representing the emperor to the prime fiscal-administrative unit of the empire, which for Justinian was the city, but for the Isaurians was the *chōrion*. Indeed, it is possible that the *akroatai*, like the *defensor* before them, were jointly responsible with other officials for the collection of taxes, as well as upholding law and order.[133] Certainly, NG.18–19 covered issues intimately connected to the issue of tax payment, and as they tied permissible usufruct of another's land to payment of taxes, they inform us that the fundamental concern of the state vis-à-vis the agricultural world was revenue collection.[134]

Further, it is interesting that in the NG there is little idea of movement of litigants to *akroatai*. The only suggestion is of *akroatai* actively investigating litigants and places of dispute.[135] Indeed, given the lowly status of many of the litigants and the frequently small

[130] Haldon, *Seventh Century*, 99–102. [131] N.15.3.2, 4.

[132] E.10.1.2.547. [133] N.15.3.

[134] Cf. Lemerle, *Agrarian History*, 40–1, 65. J. Lefort, 'The rural economy, seventh–twelfth centuries', in *EHB*, 231–310, esp. 281.

[135] E.g. NG.7 says that a landmark was to have primacy when the *akroatai* were adjudicating between *chōria* on their respective boundaries, implying that some form of inquiry of the physical artefact by the judges, or their appointed representatives, was necessary.

issues involved, this might imply that travel to a distant centre of justice for uncertain adjudication would often have been too great a certain cost for too little potential gain to warrant such cases. Plausibly, then, the *akroatai* went to the village, rather than the villagers going to the *akroatai*. There was one certain point when the imperial authorities actively interacted with the people: when taxes were collected.[136] One can therefore reasonably imagine the *akroatai* accompanying tax collectors, administering justice and resolving disputes in order to maintain law and order, and thus to ease the strains resultant from tax collection.

As discussed in Chapter 2, the derivation of *akroatai* is obscure, but it is probably biblical. Nor is it the only element in the NG to betray biblical influences and language. For instance, the NG frequently employs the semantic reduplication of participle and verb to reinforce the emphasis that is a motif of the *Septuagint*.[137] Thus NG.21 uses the phrase *ananeuōn ananeusē*, 'strictly forbidden', found (among many instances) in Exodus 22:16 = NM.25.[138] Moreover, the NG evinces the same ideas and concerns as several biblical passages, and not just its language. NG.61 is an article without precedent in Roman law, ordaining that if people enter another's figyard or vineyard to eat, they should go free, but if they enter to steal, then they are to be beaten, based on Lev. 19:9–10 and Deut. 24:1–2.[139] Moreover, the couplet of vines and figs, which are only mentioned in the NG here, is a distinctly biblical one, with the emphasis on peaceful self-sufficient peasantry, sitting under the vine and fig-tree.[140] Furthermore, the complex NG.67, as plausibly reconstructed by Laiou, states that if anyone secured a loan against his land, for the first seven years half the revenue was marked against the principal, presumably with the rest for interest, while after that point an *akroatēs* was to take note, and then the whole of the revenue was set aside the principal, so that no further interest could be paid.[141] As Laiou noted, like Ashburner

[136] See the description in Brown, *Power and Persuasion*, 26.

[137] Svoronos, 'Notes sur l'Origine et la Date du code Rural', 493–4. Schminck, 'Nomos Mosaikos', 258–61.

[138] Schminck, 'Nomos Mosaikos', 259.

[139] Ashburner, 'Farmer's Law II', 92 n. 32.

[140] See for example Deut. 8:8, IV Kings 18:31, Is. 36:16. The couplet is also used when God is destroying the transgressors' produce, e.g. Jeremiah 8:13, Ps. 105:33. Cf. A. Laiou, 'Economic thought and ideology', in *EHB*, 1123–44, esp. 1125–6.

[141] Laiou, 'Chapter 67'.

before, this regulation has no precedent in Roman law, and indeed would have a short life.[142] It severely limited the degree of profit that could be made by lending against the land, and so protected the debtor. Moreover, it actively encouraged the debtor to apply to imperial justice, through the *akroatēs*, to seek protection. The only precedent is found in Deut. 15:1–2, where after seven years, debts were remitted. Thus we have a judicial authority strongly associated with the Isaurians, enforcing a decree based on the Old Testament, for a vital constituency, the farmer-taxpayer. As Laiou argues, this is not proof of Isaurian authorship, but it is certainly suggestive.[143] Indubitably, it is evidence of the strong influence of the Bible, and in particular the Old Testament, on the NG. Furthermore, these rare examples in the NG of new law, particularly new criminal law, were buttressed through appeal to Scripture, in a manner reminiscent of the *Ecloga*.

Moreover, most of those appropriations of ideas and phrases are also found in the NM. For instance, NG.39 stipulates that if one accidentally killed an animal, one must render *psuchēn anti psuchēs*, 'soul for soul', the exact phrase as Lev. 24:18 = NM.47.[144] These are more than just borrowed phrases, for the idea behind NG.39 is the same as NM.47 and not just expressed in the same way. NG.70's condemnation of unjust measures and weights is taken directly from Lev. 19:35 = NM.9. NG.78 punished those who harvested early and let in their animals, which then harmed their neighbour's crop, and NG.79 extended this to the vineyard. NM.18 = Ex. 22:5 contains both infringements in the same order as they appear in the NG. NG.64 covers the same ground as NM.20 = Ex. 22:6, the burning of a threshing-floor, *halōn*, employing the same rare term.[145] The most significant overlap is the focus on the damage done to and by animals.[146] There is a particularly close association with NG.23–29 concerning herdsmen, especially NG.26–28, which allows the herdsman to deny liability of any lost animal through an oath to God that he was not to blame, taken from Ex. 22:10–13 = NM.13. Evidently, as Svoronos and Schminck maintain, there is a close correlation between

[142] Laiou, 'Chapter 67', 202; Cf. Ashburner, 'Farmer's Law II', 93 n. 35.

[143] Laiou, 'Chapter 67', 202.

[144] NG.39, ed. Medvedev, 112.

[145] NG.64, ed. Medvedev, 120. *thēmōnia*, 'stack', is another rare Greek word from the *Septuagint*, this time Ex. 8:14.

[146] NM.12–15, 18–19, 21, 47.

the NM and NG, implying more than simple interest in the Bible but suggesting a degree of contemporaneity.[147] However, instead of the fifth or ninth centuries, both better suit the period after the promulgation of the *Ecloga.*

THE DATE, NATURE, AND AUTHORSHIP OF THE NG

Having perused the evidence, it is now possible to proffer answers to those three interlocked queries: the date, character, and authorship of the NG. Firstly, the manuscript, stylistic format, and content overlap between the NG and the *Ecloga*, AE, NM, NS, and NN strongly implies a measure of contemporaneity. Considering the very precise dovetailing of the NG with the *Ecloga*, with the former not repeating but expanding the latter, and missing elements that were in the *Ecloga* and that were surely relevant to law at the level of the *chōrion*, this would suggest that the NG was produced after the *Ecloga* as a deliberate supplement. Moreover, it is highly unlikely that it was produced with the *Ecloga* or immediately after it, for then one would expect the manuscript correspondence to be closer than it is. Further, the NG was clearly constituted as a separate *nomos* offering additional titles to the body of the *Ecloga*, designed for a particular judicial authority, the *akroatai.* This would imply production in the generation after 741, as a professional judiciary buttressed the *Ecloga* with additional Justinianic material and discovered practical areas uncovered or underexplored by the *Ecloga*, in the process creating both a definite AE and a wider appendix of associated texts, including the NG.

A plausible *terminus ante quem* is the Macedonian reforms of the later ninth century, for on several issues the NG is closer to the *Ecloga* than the Macedonian handbooks.[148] For instance, the *Eisagoge*—which incidentally has no significant manuscript association with the NG[149]—provides an entirely different schema for loans than

[147] Svoronos, 'Notes sur l'Origine et la Date du code Rural', 493–4. Schminck, 'Nomos Mosaikos', 258–61.

[148] Wickham, *Framing*, 463 n. 60 relays a personal comment by John Haldon that the NG must be before the *Basilika* due to differences in terminology and the tax law.

[149] See Appendix, Table 14.

NG.67, and the prime judicial authority is no longer the *akroatai* in either the *Eisagoge* or the *Prochiron*.[150] Furthermore, if one were to follow Schminck's dating of the NG to 867, there would seem little reason why the NG would be associated at all with the *Ecloga*, a position bordering on the incredible. The reference to a *nomos geōrgikos* in the early ninth-century *Letters of Ignatios the Deacon* would further strengthen the notion that the NG had a contemporary recognized authority in agricultural relations, and there is no sense that this is something recent implying a late eighth-century reception of the text at the latest, although it is possible that this is merely a topos.[151] A final consideration is the low profile of coinage in the NG, with only small-change *folles* mentioned.[152] Moreover, NG.9–10 give the impression of rent paid in kind, as do the contracts of NG.11–15. Furthermore, NG.19 describes the regular land tax as *ta ekstraordina tou dēmosiou logou*, 'the extraordinary taxes of the public treasury',[153] which Haldon plausibly suggests was expressed in this way because it was paid in kind, deriving from the old practice of force-purchase, *synōnē*.[154] This relatively under-monetized (although not demonetized) economy and taxation dominated by kind is exactly the picture given by other sources for the seventh and eighth centuries, but not for the ninth century.[155] In particular, Constantine V's probable decision in 769 to commute some (if not all) of the land tax into money payments revitalized the circulation of coinage, and might be taken as a *terminus ante quem*.[156] More certainly, it reveals Isaurian interest in the tax system and the countryside, and a time frame of a quarter-century after the publication of the *Ecloga* would provide a suitable gestation period for such an interdependent but still separate document. That this was also the period of renewed imperial control over Asia Minor following the stabilization of the Arab front, including the imposition of new taxes and major reorganization of the

[150] Laiou, 'Chapter 67', 201.

[151] *Letter* 1, line 14, ed. C. Mango with S. Efthymiadis, *The Correspondence of Ignatios the Deacon: Text, Translation, and Commentary* (Washington DC, 1997), 28. See Howard-Johnston, 'Social change', 47.

[152] NG.22, 62.

[153] NG.19, ed. Medvedev, 104; trans. Ashburner, 'Farmer's Law II', 89.

[154] Haldon, *Seventh Century*, 147–8.

[155] In general see C. Morrisson, 'Byzantine money: its production and circulation', in *EHB*, 909–66.

[156] See Oikonomidès, 'The role of the Byzantine state in the economy', 981.

provinces (not to mention a period of legal codification), further underscores the mid-to-late eighth century as the most plausible period for the creation and dissemination of the NG.[157]

The character and origins of the articles in the NG are primarily Justinianic, just as its title proclaims they are. More precisely, the vast majority of chapters are case studies and practical examples of delict law and theft, manifesting the general principles of Roman law, in particular as contained in the *Digest*. In the realm of civil law, the NG mostly concerns forms of contract unknown to Justinianic law, although hardly inherently alien to it. Moreover, the NG does not cover known Roman contract and tenure law, such as *emphyteusis* and leases, because the *Ecloga* had already covered them. Thus, here the changing practice on the ground was regulated through the NG and set within a broader system of Roman law. The amount of truly new legislation that is inexplicable through the simple evolution of Roman law is vanishingly small, with only NG.61 and 67 evidently so. That these were justified through exegesis, combined with the percolation of biblical rhetoric, chime with an eighth-century date and demonstrate the power of Scripture in reformulating (or at least re-expressing) Roman law. However, the vast bulk of the NG is essentially Justinianic law as it had evolved on the ground over two centuries of significant socio-economic change.

Further, any categorization of this law as 'vulgar' is more a hindrance than help.[158] This slippery term has been chiefly defined either as the denigration of classical law through intermingling with non-Roman ideas, or the continued existence of customary or provincial law, which then interacted with Roman law.[159] However, what is striking about the NG is the extent to which it follows the essential principles of the *Digest* on delict and theft. Punishment had shifted towards the corporal, and some previous forms of contract had declined and others had risen. Such alteration is exactly what one would expect over two turbulent centuries. Moreover, considering that next to nothing is known of customary law in this period it is difficult to demonstrate any particular article being influenced by it, although it is also difficult to disprove it. More fundamentally, Greece

[157] See Conclusion, 261–5.

[158] Pieler, 'Rechtsliteratur', 440–2. See Introduction, 9 n. 36.

[159] For a good recent examination of vulgar law in the post-Roman west, for which the concepts have more validity, see Barnwell, 'Emperors, jurists and kings'.

and Asia Minor had been part of the Roman Empire for almost a millennium by the mid-to-late eighth century, and indeed had contained the capital of an ever-intensifying and litigious state for four centuries. As far as it is possible to tell, the customary law of the Byzantine heartlands was Roman law. Moreover, if anything, in the seventh century, state power and control over the shrinking territories of the empire had deepened as the state sucked in all surplus resources to survive.[160] As its tentacles sank ever further, so, most probably, did Roman law. No other constellation of power and authority could match the state, and indeed the classical intermediaries of the cities and the senatorial aristocracy shrivelled in the period almost (if not quite) to the point of irrelevance.[161] Only one other system of authority and law, the Church, endured—even flourished—but it was one inherently intertwined with the imperial structure. Certainly, despite its well-recorded power, there is no great indication of canon law in the NG. Given all this, it seems highly unlikely that any separate sphere of customary law, in the sense of either provincial law or some distinct non-Roman system, existed, or that the authors of the NG would have used it.

Furthermore, to describe the NG and other contemporaneous codes as 'vulgar' law is to impose a set of unhelpful paradigms. It implies degradation from classical heights. It entombs Roman law as a precise thing, rather than as a dynamic process interacting with reality. It can imply a dichotomy between urban, elite, civilized Romans, who used proper law, and the rural, poor, uneducated, often barbarous populace, who either had their own customs, or misunderstood and misapplied Roman law. Considering that by the eighth century the inhabitants of the empire had been officially Roman citizens for five centuries, and for the past two had been governed by a Greek-speaking administration, there would have been little linguistic or cultural barrier to accessing Roman law. Moreover, while the empire of Justinian was vast and heterogeneous, ethnically and linguistically, with state power checked by the tyranny of distance, and therefore forced to recognize the existence and

[160] This relative intensification of state power, and the abatement of the cities and the old elites as centres of power, is a uniting theme of the most recent scholarship of the period, in particular Zuckerman, 'Learning from the enemy'; Auzépy, 'State of emergency'; and Brubaker and Haldon, *History*.

[161] See Brubaker and Haldon, *History*, 531–72 for the decline and reordering of cities, and 573–624 for the reconfiguration of elites.

validity of customary law, the compact and relatively homogenous Isaurian empire neither needed to nor did. The *Ecloga* gives no hint of any other form of legal system, even combining theoretically the law of the Bible with that of the emperors into one system. There is no notion of, and indeed no room for, 'vulgar' law as provincial law. What the law of the *Ecloga* and the NG declared and thought itself to be was Justinianic law, now corrected and aligned with Scripture. Therefore, the best description of the NG is as primarily a collection of Justinianic legislation as it had evolved on the ground, combined with a sprinkling of new legislation, set within biblical ideas and expressed through biblical phrases, following the pattern set by the *Ecloga*.

Moreover, one can reject the notion of Slavic influence. Not a single Slavic term is found in the text.[162] The conditions of agrarian life, which on close inspection do not appear radically different from what had come before, were produced by inherently endogenous socio-economic changes and external political shock, without need for any mass Slavic migration.[163] Furthermore, the NG, whether 'official' or not, became the recognized law of the land for centuries and across the empire. Evidently, the law contained therein was considered applicable to all *chōria*, meaning that it must have reflected the perceived reality of agrarian life across the empire.

It is perhaps also possible to postulate something concerning the immediate sources and construction of the NG. Ashburner certainly thought that apparent repetitiousness of the NG might reasonably imply that its authors merely stitched together separate existing works excerpting Justinianic law, intermingled with new regulations and customary law.[164] For instance, NG.23–29 does seem to form a unit, with some manuscripts including a title *peri agelariōn*, 'concerning herdsmen'.[165] Yet this may well have sprung from the simple repetition of the word *agelarios* in the articles, rather than having been part of an original separate text. Furthermore, the principle of association laid out above would seem to explain the structure of the code. Perhaps the articles after NG.70, which conspicuously ends

[162] Kazhdan, 'Farmer's Law'.

[163] In general see Lefort, 'The rural economy'; Laiou and Morrisson, *Byzantine Economy*, 38–49, 64–70.

[164] Ashburner, 'Farmer's Law I', 85–6, and 'Farmer's Law II', 70.

[165] Medvedev, NG, 105.

where NG.1 started, with an insistence on justice, and after which the NG becomes less well ordered (or not obviously so), were a later addition. Yet with the appearance of manuscripts only in the eleventh century, it is difficult to offer a definite answer to the possibility of multiple recensions, interpolations, and accretions.

Moreover, the NG's utilitarian nature should be stressed. This is not a text laden with rhetoric or legal theory. It is meant to aid the administration of justice, not in itself to trumpet ideology and propaganda. However, this is not to say that it is not affected by grander discourses. From its claimed authority from Justinian to its use of exegesis, the NG reveals that it is part of a broader legal and symbolic world. Further, its very utility was designed for political and ideological ends: the maintenance of law and order within the tax base, the securing of divine support, and eventual salvation for the emperors and their subjects. This pragmatic text then had political ramifications.

Furthermore, like the NN, the authors of the NG evidently felt no need to organize its contents into titles, nor, considering its popularity, did people find its associative style difficult to use. It is therefore strange for modern scholars to decry its supposed lack of structure as evidence of its private authorship, postulating that a legal commission would have done better.[166] This seems to ignore its success, and unnaturally raise the skills of legal commissions. Indeed, to declare it a private text seems to evince a scepticism towards the legal and administrative ability of eighth-century Byzantine government that would jar with everything we know of the period. Contrarily, such a text, in such a format, with such rhetoric and intent, would fit the policies, politics, and propaganda of the Isaurians perfectly.

Moreover, attempts to tie the NG to a particular place within the empire, and thereby to demonstrate how it emerged to deal with a specific context, are a chimera.[167] Firstly, the NG self-evidently was thought to be universally applicable, and was probably designed as such. The picture it paints of rural society was common across the pre-modern world, explaining the NG's enduring popularity, and its appeal to non-Byzantine societies. Further, one frequently noted

[166] Cf. Dölger, 'Ist der Nomos Georgikos ein Gesetz des Kaisers Justinians II?', 45–7.

[167] Cf. Kazhdan, 'Farmer's Law'; Haldon and Brubaker, *Sources*, 290; Wickham, *Framing*, 463.

aspect of the NG, that it does not mention the olive, has been used to position the text, with the Balkans, Southern Italy, and the interior of Asia Minor all suggested. Such diffusion relates the dangers of using the NG to paint a rural world that can then be pinpointed. Moreover, this is no evidence for the NG's supposed provincial provenance, for olives were not grown either in the vicinity of Constantinople or in the surrounding region of Thrace in the eighth century.[168] Indeed, olives do not seem to have been a major factor in Byzantine state thinking or the economy of Constantinople, judging from the tenth-century *Book of the Eparch*, which does not mention olives *per se* and olive oil only rarely, but does regulate soap and candle-makers.[169] Considering the focus in the NG on practical cases that expanded upon the issues of the *Ecloga*, it is plausible that the NG's authors combined both existing texts and local case records, which, if written in Constantinople, would have meant short shrift for the olive. Certainly there is nothing in the NG that demonstrates an origin outside the capital. Rather, all the evidence, from the NG's association with the *Ecloga* to its utilitarian focus and intended audience, suggests it was always an 'official' production by the legal administration of Constantinople, or at the very least very quickly incorporated by them into an official corpus appending the *Ecloga*.

Furthermore, even if the NG were a private text, it reveals much about the legal and ideological, as well as the socio-economic, world of Byzantium in the Iconoclast era. Firstly, the law and the justice system sought to appear—and to a remarkable degree were—ubiquitous down to the lowest levels of society. Disputes were being settled, and were encouraged to be settled, through the imperial administration. A vast range of cases were being heard by a specialized, salaried judiciary, with clear, established rules on testimony and a preference for written evidence. The compilation of the NG itself

[168] See B. Greger, 'Physical factors in the evolution of the landscape and land use', in *EHB*, 31–45. Constantinople's immediate hinterland is too cold to permit the growing of olives. Considering that the evidence points to a colder climate in the sixth–ninth centuries, and considering significant regional political turmoil, it is even less likely that olives were grown anywhere in Thrace. It was only later that olives started to appear as a major element in the economy of the Chalkidike and parts of Bithynia.

[169] *Book of the Eparch*, ed. J. Koder, *Das Eparchenbuch Leons des Weisen* (Vienna, 1991). For a general introduction, see A. Kazhdan, 'Book of the Eparch', in *ODB*, vol. 1, 308.

stands witness to the perceived necessity to provide judges with manuals of accurate, comprehensive, and relevant law, with the purpose of aiding the administration of justice. Further, the law they were applying was based firmly on the principles of Justinianic law. Even if there was a shift in emphasis or punishment, those principles endured, and indubitably the compilers of the NG deliberately set it within the paradigm, established by the *Ecloga*, of selections from the official Justinianic *Corpus*. This is proof that someone in the period had a concern to promote legal administration at the village level, or in cataloguing the law, or in positing links with Justinian I, or—most plausibly—all three. The NG informs us that there was a focus on delict law, an impression reinforced by the NS, NN, and indeed NM. Further, the bulk of the NG's ordinances deal with petty disputes over land and beasts. These must have represented not only the cynosure of the *akroatai* for whom the NG was written, but the actual majority of cases.

These disputes arose naturally from an existing, sophisticated, agrarian society interlocked with a powerful, tax-gathering state. In the NG we see one level of that interaction of polity and people, one method by which the state projected its power and maintained control, but also one justification for its existence: the provision of justice. Into that mesh of law, society, and state the NG also offers a glimpse of the omnipresent percolation of the Bible. Its phrases and ideas were intermingled with every aspect and register of Byzantine society, reformulating its self-expression, self-imagination, and even day-to-day existence. More specifically, the law of this period was positioned within a biblical schema to such an extent that what new law we can indubitably see in the NG was both justified by and drew inspiration from Scripture.

All this would be true if the NG were 'official' or 'private'. But, if it were (as the evidence suggests) an official document, all these aspects would be sharpened with particular political connotations.[170] For it would convey the impression of the Isaurians reclaiming, restating, reforming, and repositioning Roman law, both symbolically and substantively. It would imply a deliberate attempt to regulate, control, and impose a justice system reliant on the state and central to the ideological order evinced by the Isaurians, upon every level of society,

[170] See Howard-Johnston, 'Social change in early medieval Byzantium', 49.

with a particular focus here on the foundation of the tax system, and therefore the state itself. Moreover, it would portray emperors who wished to be seen to be bringing justice to all, a justice inherently founded on Scripture and designed in part for the realization of heavenly commandments. Thus, an official NG would be both tool and claim, a component of a broader policy of reformed and restored law as the instrument for imperial rejuvenation and moral absolution. This political and ideological intent would chime with the stated aims of the *Ecloga* and the wider picture of Isaurian policy. Therefore, the NG should be seen as an addendum to the *Ecloga* and an integral part of a grander Isaurian renaissance.

CONCLUSIONS

The NM, NN, and NG all share a common function: the extension and augmentation of the *Ecloga*. In this they are similar to the texts examined in Chapter 3, yet crucially these present works that from their inception were portrayed as defined and separate texts. Thus, even though intended to be associated with a particular foundational text, they could be more easily juxtaposed with a variety of works than those texts whose format linked them more strongly with the *Ecloga*. This and their apparent popularity, presumably linked to their utility, led to the marked variety of the manuscript tradition. All three additionally are presented as selections from an identified and unquestionable authority, ones also notable for their antiquity. There is nothing in the title or presentation of any of these three to suggest that they contain anything but established and received law. In truth there was little that was new—or more importantly what an eighth-century audience thought was new—in either the NN or NG, while the NM was of course composed from the immutable word of God. All, therefore, speak of a legal discourse that was highly conservative, especially in its ideological bearings. The legitimate (and presumably relevant) past was being collected and arranged for the benefit of the present.

Yet these texts that were evidently contemporaneous and contained so much in common had markedly different fates. For while the NN and NG multiplied prolifically throughout the legal tradition, combining with the NS, reworked into a *nomos*, to form a recognized corpus, an almost indispensable appendix to all future legal handbooks, the NM fell out of the legal tradition. These divergent futures contrasting with a shared past was the natural result of their different intent. For although the NG, NN, and NS were all designed to supplement the *Ecloga*—to such an extent that they make little sense without it, and indeed were impregnated with the language and thought of the eighth century—they were primarily practical texts, drawn from the unimpeachable authority of Justinian. There is little inherent in them to anchor them indelibly to the Isaurians. Further, their innate conservatism in presenting themselves as excerpts from an established authority rather than as creations of a particular time, let alone dynasty, manifestly permitted easy appropriation by the Macedonians as appendices for their legal works, if indeed they were not so deeply integrated into legal practice by the ninth century that uprooting them was deemed impossible. The NM, on the other hand, was a more independent text than either the NN or NG, with a defined thematic structure, composed from a source of indubitable, unchangeable legitimacy and, to the Byzantine mind, relevance. Yet it was inextricably bound to the ideological programme of the Isaurians, and particularly the *Ecloga*. It was the testament that the Isaurians were legislating in the model of Moses, aligning the new law with the old. This potent ideological construct destined the NM for isolation, as the successors of the Isaurians sought to undo or appropriate their works, the legal element of which forms the focus of the following chapter.

6

Three Reactions

Irene, Leo V, and the Macedonians

It has been argued already that the Isaurians inaugurated a period of legal reform, marked by the creation of excerpts of established law, gathered into concise texts intended for both practical and ideological purposes. Furthermore, they set that law within an Old Testament discourse, in expression, substance, and most importantly conception, reimagining their inherited Roman law as a new covenant between God and the new Chosen People. In this schema the Isaurians were the new Moses, delivering divinely sanctioned law for moral reformation, thus safeguarding the state against the foes that besieged it. This was such a potent mixture that the Isaurians' successors had to react to it, and the ways in which they did so, and their limits, underscore much of the message of the Isaurian legal programme. In particular, Irene (r.797–802), Leo V (r.815–20), and the Macedonians Basil I (r.867–886) and Leo VI (r.886–912) reacted in markedly different and illuminating ways to the Isaurian legal legacy. Those reactions are here only sketched, yet even in brief, the salient points demonstrate the remarkable potency and longevity of the Isaurian programme.

THE NOVELS OF IRENE: THE REPUDIATION OF THE ISAURIAN SYSTEM

When Constantine V died in 775, he left behind a stable empire and a secure dynasty. His son Leo IV was only 25, and already had his own son, Constantine VI. The Isaurian dynasty was popular and had no serious rivals. Indeed, its only major problem seemed to be a surplus of members, with Leo IV's five half-brothers the centre of successive conspiracies over the following two decades. The frontiers were relatively stable, and the army loyal. The economy was recovering, and the urban fabric of Constantinople had been renewed. Evidently heaven seemed to be pleased, and as a result the policy of iconoclasm was little challenged. The Isaurian recipe for the reformation of the Empire, prominently including their legal policies, could only be judged a success.[1]

It took the intervention of chance so surprising that Theophanes described it as a miracle to change things.[2] For in 780 Leo IV died abruptly, leaving behind the nine-year-old Constantine VI as emperor, and his mother Irene as regent. Thus began a complex struggle, firstly between Irene, the sons of Constantine, and their supporters in the Church and the army, and then, as Constantine VI grew up, between the young emperor and his mother.[3] Throughout this, Irene had to contend with the facts that she was only a member of the dynasty through marriage, that her authority therefore stemmed from her position as wife of Leo IV and mother of Constantine VI, and finally that she was a woman ruling in a world used to martial, masculine emperors. These flaws in Irene's legitimacy were evidently felt among many of the key actors in Byzantine power politics, given the tangled web of conspiracies, coups, and rebellions witnessed between 780 and Irene's eventual overthrow in 802. Clearly, she had been dealt a difficult hand to play. But the empress would prove extraordinarily tenacious, for the most part successfully dividing her enemies while attempting to forge a new regime.

This was the situation that gave rise to the dominant theme of Irene's rule, the deliberate differentiation between herself and the policies of her Isaurian successors; this campaign reached its crescendo during her brief but remarkable personal reign (797–802). So,

[1] For the situation at Constantine V's death, see Brubaker and Haldon, *History*, 248.

[2] Theophanes, 454.

[3] For an introduction to this period and Irene's reign, see the many works of Judith Herrin, inter alia 'The imperial feminine in Byzantium', *Past and Present* 169 (2000), 3–33. See also P. Speck, *Kaiser Konstantine VI. Die Legitimation einer fremden und der Versuch einer eigenen Herrschaft* (Munich, 1978).

unlike the martial Isaurians, Irene made peace rather than war.[4] Instead of highlighting dynasty, she extirpated it, having her own son Constantine VI killed, and then proclaiming her solo reign by having herself portrayed on both sides of her *solidi*.[5] Most famously, Irene restored icons through the Second Council of Nicaea in 787.[6] It is in this context of deliberate difference that her two extant novels should be read, for they reveal both the extent of Irene's attempt to break the Isaurian imperial model, and the real limits to that effort.

Irene promulgated two novels, undated except to her personal reign, one on oaths and the other on marriage.[7] Both were of exceedingly minor legal import.[8] By far the longer is that on oaths. By the late eighth century, oaths were a central part of Byzantine legal and political life.[9] The *Ecloga* had sanctioned the use of oaths to ensure valid testimony, and to help settle disputes.[10] Moreover, it authorized tongue amputation for perjury after a suitor had sworn on the Gospels.[11] The Isaurians also made widespread use of oaths politically.[12] Constantine V employed oaths of loyalty to reinforce his dynasty's hold on power and the policy of iconoclasm.[13] Leo IV, in a move clearly designed to secure his position in respect to his half-brothers, in 776 crowned his son as co-emperor and extracted an oath from the army, civic notables, and the people of Constantinople that they would accept no emperor other than Leo or Constantine; this oath was signed and deposited in Hagia Sophia.[14] Most recently, in

[4] For this and following comparisons, see Auzépy, 'State of emergency', 277.

[5] See *DOC* III, 1:181, 347–8.

[6] See inter alia Brubaker and Haldon, *History*, 260–84.

[7] Irene, *Novels*, ed. L. Burgmann, 'Die Novellen der Kaiserin Eirene', *FM* IV (Frankfurt, 1981), 1–36. See Dölger, *Regesten* 358–9 for an older but still useful description.

[8] Burgmann, 'Die Novellen der Kaiserin Eirene', 28–36.

[9] For a general introduction into the importance of oaths, see L. Burgmann, 'Oath', in *ODB*, vol. 3, 1509. For their manifest and widespread use politically and legally by the Isaurians, see Nichanian, 'Iconoclasme et prestation de serment à Byzance?'; and for their continued importance throughout Byzantine history, see N. Oikonomidès, 'Le serment de l'impératrice Eudocie (1067)', *Revue des Études Byzantines* 21 (1963), 101–28.

[10] E.g. E.6.4.3 on the settlement of debts accrued by an estate, and E.14.4 where witnesses are to put on oath.

[11] E.17.2.

[12] See Auzépy, 'State of emergency', 275–8; Nichanian, 'Iconoclasme et prestation de serment à Byzance?'.

[13] Nichanian, 'Iconoclasme et prestation de serment à Byzance?', 84–93.

[14] Theophanes, 449. See Auzépy, 'State of emergency', 274.

c.790–1, Irene and her son Constantine VI had tried to outbid each other for political power by having soldiers swear oaths to them alone.[15] The importance placed upon oaths is seen in Theophanes' complaint about the soldiers' eventual support for Constantine:

> They acclaimed Constantine emperor, not understanding, wretches that they were, that they should not have taken contrary oaths; for it is inevitable that perjury should result from contrary oaths, and perjury is a denial of God.[16]

Evidently, oaths were taken seriously and believed to be a potent tool of power.

The fundamental problem for the Byzantines with oaths was not legal or political, but theological, stemming from Christ's prohibition of them in the Sermon on the Mount.[17] Consequently, it is not surprising that criticism of the Isaurians' increased use of oaths was led by churchmen, especially their iconophile opponents.[18] Indeed, Theophanes' concern was shared as a justification for Irene's novel: 'the present edict has been created since perjury is brought forth from oaths, which is a denial of God.'[19] Further, Theodore the Studite praised Irene's reduction of the tax burden in part because it removed the need for multiple oaths, and the resultant temptation to give false oaths, a further insight into the general import of oaths to Byzantine administration.[20] For Irene to attack oaths, therefore, was a natural part of her repudiation of the Isaurians, and this was pleasing to her theological supporters. It also served to blacken the Isaurians in general, and those who had broken their oaths of loyalty to her in particular. The *prooimion* to Irene's novel introduced the issue as follows:

> Knowing that God is the Giver, Creator, and Master of all good things, and trusting in the fulfilment of his holy commandments to prosper our empire and to advance the Christian people entrusted to us in goodness, and calling upon Him to be a helper and assistant for us in all the affairs

[15] Theophanes, 464–6.

[16] Theophanes, 466, trans. Mango and Scott, 641.

[17] Mt. 5:33–7. See Burgmann, 'Die Novellen der Kaiserin Eirene', 28.

[18] Cf. Nicephorus, *Antirrhetici* III.62, PG 100.487–8. See Auzépy, 'State of emergency', 277.

[19] Irene, *Novel* I.24–25.

[20] Theodore the Studite, *Letters*, ed. G. Fatouros, *Theodori Studitae Epistulae* (Berlin, 1992), no. 7.37–41.

> assigned to us by him, for this reason we have deemed it necessary to publish a chapter concerning the eradication of oaths.[21]

However, despite the grandiloquent claim of the *prooimion* and repeated intimations throughout the remainder of the novel to their general unworthiness, oaths per se were not eradicated. The actual legal restrictions in the novel were minor.[22] Contracts and agreements were, preferably, to be written.[23] If the party responsible for drafting the document was unable to write, then he should prefix the agreement with a Cross and the remainder was written by a notary.[24] If previously oral agreements were disputed, a holographic document should be created by the litigants and the witnesses to record the settlement, and deposited in a church.[25] A formula was provided for these holographic documents, beginning with an invocation to God and the church in which the document was to be deposited, to act as witnesses.[26] The degree of an actual repudiation of oaths is measured by this invocation, and a previous call on God to be a witness, as both are so close to being oaths that Burgmann described the difference as 'hair-splitting'.[27] Furthermore, the catalogue of cases and credible witnesses given generally follows the schema of the *Ecloga*, with only insignificant changes.[28] Even these tiny changes do not seem to have lasted, with the sworn oath for testimony remaining an indispensable part of Byzantine judicial process.[29] Few pieces of legislation can have such a gulf between rhetoric and legal reality.

This disconnect tells us, however, that this novel was not really about oaths at all.[30] That was simply a useful legal and theological peg around which to mount a rhetorical broadside against the Isaurians using their favoured medium, the law. This supposition is supported by the *prooimion*'s relative length of 46 lines compared to 59 of the legal section of the novel, a dominance of rhetoric almost unparalleled

[21] Irene, *Novel* 1.3–9.

[22] For an overview, see Burgmann, 'Die Novellen der Kaiserin Eirene', 29–33.

[23] Irene, *Novel* 1.56–62.

[24] Irene, *Novel* 1.72–5.

[25] Irene, *Novel* 1.78–86.

[26] Irene, *Novel* 1.87–96.

[27] Previous use at *Novel* 1.66; Burgmann, 'Die Novellen der Kaiserin Eirene', 28, 'Spitzfindigkeit'.

[28] Irene, *Novel* 1.49–58; for comparison with the *Ecloga*, see Burgmann, 'Die Novellen der Kaiserin Eirene', 29–31.

[29] Burgmann, 'Die Novellen der Kaiserin Eirene', 35; and Burgmann, 'Oath'.

[30] See Burgmann, 'Die Novellen der Kaiserin Eirene', 28.

in Byzantine law.[31] Moreover, it is an exceedingly well-crafted polemic attacking the fundamental structures and motifs of Isaurian legislation. For as we have seen, the Isaurians had aspired to redefine Roman law as a direct successor to the law of the Old Testament, and themselves as the heirs of Moses. This novel, however, announced that:

> For all those who are not ignorant of Holy Scripture it is manifestly clear that the law given through Moses is a shadow of future goodness, not itself the icon of things, due to the imperfection and immaturity of those who received it.[32]

This law, in language deliberately echoing that of the *Ecloga* and the NM, thus downgraded the symbolic importance of Moses. Moreover, it described those who disagreed as fundamentally ignorant of the Bible. Furthermore, the whole Old Testament was cast through the interpretive lens of the New, as Mosaic Law lacked perfection because it did not know of the Incarnation.[33] As Christ had fulfilled the law, the implicit argument is that reference solely to it and the Old Testament in general (a central pillar of Isaurian ideology) was false logic, as it ignored Christ.[34] Thus the Isaurians were impious ignoramuses, uneducated in the Scriptures, misusing and misunderstanding the little they knew.

From this schematic basis, the novel paraphrases the Sermon on the Mount's recitation of certain key crimes in the Old Testament—adultery, murder, oath-breaking—and the radical Christian response to each.[35] Considering all three were prominent in the *Ecloga*, the final injunction against any oath-swearing at all was a clever and damning rhetorical pivot.[36] In the following sections, a host of biblical figures are paraded to castigate oath-swearing, including the Old Testament Isaurian favourites Isaiah, Moses, and Solomon.[37] This was a stark rejoinder to the attitude of the NM, with NM.1 beginning with the importance of just witnesses, while NM.12–13 endorsed the using of oaths to settle disputes. Indeed, the *prooimion* of the novel reads more like a theological text and biblical florilegium than a work of law.[38]

[31] Burgmann, 'Die Novellen der Kaiserin Eirene', 28.
[32] Irene, *Novel* 1.10–14. [33] Irene, *Novel* 1.14–16.
[34] Irene, *Novel* 1.16–18. Incidentally, this rhetoric is by far the more impressive if it assumes the existence of the NM firmly associated with the iconoclast emperors.
[35] Irene, *Novel* 1.18–23; Cf. Mt. 5:21–34. [36] See Chapter 2, 107, 121.
[37] Irene, *Novel* 1.36–44.
[38] This attack would further support the notion that the NM was produced in the eighth century before the present Novel.

Furthermore, hints of a wider discrediting of the Isaurians, and particularly their policy of iconoclasm, are noticeable. In particular, Mosaic Law was said to be not an icon of the real goodness of the Incarnation.[39] This intertwined with iconophile thinking, which proclaimed icons to be true Aristotelian representations of their prototypes, and thereby worthy of production and veneration.[40] Its use here, then, implies firstly that an icon is itself a good thing, and secondly that the Mosaic Law fails to be an icon. Moreover, iconophile propaganda is in evidence when the practice of oath-making is called 'profoundly Hebrew', echoing the polemic that linked iconoclasm with Judaism.[41] Furthermore, the charge of ignorance strongly echoes that of *amathia*, 'lack of education/culture', which iconophiles also flung at the Isaurians, particularly for their failure to understand Scripture.[42] Above all, the Mosaic prohibition of idols was the centrepiece of the iconoclast critique, which the iconophiles primarily countered by referencing the changes wrought by the Incarnation, fulfilling the old law and allowing the new dispensation, including icons.[43] This novel is saturated with such thought. However, just as Isaurian scepticism of icons flowed from a revitalized imperial office reconceptualized as an Old Testament kingship, rather than vice versa, Irene was using the thought and heat of the iconophile reaction to mount a broad attack on the altered imperial office, rather than on iconoclasm per se.[44]

The combined effect of this prolixity is a polemical demolition of the first order. The Isaurians misunderstood Scripture and ignored the Incarnation. They broke the clearest injunctions of Christ, causing the people to sin. Thus they were leading the people to destruction:

> For if the most grandiloquent prophet Isaiah exclaimed 'Those who made the people sin in words have been destroyed', how much more so with an oath?[45]

[39] Irene, *Novel* 1.11–12.

[40] See C. Barber, *Figure and Likeness. On the Limits of Representation in Byzantine Iconoclasm* (Princeton, 2002), 107–23.

[41] Irene, *Novel* I.26: *eipein de mallon ōs ta polla Hebraikē*. For the use of 'Jewish-minded' as an insult, see M.-F. Auzépy, 'Les enjeux de l'iconoclasme', *Settimane di studio del centro italiano di studi sull'alto medioevo* 51 (2004), 127–69, esp. 146–51. See also S. Wessel, 'The *Nouthesia* and the Law of Moses', *Byzantion* 73 (2003), 530–42.

[42] See Auzépy, 'State of emergency', 278–9.

[43] See, Barber, *Figure and Likeness*, 39–60; cf. Brubaker and Haldon, *History*, 135–40.

[44] Dagron, *Emperor and Priest*, 158–91.

[45] Irene, *Novel* 1.36–8.

The rulers who had founded their laws on Scripture, and liberally quoted from it, were attacked by a *florilegium* proving their lack of understanding. The Isaurians were implicitly presented as not just essentially Jewish, but bad Jews at that, as they broke Moses' own commandments which they had sought to appropriate. Legally, this novel may have changed nothing substantial, but rhetorically, it assaulted the fundamentals of Isaurian ideology.

The second (far shorter) novel on marriage presents a similar balance between law and rhetoric. It banned third and further marriages, declaring them to be 'unlawful and bestial'.[46] Marriage between a master and his slave was also prohibited, with any resulting children declared illegitimate.[47] However, this was the implicit existing legal position. The *Ecloga* repeatedly implies that remarriage should be avoided, and only talks about second marriages, suggesting a prohibition on further marriages.[48] Indeed, this novel explicitly refers to 'the second title' of the *Ecloga*, which dealt with marriage.[49]

Yet, if legally unimportant, the novel is, in the slightly hyperbolic words of Burgmann, 'a small rhetorical masterpiece'.[50] It is couched in the words of Moses, Paul, and Basil, central figures respectively in the Old Testament, the New, and the church fathers.[51] Although explicitly announcing that the novel was adding nothing new, quoting Moses saying 'it is not to be added to, nor taken away from', and confirming the *Ecloga*, it implicitly positioned Irene as the interpreter of the *Ecloga* specifically, and law in general.[52] Thus, the novel also portrayed the *Ecloga* as in need of interpretation and emendation. Moreover, it had a direct political purpose, for Constantine V himself had married three times. Thus the clarification and restipulation of the *Ecloga*'s law, buttressed as it was by those same authorities that Constantine claimed supported his policies, was a deliberately ironic assault on the legitimacy of the emperor against which Irene most reacted. Furthermore, as she herself had been married to the child of Constantine V's first wife, while the children of his third wife had repeatedly featured in the factional plotting against her, this law

[46] Irene, *Novel* 2.8; cf. Basil c.80. [47] Irene, *Novel* 2.11–15.

[48] E.g. E.2.8.rubric; 2.5. [49] Irene, *Novel* 2.6, *en tō deuterō titlō*.

[50] Burgmann, 'Die Novellen der Kaiserin Eirene', 35, 'eine kleine rhetorische Meisterleistung'.

[51] Irene, *Novel* 2.4–8.

[52] Irene, *Novel* 2.4–5; quote from Deut. 4:2=13:1.

delegitimized them and the father who had begat them from an illicit marriage, while maintaining her own legitimacy.[53]

Furthermore, the very issuing of novels implied the necessity of new law, rejecting the previous half-century since the issuing of the *Ecloga* which had overwhelmingly focused on the gathering and representing of old, in particular Justinianic, law. Moreover, the only incontestable allusion in the *Ecloga* to an Isaurian novel is to one concerning marriage, with the specific issue of making written marriage contracts before three credible witnesses.[54] It is therefore plausible (if impossible to prove) that Irene's novels deliberately countered the very issues of marriage and witnesses that the Isaurians' own only novel had dealt with. Certainly, Irene was returning to a prime issue of the Isaurians, inferring that even after all their attention and rhetoric, they had failed to provide adequate legislation.[55] This tiny novel, therefore, combined the leitmotifs of Isaurian legislation—the use of the Bible to make clear and amend the legislation of the past, and a concern for the sanctity and propriety of marriage—and strove to employ them to discredit their advocates.

However, these novels are also evidence of the legal and ideological restrictions to Irene's own campaign of iconoclasm against her predecessors. The fact that these novels changed little legally, and seem to have no or little lasting effect, is testament to the strength of the legal system refounded by the Isaurians. The *Ecloga* and related legislation had so firmly set the standard on what was both the law and legal process that it proved nigh-on impossible to change. Moreover, the need to create novels at all, let alone such powerful polemic, suggests the high degree of ideological power the Isaurians had successfully reaffirmed to imperial legislation. Thus the fact that Irene felt compelled to legislate is evidence of both the importance of law to the Isaurians, and also the existence a base of legal knowledge. As in other literary genres, the Isaurians' own success at rejuvenation was now being used against them.[56]

Rhetorically, the sheer breadth and potency of her response is a backhanded compliment to the efficacy of the imperial model established by the Isaurians, especially in the arena of law. In style, the novels may attempt to subvert, but they still use the methods of the

[53] For the repeated troubles with Constantine V's sons, see P. Hollingsworth, 'Nikephoros', in *ODB*, vol. 3, 1476.

[54] E.2.3.

[55] See Chapter 2, 113–18.

[56] See Conclusion, 270–1.

Isaurians. Legislation now had to be framed in biblical thought, exegesis justifying the central points. Roman law was naturally seen as somehow flowing from the Bible, the debate being over how to interpret that text. Correspondingly, the function of law was a moral one, with the potential of dire consequences from divine wrath driving the need to proclaim and enforce correct law. Furthermore, Irene was returning to the issue of marriage, which was a recurring concern of Byzantine, and indeed Roman law.[57] The difference for the Isaurians was the predominant interest in the morality of marriage, viewing it as they did through a thoroughly Christian lens as a societal good in need of protection. This perception is replicated entirely in Irene's novel. In all this, these novels are similar to those of Heraclius two centuries previously, in implicitly accepting the existing schema. Despite the florid oratory, these novels failed to break the ideological supremacy of the system created by Leo III and his successors.

THE NOVEL OF LEO V: THE ISAURIAN SYSTEM REAFFIRMED

That failure is reflected in the novel of Leo V, an emperor who returned to the model of emperorship established by the Isaurians as deliberately and assuredly as Irene had attempted to demolish it.[58] Famously, the *Scriptor Incertus* had described Leo's resuscitation of iconoclasm as a strategy to imitate the Isaurians, and their long and successful reigns, in stark contrast to Irene and her successors.[59] As part of this strategy, he named his son and co-emperor Constantine, and modelled his coins on those of Leo III's so closely that they have frequently been confused.[60] Similarly, this novel had been variously ascribed to Leo III and Constantine V, and Leo IV and Constantine

[57] Burgmann, 'Die Novellen der Kaiserin Eirene', 34.

[58] Leo V, *Novel*, ed. D. Simon, 'Zur Ehegesetzgebung der Isaurier', *FM* I (Frankfurt, 1976), 16–43, edn. 21–29. Cf. Dölger, *Regesten* 338.

[59] *Scriptor incertus de Leone Armenio*, in *Leonis Grammatici Chronographia*, ed. I. Bekker (Bonn, 1842), 335–62, 349.

[60] *DOC* III, 1, 371–2.

VI, before Kresten firmly established Leo V as its author.[61] Leo V thus carried his strategy of legitimation through association into that most Isaurian of mediums, the law, and the fact that he (like Irene) felt the need and ability to do so reflects the ideological import attached by this point to legislation.

The *prooimion* of Leo's novel was a deliberate echo of the *Ecloga*, emphasizing Leo's divinely appointed and sanctioned role as emperor, entrusted with the task of ceaseless watching over his people, to help guide them on the path of salvation and to provide the benefit of philanthropic care.[62] Its subject was, yet again, marriage. More particularly, it concerns the subject of divorce, where the *Ecloga* had instituted major innovations strictly limiting the legal grounds for it.[63] The *Ecloga* had also tightened the restrictions on whom one could marry, most importantly, in this instance, adopting the canonical regulation proposed at Trullo prohibiting the marriage of a godparent to their godchild or their parent into civil law.[64] This regulation, however, was being used by parents to gain a divorce by standing as godparents to their own children. To close this loophole, and following clear precedents in the *Ecloga*, Leo V promulgated a series of punishments based on circumstance.[65] The unpropertied were to be *sphodrōs aikisthēsetai*, 'vehemently tortured', while the propertied were essentially to lose their property to their wronged partners and their children.[66] All guilty, propertied or unpropertied, husband or wife, were to be banished for seven years and prohibited from a second marriage. If they dared to marry again, the marriage would be declared illegitimate, along with any offspring, and punished with permanent banishment. In this, Leo V was using the example and tools of Leo III, in order to maintain the legal and moral system established by the Isaurians. This essential continuity in ideology, method, and law between the *Ecloga* and this novel is reflected in the manuscripts, where of its four MSS, two are found directly after the *Ecloga Privata* and the *Krisis peri gambrōn stratiōtōn*, and the others accompanying the AE.[67] These later compilers

[61] O. Kresten, 'Datierungsprobleme "isaurischer" Eherechtsnovellen I. Coll. 1.26', *FM* IV (Frankfurt, 1984), 37–106.

[62] Leo V, *Novel*.5–16. Cf. E.pr.11–31.

[63] E.2.9. See Chapter 2, 116–18.

[64] E.2.2.

[65] For the various gradations of punishment, see Simon, 'Ehegesetzgebung', 31–7.

[66] Leo V, *Novel*.134. Cf. E.17.26.846.

[67] Respectively *RHBR*.53, 244, 319, and 327.

thus gave Leo V the highest praise he could have wished: to be treated as a continuator of the Isaurians.

In their respective opprobrium and adulation, the novels of Irene and Leo V testify to the enduring potency of Isaurian ideology, especially as espoused through law. This law had become, as in the days of Justinian, a vital manifestation of imperial glory, as well as a tool of propaganda and control. Indeed, Irene and Leo were in the same respective position as Justinian's successors, essentially maintaining and mildly modifying, as necessity demanded, the corpus of law they had inherited, always set within an ideological and rhetorical schema that they could not break. Although Irene fervently tried to destroy this mould, the historical failure of her novels to resonate, and the equally determined return prosecuted by Leo V, indicate the power of the imperial office constructed by the Isaurians.

THE MACEDONIANS: APPROPRIATION AND CONDEMNATION

The Macedonian dynasty would succeed where Irene had failed, appropriating the Isaurian legal inheritance, while denigrating its authors. Indeed, their motivation was similar to Irene's.[68] Firstly, a system so indelibly associated with the iconoclast emperors and their reverence for Mosaic Law sat uncomfortably with triumphant iconophiles who had strenuously argued against an over-literal reading of the Old Testament. Secondly, both were usurpers. They therefore urgently needed to legitimize themselves and delegitimize their predecessors. That the most prominent way Basil I (r.867–86) sought to do this was through comprehensive legal reform was a backhanded compliment to the system created by the Isaurians.

The first manifestation of this was the *Prochiron*, issued *c.*870–9, as a deliberate replacement for the *Ecloga*.[69] Indeed, it attacked the

[68] For the general period, see Pieler, 'Rechtsliteratur', 445–72. Cf. Fögen, 'Reanimation of Roman law in the ninth century'.

[69] Here I follow the traditional dating given to the *Prochiron* and *Eisagoge*, upheld convincingly (in my view) by Van Bochove, *To Date?*. This rejected the redatings proposed by Schminck, *Rechtsbüchern*, which dated the Eisagoge to 885/6 and the Prochiron to 907. This debate is beyond the scope of this inquiry, yet even if Schminck is correct, it would little alter the implications of this section.

Ecloga as 'the author's perversion of good laws, harmful to the state and fit only to perpetuate foolishness'.[70] Instead, the *Prochiron* would act as the synopsis of a law 'cleansed', *anakatharsis*, with the redundant removed, the 'perversions' of the past deleted, and the obscure Latin terminology tenaciously embedded in the legal discourse from the original Justinianic codification translated into Greek.[71] Furthermore, the *Prochiron* was given an explicitly didactic purpose, obliquely implying that the *Ecloga* had become the standard primer in legal education.[72] The *Prochiron*'s successor, the *Eisagoge*, issued *c*.879–83, was even more strident in its denunciation of the Isaurians.[73] They and their works were attacked as that 'nonsense promulgated by the Isaurians in contradiction to the said divine doctrines and to the detriment of the laws that bring salvation'.[74]

Ironically both the *Prochiron* and *Eisagoge* were heavily modelled on the *Ecloga*.[75] Their very format of a concise legal manual or handbook followed that of the *Ecloga*. Their *prooimia* were littered with biblical citations. Substantively, while in matters of civil law they adhered more closely to Justinianic legislation, in criminal law they adopted E.17 almost wholesale.[76] These texts' strident polemic, combined with an inability to shake off the model of the *Ecloga*, speaks volumes on the potency of the Isaurian work. Similarly, as we have seen, the *Prochiron*, *Eisagoge*, and their respective derivatives were appended with the NS, NN, and NG almost as a matter of course—evidence of the utility of these three and how far they had become embedded in legal discourse, and most probably practice as well.

The apogee of the Macedonian programme, however, was the creation of the *Basilika*, rightly seen as the beginnings of a new epoch in Roman/Byzantine law.[77] The *Basilika* represented the collection and reorganization of the entire Justinianic *Corpus* rendered

[70] Schminck, *Rechtsbüchern*, 60.66; trans. E. Freshfield, *A Manual of Eastern Roman Law: The Procheiros nomos* (Cambridge, 1928), 51.

[71] Schminck, *Rechtsbüchern*, 60.77; See Van Bochove, *To Date?*, 73–86; P. Pieler, *Anakatharsis tōn palaiōn nomōn* und makedonische Renaissance', *Subseciva Groningana* 3 (1989), 61–77.

[72] Schminck, Rechtsbüchern, 58.45–51. See Van Bochove, *To Date?*, 63–4, 73–5.

[73] For date, see Van Bochove, *To Date?*, 23–5.

[74] Van Bochove, *To Date?*, 77.

[75] Van Bochove, *To Date?*, 68.

[76] Burgmann, *Ecloga*, 121–2.

[77] *Basilika*, ed. H. Scheltema et al., *Basilicorum libri LX*, Series A (Text), 8 vols, Series B (Scholia), 9 vols (Groningen, 1953–88). For its place in Byzantine law, see Pieler, 'Rechtsliteratur', 445–57.

into Greek. Its materials were the very same works of the sixth-century *antecessores* that formed the bulk of the *Ecloga* and its appendices, yet on an utterly vaster scale.[78] Justinianic law was appropriated *in toto* by the Macedonians, in the words of Fögen, 'making Roman law Byzantine intellectual property'.[79] Fögen convincingly posits that the impetus for this was to reassert ownership of the Roman past in the face of a western world busily appropriating it for themselves and denying the 'Greeks' their Roman status.[80] Yet one should not ignore the role of the Isaurians. For firstly, the *Basilika* gave credence to the claims of the *Prochiron* and *Eisagoge* that the *Ecloga* was based on corrupted Justinianic law, intermixing it with deviant sources, therefore necessitating the return to the pure original. Secondly, the *Ecloga*'s sponsoring of a specialized legal administration and the Isaurian project to collect, edit, and disseminate Justinianic law provided a model for the Macedonians, and plausibly provided the momentum in the academic study of Justinianic law that produced the means for the creation of the *Basilika*. If so, the Isaurians were excoriated by a discourse whose revival they could justly claim credit for.

Nor was this the end of the Macedonian legal outpouring, for Leo VI (r.886–912) would issue 113 novels.[81] These constantly repeated the idea that law, government, and society needed cleansing.[82] Moreover, they underlined the Macedonians' appropriation of Justinian I from the impious clutches of the Isaurians. Furthermore, they re-established the model of the novel as the principle means of imperial lawmaking, stepping away from the handbooks favoured by the Isaurians. Not that the utilitarian book of law was dead—for in 911 or 912, Leo promulgated the *Book of the Eparch*, an assemblage of regulations touching on some of the guilds of Constantinople under the jurisdiction of the *Eparch*.[83] Its small preface even contains an

[78] Fögen, 'Reanimation of Roman law', 14.

[79] Fögen, 'Reanimation of Roman law', 17.

[80] Fögen, 'Reanimation of Roman law', 17–22.

[81] Leo VI, *Novels*, ed. P. Noailles and A. Dain, *Les Novelles de Léon le Sage* (Paris, 1944).

[82] J. Shepard, 'Equilibrium to expansion (886–1025)', in Shepard (ed.), *The Cambridge History of the Byzantine Empire, c.500–1492* (Cambridge, 2008), 493–536, 497.

[83] *Book of the Eparch*, ed. J. Koder, *Das Eparchenbuch Leons des Weisen* (Vienna, 1991).

allusion to the Law of Moses.[84] Evidently the Isaurian model continued to have an impact, although it was now thoroughly appropriated by the Macedonians.

Overall the Macedonian legal works brought four shifts within imperial ideology from the world of the Isaurians. The links with late antiquity and *Romanitas* were symbolically resoldered. In this regard we should consider the *Taktika* of Leo VI, a work which declared itself legislation, indeed a partner of the *Prochiron*, which presented the military wisdom of the glorious past as the solution to the problems of the present.[85] The criticism about the intervening rulers, and particularly the iconoclasts, was that their boorishness had undermined the wisdom of the past, leading to the decay of good order, which the Macedonians were now putting right through restoring the old order and cleansing it of any accretions.[86]

With the restoration of the Roman past came a downplaying and reworking of the significance of the Old Testament. Never again would a regime 'attempt to apply the letter of the Old Testament law to the reality of Byzantine life'.[87] By the late ninth century, Byzantium had weathered the storms that had created an atmosphere propitious to assertion of such a close association with the tribulations of the Hebrews. Set for a period of prosperity, the Old Testament was relegated in favour of and interpreted analogously through the New, rather than the more literal approach of the Isaurians.[88] Indeed, the Byzantine emperors were thereon most strikingly linked with Christ, indicated by Justinian II's abortive coinage being revived as the standard imperial type.[89]

Similarly, after the early Macedonians, the importance of Justinian as an imperial role model was increasingly downgraded in favour of Constantine I.[90] Indeed, even in the novels of Leo VI, Justinian would

[84] *Book of the Eparch*, 72.

[85] *Taktika*, ed. G. Dennis, *The Taktika of Leo VI* (Washington DC, 2010).

[86] For the cleansing of the law, see Pieler, '*Anakatharsis*'; for the broader cultural movement, see Mango, 'The revival of learning'.

[87] Magdalino and Nelson, 'Introduction', *Old Testament*, 21.

[88] Magdalino and Nelson, 'Introduction', 29. For this general period of prosperity, see Shepard, 'Equilibrium to expansion'; Whittow, *Formation*, 310–57.

[89] P. Grierson, *Byzantine Coinage* (2nd edn., Washington DC, 1999), 9.

[90] For the rise in the significance of Constantine I from the eighth century onwards, see A. Kazhdan, '"Constanin Imaginaire": Byzantine legends of the ninth century about Constantine the Great', *Byzantion* 57 (1987), 196–250; for a greater emphasis on the upswing in intensity on the first Christian emperor in the ninth

be criticized as introducing uncertainty in the law through excess of legislation.[91] Of course, Justinian remained important within the imperial imagination, forming, along with Constantine, an almost semi-divine imperial model, by which emperors could legitimize themselves and be judged by others. But the emphasis had shifted between the two.

Moreover, after Leo VI's own impressive outpouring, imperial legislation was hardly vast and never imbued with the power and centrality ascribed to it in the reigns of Justinian and Leo III. Law became a more minor attribute of imperial ideology, dwarfed by imperial 'management of the sacred'.[92] Emperors were increasingly enmeshed in a web of ceremonies and rituals, which prominently included the use and control of relics, orchestrated to map onto earth the court of heaven. These developments lie well beyond the scope of this study, yet they remind us that law is always part of a greater social, cultural, and symbolic world, contingent on it for its role and position within a given society. The world of Leo VI was not that of Leo III, and their respective laws reflect that. However, the Macedonians' efforts to appropriate the Isaurian legacy while condemning the iconoclast emperors indicates that the Isaurians had indelibly shaped the Byzantine world, and in particular the legal sphere. Those legal changes of the iconoclast era were, however, but one thread in a complex tapestry. To truly appreciate them we must try to glimpse the whole, and the place of the law within it. It is to this context that the Conclusion shall turn.

century, see P. Magdalino, 'Introduction', in Magdalino (ed.), *New Constantines: The Rhythm of Imperial Renewal in Byzantium, 4th–13th Centuries* (Aldershot, 1994), 1–9, esp. 3. In the same collection see J. Haldon, 'Constantine or Justinian? Crisis and identity in imperial propaganda in the seventh century', 95–107; L. Brubaker, 'To legitimize an emperor: Constantine and visual authority in the eighth and ninth centuries', 139–58; and A. Markopoulos, 'Constantine the Great in Macedonian historiography: models and approaches', 159–70.

[91] Leo VI, *Novels*, ed. P. Noailles and A. Dain, *Les Novelles de Léon le Sage* (Paris, 1944), 1.

[92] Dagron, *Emperor and Priest*, 219.

Conclusion

> Let those who have been appointed by our piety to judge cases and entrusted with the just weighing of our pious laws consider and understand these things, and conduct themselves accordingly. For by these things we endeavour to serve God who entrusted us with the sceptre of the Empire; with these weapons, by His power, we wish to firmly resist our enemies; by these we trust to increase in goodness and prosper the flock signified by Christ, subjected by his authority to our clemency; and with these we hope for the restoration of the ancient jurisdiction of the state by us. . . . For it is written, 'Woe to them who justify the ungodly for rewards,[1] and pervert the way of the humble,[2] and take away Justice from the righteous; their root shall be as chaff, and their flower shall go up as dust, for they were not willing to fulfil the law of the almighty Lord.'[3]

This section from the *prooimion* of the *Ecloga* is a representative summation of Isaurian legal ideology and policy. The divinely appointed emperors, armed with the law, are cast as the defenders against external enemies and internal sin. Their pursuit of justice, both in the collection of law and through its enforcement by a competent and just judiciary, was a mission ordained by heaven, the vigorous pursuit of which ensured divine favour, the fundamental basis of the Christian state. These ideological threads underlie the diverse texts explored above. Together they formed a consistent and coherent programme, evidence of a determined and broadly successful campaign to restore imperial authority and remake the image of the state in the wake of defeat. We shall examine the parameters of that programme and the broader transformation in the Byzantine

[1] Is. 5:23. [2] Amos 2:7 [3] Is. 5:24. E.pr.87–95, 98–101.

symbolic universe, through both the evidence of the legal sources and the narratives drawn from the non-legal material. Yet before that, we must summarize the development of law in the Iconoclast era, and how it interacted with the Justinianic world it had inherited.

LAW IN THE ICONOCLAST ERA

The first and highly significant aspect of law to note in this period, testified through all the texts explored above, is the persistence and deep continuity of the Roman legal tradition, in particular in the reformulated form bequeathed by Justinian I. In the first instance, the substantive legal content of the overwhelming bulk of these texts adheres to Justinianic ordinances or the broader inheritance of the antique world. From Trullo's restatement of canons from fourth-century councils and the *Ecloga*'s repetition of the *Digest*'s condemnation of arson, to the NG's elucidation on delict law and NS's restipulation of best practice maintained in the *Strategikon*, law in the Iconoclast era largely retained and maintained the law of late antiquity.

Furthermore, in both Trullo's canons and the civil law of the Isaurian works, a significant proportion and perhaps the majority of the raw material that composed these texts emanated from late antiquity. Due to the opacity of the processes of transmission, it is impossible to examine precisely the extent to which contemporary texts reworked that material. Yet, from the evidence we do possess, it is clear that the whole gamut of responses was employed, ranging from outright copying of an extant work, through truncation and simplification, to amalgamation and emendation. Moreover, much of that inherited legal material was rephrased, from mere compression to expression through exegesis. Finally, that heritage was repackaged within novel formats, such as the anthology-cum-manual of the *Ecloga* and NM, or the NN, NS, and NG's excerpts of law relevant to a particular section of society. Indeed, the dominant mode of contemporary legal activity was one of partial selection, codification, and restipulation of the past, especially the Justinianic past.

Moreover, the very creation of multiple texts of manifold nature, combined with their popularity in the manuscript tradition that is probably indicative of repeated production and dissemination during this period, is testament both to the demand for such works, whether from the central imperial authorities, judges, and lawyers themselves, or individuals and institutions for whatever reason concerned with the law, and to the ability to supply. Therefore, these varied and diverse texts, with their marked propensity towards the practical, cumulatively speak of an age of continued legal competence and practice.

Further, these works were not mere academic catalogues of the past, but intended for present, practical purposes. Above all, they were designed for all those involved in the administration of justice, and as such they provide evidence of a continuing judicial system. The *Ecloga* documents a world replete with judicial and legislative institutions, from the central authorities of the emperors and *Quaestor*, through to multiple types of judges and notaries. Indeed, the *Ecloga*, its extensions, and associated texts were all aimed at providing presiding magistrates with clear and concise compendia of legal guidelines of likely cases. As such, they have an evident bias towards such practical issues as property law and delict, over the sometimes abstruse and abstract intricacies of Justinianic law.

Furthermore, these texts were instruments intended not just to aid magistrates, but also to stamp central control over them. Firstly and significantly, the *Ecloga*'s *prooimion* and the NM in particular contain considerable rhetorical encouragement for good judgement, and attack venal or incompetent judges. More importantly, there is a marked propensity to prescription, the need to state categorically what the law was and what the judicial response should be. Thus these codes represent a major restriction on judicial discretion and independence. This is most obvious in criminal law and punishments, for whereas judges in late antiquity had been given a large degree of discretion in the choice of punishment, in the Isaurian legislation there is a precise punishment designed for every crime. In this, these texts reflect an imperial ambition to reassert control, to regularize and systematize, to impose imperial order on threatened chaos, and to organize and penetrate all levels of society. The final aspect of this programme was the creation of state remuneration for all involved with judicial administration. This could only strengthen central control, but would also naturally propel the emergence of a more specialized legal establishment.

Therefore, the world described by these texts is no legal desert but positively verdant. Moreover, there was considerable growth, with the proliferation of texts testament to an increased desire to extend the

Ecloga and continue its project of collecting and restipulating the Justinianic legal past. Indeed, the creation of a centrally salaried legal officialdom, combined with the model of the *Ecloga* and probable continued imperial encouragement, must have spurred this process, laying the foundations for the legal outpouring of the ninth century. Further, although the process is murky, these texts, their practical aim, the creation of salaries, the apparent specialization of the still-extant provincial administration on judicial affairs, and the prominence of the previously little known *akroatai* who appear as ubiquitous investigating magistrates (many probably operating at the sub-provincial level) all tell of a marked strengthening in provincial jurisprudence across the eighth century. Therefore, the best description of the trajectory of law in this period is that after an abatement, rather than collapse, of Roman law in the seventh century, with the probable diminution of legal education and judicial practice combined with virtual cessation of imperial legal activity, there was a marked intensification under the Isaurians.[4] Importantly, at no point did the Roman legal tradition and practice break, despite huge stress leading to undeniable subsidence, and the Isaurians in the eighth century self-consciously utilized a discourse fundamentally anchored in the Justinianic legal revolution. Yet the upswing in legal activity from the promulgation of the *Ecloga* in 741 is undeniable.

Moreover, significant continuity did not mean an end to legal change. Rather, in manifold ways, major and minor, the inherited corpus was not just reworked and re-expressed, but amalgamated with novel material to reflect the changing priorities of the time. Indeed, from what was selected from the past, how those selections were amended, and the truly novel, one can detect several important shifts in focus. In particular, a leitmotif of the entire period was a concern for correct practice, which was manifested in manifold ways. Perhaps most strikingly and consistently, from the Trullan canons onwards there was a repeated and prominent interest in issues of personal morality, and in particular of sexual conduct and marriage, and in ensuring correct religious practice. Moreover, in the Isaurian texts, crime and punishment loom large, with a growing interest in delict law. In all this there was a marked extension and refocusing of

[4] For this language of 'abatement' versus 'intensification' in a primarily economic sense, see P. Horden and N. Purcell, *The Corrupting Sea: A Study of Mediterranean History* (Oxford, 2000) 263–70.

legal activity towards the quotidian and spiritual lives of everyone, away from the complexities of Roman law aimed primarily at the rich and powerful. Further, this shift was embedded within a grander conceptual transformation in how law was conceived, to which we shall now turn.

LAW AND THE BYZANTINE SYMBOLIC UNIVERSE

Whereas substantively the law of the Iconoclast era upheld Justinianic law, conceptually and rhetorically there is a chasm between the legal worlds of Justinian I and Leo III, with Justinian II at Trullo standing on the very cusp of transition. The first aspect of this was the reimagining of what the function of law was. The Justinianic *Corpus* retained the essentially Hellenistic principle that law's purpose was to help men 'live honourably, harm nobody, give everyone his due'.[5] By Trullo, the civil law was in suspended animation, awaiting normality to be such an aid once again. Instead, what was prescribed as needed were canons, designed as part of an eschatological plan to heal the souls of the sinful sick, in order to restore health to the empire. In the Isaurian world, the urgency and immediacy of Trullo's providential canons was extended to civil law, which itself was elided with Mosaic Law, if moderated through *philanthropia*. Thus the law was conceived as a heaven-sent implement of correction, which would advance Christian morality by protecting the weak, deterring those with any propensity to evil and punishing the wicked, both for the sake of stern justice in upholding God's commandments, and for the purgation of sin. Further, the law was the Byzantines' covenant with God, whose application thereby ensured God's promised support, which was the foundation of the state.

Similarly, the proclaimed origins and identity of law fundamentally altered. The law of Justinian was explicitly and definitely Roman. Its origins lay in the ordinances and customs of the Roman people, the proclamations of its senate, and the statutes of the Roman emperor, and expounded in the writings of Roman jurists.[6] Law was finely

[5] I.1.1.3; trans. Birks and McLeod, *Institutes*, 37.
[6] D.1.1–4; I.1.1–2.

graded and classified, conceived as divided between *lex* and *ius*, between public and private, and between *ius naturale*, *ius gentium*, and *ius civile*.[7] One of Justinian's achievements was to create a canon of Roman law that was subjected to imperial authority, and ultimately to that of heaven—and a heaven that was expressly Christian. Yet the more immediate origins and the diversity of different legal systems were admitted. Similarly, the Trullan canons, despite emphasizing the role of Justinian II and the need for new legislation, enumerated their late antique inheritance and the function of synods as legislators. However, Trullo's canons were unavoidably Christian, to a far greater extent than even the invocations of the Almighty in Justinian I's novels. This in itself was hardly radical, for the law of the Church is inescapably Christian and conceived as ultimately God-given. Yet the fact that Justinian II chose to utilize a medium that had little 'Roman' about it as the tool to restore the Justinianic empire is a measure of how far imperial rhetoric had travelled by the end of the seventh century. Far more radical, however, was the conception of law expounded in the Isaurian texts. Here the present law was not just divinely sanctioned, but was in actuality the successor to that delivered through the prophets of the Old Testament. Thus, although substantively very much Roman law, it was expressed as Christian law, which was Mosaic Law perfected through *philanthropia*.

Corresponding to these shifts, three different identities were given to the people subject to the law. In Justinian's laws, the prime signifier was still Roman. The components of that identity were shifting in importance, with the rise of Christianity and, more specifically, a focus on the Orthodox. However, the people were still primarily defined as Roman citizens, living under Roman law, living in the Roman Empire, and governed and protected by the Roman state and emperor.[8] By the time of Justinian II at the Council in Trullo, Christianity had become the hegemonic idea, with an inherently stronger focus on Orthodoxy versus heresy as the division between us and them. Yet although the empire and its inhabitants were clearly Christian, they were still unquestionably Roman, with an imperial ideology focused on restoring the world of Justinian I.

[7] D.1.1; I.1.2.

[8] For example, in I.pr.–1.2 the qualifier *Romanus* is used no fewer than seven times, linked to the state, empire, law, and people. Apart from the invocation to Christ at the beginning of the text, no Christian term is employed.

The *Ecloga* presents a different world. The word 'Roman' is completely absent. The only signifier is 'Christian'. The people entrusted to the emperors' care were *christosēmeiōtos*, 'marked/signified as Christians'.[9] Betrothal and marriage were explicitly 'of Christians', the implications being that betrothal and marriage were inherently Christian institutions and that the only people that constituted true citizens of the state were Christians.[10] The state was described as 'of Christians', and conspiracy against it and its sovereigns was punishable by death.[11] Those who fell into enemy hands and renounced the Christian faith were thus exiled from Church and community, portrayed here as virtually coterminous.[12] Importantly, there is no internal 'Other' in the *Ecloga*, except perhaps the limited reference to slaves. All are assumed to be Christian, with no mention of Jews or pagans, and the briefest mention of heretics; nor indeed is there use of 'barbarian'. The 'other' is specifically external—the enemy or enemies who constantly threaten the Christian realm, implicitly above all the Islamic Caliphate. The Christian people were, therefore, established in an overriding martial paradigm.

The subsequent legislation nuanced this assertion of identity. The AE, through its restatement of Justinianic ordinances against Jews, heathens, and deviant practices, punished the archetypal others of the Christian world.[13] The NS did use the word 'Roman' and compared it to 'barbarian', yet only in those sections belonging to the recension dated to the mid-seventh century.[14] The section that has been argued was an Isaurian addition only uses the dichotomy of soldiers and enemies. Neither the NG nor NN give any specific identity beyond occupation and societal status to their subjects. Most importantly, the NM advanced the claims of the *Ecloga* to a people defined by their relationship with God. Indeed, both the *Ecloga* and NM present a fundamental difference with the identity claimed at Trullo, for in the former, Christian is understood through an avowedly Old Testament

[9] E.pr.92. [10] E.1.1.112, 2.1.140. [11] E.17.3.774.
[12] E.17.6.790. [13] AE.III–VIII.
[14] NS.23=Ashburner 38 punishes betrayal of the Romans; NS.24=Ashburner 6 and 39 states that anyone deserting to the barbarians, including any inhabitant of Roman territory, is to be executed; NS.25=Ashburner 40 punishes the scouts of the Roman army divulging the 'secrets of the Romans'. The only other mentions are of barbarians in NS.36=Ashburner 6 and of secrets of Romans NG.47=Ashburner 27, both repeating earlier material. Incidentally, the neat unit of NS.23–5 punishing desertion is further evidence of the superiority of *RHBR*.274 as the best exemplar of the NS.

prism. The Christians were the New Israelites, and like the old, their identity was based on a covenant with God. Indeed, to a great degree it was the same legal covenant that had defined the old elect, if now corrected through Christian grace. In all this, one central continuity was the importance accorded to law in the formation of identity. To be Roman was to be under Roman law; to be Christian was to be subject to God's law. What had changed were the identification, legitimizing authority, and function of that law, and the identity of the people subject to it.

These different identities were enmeshed within variant expounded pasts. The laws of Justinian I explicitly and repeatedly invoked the past glory of Rome, in particular its imperial past, which Justinian was restoring. At Trullo, Justinian II again looked back, this time to the imperial world of his namesake. However, this was conceived as foremost a Christian world. More significantly, Trullo situated itself within Christian cosmological history, as the hinge between the current decline of the Christian empire, caused by moral and religious laxness, and the grander battle between God and Satan over the souls of men, begun in the beginning and only to end at the end of days. However, in the Isaurian world, it was the past contained in the Old Testament that provided the nexus of identity, a past espoused through prophets, followed by kings like Solomon and emperors such as Justinian, leading to the present Christian state being corrected through the law of the *Ecloga* and associate texts, culminating in the curing of souls for heaven and the end of time. Moreover, the Isaurian legal texts were self-consciously presented as a selection from the past. However, they were more than just anthologies, but conceived as improvements. The law was both catalogued and corrected. There was a clear conception of disjuncture with the past, even as the imperial past was elided with the biblical. This recognition is borne out in the perceived need not only to repeat law that is described as both ancient and in danger of becoming confused or unknown, but also to alter it for the sake of humanity. Importantly, the recognition of disjuncture did not produce the classic Roman response of restoration of the past, even if in reality it was a rhetorical cloak for innovation, as it had under Augustus, Diocletian, and Justinian.[15] Instead, correction even to the point of innovation was an avowed

[15] For Justinian in particular, see Maas, 'Roman history and Christian ideology'.

and approved part of the programme from the beginning, even when the legal content was frequently little changed. There is a sense of a creation of a new empire, from the cleansed and sifted strands of the old, with Christian emperors at its head and armed with the law.

Within this reworked and simplified ideological framework, the role of the emperor was also reimagined. Justinian I was God's vicegerent, who would overshadow and outdo his imperial predecessors. Justinian II would restore the world of Justinian I, but was also associated repeatedly and stridently with Christ. However, the Isaurians were the heirs of Moses, Solomon, and the Maccabees. The only Roman emperor mentioned in their legal corpus is Justinian, presented as the great lawgiver, but more within a biblical model than the Roman.[16] The emperors were entrusted with power to reform the people, primarily through the aegis of law. Leading a purified people, and armed with divine favour, the enemies of the Christian state could be repelled by Isaurian military leadership. The emperors were the shepherds of society, leaders, protectors, and correctors combined in one office. Moreover, they were the mediators between heaven and earth, responsible for bringing God's law to the people and for ensuring divine favour for the state. All segments of society—civil and military, lay and clerical—were the responsibility of the emperor and subject to his law as a matter of course. In this the Isaurians maintained the late antique paradigm, and in particular the role staked out by Justinian.[17] Yet the Isaurians vigorously reaffirmed this standard, and in many respects expanded the moral ambitions of imperial government, which were justified, conceptualized, and expounded through Scripture.

Cumulatively, these conceptual shifts elucidate a marked transformation in imperial ideology as expressed through the medium of law. For Justinian I proclaimed a Christian-Roman empire, with the two terms distinct but inherently conjoined by providence and the pious and glorious rule of Justinian himself. By the time of Justinian II, the Roman half of this conception had receded into obscurity. It was not that late seventh-, or indeed eighth-century Byzantines, let alone the imperial government, would have denied their essential 'Roman-ness', but it had become a peripheral and barely perceivable

[16] E.pr.5; NG.title. [17] Dvornik, *Byzantine Political Philosophy*, 724–850.

aspect of imperial rhetoric and projection of identity.[18] Justinian II, however, definitely and defiantly claimed to rule the empire of Christians, the sole legitimate Christian polity, whose territories had only been temporarily invaded by the armies of Islam, as a punishment for Christian sin. Defeat and the crushing subsequent realization of Byzantium's relegation from superpower status led to the Isaurians' reformulation of Byzantine identity, with the abatement of the imperial notion. Again, this was not a complete abandonment, but a marginalization of a hitherto dominant theme. Instead, the Isaurians proffered a Christian kingdom, fundamentally aligned with the model and rhetoric of the Old Testament. Thus they concentrated imperial ideology almost completely upon a theme that had previously formed just one strand (if a growing one) of the rich embroidery of imperial power. This was a brutal rationalization of a complex inherited world, on both practical and ideological planes, in reaction to a struggle for survival. Moreover, it is a phenomenon that can be traced in all the policies and propaganda contained in other extant media. That evidence shall now be briefly examined as far as it buttresses the picture conveyed by the legal material.

THE REFASHIONING OF THE IMPERIAL IMAGE

A similar pattern to the legal evidence can be drawn from that other prime, imperial medium maintained from late antiquity: coinage.[19] Throughout the Iconoclast era, it retained its traditional importance as one of the few media that would circulate widely, and as a vital part of the fiscal machinery. Indeed, late antiquity had bequeathed a medium gravid with a vast array of symbols that later rulers were not slow to use. Thus Justinian II introduced a radical new coinage as part of his ideological campaign against the Arabs, employing a bust of Christ for the first time in Roman numismatics.[20] Thereby he

[18] For this falling away of 'Roman' between Justinian I and II, see Cameron, 'Images of authority', esp. 24–9.

[19] For a good introduction into Byzantine numismatics, see Grierson, *Byzantine Coinage*. For detailed overviews of eighth- and ninth-century coinage, see Hendy, *Byzantine Monetary Economy*, 500–5; Brubaker and Haldon, *History*, 146–9, 226–7, 352–5.

[20] *DOC* II.2, 568. For analysis, see Breckenridge, *The Numismatic Iconography of Justinian II.*

reified the message contained in Trullo's *Logos* of the closeness between himself and Christ, and broadcast it through the monetary system. This type ceased with Justinian II's fall, and the Isaurians inherited the system as created in late antiquity.

This inheritance they proceeded to simplify and rationalize as fundamentally as they had the law. Firstly, all fractional denominations stopped, leaving just one per metal.[21] Secondly, imperial portraiture was abandoned.[22] Instead a standardized imperial image was portrayed, one Isaurian emperor blending into another. This reinforced two central messages of Isaurian ideology: firstly, the centrality of the imperial office; and secondly, the continuity of its current dynastic holders. This dynastic aspect was first pronounced in 720, when, to proclaim the elevation of Constantine V as co-emperor, Leo III issued a new *nomisma*.[23] Here the traditional cross-on-steps motif on the reverse was replaced by a bust of Constantine, virtually identical to that of his father on the obverse. Thus the centrality of dynasty trumped even religious symbolism. Moreover, this would become the defining feature of Isaurian coins, with deceased ancestors unprecedentedly retained as a celebration of dynastic success.[24]

The Isaurians also introduced a new silver coin, the *miliaresion*.[25] Although its design was very similar to the contemporary Islamic *dirham*, the *miliaresion* was stamped with a stridently Christian message. For on the reverse the cross-potent was surrounded by the inscription *Iesus Christus Nika*, 'Jesus Christ Victorious', the triumphant message of the Cross and the ultimate point of disagreement between Islam and Christianity.[26] Further, the Cross and this defiant tag had long and specifically imperial connotations from the reign of Constantine I onwards.[27] On the obverse was the inscription, 'Leo and Constantine by [grace of] God, emperors'. This was the first time *basileus* was employed on coins as the official title of the emperor, a title which, as we explored in relation to Heraclius, had important Scriptural resonances, both with the Old Testament kings and with Christ.[28] When combined with the Cross, it conveyed an

[21] Grierson, *Byzantine Coinage*, 2. [22] Grierson, *Byzantine Coinage*, 8.
[23] *DOC* III.1, 226–30. [24] Grierson, *Byzantine Coinage*, 27.
[25] *DOC* III.1, 5, 62, 179, 182, 227, 231–2.
[26] See G. King, 'Islam, iconoclasm and the declaration of doctrine', *Bulletin of the School of Oriental and African Studies* 48 (1985), 267–77.
[27] See Moorhead, 'Iconoclasm, the Cross and the imperial image'.
[28] *DOC* III.1, 63–4. See Introduction, 31–4.

exceedingly close link between divine and imperial authority. Moreover, considering that the Isaurians' new *nomismata* also dropped the title *Augustus*, these coins express the recedence of the employment of Roman imperial signifiers and expressions of legitimate authority in favour of specifically Christian ones also elucidated in the legal material. Further, this pattern was replicated, at exactly the same time, on imperial seals, where a varied heritage was replaced with a standardized image, indeed the same as used on the *miliaresion*.[29] Together, they portray a fundamental reconfiguration of imperial representation beginning in *c.*720, with the creation of a single, coherent image of imperial centrality, dynastic success, and Christian kingship symbolized in the Cross.

This message was replicated in the Isaurians' architectural campaigns, literally in the case of the walls of Nicaea, which included the slogan *Iesus Christus Nika*.[30] Considering that it, along with Constantinople whose walls were also renovated, had survived Islamic sieges under the Isaurians, this represented a strident reassertion of Christian rule in the face of Islamic armies.[31] Furthermore, as noted in Chapter 2, Leo is reported as erecting an image of the prophets and apostles around the Cross, a setting reminiscent of the *Ecloga*'s *prooimion*, as Auzépy notes.[32] This glorification of the Cross as the symbol of imperial Christianity reached a sumptuous apogee in the apse of the rebuilt Hagia Eirene, which was filled with an impressive mosaic of the Cross, flanked by excerpts from Scripture.[33] Similarly, the focus on dynasty was given physical expression by the Isaurians' probable construction of the famous porphyry chamber of the palace, designed for the labour of legitimate empresses to produce sons 'born in the purple'.[34] Finally, the restoration of the aqueduct of Valens in the 760s dovetails neatly with the contemporary legal endeavours such as the AE, with the restoration of an imperial service fallen

[29] G. Zacos and A. Veglery, *Byzantine Lead Seals*, vol.1 pt. 1 (Basel, 1972), 31–2. It must be noted, however, that the only innovation in these seals is that they do describe the emperors as Roman.

[30] Brubaker and Haldon, *Sources*, 18; Brubaker and Haldon, *History*, 161.

[31] Brubaker and Haldon, *History*, 161.

[32] Germanus, *Letter to Thomas of Klaudioupolis*, Mansi XIII, 108 A7–128 A12. For analysis, see M.-F. Auzépy, 'La destruction de l'icône du Christ de la Chalcé par Léon III: propaganda ou réalité?', *Byzantion* 60 (1990), 445–92, esp. 446–8; Magdalino, 'The other image'.

[33] Brubaker and Haldon, *History*, 212–14.

[34] J. Herrin, *Women in Purple: Rulers of Medieval Byzantium* (London, 2001), 65.

into disrepair.[35] Moreover, like the legal campaign, this reconstruction was primarily espoused through a religious vein, given that it formed the backdrop for multiple myths involving Constantine and his slaying of a dragon to restore the waterway.[36] This surely represents Constantine slaying the dragon of sin and heresy to restore the healing balm of Christian water, the element of baptism and rebirth.

Thus the capital was refounded through Isaurian leadership within an explicitly Christian realm. All these media expound a markedly similar paradigm of ideological reformulation as contained in the legal sources, an ideology that sought to symbolically refound the empire, to reassert the centrality of the imperial office, and to glorify and proclaim the piety of its current holders, within an overtly and stridently Christian framework.

THE RESTRUCTURING OF THE STATE

This ideological reorientation went lockstep with a restructuring of the state. In essence, the Isaurians inherited an administration marked by ad hoc additions and modulations to the late antique system.[37] Militarily, throughout the seventh century, the armies were essentially the same units pulled back in the 640s and garrisoned (supposedly temporarily) above the still-existing provincial structures of Asia Minor, whose pay at some point was switched chiefly to kind.[38] From these positions, emperors down to Justinian II sought to engage in military operations against the Caliphate that only make sense if the Romans thought themselves, at the least, potentially equal to the Arab enemy.[39] It was only in the eighth century that new tactics

[35] Theophanes, 440; Nicephorus, 160.

[36] See C. Zuckerman, 'The reign of Constantine V in the miracles of St Theodore the Recruit (BHG 1764)', *Revue des Études Byzantines* 46 (1988), 191–210, 200; M.-F. Auzépy, 'Constantin, Théodore et le dragon', in *Toleration and Repression in the Middle Ages* (Athens, 2002), 87–96. For a comparative analysis between the rebuilding of this aqueduct with contemporary Frankish and Abbasid urban development, see A. Stoclet, 'From Baghdad to Beowulf: eulogising "imperial" capitals east and west in the mid-eighth century', *Proceedings of the Royal Irish Academy, Section C* 105 (2005), 151–95.

[37] For detailed study, see Brubaker and Haldon, *History*, 665–771.

[38] Haldon, *Seventh Century*, 208–53.

[39] Howard-Johnston, *Witnesses to a World Crisis*, 500–1, 507–12.

of harassment and containment emerged, combined with the building of more fortresses and the deliberate depopulation of the border zone with the Caliphate.[40] This speaks of a broad strategic realization that the Byzantine Empire was no longer a great power, being fundamentally weaker than its principal enemy. Instead of reconquest, survival and retention became the goal of imperial policy.

In the fulfilment of this strategy, Leo III and Constantine V would prove themselves to be capable soldiers, stabilizing the eastern frontier in the 730s and winning a major victory at the battle of Akroinon in 740.[41] In the process, they accrued great prestige and popularity to themselves, and created a breathing space for reform. Thus their reforms, both ideological and structural, including their legal programme, were to a large extent contingent on the military situation. Further, after the civil war of *c.*742–3, Constantine V sought to reorganize the army in order to minimize the threat of its rebellious tendencies, and to maximize imperial control over this crucial institution, while improving military efficiency. Thus, he broke up the over-powerful *Opsikion* theme while creating a new central, professional army, the *tagmata*, paid in coin and directly under imperial control.[42] It is in this context of reassertion of imperial control and internal discipline that the Isaurians' legal changes concerning the military should be viewed, in particular the creation of the NS. Through these laws the emperors were posing as the patrons and defenders of the soldiery, while attempting to ensure that soldiers, who were more embedded in local society than ever before, were loyal above all to the emperors and not to their localities. Thus, although the Isaurians inherited a military system that, although perforce had evolved to engage in constant warfare against a richer foe, was still enmeshed in ad hoc structures founded on the expectation of eventual imperial restoration, they successfully redesigned it to defend a smaller and reconceived realm, with themselves the central fulcrum.

The Isaurians also significantly overhauled the fiscal administration.[43] Repeatedly there are hints of the attempt to squeeze extra

[40] Brubaker and Haldon, *History*, 163–8.

[41] Brubaker and Haldon, *History*, 163–8, 552–4.

[42] Brubaker and Haldon, *History*, 740–3. For the significance of the *tagmata* in particular, see Haldon, *Byzantine Praetorians.*

[43] Brubaker and Haldon, *History*, 665–722. Cf. Brandes, *Finanzverwaltung in Krisenzeiten.*

income from relatively stable and sheltered parts of the empire, principally through revised censuses, which would lead to several rebellions.[44] However, a far more significant reorganization occurred *c.*730. The *genikoi kommerkiarioi*, the aptly described 'fiscal crisis managers' of the previous century, who had general (if ad hoc) responsibilities for supplying the armies, disappear.[45] Instead, a lower rank of *kommerkiarioi* re-emerge firmly associated with the taxation and regulation of trade, eventually associated with the *kommerkion* customs levy that is first mentioned in the later eighth century.[46] In those areas firmly under imperial control, new officials called *basilika kommerkia* appear, coupled to provinces that supported the Thematic armies.[47] Finally, the *dioikētai*, the tax collectors under the overall authority of the *logothete* of the *genikon*, were for the first time also associated with specific groupings of provinces named after the army stationed in them.[48]

This was plainly a centrally conceived and arranged reorganization.[49] Effectively, the ad hoc measures that had arisen from the pressures of the seventh century were replaced with a more permanent fiscal administration. Moreover, that administration was arranged to match the military infrastructure directly, a sign of their immediate and overriding purpose: the supply of the army. Furthermore, the emergence of names for groups of provinces taken from the army commands reflects the rise of both a greater sense of regionalism but also the omnipresent militarism that pervaded Byzantine society in the eighth century.[50] Finally, this reorganization also recognized the fundamental transformation of the empire from a matrix of cities into a network of villages.[51] Constantine V further developed this system with the emergence of a separate department of the *dromos* under its own *logothete* by the 750s and the possible commutation of some taxes in kind into cash *c.*769.[52] Moreover, his large-scale population

[44] For instance, the rebellion in Italy led by the papacy in the early 720s began as a tax revolt; see Zuckerman, 'Learning from the enemy', 84–95.

[45] Brubaker and Haldon, *History*, 695.

[46] Brubaker and Haldon, *History*, 695–704. The *kommerkion* is first mentioned for the year 795 in Theophanes, 469–70.

[47] Brubaker and Haldon, *History*, 695–704.

[48] Brubaker and Haldon, *History*, 668–9, 705, 710.

[49] Brubaker and Haldon, *History*, 705.

[50] Brubaker and Haldon, *History*, 668–9.

[51] Brubaker and Haldon, *History*, 463.

[52] For the reorganization of the *dromos*, see Brubaker and Haldon, *History*, 705–9.

transfers and stabilization of the frontiers were probably accompanied by revised censuses and land registers, all ensuring maximized extraction of resources for the fisc and the penetration of imperial power into every section of society, providing the context for the Isaurian interest in property law, in particular the creation of AE.II and the NG.

Finally, this fiscal reorganization would have impacted on the judicial structures of the empire, which had always been entwined with the fiscal system. Indeed, the recognition that cities had ceased to form viable jurisdictional units probably spurred the creation, or at least increased prominence and imperial interest in sub-provincial magistrates, in particular the *akroatai* of the *Ecloga* and NG. At the provincial level, the survival of the old provincial structures implies that certainly by this point governors were overwhelmingly concerned with the administration of justice. Indeed, the survival in the seal evidence and the *Taktikon Uspenskij* of *anthypatoi* and *praitores*, proconsular and ordinary governors respectively, implies the continuance of some kind of chain of command and appellate structure.[53] Indeed, since in the *Taktikon Uspenskij* they were called *anthypatoi* of the Themes, and there exist two ninth-century seals for an *anthypatos* of the *Anatolikoi*, it is possible that like the fiscal administration, the judicial had been made to match the military, with each military command having their own *anthypatos* to which the more junior *praitores* could appeal.[54] However, these questions and others, such as the extent to which villages could act as their own local courts, await future research.[55]

Together, these judicial, financial, and military reorganizations set the context for the publication of the *Ecloga* in 741. Firstly, reasserted imperial control over the provinces and a securer frontier created a breathing space, both practical and ideological, for a project on the

[53] Oikonomidès, *Listes de Préséance*, 49–53, 343–4.

[54] Oikonomidès, *Listes de Préséance*, 51. The seals are *ZV* 1901 and 2049. For general discussion, see Brubaker and Haldon, *History*, 674–8.

[55] Village-level courts headed by *oikodespotai* are known in later Byzantine history; see M. Angold, *Church and Society in Byzantium under the Comneni, 1081–1261* (Cambridge, 1995), 249, 325–8. The term describing the leading households of the village is known in the seventh century, although with little hint of any formal judicial role; see S. Mitchell, *Anatolia: Land, Men, and Gods in Asia Minor*, 2 vols (Oxford, 1993), vol. 2, 133. However, it is plausible they had some de facto responsibility for overseeing village life, and might be equated with 'the commonalty of the village', *hē tou chōriou koinotēs*, of NG.81.

scale of the *Ecloga*. Secondly, that reassertion itself may have acted as a prompt to central government as the shortcomings of present legal knowledge and diversity of proceedings became clearer. Further, the creation and promulgation of the *Ecloga* and succeeding legislation was an ideological adjunct to those structural changes, part of the symbolic reclamation of central authority. Thus, as imperial power was reimposed and strengthened over the remnants of the empire, so was the legal system, both as a tool of control and as a source of legitimization.

THE ENFORCING OF ORTHODOXY

The final element of Isaurian rule was the dynasty's religious policies, normally subsumed under the title 'iconoclasm'. With limited space and controversial sources, this is not the place to provide a detailed narrative. Rather, what can their religious policies tell us about the Isaurians and their rule, and how does that correspond with the picture from the legal evidence?

Firstly, whatever theological and intellectual currents it eventually tapped, iconoclasm was in its origins based on ideas drawn from the Old Testament, above all the sin of idolatry.[56] This was the cardinal and recurrent Israelite transgression, the prime reason for repeated punishments from God. Most famously, idolatry was condemned by the Second Commandment given to Moses, repeated prominently in NM.2. Given their sustained ideological effort to imagine the Byzantines as New Israelites and themselves as the heirs to the prophets and kings, it is hardly surprising that the Isaurians would come to believe idolatry had returned and was the source of God's evidently great wrath. The Christian state, once purified from this immoral practice, could be refounded, secure in fulfilling the commandments of heaven.

Secondly, iconoclasm was about the promotion of authoritative, centrally approved symbols from the past reaffirmed in this new world.[57] Whereas the icon was an unlawful, unnecessary, and useless conduit to heaven, the Cross and the Eucharist were the true signs of

[56] Barber, *Figure and Likeness*, 39–60.

[57] In particular see P. Brown, 'A Dark Age crisis: aspects of the iconoclastic controversy', *English Historical Review* 88 (1973), 1–34.

Christ. Moreover, they had been central to Christian worship, it was claimed, since the foundation of the Church, while icons were castigated as a pagan accretion to traditional, righteous, divinely sanctioned practice. Furthermore, the focusing on such central symbols was a reproof to both Jews and Muslims, being signs of the fundamental belief in the Incarnation and Resurrection of Christ, while neatly sidestepping any critique concerning the worship of figural images. The elevation of the Cross and Eucharist was, therefore, both Christian defiance and a deliberate selection from the past of symbols imbued with peculiar significance and beyond reproach.[58] This preference for centrally approved symbols and purificatory mindset might also underlie the iconoclast attitude to relics, for as has been convincingly shown, the iconophile invective stating that iconoclasts were also relic destroyers is a fabrication.[59] However, Auzépy plausibly argues that iconoclasts may have deliberately kept relics out of altars, so as to keep the Eucharist untainted and the cynosure of Church ritual, a policy deliberately reversed at the Council of Nicaea 787.[60]

Thirdly, iconoclasm involved the general reassertion of central control over centrifugal tendencies, and the emperor's role within the Church.[61] The Cross and Eucharist were both symbols under the control of Church and state. The former had manifest and long-established imperial and martial connotations, while the latter could only be administered by ordained, centrally regulated, and salaried clergy. Further, the acceptance of imperial policy on icons was a public display of loyalty and confidence in the emperors' piety, and thus a useful tool of political control over lay and clerical alike. For instance, Leo III used iconoclasm to force the resignation of the patriarch Germanus in 730 and elevated a more dependable ally to the patriarchal throne. Constantine V similarly used the occasion of the Council of Hiereia to promote a new patriarch, the choice of whom the sources clearly state had been the emperor's.[62] Evidently,

[58] For the Cross in particular, see Moorhead, 'Iconoclasm, the cross and the imperial image'.

[59] J. Wortley, 'Iconoclasm and leipsanoclasm: Leo III, Constantine V and relics', *Byzantinische Forschungen* 8 (1982), 253–79.

[60] M.-F. Auzépy, 'Les Isauriens et l'espace sacré: l'église et les réliques', in M. Kaplan, *Le sacré et son inscription dans l'espace à Byzance et en Occident: études comparées* (Paris, 2001), 13–24.

[61] Auzépy, 'State of emergency', 286–7.

[62] Theophanes, 428; Nicephorus, 72.

the picture of the emperor in the *Ecloga* as the sole and undisputed leader of society, with the Church subordinate to his authority and regulatory care, had considerable truth in reality.

While asserting their own central role within the Church as patron, protector, regulator, and enforcer of Orthodoxy, the Isaurians also stressed the authority of the episcopal church, especially over monks whose order had begun to flourish under the stable conditions of Isaurian rule, and indeed who enjoyed significant imperial patronage.[63] Isaurian policy towards monks has been distorted in a similar way to their actions concerning icons and relics.[64] Yet it is possible to discern an attempt to place monasteries more definitively under the authority of bishops, and to restrict the role of monks to charity, prayer, and exemplary living.[65] Any numinous authority of the holy man, with the power of intercession and attendant miracles, was firmly denied, and the populace directed to the true presence of the Eucharist and personal, spiritual reflection on the Scriptures and saints as pointers to the truth and the intercession of heaven.[66]

Moreover, whatever one thinks of Leo III's role in iconoclasm, it is evident that Constantine V became the principal mover and thinker of the iconoclasts.[67] Through his *Peuseis*, Constantine revealed his pretensions as a scholar and as an active leader of events.[68] Further, the arguments of the *Peuseis*, considered together with their slightly altered form adopted at Hiereia in 754, indicate a constant desire to justify present policy through linking it with the authoritative statements of the past. When combined with Constantine's personal command in various military campaigns, his military reforms, his highly active diplomacy, and his extensive building programmes, the impression is of an activist emperor, perfectly prepared and able to pursue reforms personally. It is easy to imagine such an emperor taking a considerable hand in the legal texts produced after the *Ecloga*, especially considering the overlap of such as AE.III and the

[63] For the flourishing of monasteries in this period, particularly in the capital, see P. Hatlie, *The Monks and Monasteries of Constantinople ca.350–850* (Cambridge, 2007), 312–52. See also K. Ringrose, 'Monks and society in iconoclastic Byzantium', *Byzantine Studies* 6 (1979), 130–51.

[64] Auzépy, 'State of emergency', 284; Brubaker and Haldon, *History*, 234–47.

[65] Brubaker and Haldon, *History*, 244–5.

[66] See Anastos, 'The ethical theory of images'.

[67] Gero, *Constantine V*; cf. Brubaker and Haldon, *History*, 176–212, 234–47.

[68] Gero, *Constantine V*, 37–52; Auzépy, 'State of emergency', 283.

NS with Constantine's well-documented theological and military concerns, and the similar use of established, authoritative texts to legitimize present actions. Although it is impossible to prove any personal involvement of Constantine V with any of the texts explored above, save for the *Ecloga*, it certainly would be in keeping with the picture that can be drawn from his involvement in iconoclasm.

Thus, in their religious policies the Isaurians revealed both a set of attitudes and a coherent programme that chimed with their other campaigns. The role of the emperor within the Church, elaborated by Justinian I, was resolutely asserted, and ecclesiastical authority intertwined even further with imperial power. An immoral practice was combated, a process justified and expounded through exegesis. The purified state and people were united under the clear and resolute leadership of the Isaurians, who promoted a verified selection of traditional symbols for the new Chosen People.

THE ISAURIAN LEGAL RENAISSANCE AND THE FORMATION OF BYZANTIUM

Underpinning all the above were two interlocked processes. Firstly and most importantly was the rise of Islam. Militarily and politically, the Arab conquests strained then broke Roman hegemony in the Near East and Mediterranean. Perforce, the polity founded on Constantinople was circumscribed and reduced to a compact kernel. Intellectually and ideologically, this rapid advance of an increasingly distinct religious community challenged the very foundations of Christian and Roman thought that had aggregated over centuries of interaction. In particular, Islam forced Christians to examine, defend, or alter their religious practice and private morality in response to the evident displeasure of heaven.

Confronted by this unprecedented challenge, the imperial response was first to invest more heavily in the comforting conceit of the universal power of the Christian Roman Empire, and aim for the supposedly inevitable reconquest and restoration of normality. Yet any such belief was brutally shattered during the quarter-century of coups, rebellions, and defeats that intervened between the hopes espoused at Trullo, and the rise of Leo III and the siege of Constantinople in 717–18. In the wake of crushing defeat, and the continued threat of annihilation, the imperial dream was jettisoned. Instead the Isaurians, informed by a grasp on strategic realism, oversaw a coherent and coordinated programme of retrenchment and reorganization of resources, both mental and material, to fit the needs of a shrunken and besieged realm.

Throughout this, law was a joining thread, both as a genre and system, and as an inherent component of imperial ideology and power. Yet as the imperial matrix of rhetoric and reality became increasingly tattered, and finally reformulated altogether in the eighth century, that thread was altered, reconceived, and reset within a fast-changing world. Thus at Trullo, Justinian II emulated Justinian I's grand project of imperial restoration, but tellingly reached for canon law instead of civil to realize this vision of imperial restoration. Moreover, throughout, Trullo employed a rhetoric shaped by the tumults of the times, and displayed the altered anxieties of the period, both of which pointed firmly to the symbolic universe of eighth-century Byzantium, not sixth-century New Rome. The loss of superpower status cut this Gordian knot, permitting the Isaurians' laws, and above all the *Ecloga*, to employ the language of Scripture within a discourse now utterly monopolized by the Old Testament. Here the Isaurians found the analogue of the elect constantly attacked by superior earthly powers while maintaining a special relationship with God. Moreover, they reaffirmed and focused in on the reasons for their defeat—namely incorrect and impious religious rites, especially the idolatry of icon worship, and private immorality, in particular sexual misconduct.

Furthermore, as the Byzantine state stabilized, reasserted control over its provinces, and sank its tentacles into the new political-economic landscape in order to ensure the extraction of resources to feed a militarized society, the Isaurians turned to law as a tool of enforcement and dispute settlement, as well as a means of garnering legitimacy. Therefore, the most relevant sections of the Justinianic *Corpus* were excised, compressed, and reordered with the deliberate pragmatic aim of ensuring just enforcement and the maintenance of law and order, thus smoothing the running of a system redesigned towards continual warfare. Yet it was also reimagined as an extension of Mosaic Law, whose reimposition would purify the people and guarantee divine sanction for the reconceived empire. Thus that most quintessentially Roman and imperial of inheritances from late antiquity was transformed for a post-Roman world.

Significantly, similar developments were occurring in the other two heirs of Rome, the Carolingian Frankish kingdom and the Caliphate. Both, particularly in the latter half of the eighth century, began cataloguing and re-expressing their laws, as part of a broader encyclopaedic movement that sought to reconnect with a now clearly discontinuous Roman past, and to appropriate it within new paradigms.[69] All three societies were spurred on by an economic and demographic revival from the nadir of the early eighth century, as the plague petered out and general geopolitical stability provided a better platform for growth.[70] The combination of enlarged court patronage with broader prosperity propelled a literary and intellectual effervescence. Whereas the Carolingian and Abbasid 'Renaissances' are well documented, the cultural revival of Byzantium is normally situated in the ninth century under the Macedonians, due to the distorting miasma of iconophile rhetoric.[71] Yet the very flourishing of hagiography and resumption of historical writing from the latter eighth century, which proceeded to vilify the Isaurians for their heresy and ignorance, is testament to the general resurgence begun under their rule. Indeed, one can perceive the legal programme as the outlier of this intellectual intensification, cataloguing the ancient past for use in the present.

Further, the invention of Greek minuscule *c.*780, which is roughly coincidental with the better documented creation of Latin minuscule, was indicative of a growing demand for the written word, necessitating a more utilitarian script. Moreover, as Auzépy plausibly suggests, this development could have been led by increased volume of writing emanating from the imperial administration, in which the legal texts would be an obvious component.[72] Indeed, it is notable that all the works accredited to the Isaurians in this study are concise, practical

[69] For the Carolingians' legal activity, see R. McKitterick, *The Carolingians and the Written Word* (Cambridge, 1981); for the general Carolingian Renaissance, see McKitterick (ed.), *Carolingian Culture*. For the Islamic legal reforms, see B. Jokisch, *Islamic Imperial Law: Harun-al-Rashid's Codification Project* (Berlin, 2007); for the general cultural effervescence, see Kennedy, *The Court of the Caliphs*. One could also note the later flourishing of Anglo-Saxon law, for which see P. Wormald, *The Making of English Law, Vol. 1: Legislation and its Limits* (Oxford, 2001).

[70] McCormick, *Origins*, esp. 115–19, 433–41.

[71] For the traditional schema, see P. Lemerle, *Le Premier Humanisme byzantin* (Paris, 1971); cf. Auzépy, 'State of emergency', 278–9. See also Mango, 'The revival of learning', which at 214–15 notes the contemporaneity of all three intellectual movements.

[72] Auzépy, 'State of emergency', 279.

documents that appear frequently to occupy some multiple of four folios, suggestive of a quire.[73] This might plausibly imply an original format for easily created and carried documents, designed for ease of use by judges. Further, such a pattern of promulgation would explain the large degree of variability in arrangement found in the manuscript tradition, as units could be readily rearranged to suit the user or the creator of the codex. Although the manuscript evidence renders any such conclusion only possible, it would strengthen the impression, conveyed both in the legal tradition and in everything else known about the Isaurians, of a strong, central government utilizing all means in their possession to reimpose imperial authority over a shrunken and reconceived realm.

The irony of Isaurian success was that they ushered in a world that no longer needed them. As external pressures eased, and indeed allowed gradual Byzantine expansion, the necessity for an imperial ideology founded so closely on the Old Testament, and for the policy of iconoclasm that sprouted from it, faded. Indeed, the iconophile writers led the way in restressing those elements of imperial ideology that had receded into the background.[74] Thus the New Testament rather than the Old came to dominate, and emperors were once more visually associated with Christ. Further, spurred on by the creation of a rival western empire, Byzantine claims to being Roman re-emerged, as did the ideal of universal empire. Even the Isaurians' legal programme was theoretically condemned, while at the same time being continued and appropriated. Indeed, to a great extent it was the contentions of the Iconoclast era, and their eventual resolution, that created the Byzantine world.

In the centre of that storm, as a marker of both structural continuity and ideological transformation, was the law. Through the texts examined in this work, this formative period comes into sharper focus. Further, it is evident that the medium of law was not merely a passive bystander, simply marking the effect of those changes, but was actively utilized as a vital tool of imperial power, both practically

[73] See the *RHBR* for details of the manuscripts.

[74] For the general rewriting of history by the iconophiles, see Brubaker and Haldon, *History*, 787–99. For the years *c.*800 as a turning point in the realization of discontinuity with the Roman past, see P. Magdalino, 'The distance of the past in early medieval Byzantium (VII–X centuries)', *Settimane di studio del centro italiano di studi sull'alto medioevo* 46 (1999), 115–46; and I. Ševčenko, 'The search for the past in Byzantium around the year 800', *DOP* 46 (1992), 279–93.

and symbolically. In particular, the legal evidence reveals the fundamental reconfiguration of the Byzantine symbolic universe under the Isaurians, as the Roman past was selected, reconceived, and reset. In short, the legal material illuminates that crucial transition, when from the wreckage of the Roman world system Byzantium emerged, and the ancient world ultimately gave way to the medieval.

APPENDIX OF MANUSCRIPT TABLES

The following is a collection of tables of manuscripts of the texts studied in this work. For an introduction in how to read them, see Note on Language and Tables. Although overwhelmingly the evidence for these tables has been drawn from the *RHBR*, those manuscripts known to the author that are not and are relevant to the present enquiry, are for ease of use ascribed the following letters:

Athens, Ethnikē Bibliothēkē, 1377.	A
Athens, Ethnikē Bibliothēkē, 1379.	B
Athous, Megistēs Lauras, Θ 220.	C
Basel, Universitätsbibliothek, A III.6.	D
Cambridge, Trinity College Library, 1255.	E
Escorial, Biblioteca, X. III. 2.	F
Escorial, Biblioteca Ψ. II. 20.	G
Florence, Biblioteca Laurenziana, V.2.	H
Meteora, Metamorphōseōs, 43.	I
Moscow, Gosudarstvennyj Istoričeskij Muzej (GIM), 318.	J
Moscow, Gosudarstvennyj Istoričeskij Muzej (GIM), 336.	K
Oxford, Bodleian Library, Barocci 196.	L
Oxford, Bodleian Library, Misc. 170.	M
Paris, Bibliotheque Nationale, gr. 1320.	N
Sinai, Monē tēs Hagias Aikaterinēs, 1117.	O
Sinai, Monē tēs Hagias Aikaterinēs, 1121.	P
Vatican, Bibliotheca Apostolica Vaticana, gr. 1137.	Q
Vatican, Bibliotheca Apostolica Vaticana, gr. 1167.	R
Vienna, Österreichische Nationalbibliothek, hist. gr.24.	S
Vienna, Österreichische Nationalbibliothek, iur. gr.16.	T

Table 9. The manuscripts of the *Ecloga* according to the *RHBR*

RHBR	K	AE	NS	NM	NN	NG	C.
6.4	x				x	x	15
9.13		x	x	x			17
21.72		x		x			12
25.3		x	x			x	16
27.5			x				13
29.43		x		x	x		11
55.46	x	x	x	x	x		16
61.61		x	x	x	x		12
109.8	x		x	x	x	x	15
134.11		x		x	x		14
135.32						x	14
141.3	x			x			12/13
151.5	x	(x)	x	(x)	x	x	14
197.4		x	x			x	14
222.19						(x)	15
226.3						x	16
241.6	x					x	14
272.1		(x)	(x)		(x)	(x)	14
274.40		x	x				11
310.29		x	x		x		14
327.20		x	x		x	x	13/14
Total: 21	6	(13) 11	(12) 11	(9) 8	(10) 9	(11) 9	

Table 10. The manuscripts of the AE according to the *RHBR*

AE	I	II	III	IV	V	VI	VII	VIII	IX	X	XI	XII	XIII	XIV	NS	NM	E	ED	NN	NG	Pr.
9	x	x	x	x	x	x	x	x	x						x	x	x				
21		x							x							x	x				
25	x	x	x	x	x	x				x					x		x			x	
29		x														x	x		x		
47									x												
48									x												
55	x	x	x	x	x	x	x	x	x	x	x	x	x		x	x	x		x		
61	x	x	x	x	x	x			x	x					x	x	x		x		
78		x							x							x					
79									x									x	(x)	(x)	
82									x												
90									x												
110									x												
124	x	x													(x)				x	x	x
127	x	x	x	x	x	x	x	x	x	x		x		x	x	x		x	x	x	
134		x														x	x		x		
148	x	x	x	x	x	x	x	x		x	x	x	x		x				x		x
151									x						(x)	x	(x)		(x)	(x)	(x)
169									x												
188			x	x	x			x	x	x	x	x	x		x	x		x	x	x	x
193	x	x	x	x	x	x	x	x	x	x					x			x	(x)	x	
197	x	x	x		x	x				x					x		x			x	
221		x		x	x																
244									x												
249	x	x													(x)						

(*continued*)

Table 10. Continued

AE	I	II	III	IV	V	VI	VII	VIII	IX	X	XI	XII	XIII	XIV	NS	NM	E	ED	NN	NG	Pr.
253									x												
263	x	x	x	x	x	x	x	x		x					x	(x)			x	(x)	
264									x											(x)	
272	x	x									x				(x)		(x)		(x)	(x)	
274	x	x	x	x	x	x	x	x	x	x		x			x		x				
280															x	x		x	x		x
282		x														x					
294									x												
298	x	x	x	x	x	x	x	x		x					x				x		
310	x	x	x	x	x				x	x	x	x	x	x	x		x		x		x
319	x	x	x	x	x	x	x	x	x	x	x		x		x				x	x	x
321	x	x			x			x				x	x					x			
327	x	x	x	x	x	x					x				x		x		x	x	
352									x												
354									x												
360									x												
380									x												
396									x												
397									x												
A		x							x							x					
B		x							x												
C		x														x					
D		x							x							x					
H		x							x							x					
I		x														x					
50	18	30	15	15	17	13	9	11	33	13	7	7	6	2	(20) 16	(18) 17	(13) 11	6	(18) 14	(13) 8	(7) 6

Table 11. The manuscripts of the NS according to the *RHBR*

NS	E	ED	AE	NM	NN	NG	Pr.	PD	Eis.	EA	Epitome	C.
9.15	x		x	x								17
25.5	x		x			x	(x)					16
27.6,8	x											13
55.53	x		x	x	x							16
61.63	x		x	x	x							12
79.2		(x)			x	x		x				12/13
80.2					x						x	13
81.2		(x)			x	x		x				14
87.9					x	x				x		14
100.4					x	x				x		16
101.4					x	x				x		16
102.2					x	x	x					14
109.5	x			x	x	x						15
122.5					x	x				x		14
124.22			(x)		x	(x)	(x)					14
127.13		x	x		(x)	x		x				12
129.6,24					x	x		x				14
130.5					x	x	x					16
140.4					x	x				x		13
144.29					x	x	x					16
148.46			x		x		x					10
149.5					x	x				x		15/16
151.14	x		(x)	(x)	x	x	x					14
171.4						x				x		16
182.13					x	x		(x)				11/12

(*continued*)

Table 11. Continued

NS	E	ED	AE	NM	NN	NG	Pr.	PD	Eis.	EA	Epitome	C.
185.4						x				x		13
187.4					x	x				x		12
188.4		x	x	x	x	x	x					12
189.11						x						15
193.22		x	x		x	x	(x)					14
197.6	x		x			x	(x)					14
212.10						(x)		(x)				14
229.38					x	x	x					14
242.4		x		(x)	x	x		x				11
243.27					x	x	x					16
249.15			(x)		(x)	(x)					x	10
263.4,29			x	(x)	x	x			x		x	16
272.13	(x)		(x)		x	x		x				14
274.42	x		x									11
276.13					x	x	x					11
278.15					x	x				x		14/15
280.6		x	x	x	x		x					11
289.12				(x)	x	(x)					x	12
298.4			x		x				x			15
302.3,6					x	x		x			x	11
309.2,36		x				(x)		(x)				14
310.34	x		x		x		x					14
319.7,19			x		x	x	x					14
327.12	x		x		x	x	x					13/14
Total 49	(12) 11	(8) 6	(20) 16	(10) 6	(39) 37	(39) 34	(17) 13	(10) 7	2	10	5	

Table 12. The manuscripts of the NM according to the *RHBR*

NM	NMA	NMB	E	ED	AE	NS	NN	NG	Pr.	PD	Eis.	Epitome	C.
3.73	x												14
9.11	x		x		x	x							17
21.70	x		x		x								12
29.41	x		x		x		x						11
55.50	x		x		x	x							16
61.59	x		x		x	x	x						12
78.114	x				x								14
109.6	x		x			x	x	x					15
127.4	x			x	x			(x)		(x)			12
134.9	x		x		x		x						14
138.2	Unknown												15
141.5	x		x										14
151.59	x		(x)		x	(x)	(x)	(x)					14
188.6	x			x	x	x	x	x	x				12
242.13		x		(x)		(x)	(x)	(x)		(x)			11
263.37	x				(x)	(x)	(x)	(x)			(x)	x	16
280.7	x			x	x	x	x		x				11
282.13	Unknown				x								16
286.50		x							x		(x)		10
289.21	x					(x)	(x)	(x)				x	12
347.33	Unknown						x	x					11
A	x				x								13
C	x?				x								14
D	x				x								13
E	x												17

(*continued*)

Table 12. Continued

NM	NMA	NMB	E	ED	AE	NS	NN	NG	Pr.	PD	Eis.	Epitome	C.
F	x												13
G	x												13
H	x				x								14
I	x				x								17
J		x											11
K	Unknown												17
L		x											11
M	Unknown												11
N		x											11
O	x												14
P	x												14/15
Q	x												16
R	x												14
S		x											16
T		x											14
Total: 40	28	7	(9) 8	(4) 3	(18) 17	(10) 6	(11) 7	(8) 3	3	(2) 0	(2) 0	2	

Table 13. The manuscripts of the NN according to the *RHBR*

NN (II+III)	E	ED	AE	NM	NS	NG	Pr.	PD	Eis.	EA	Epitome	C.
29.44	x		x	x								11
55.58, 61	x		x		x							16
61.64	x		x	x	x							12
79.3		(x)	(x)		x	x		x				12/13
81.3		(x)			x	x		x				14
96.4												16
100.5					x	x				x		16
101.5					x	x				x		16
102.4					x	x	x					14
129.7					x	x		x				14
130.3					x	x	x					16
134.13	x		x	x								14
144.31					x	x	x					16
148.45			x		x		x					10
170.25						x		(x)				14
182.3,16					x	x		x				11/12
188.5		x	x	x	x	x	x					12
193.35		x	(x)		x	x	(x)					14
229.40					x	x	x					14
230.6						x		x				12
231.3									x			14
242.5		x		(x)	x	x		x				11
243.29					x	x	x					16
249.12					(x)	x					x	10
251.44						x						11
263.2,22			x	(x)	x	x			x		x	16
276.12					x	x	x					11
280.5		x	x	x	x		x					11
289.5,13				(x)	x	x					x	12
333.4												13
335.4												16

(continued)

Table 13. Continued

NN (II+III)	E	ED	AE	NM	NS	NG	Pr.	PD	Eis.	EA	Epitome	C.
336.5												16
337.3												16
348.3												16
427.4												16
Total: 35	4	(6) 4	(10) 8	(8) 5	(22) 21	21	(10) 9	(7) 6	2	2	3	
NN (III)	E	ED	AE	NM	NS	NG	Pr.	PD	Eis.	EA	Epitome	C.
6.9	x					x	x					15
68.8						x					x	15
80.3					x						x	13
87.10					x	x				x		14
88.1												11
109.4	x			x	x	x						15
122.6					x	x				x		14
123.1						x						11/12
124.13			x		x	x	x					14
127.23		(x)	x		(x)	x		x				12
140.5					x	x				x		13
149.6					x	x				x		15/16
151.10	x		(x)	(x)	x	x	x					14
187.5					x	x				x		12
213.3						x						14
272.14	(x)		(x)		x	x		x				14
278.16					x	x				x		14/15
298.2			x		x				x		x	15
302.5					x	x					x	11
310.33	x		x		x		x					14
319.8			x		x	x	x					14
327.13	x		x		x	x	(x)	x				13/14
347.35				x		x						11
Total: 23	(6) 5	(1) 0	(8) 6	(3) 2	(17) 16	19	(6) 5	3	1	6	4	
Total: 58	(10) 9	(7) 4	(18) 14	(11) 7	(39) 37	40	(16) 14	(10) 9	3	8	7	

Table 14. The manuscripts of the NG according to the *RHBR*

NG	E	AE	NM	NS	NN	ED	Eis.	EA	Pr.	PD	Epitome	C.
6.8	x				x				x			15
20.23												15
25.11	x	x		x					(x)			16
68.7					x						x	15
79.5		(x)		x	x	(x)				x		12/13
81.4				x	x	(x)				x		14
87.8				x	x			x				14
100.3				x	x			x				16
101.3				x	x			x				16
102.3				x	x				x			14
109.19	x		x	x	x							15
119.1												13
122.4				x	x			x				14
123.2					x						x	11/12
124.12		x		(x)	x				x			14
127.15		x	(x)	x	x	(x)				x		12
129.15				x	x					x		14
130.2				x	x				x			16
135.27	x								x			14
140.3				x	x			x				13
144.30				x	x				x			16
149.4				x	x			x				15/16
151.8	x	(x)	(x)	x	x				x			14
165.12										(x)		15

(*continued*)

Table 14. Continued

NG	E	AE	NM	NS	NN	ED	Eis.	EA	Pr.	PD	Epitome	C.
170.5					x					x		14
171.3				x				x				16
182.12				x	x					(x)		11/12
183.22										x		15
185.3				x				x				13
187.3				x	x			x				12
188.9		x	x	x	x	x			x			12
189.12				x								15
193.26		x		x	x	x			(x)			14
197.9	x	x		x								14
212.4				(x)						x		14
213.2					x						x	14
222.3	(x)											15
226.4	x											16
229.39				x	x				x			14
230.2					x					x		12
240.23										(x)		14
241.3	x								x			14
242.6			(x)	x	x	x			x			11
243.28				x	x				x			16
245.3										x		14
249.13				(x)	x						x	10/11
251.42					x							11/12
263.23		(x)	(x)	x	x		(x)				x	16
264.5		(x)							x			14
272.15	(x)	(x)		x	x					x		14

273.13									x			13
276.11				x	x				x			11
278.14				x	x			x				14/15
289.6			(x)	(x)	x						x	12
302.4				x	x					x	x	11
309.29				(x)						x		14
319.9		x		x	x				x			14
327.14	x	x		x	x				(x)			13/14
347.33			x		x							11
Total: 59	(11) 9	(13) 8	(8) 3	(39) 34	40	(6) 3	(1) 0	10	(19) 16	(15) 12	7	

Bibliography

Primary Sources

Agapetus, *Ekthesis*, ed. R. Riedinger, *Der Fürstenspiegel des Kaisers Justinianos* (Athens, 1995).

Anastasius of Sinai, *Questiones et Responsiones*, ed. M. Richard and J. Munitiz (Turnhout, 2006).

Appendix Eclogae, ed. L. Burgmann and S. Troianos, *FM* III (Frankfurt, 1979), 24–125.

Aristotle, *Politics*; trans. S. Everson, *Aristotle: The Politics and the Constitution of Athens* (Cambridge, 1996).

Basil of Caesarea, *In Principium Proverbiorum*, PG 31 (Paris, 1857), 385–424.

Basilika, ed. H. Scheltema, N. Van Der Wal, and D. Holwerda, *Basilicorum libri LX*, Series A (Text), 8 vols, Series B (Scholia), 9 vols (Groningen, 1953–88).

Book of the Eparch, ed. J. Koder, *Das Eparchenbuch Leons des Weisen* (Vienna, 1991).

Cicero, *De legibus*, ed. C. Keyes, *De re publica, De legibus* (Loeb Classical Library, London, 1928).

Collatio legum Mosaicum et Romanum, ed. M. Hyamson (London, 1913).

Collectio Tripartita, ed. N. Van der Wal and B. Stolte, *Collectio Tripartita: Justinian on Religious and Ecclesiastical Affairs* (Groningen, 1994).

Collectio 25 capitulorum, ed. G. Heimbach, *Anekdota*, vol. 2 (Leipzig, 1840), 145–201.

Collectio 87 capitulorum, ed. I. B. Pitra, *Iuris ecclesiastici graecorum historia et monumenta*, vol. 2 (Rome, 1868), 385–405.

Constans II, *Typos*, ed. R. Riedinger, *ACO* 2.1 (Berlin, 1984), 208–10.

Constantine Harmenopoulos, *Hexabiblos*, ed. G. Heimbach, *Constantini Harmenopuli: Manuale legum sive Hexabiblos* (Leipzig, 1851).

The Council of Constantinople I of 381: The Second Ecumenical Council, ed. Mansi III (Florence, 1759), 521–600.

The Council of Constantinople II of 553: The Fifth Ecumenical Council, ed. J. Straub, *ACO* 4:1 (Berlin, 1971).

The Council of Constantinople III of 680–1: The Sixth Ecumenical Council, ed. R. Riedinger, *ACO* 2.2, 3 vols (Berlin, 1990–95).

The Council in Trullo, ed. H. Ohme, *Das Konzil Quinisextum* (Turnhout, 2006). Previous edition P.-P. Joannou, *Discipline génerale antique*, vol. 1 (Grottaferrata, 1962), 101–241; improved and given an English translation in G. Nedungatt and M. Featherstone (eds), *The Council in Trullo*

Revisited (Rome, 1995). Signatory list ed. H. Ohme, *Das Concilium Quinisextum und Seine Bischofsliste* (Berlin, 1990).

Ecloga, ed. L. Burgmann, *Ecloga: Das Gesetzbuch Leons III. und Konstantinos V.* (Frankfurt, 1983). Old edition by A. Momferratos, *Ecloga Leonis et Constantini cum appendice* (Athens, 1889); trans. E. Freshfield, *A Manual of Roman Law, The Ecloga* (Cambridge, 1926).

Ecloga Aucta, ed. D. Simon and S. Troianos, 'Eklogadion und Ecloga private aucta', *FM* II (Frankfurt, 1977), 45–86.

Ecloga ad Prochiron mutata, ed. K. Zacharia von Lingenthal, *IGR* IV (Leipzig, 1865), 49–170 = Zepos, *IGR* VI (Athens, 1931), 217–318.

Ecloga Privata; see L. Burgmann, *Ecloga: Das Gesetzbuch Leons III. und Konstantinos V.* (Frankfurt, 1983), 51–2.

Ecloga Privata Aucta, ed. K. Zacharia von Lingenthal, *IGR* IV (Leipzig, 1865) 1–48 = Zepos, *IGR* VI (Athens, 1931), 1–47.

Ecloga Privata Aucta Sinaitica, ed. D. Simon and S. Troianos, 'EPA Sinaitica', *FM* III (Frankfurt, 1979), 168–77.

Edictum Theoderici, ed. G. Pertz et al., *Monumenta Germaniae Historiae: Leges V* (Hanover, 1875–89), 145–79.

Eisagoge, ed. K. Zacharia von Lingenthal, *Collectio librorum juris Graeco-Romani ineditorum* (Leipzig, 1852), 61–217 = Zepos, *IGR* II, 236–368.

Eisagoge Aucta, ed. K. Zacharia von Lingenthal, *IGR* IV 180–370 (Leipzig, 1865) = Zepos, *IGR* VI (Athens, 1931), 57–216.

Epitome, ed. K. Zacharia von Lingenthal, *IGR* II (Leipzig, 1856), 277–431, and VII (Leipzig, 1884), 1–199 = Zepos, *IGR* IV (Athens, 1931), 276–585.

George of Pisidia, *Heraclias*, ed. A. Pertusi, *Giorgio di Pisidia. Poemi I: Panegirici epici* (Ettal, 1959), 240–61.

Germanus, *Letter to Thomas of Klaudioupolis*, Mansi XIII (Florence, 1767), 108 A7–128 A12.

Heraclius, *Novels*, ed. J. Konidaris, 'Die Novellen des Kaisers Herakleios', *FM* V (Frankfurt, 1982), 33–106.

Heraclius, *Ekthesis*, ed. R. Riedinger, *ACO* 2.1 (Berlin, 1984), 156–62.

Ignatios the Deacon, *Letters*, ed. C. Mango with S. Efthymiadis, *The Correspondence of Ignatios the Deacon: Text, Translation, and Commentary* (Washington DC, 1997).

Irene, *Novels*, ed. L. Burgmann, 'Die Novellen der Kaiserin Eirene', *FM* IV (Frankfurt, 1981), 1–36.

John Malalas, *Chronicle*, ed. H. Thurn, *Chronographia* (Berlin and New York, 2000).

John Scholasticus, *Synagoga L Titulorum*, ed. V. Beneševič (Munich, 1937).

Justinian I, *Digest*, ed. P. Krüger and T. Mommsen, vol. 1 of *Corpus iuris civilis* (16th edn., Berlin, 1928); trans. A. Watson, *The Digest of Justinian* (Philadelphia, 1985).

Justinian I, *Institutes*, ed. P. Krüger and T. Mommsen, vol. 1 of *Corpus iuris civilis* (16th edn., Berlin, 1928); trans. P. Birks and G. McLeod, *Justinian's Institutes* (London, 1987).

Justinian I, *Novellae*, ed. R. Schöll and G. Kroll, vol. 3 of *Corpus iuris civilis* (6th edn., Berlin, 1928).

Justinian I, *Codex Iustinianus*, ed. P. Krüger, vol. 2 of *Corpus iuris civilis* (11th edn., Berlin, 1929); trans. S. Scott, *The Civil Law*, 17 vols (Cincinnati, 1932), and F. Blume, *Annotated Justinian Code*, ed. T. Kearley, <http://www.uwyo.edu/lawlib/blume-justinian>.

Krisis peri gambrōn stratiōtōn, ed. D. Simon, 'Byzantinische Hausgemeinschaftsverträge' in F. Baur, K. Larenz, and F. Wieacker (eds), *Beiträge zur europäischen Rechtsgeschichte und zum geltenden Zivilrecht: Festgabe für J. Sontis* (Munich, 1977), 91–128, text at 94.

Leder, S. (ed.), *Die arabische Ecloga* (Frankfurt, 1985).

Leo V, *Novel*, ed. D. Simon, 'Zur Ehegesetzgebung der Isaurier', *FM* I (Frankfurt, 1976), 16–43.

Leo VI, *Novels*, ed. P. Noailles and A. Dain, *Les Novelles de Léon le Sage* (Paris, 1944).

Leo VI, *Taktika*, ed. G. Dennis, *The Taktika of Leo VI* (Washington DC, 2010).

Liber Pontificalis, ed. L. Duchesne, 3 vols (Paris, 1886–1957).

Nicephorus, *Antirrhetici*, PG 100 (Paris, 1865), 205–533.

Nicephorus, *Breviarium*, ed. C. Mango, *Nikephoros, Short History* (Washington DC, 1990).

Nomokanon in XIV Titles, ed. I. B. Pitra, *Iuris ecclesiastici graecorum historia et monumenta*, vol. 2 (Rome, 1868), 433–640.

Nomos Georgikos, ed. I. Medvedev et al., *Vizantiĭskiĭ zemledel'cheskiĭ zakon* (Leningrad, 1984). Old edition see W. Ashburner, 'The Farmer's Law I', *JHS* 30 (1910), 85–108 (Edition), 'The Farmer's Law II' *JHS* 32 (1912), 68–95 (commentary and translation).

Nomos Mosaikos, ed. L. Burgmann and S. Troianos, *FM* III (Frankfurt, 1979), 126–67.

Nomos Rhodion Nautikos, ed. W. Ashburner, *The Rhodian Sea-Law* (Oxford, 1909).

Nomos Stratiotikos, ed. W. Ashburner, 'The Byzantine mutiny law', *JHS* 46 (1926), 85–109.

Orosius, *History Against the Pagans*, ed. C. Zangemeister, *Pauli Orosii Historiam adversam Paganos* (Vienna, 1882), trans. I. Raymond, *The Seven Books of History Against the Pagans* (New York, 1936).

Plato, *The Republic*, trans. D. Lee (2nd rev. edn., London, 1974).

Pliny the Younger, *Letters*, trans. P. Walsh (Oxford, 2006).

Prochiron, ed. K. Zacharia von Lingenthal, *Ho Procheiros Nomos* (Heidelberg, 1837); trans. E. Freshfield, *A Manual of Eastern Roman Law: The Procheiros Nomos* (Cambridge, 1928).

Ps.-Methodius, *Apocalypse*, Syriac version ed. G. Reinink, *Die syrische Apokalypse des Ps.-Methodius* (Louvain, 1993); Greek and Latin version ed. W. Aerts and G. Kortekaas, *Die Apokalypse des Pseudo-Methodius. Die ältesten griechischen and lateinischen Übersetzungen* I–II (Louvain, 1998).

Rhopai, ed. F. Sitzia, *Le Rhopai* (Naples, 1984).

Rutilius Namantianus, *De reditu suo*, ed. and trans. A. Duff, *Minor Latin Poets* (Loeb Classical Library, London, 1934).

Scriptor incertus de Leone Armenio, in *Leonis Grammatici Chronographia*, ed. I. Bekker (Bonn, 1842), 335–62.

The Septuagint, ed. and trans. L. Brenton, *The Septuagint with Apocrypha: Greek and English* (London, 1851).

Strategikon, ed. G. Dennis and E. Gamillscheg, *Das Strategikon des Maurikios* (Vienna, 1981).

Taktikon Uspenskij, ed. N. Oikonomidès, *Les Listes de préséance byzantines des IXe–Xe siècles* (Paris, 1972), 47–63.

Theodore the Studite, *Letters*, ed. G. Fatouros, *Theodori Studitae Epistulae* (Berlin, 1992).

Theodore Syncellus, *Sermo* I, ed. L. Sternbach, *Analecta Avarica* (Kraków, 1900), 298–320.

Theodosius II, *Codex Theodosianus*, ed. T. Mommsen and P. Meyer, *Theodosiani libri XVI cum constitutionibus Sirmondianis*, 2 vols (Berlin, 1905).

Theophanes Confessor, *Chronicle*, ed. C. de Boor (Leipzig, 1883–5); trans. C. Mango and R. Scott, *The Chronicle of Theophanes Confessor: Byzantine and Near Eastern history, AD 284–813* (Oxford, 1997).

Theophylact Simocatta, *History*, ed. C. de Boor and P. Wirth, *Theophylacti Simmocattae Historiae* (Stuttgart, 1972); trans. Mi. and Ma. Whitby, *The History of Theophylact Simocatta* (Oxford, 1986).

Virgil, *Aeneid*, trans. C. Day Lewis (Oxford, 1986).

Source Collections, *Repertoria*, and Dictionaries

Abbott-Smith, G., *A Manual Greek Lexicon of the New Testament* (Edinburgh, 1999).

Avotins, I., *On the Greek of the Code of Justinian* (Hildesheim, 1989).

Avotins, I., *On the Greek of the Novels of Justinian* (Hildesheim, 1992).

Burgmann, L., Fögen, M.-T., Schminck, A., and Simon, D. (eds), *Repertorium der Handschriften des byzantinischen Rechts: Teil I Die Handschriften des weltlichen Rechts* (Frankfurt, 1995).

Dölger, F., *Regesten der Kaiserurkunden des oströmischen Reiches von 565–1453*, 5 vols (Munich, 1924–65).

Evans Grubbs, J., *Law and Family in Late Antiquity: the Emperor Constantine's Marriage Legislation* (Oxford, 1995).

Evans Grubbs, J., *Women and the Law in the Roman Empire: A Sourcebook on Marriage, Divorce and Widowhood* (Abingdon, 2002).

Grierson, P., *Catalogue of the Byzantine Coins in the Dumbarton Oaks Collection and in the Whittemore Collection, II: Phocas to Theodosius III, 602–717*, 2 vols (Washington DC, 1968); *III: Leo III to Nicephorus III, 717–1081*, 2 vols (Washington DC, 1973).

Jones, A. H. M., et al. (eds), *Prosopography of the Later Roman Empire*, 3 vols (Cambridge, 1971–92).

Kazhdan, A., et al. (eds), *The Oxford Dictionary of Byzantium*, 3 vols (Oxford, 1991).

Lampe, G. W. H., *A Patristic Greek Lexicon* (Oxford, 1961–8).

Lilie, R.-J., et al. (eds), *Prosopographie der mittelbyzantinischen Zeit* I: *(641–867)*, 6 vols (Berlin, 1998–2002).

Maas, M., *Readings in Late Antiquity: A Sourcebook* (Abingdon, 2000).

Schminck, A. and Getov, D. (eds), *Teil II Die Handschriften des kirchlichen Rechts I* (Frankfurt, 2010).

Talbot, A.-M. (ed.), *Byzantine Defenders of Images: Eight Saints' Lives in English Translation* (Washington DC, 1998).

Trapp, E., et al. (eds), *Lexikon zur byzantinischen Gräzitat: besonders des 9.–12. Jahrhunderts*, 7 vols to date (Vienna, 1994–).

Zacos, G. and Veglery, A., *Byzantine Lead Seals*, vol. I (Basel, 1972).

Secondary Literature

Ahrweiler, H., *Byzance et la mer: la marine de guerre, la politique et les institutions maritimes de Byzance aux VIIe–XVe siècles* (Paris, 1966).

Alexander, P., *The Byzantine Apocalyptic Tradition* (London, 1985).

Anastos, M., 'The ethical theory of images formulated by the iconoclasts in 754 and 815', *DOP* 8 (1954), 151–60.

Ando, C., *Imperial Ideology and Provincial Loyalty in the Roman Empire* (London, 2000).

Ando, C., *Law, Language, and Empire in the Roman Tradition* (Philadelphia, 2011).

Angold, M., *Church and Society in Byzantium under the Comneni, 1081–1261* (Cambridge, 1995).

Angold, M., *Byzantium: The Bridge from Antiquity to the Middle Ages* (London, 2001).

Angold, M., 'The Byzantine political process at crisis point', in P. Stephenson (ed.), *The Byzantine World* (London, 2010), 5–21.

Arjava, A., 'Paternal power in late antiquity', *Journal of Roman Studies* 88 (1998), 147–65.

Auzépy, M.-F., 'La destruction de l'icône du Christ de la Chalcé par Léon III: propaganda ou réalité?', *Byzantion* 60 (1990), 445–92.

Auzépy, M.-F., 'Les Isauriens et l'espace sacré: l'église et les réliques', in M. Kaplan, *Le sacré et son inscription dans l'espace à Byzance et en Occident: études comparées* (Paris, 2001), 13–24.

Auzépy, M.-F., 'Constantin, Théodore et le dragon', in *Toleration and Repression in the Middle Ages* (Athens, 2002), 87–96.

Auzépy, M.-F., 'Les enjeux de l'iconoclasme', *Settimane di studio del centro italiano di studi sull'alto medioevo* 51 (2004), 127–69.

Auzépy, M.-F., *L'histoire des iconoclastes* (Paris, 2007).

Auzépy, M.-F., 'State of emergency', in J. Shepard (ed.), *The Cambridge History of the Byzantine Empire c. 500–1492* (Cambridge, 2008), 251–91.

Banaji, J., *Agrarian Change in Late Antiquity: Gold, Labour, and Aristocratic Dominance* (2nd edn., Oxford, 2007).

Barber, C., *Figure and Likeness. On the Limits of Representation in Byzantine Iconoclasm* (Princeton, 2002).

Barnwell, P., 'Emperors, jurists and kings: law and custom in the Late Roman and early medieval west', *Past and Present* 168 (2000), 6–29.

Bell, P., *Three Political Voices from the Age of Justinian* (Liverpool, 2009).

Booth, P., *Crisis of Empire: Doctrine and Dissent at the End of Late Antiquity* (London, 2014).

Brand, C., *Roman Military Law* (Austin, 1968).

Brandes, W., *Finanzverwaltung in Krisenzeiten. Untersuchung zur byzantinischen Administration im 6.–9. Jahrhundert* (Frankfurt, 2002).

Brandes, W., 'Orthodoxy and heresy in the seventh century: prosopographical observations on monotheletism', in A. Cameron (ed.), *Fifty Years of Prosopography: The Late Roman Empire, Byzantium and Beyond. Proceedings of the British Academy* 118 (Oxford, 2003), 103–18.

Breckenridge, J., *The Numismatic Iconography of Justinian II* (New York, 1959).

Bréhier, L., 'Le protocole impérial depuis la fondation de l'empire Romain jusqu'à la prise de Constantinople par les Turcs,' *Comptes-rendus des séances de l'Académie des Inscriptions et Belles-Lettres* 1 (1905), 177–82.

Bréhier, L., 'L'origine des titres impériaux à Byzance', *BZ* 15 (1906), 161–78.

Brown, P., *The World of Late Antiquity* (London, 1971).

Brown, P., 'A Dark Age crisis: aspects of the iconoclastic controversy', *English Historical Review* 88 (1973), 1–34.

Brown, P., *Power and Persuasion in Late Antiquity* (Madison, 1992).

Brown, P., *The Rise of Western Christendom: Triumph and Diversity, AD 200–1000* (2nd edn., Oxford, 2003).

Brubaker, L., 'To legitimize an emperor: Constantine and visual authority in the eighth and ninth centuries', in P. Magdalino (ed.), *New Constantines: The Rhythm of Imperial Renewal in Byzantium, 4th–13th Centuries* (Aldershot, 1994), 139–58.

Brubaker, L., 'Icons before iconoclasm', *Settimane di studio del Centro italiano di studi sull'Alto Medioevo* 45 (Spoleto, 1998), 1215–54.

Brubaker, L., 'In the beginning was the Word: art and orthodoxy at the Council of Trullo (692), and Nicaea II (787)', in A Louth and A. Casiday (eds), *Byzantine Orthodoxies* (Aldershot, 2006), 95–101.

Brubaker, L. and Haldon, J., *Byzantium in the Iconoclast Era, c.680–850: The Sources* (Aldershot, 2001).

Brubaker, L. and Haldon, J., *Byzantium in the Iconoclast Era, c.680–850: A History* (Cambridge, 2011).

Bryer, A. and Herrin, J., *Iconoclasm: Papers Given at the Ninth Spring Symposium of Byzantine Studies, University of Birmingham, March 1975* (Birmingham, 1977).

Burgmann, L., 'Ist der Nomos Georgikos vorjustinianisch?', *Rechtshistorisches Journal* 1 (1982), 36–9.

Burgmann, L., 'Delict', in *ODB* (1991), vol. 1, 601.

Burgmann, L., 'Ecloga', in *ODB* (1991), vol. 1, 672–3.

Burgmann, L., 'Law in the east, Byzantine', in *ODB* (1991), vol. 2, 1195–6.

Burgmann, L., 'Law in Slavic countries, Byzantine', in *ODB* (1991), vol. 2, 1195.

Burgmann, L., 'Noxal actions', in *ODB* (1991), vol. 3, 1500.

Burgmann, L., 'Oath', in *ODB* (1991), vol. 3, 1509.

Burgmann, L., 'Reformation oder Restauration? Zum Ehegüterrecht der Ecloga', in D. Simon (ed.), *Eherecht und Familiengut in Antike und Mittelalter* (Munich, 1992), 29–42.

Burgmann, L., 'Die Gegenwart der Vergangenheit im Byzantinische Recht', *Settimane di studio del centro italiano di studi sull'alto medioevo* 46 (1999), 591–612.

Burgmann, L., 'Die Nomoi Stratiotikos, Georgikos und Nautikos', *Zbornik Radova Vizantološkog Instituta* XLVI (2009), 53–64.

Burgmann, L. and McGeer, E., 'Nomos Stratiotikos', in *ODB* (1991), vol. 3, 1492.

Burns, J. (ed.), *The Cambridge History of Medieval Political Thought* (Cambridge, 1988).

Burton, G., 'Provincial procurators and the public provinces', *Chiron* 23 (1993), 15–28.

Bury, J. B., *A History of the Later Roman Empire: From Arcadius to Irene (395 A.D. to 800 A.D.)*, 2 vols (London, 1889).

Bury, J. B., 'Graeco-Roman law', Appendix 11 in E. Gibbon, *The History of the Decline and Fall of the Roman Empire*, ed. J. B. Bury with an Introduction by W. E. H. Lecky, 12 vols (New York, 1906), vol. 8, 261–5.

Bury, J. B., *The Imperial Administrative System in the Ninth Century, with a Revised Text of the Kletorologion of Philotheos* (London, 1911).

Cameron, A., 'Images of authority: elites and icons in late sixth century Byzantium', *Past and Present* 84 (1979), 3–35.

Cameron, A., *Procopius and the Sixth Century* (London, 1985).

Cameron, A., *Christianity and the Rhetoric of Empire: The Development of Christian Discourse* (Berkeley, 1991).

Cameron, A. and Conrad, L. (eds), *The Byzantine and Early Islamic Near East I: Problems in the Literary Source Material* (Princeton, 1992).

Cappel, A., 'Emphyteusis', in *ODB* (1991), vol. 1, 693–4.

Cassirer, E., *An Essay on Man: An Introduction to a Philosophy of Human Culture* (New Haven, 1944).

Chambliss, W. and Seidman, R., *Law, Order, and Power* (2nd edn., Reading MA, 1982).

Christides, V., 'Raid and trade in the eastern Mediterranean', *Graeco-Arabica* 5 (1993), 63–102.

Christophilopulos, A., '*Akroatēs*', *BZ* 44 (1951), 86–8.

Chrysos, E., 'The title *Βασιλεύς* in early Byzantine international relations', *DOP* 32 (1978), 29–75.

Constantelos, D., *Byzantine Philanthropy and Social Welfare* (New Brunswick NJ, 1968).

Corcoran, S., *The Empire of the Tetrarchs: Imperial Pronouncements and Government, AD 284–324* (rev. edn., Oxford, 2000).

Corcoran, S., 'The sins of the fathers: a neglected constitution of Diocletian on incest', *The Journal of Legal History* 21 (2000), 1–34.

Crook, J., *Law and Life of Rome* (London, 1967).

Crook, J., 'Legal history and general history', *Bulletin of the Institute of Classical Studies* 41 (1996), 31–6.

Crone, P., 'Islam, Judeo-Christianity and Byzantine iconoclasm', *Jerusalem Studies in Arabic and Islam* 2 (1980), 59–95.

Dagron, G., 'Lawful society and legitimate power', in A. Laiou and D. Simon (eds), *Law and Society in Byzantium: Ninth–Twelfth Centuries* (Washington DC, 1994), 27–51.

Dagron, G., 'The urban economy, seventh–twelfth centuries', in *EHB* (2002) vol. 2, 393–461.

Dagron, G., *Emperor and Priest: The Imperial Office in Byzantium* (Cambridge, 2003), trans. J. Birrell.

Donner, F., *Muhammad and the Believers at the Origins of Islam* (London, 2010).

Drake, H., *Constantine and the Bishops: The Politics of Intolerance* (Baltimore, 2000).

Dölger, F., 'Ist der Nomos Georgikos ein Gesetz des Kaisers Justinians II?', in *Festschrift für Leopold Wenger Vol. II* (Munich, 1945), 18–48.

Dölger, F., *Harmenopulos und der Nomos Georgikos* (Thessalonica, 1951).

Dvornik, F., *Early Christian and Byzantine Political Philosophy*, 2 vols (Washington DC, 1966).

Englezakis, P. B., *Cyprus Nea Justinianoupolis* (Nicosia, 1990).

Evans, J., *The Age of Justinian: The Circumstances of Imperial Power* (London, 1996).
Evans-Grubbs, J., *Law and Family in Late Antiquity* (Oxford, 1999).
Fögen, M.-T., 'Legislation in Byzantium: a political and bureaucratic technique', in A. Laiou and D. Simon (eds), *Law and Society in Byzantium: Ninth–Twelfth Centuries* (Washington DC, 1994), 53–70.
Fögen, M.-T., 'The legislator's monologue: notes on the history of prologues', *Chicago-Kent Law Review* 70 (1994–5), 1593–620.
Fögen, M.-T., 'Reanimation of Roman law in the ninth century: remarks on reasons and results', in L. Brubaker (ed.), *Byzantium in the Ninth Century: Dead or Alive?* (Aldershot, 1998), 11–22.
Fowden, G., *Empire to Commonwealth: Consequences of Monotheism in Late Antiquity* (Princeton, 1993).
Frakes, R., *Compiling the Collatio Legum Mosaicum et Romanum in Late Antiquity* (Oxford, 2011).
Frembergen, J., 'Honour, shame, and bodily mutilation. Cutting off the nose among tribal societies in Pakistan', *Journal of the Royal Asiatic Society* 16 (2006), 243–60.
Freshfield, E., *Roman Law in the Later Roman Empire: The Isaurian Period* (Cambridge, 1932).
Frendo, J., 'The poetic achievement of George of Pisidia', in A. Moffatt (ed.), *Maistor* (Canberra, 1984), 159–87.
Gallagher, C., *Church Law and Church Order in Rome and Byzantium: A Comparative Study* (Aldershot, 2002).
Galsterer, H., 'Roman law in the provinces: some problems of transmission', in M. Crawford (ed.), *L'impero Romano e le strutture economiche e sociali delle province* (Como, 1986), 13–27.
Garnsey, P., 'Why penal laws became harsher: the Roman case', *Natural Law Forum* 13 (1968), 141–62.
Garnsey, P., *Social Status and Legal Privilege in the Roman Empire* (Oxford, 1970).
Garnsey, P., 'Roman citizenship and Roman law in the late empire', in S. Swain and M. Edwards (eds), *Approaching Late Antiquity* (Oxford, 2004), 132–55.
Garnsey, P. and Saller, R., *The Roman Empire: Economy, Society and Culture* (London, 1987).
Geertz, C., *The Interpretation of Cultures* (New York, 1973).
Geertz, C., *Local Knowledge: Further Essays in Interpretative Anthropology* (3rd edn., New York, 2000).
Gero, S., *Byzantine Iconoclasm During the Reign of Leo III with Particular Attention to the Oriental Sources* (Louvain, 1973).
Gero, S., *Byzantine Iconoclasm During the Reign of Constantine V with Particular Attention to the Oriental Sources* (Louvain, 1977).

Górecki, D., 'The Slavic theory in Russian pre-Revolutionary historiography', *Byzantion* 56 (1986), 77–107.

Górecki, D., 'The Slavic theory of the Byzantine rural community in Soviet and post-Soviet historiography', *Byzantinoslavica* 67 (2009), 337–64.

Gray, P., 'Through the tunnel with Leontius of Jerusalem: the sixth-century transformation of theology', in P. Allen and E. Jeffreys (eds), *The Sixth Century: End or Beginning?* (Brisbane, 1996), 187–96.

Greger, B., 'Physical factors in the evolution of the landscape and land use', in *EHB* vol. 1 (2002), 31–45.

Grierson, P., *Byzantine Coinage* (2nd edn., Washington DC, 1999).

Haldon, J., *Byzantine Praetorians* (Bonn, 1984).

Haldon, J., 'The works of Anastasius of Sinai: a key source for the history of seventh-century east Mediterranean society and belief', in A. Cameron and L. Conrad (eds), *The Byzantine and Early Islamic Near East I: Problems in the Literary Source Material* (Princeton, 1992), 107–47.

Haldon, J., 'Military service, military lands, and the status of soldiers: current problems and interpretations', *DOP* 47 (1993), 1–67.

Haldon, J., 'Constantine or Justinian? Crisis and identity in imperial propaganda in the seventh century', in P. Magdalino (ed.), *New Constantines: The Rhythm of Imperial Renewal in Byzantium, 4th–13th Centuries* (Aldershot, 1994), 95–107.

Haldon, J., *Byzantium in the Seventh Century: The Transformation of a Culture* (rev. edn., Cambridge, 1997).

Haldon, J., 'The reign of Heraclius: a context for change', in G. Reinink and B. Stolte (eds), *The Reign of Heraclius (610–41): Crisis and Confrontation* (Leuven, 2002), 1–16.

Haldon, J., 'The fate of the late Roman senatorial elite: extinction or transformation?', in J. Haldon and L. Conrad (eds), *Elites Old and New in the Byzantine and Early Islamic Near East* (Princeton, 2004).

Halsall, G., *Barbarian Migrations and the Roman West, 376–568* (Cambridge, 2007).

Hankinson, R., 'Stoicism and medicine', in B. Inwood (ed.), *The Cambridge Companion to the Stoics* (Cambridge, 2003), 295–309.

Harries, J., 'Constructing the judge: judicial accountability and the culture of criticism in late antiquity', in R. Miles (ed.), *Constructing Identities in Late Antiquity* (London, 1999), 214–33.

Harries, J., *Law and Empire in Late Antiquity* (Cambridge, 1999).

Harries, J., *Law and Crime in the Roman World* (Cambridge, 2007).

Harries, J. and Wood, I. (eds), *The Theodosian Code: Studies in the Imperial Law of Late Antiquity* (2nd edn., London, 2010).

Hatlie, P., *The Monks and Monasteries of Constantinople c.350–850* (Cambridge, 2007).

Heather, P., 'New men for new Constantines? Creating an imperial elite in the eastern Mediterranean', in P. Magdalino (ed.), *New Constantines: The Rhythm of Imperial Renewal in Byzantium, 4th–13th Centuries* (Aldershot, 1994), 11–44.

Heather, P., 'Senators and senates', in A. Cameron and P. Garnsey (eds), *The Cambridge Ancient History Vol. XIII: The Late Empire, A.D. 337–425* (Cambridge, 1998), 184–210.

Heather, P., *The Fall of the Roman Empire* (London, 2005).

Heimbach, G., *Anekdota*, 2 vols (Leipzig, 1838–40).

Heimbach, G., 'Griechisch-römisches Recht im Mittelalter und in der Neuzeit', in J. Ersch and J. Gruber (eds), *Allgemeine Encyclopädie der Wissenschaften und Künste in alphabetischer Folge. Section I Pt.86* (Leipzig, 1868), 191–471.

Hendy, M., *Studies in the Byzantine Monetary Economy, c.300–1450* (Cambridge, 1985).

Herrin, J., *The Formation of Christendom* (Oxford, 1987).

Herrin, J., 'The imperial feminine in Byzantium', *Past and Present* 169 (2000), 3–33.

Herrin, J., *Women in Purple: Rulers of Medieval Byzantium* (London, 2001).

Herrin, J., 'The Quinisext Council (692) as a continuation of Chalcedon', in R. Price and M. Whitby (eds), *Chalcedon in Context: Church Councils 400–700* (Liverpool, 2009), 148–68.

Hollingsworth, P., 'Nikephoros', in *ODB* (1991), vol. 3, 1476.

Honoré, T., *Tribonian* (London, 1978).

Honoré, T., *Emperors and Lawyers* (London, 1981).

Honoré, T., 'Roman law AD 200–400: from cosmopolis to Rechtstaat?', in S. Swain and M. Edwards (eds), *Approaching Late Antiquity* (Oxford, 2004), 109–32.

Honoré, T., *Justinian's Digest: Character and Compilation* (Oxford, 2010).

Hopper, V., *Medieval Number Symbolism: Its Sources, Meanings and Influence on Thought and Expression* (New York, 1938).

Horden, P. and Purcell, N., *The Corrupting Sea: A Study of Mediterranean History* (Oxford, 2000).

Howard-Johnston, J., 'The two great powers in late antiquity: a comparison', in A. Cameron (ed.), *The Byzantine and Early Islamic Near East II: States, Resources and Armies* (Princeton, 1995), 157–226.

Howard-Johnston, J., 'Heraclius' Persian campaigns and the revival of the east Roman Empire, 622–630', *War in History* 6 (1999), 1–44.

Howard-Johnston, J., 'Social change in early medieval Byzantium', in R. Evans (ed.), *Lordship and Learning* (Woodbridge, 2004), 39–50.

Howard-Johnston, J., *Witnesses to a World Crisis: Historians and Histories of the Middle East in the Seventh Century* (Oxford, 2010).

Hoyland, R., *Seeing Islam as Others Saw It: A Survey and Evaluation of Christian, Jewish, and Zoroastrian Writings on Early Islam* (Princeton, 1997).

Hoyland, R., 'New documentary texts and the early Islamic state', *Bulletin of the School of Oriental and African Studies* 69 (2006), 395–416.

Hubel, M., 'Die Haltung zur Homosexualität im byzantinischen Reich', *Das Altertum* 49 (2004), 291–310.

Humfress, C., 'Law and legal practice in the age of Justinian', in M. Maas (ed.), *The Cambridge Companion to the Age of Justinian* (Cambridge, 2005), 161–84.

Humfress, C., 'Civil law and social life', in N. Lenski (ed.), *The Cambridge Companion to the Age of Constantine* (Cambridge, 2006), 205–25.

Humfress, C., 'Poverty and Roman law', in M. Atkins and R. Osborne (eds), *Poverty in the Roman World* (Cambridge, 2006), 183–203.

Humfress, C., *Orthodoxy and the Courts in Late Antiquity* (Oxford, 2007).

Humfress, C., 'Law and custom under Rome', in Rio (ed.), *Law, Custom, and Justice* (London, 2011), 23–47.

Humphreys, M., 'Images of authority? Imperial patronage of icons from Justinian II to Leo III', in P. Sarris, M. Dal Santo, and P. Booth (eds), *An Age of Saints? Power, Conflict and Dissent in Early Medieval Christianity* (Leiden, 2011), 150–68.

Humphreys, M., 'The "war of images" revisited. Justinian's coinage reform and the Caliphate', *The Numismatic Chronicle* 173 (2013), 229–44.

Hunger, H., *Prooimion: Elemente der byzantinischen Kaiseridee in den Arengen der Urkunden* (Vienna, 1964).

James, L. (ed.), *A Companion to Byzantium* (Oxford, 2010).

Jeffery, A., 'Ghevond's text of the correspondence between 'Umar II and Leo III', *The Harvard Theological Review* 37 (1944), 269–332.

Jeffreys, E., et al. (eds), *The Oxford Handbook to Byzantine Studies* (Oxford, 2008).

Jokisch, B., *Islamic Imperial Law: Harun-al-Rashid's Codification Project* (Berlin, 2007).

Jones, A. H. M., *The Later Roman Empire, 284–602: A Social, Economic and Administrative Survey*, 2 vols (Oxford, 1964).

Kaegi, W., *Heraclius: Emperor of Byzantium* (Cambridge, 2003).

Kaldellis, A., *Procopius of Caesarea: Tyranny, History, and Philosophy at the End of Antiquity* (Philadelphia, 2004).

Kantorowicz, E., *The King's Two Bodies: A Study in Medieval Political Theology* (Princeton, 1957).

Karayannopulos, J., 'Entstehung und Bedeutung des Nomos Georgikos', *BZ* 51 (1958), 357–73.

Kazhdan, A., '"Constanin Imaginaire": Byzantine legends of the ninth century about Constantine the Great', *Byzantion* 57 (1987), 196–250.

Kazhdan, A., 'Do we need a new history of Byzantine law?', *Jahrbuch der österreichischen Byzantinistik* 39 (1989), 1–28.
Kazhdan, A., 'Archon', in *ODB* (1991) vol. 1, 160.
Kazhdan, A., 'Book of the Eparch', in *ODB* (1991) vol. 1, 308.
Kazhdan, A., 'Erotapokriseis', in *ODB* (1991) vol. 1, 727.
Kazhdan, A., 'Farmer's Law', in *ODB* (1991) vol. 2, 778.
Kazhdan, A., 'Mosaic Law', in *ODB* (1991) vol. 2, 1413–14.
Kazhdan, A., 'State, feudal, and private economy in Byzantium', *DOP* 47 (1993), 83–100.
Kedar, B., 'On the origins of the earliest laws of Frankish Jerusalem: the canons of the Council of Nablus, 1120', *Speculum* 74 (1999), 310–35.
Kelly, C., 'Emperors, government and bureaucracy', in A. Cameron and P. Garnsey (eds), *The Cambridge Ancient History, Vol. XIII: The Late Empire, A.D. 337–425* (Cambridge, 1998), 138–83.
Kelly, C., *Ruling the Later Roman Empire* (London, 2004).
Kennedy, H., *The Court of the Caliphs: The Rise and Fall of Islam's Greatest Dynasty* (London, 2004).
Khalileh, H., *Admiralty and Maritime Laws in the Mediterranean Sea (c. 800–1050)* (Leiden, 2006).
King, G., 'Islam, iconoclasm and the declaration of doctrine', *Bulletin of the School of Oriental and African Studies* 48 (1985), 267–77.
Korzenszky, E., *Leges poenales militares e codice Laurentiano* LXXV, 6 (Budapest, 1931).
Kottje, R., *Studien zum Einfluss des Alten Testaments auf Recht und Liturgie des frühen Mittelalters* (2nd edn., Bonn, 1970).
Kresten, O., 'Datierungsprobleme "isaurischer" Eherechtsnovellen I. Coll. 1.26', *FM* IV (Frankfurt, 1984), 37–106.
Kuchma, V., '*Nomos Stratiōtikos*', *Vizantiiskii Vremennik* 32 (1971), 276–84.
Lafferty, S., 'Law and society in Ostrogothic Italy: evidence from the *Edictum Theoderici*', *Journal of Late Antiquity* 3 (2010), 337–64.
Laiou, A., 'A note on the Farmer's Law, chapter 67', *Byzantion* 41 (1971), 197–204.
Laiou, A., 'The human resources', in *EHB* (2002) vol. 1, 47–55.
Laiou, A., 'Economic thought and ideology', in *EHB* (2002) vol. 3, 1123–44.
Laiou, A. and Simon, D. (eds), *Law and Society in Byzantium: Ninth–Twelfth Centuries* (Washington DC, 1994).
Laiou, A. and Morrisson, C., *The Byzantine Economy* (Cambridge, 2007).
Laiou, A., et al. (eds), *The Economic History of Byzantium*, 3 vols (Washington DC, 2002).
Leader, R., 'The David Plates revisited: transforming the secular in early Byzantium', *Art Bulletin* 82 (2000), 407–27.

Lefort, J., 'The rural economy, seventh–twelfth centuries', in *EHB* (2002) vol. 1, 231–310.

Lemerle, P., *Le Premier Humanisme byzantin* (Paris, 1971).

Lemerle, P., *The Agrarian History of Byzantium* (Galway, 1979).

Lenski, N. (ed.), *The Cambridge Companion to the Age of Constantine* (Cambridge, 2006).

Letsios, D., 'Sea trade as illustrated in the "Rhodian Sea Law" with special reference to the reception of its norms in the Arabic Ecloga', *Graeco-Arabica* 6 (1995), 209–25.

Letsios, D., *Nomos Rhodiōn Nautikos—Das Seegesetz der Rhodier. Untersuchung zu Seerecht und Handelsschiffahrt in Byzanz* (Rhodes, 1996).

Levy, E., *West Roman Vulgar Law* (Philadelphia, 1951).

Liebeschuetz, J. H. W. G., *Continuity and Change in Roman Religion* (Oxford, 1979).

Liebs, D., 'Roman law', in A. Cameron et al. (eds), *The Cambridge Ancient History, Vol. XIV: Late Antiquity: Empire and Successors, A.D. 425–600* (Cambridge, 2000), 238–59.

Liebs, D., 'Roman vulgar law in late antiquity', in B. Sirks (ed.), *Aspects of law in Late Antiquity* (Oxford, 2008), 35–53.

Lilie, R.-J., 'Die zweihundertjährige reform: zu den Anfängen der Themenorganisation im 7. und 8. Jahrhundert', *Byzantinoslavica* 45 (1984), 27–39, 190–201.

Louth, A., 'St John Damascene as monastic theologian', *The Downside Review* 125 (2007), 197–220.

Louth, A., 'Byzantium transforming', in J. Shepard (ed.), *The Cambridge History of the Byzantine Empire, c. 500–1492* (Cambridge, 2008), 221–48.

Maas, M., 'Roman history and Christian ideology in Justinianic reform legislation', *DOP* 40 (1986), 17–31.

Maas, M., *John Lydus and the Roman Past: Antiquarianism and Politics in the Age of Justinian* (London, 1992).

Maas, M. (ed.), *The Cambridge Companion to the Age of Justinian* (Cambridge, 2005).

MacMullen, R., *Christianizing the Roman Empire (A.D.100–400)* (New Haven, 1984).

MacMullen, R., 'Judicial savagery in the Roman Empire', *Chiron* 16 (1988), 147–66.

MacMullen, R., *Christianity and Paganism in the Fourth to Eighth Centuries* (New Haven, 1997).

Magdalino, P., 'Philanthropy', in *ODB* (1991) vol. 3, 1649–50.

Magdalino, P., 'The history of the future and its uses: prophecy, policy, and propaganda', in R. Beaton and C. Roueché (eds), *The Making of Byzantine History* (Aldershot, 1993), 3–34.

Magdalino, P., 'Introduction', in Magdalino (ed.), *New Constantines: The Rhythm of Imperial Renewal in Byzantium, 4th–13th Centuries* (Aldershot, 1994), 1–9.

Magdalino, P., 'Justice and finance in the Byzantine state, ninth to twelfth centuries', in A. Laiou and D. Simon (eds), *Law and Society in Byzantium: Ninth–Twelfth Centuries* (Washington DC, 1994), 93–115.

Magdalino, P. (ed.), *New Constantines: The Rhythm of Imperial Renewal in Byzantium, 4th–13th Centuries* (Aldershot, 1994).

Magdalino, P., 'The distance of the past in early medieval Byzantium (VII–X centuries)', *Settimane di studio del centro italiano di studi sull'alto medioevo* 46 (1999), 115–46.

Magdalino, P., 'The other image at the palace gate and the visual propaganda of Leo III', in D. Sullivan, E. Fisher, and S. Papaioannou (eds), *Byzantine Religious Culture* (Leiden, 2012), 139–53.

Magdalino, P. and Nelson, R., 'Introduction', in P. Magdalino and R. Nelson (eds), *The Old Testament in Byzantium* (Washington DC, 2010), 1–38.

De Malafosse, J., 'Les lois agraires à l'époque byzantine; tradition et exégèse', *Recueil de l'Académie de Législation* 19 (1949), 1–75.

Mango, C., *Byzantium: The Empire of the New Rome* (London, 1980).

Mango, C. 'The revival of learning', in C. Mango (ed.), *The Oxford History of Byzantium* (Oxford, 2002), 214–29.

Markopoulos, A., 'Constantine the Great in Macedonian historiography: models and approaches', in P. Magdalino (ed.), *New Constantines: The Rhythm of Imperial Renewal in Byzantium, 4th–13th Centuries* (Aldershot, 1994), 159–70.

Markus, R., *The End of Ancient Christianity* (Cambridge, 1990).

Markus, R., *Gregory the Great and His World* (Cambridge, 1997).

Martin, E., *A History of the Iconoclastic Controversy* (London, 1930).

Mathisen, R. (ed.), *Law, Society and Authority in Late Antiquity* (Oxford, 2001).

Matthews, J., *Laying Down the Law: A Study of the Theodosian Code* (London, 2000).

Matthews, J., 'Roman law and barbarian identity', originally in S. Mitchell and G. Greatrex (eds), *Ethnicity and Culture in Late Antiquity* (London, 2000), 31–44, reprinted in Matthews, *Roman Perspectives*, 327–42.

Matthews, J., 'Roman law and Roman history', originally in D. Potter (ed.), *A Companion to the Roman Empire* (Oxford, 2006), 477–91; reprinted in Matthews, *Roman Perspectives*, 291–310.

Matthews, J., *Roman Perspectives: Studies in the Social, Political and Cultural History of the First to Fifth Centuries* (Swansea, 2010).

Mayr-Harting, H., *Ottonian Book Illumination* (London, 1991).

McCormick, M., *The Origins of the European Economy: Communications and Commerce A.D. 300–900* (Cambridge, 2001).

McKitterick, R., *The Carolingians and the Written Word* (Cambridge, 1981).
McKitterick, R. (ed.), *Carolingian Culture: Emulation and Innovation* (Cambridge, 1994).
Meyendorff, J., *Imperial Unity and Christian Divisions: The Church 450–680 A.D.* (Crestwood NY, 1989).
Meyer, E., *Legitimacy and Law in the Roman World: Tabulae in Roman Belief and Practice* (Cambridge, 2004).
Millar, F., *The Emperor in the Roman World: 31 BC–AD 337* (London, 1977).
Mitchell, S., *Anatolia: Land, Men, and Gods in Asia Minor*, 2 vols (Oxford, 1993).
Mitteis, L., *Reichsrecht und Volksrecht in den östlichen Provinzen des römischen Kaiserreichs* (Leipzig, 1891).
Mommsen, T., *Römisches Staatsrecht*, 3 vols (Leipzig, 1871–88).
Mommsen, T., *Römisches Strafrecht*, 2 vols (Leipzig, 1899).
Moore, S. F., *Law as Process: An Anthropological Approach* (2nd edn., Hamburg, 2000).
Moore, S. F. (ed.), *Law and Anthropology: A Reader* (Oxford, 2005).
Moorhead, J., 'Iconoclasm, the Cross and the imperial image', *Byzantion* 55 (1985), 165–79.
Morrisson, C., 'Byzantine money: its production and circulation', in *EHB* (2002) vol. 3, 909–66.
Mortreuil, J., *Histoire du Droit Byzantin*, 3 vols (Paris, 1843–6).
Munitiz, J., 'Anastasius of Sinai: speaking and writing to the people of God', in M. Cunningham and P. Allen (eds), *Preacher and Audience: Studies in Early Christian and Byzantine Homiletics* (Leiden, 1998), 227–45.
Munitiz, J., 'Anastasius of Sinai's teaching on body and soul', in L. James (ed.), *Desire and Denial in Byzantium* (Aldershot, 1999), 49–56.
Nedungatt, G. and Featherstone, M., 'Presentation', in Nedungatt and Featherstone (eds), *The Council in Trullo Revisited* (Rome, 1995), 7–14.
Nichanian, M., 'Iconoclasme et prestation de serment à Byzance?: du contrôle social à la Nouvelle alliance', in M.-F. Auzépy and G. Saint-Guillain (eds), *Oralité et lien social au Moyen Âge: Occident, Byzance, Islam: parole donnée, foi jurée, serment* (Paris, 2008), 81–102.
Nicol, D., 'Byzantine political thought', in J. Burns (ed.), *The Cambridge History of Medieval Political Thought* (Cambridge, 1988), 51–79.
Noble, T., *The Republic of St Peter: The Birth of the Papal State, 680–825* (Philadelphia, 1984).
Obolensky, D., *The Byzantine Commonwealth: Eastern Europe 500–1453* (London, 1971).
Ohme, H., 'The causes of conflict about the Quinisext Council: new perspectives on a disputed council', *The Greek Orthodox Theological Review* 40 (1995), 17–43.

Ohme, H., 'Die sogennanten "antirömischen" Kanones des Concilium Quinisextum', in G. Nedungatt and M. Featherstone (eds), *The Council in Trullo Revisited* (Rome, 1995), 307–21.

Ohme, H., 'Sources of the Greek canon law to the Quinisext Council (691/2): councils and church fathers', in W. Hartmann and K. Pennington (eds), *The History of Byzantine and Eastern Canon Law to 1500* (Washington DC, 2012), 24–114.

Oikonomidès, N., 'Le serment de l'impératrice Eudocie (1067)', *Revue des Études Byzantines* 21 (1963).

Oikonomidès, N., *Les Listes de préséance byzantines des IXe–Xe siècles* (Paris, 1972).

Oikonomidès, N., 'Middle Byzantine provincial recruits: salary and armaments', in J. Duffy and J. Peradotto (eds), *Gonimos: Neoplatonic and Byzantine Studies* (Buffalo, 1988), 121–36.

Oikonomidès, N., 'The role of the Byzantine state in the economy', in *EHB* (2002) vol. 3, 973–1058.

Olster, D., *Roman Defeat, Christian Response, and the Literary Construction of the Jew* (Philadelphia, 1994).

Olster, D., 'From periphery to centre: the transformation of late Roman self-definition', in R. Mathisen and H. Sivan (eds), *Shifting Frontiers in Late Antiquity* (Aldershot, 1996), 93–102.

Olster, D., 'Ideological transformation and the evolution of imperial presentation in the wake of Islam's victory', in E. Grypeou et al. (eds), *The Encounter of Eastern Christianity with Early Islam* (Leiden, 2006), 45–71.

Ostrogorsky, G., 'Über die vermentliche Reformtätigkeit der Isaurier', *BZ* 30 (1929–30), 394–400.

Ostrogorsky, G., *History of the Byzantine State* (2nd edn., Oxford, 1968).

Panchenko, B., *Krest'ianskaia sobstvennost' v Vizantii. Zemledel'cheskii zakon i monastyrskie dokumenty* (Sofia, 1903).

Papadakis, A., 'Pentarchy', in *ODB* (1991) vol. 3, 1625–6.

Pavlov, A., 'Vizantiiskiia "Knigi zakonnyia" v drevne-russkom perevode', *Sbornik Otdeleniia russkogo iazyka i slovesnosti Imperatorskoi akademii nauk* 38 (1885), 1–92.

Pazdernik, C., 'Justinianic ideology and the power of the past', in M. Maas (ed.), *The Cambridge Companion to the Age of Justinian* (Cambridge, 2005), 185–212.

Penner, T., 'Socrates', in C. Rowe and M. Schofield (eds), *The Cambridge History of Greek and Roman Thought* (Cambridge, 2000), 165–89.

Pieler, P., 'Byzantinische Rechtsliteratur', in H. Hunger (ed.), *Die hochsprachliche profane Literatur der Byzantiner*, 2 vols (Munich, 1978), vol. 2, 341–480.

Pieler, P., *Anakatharsis tōn palaiōn nomōn* und makedonische Renaissance', *Subseciva Groningana* 3 (1989), 61–77.

Pieler, P., 'Das Alte Testament im Rechtsdenken der Byzantiner', in S. Troianos (ed.), *Analecta Atheniensia ad ius byzantinum spectantia* (Athens, 1997), 81–113.

Prinzing, G., 'Das Bild Iustinians I. in der Überlieferung der Byzantiner vom 7. bis 15. Jahrhundert', *FM* VII (Frankfurt, 1986), 1–99.

Rapp, C., *Holy Bishops in Late Antiquity: The Nature of Christian Leadership in an Age of Transition* (Berkeley, 2005).

Rapp, C., 'Old Testament models for emperors in early Byzantium', in P. Magdalino and R. Nelson (eds), *The Old Testament in Byzantium* (Washington DC, 2010), 175–97.

Reinink, G., 'Ps.-Methodius: a concept of history in response to the rise of Islam', in A. Cameron and L. Conrad (eds), *The Byzantine and Early Islamic Near East I: Problems in the Literary Source Material* (Princeton, 1992), 149–87.

Reinink, G. and Stolte, B. (eds), *The Reign of Heraclius (610–41): Crisis and Confrontation* (Leuven, 2002).

Rhodolakes, G., *Apo to Nomo Rhodiōn sto 53o Biblio tōn Basilikōn: sumbolē stē meletē tou Buzantinou nautikou dikaiou* (Athens, 2007).

Ringrose, K., 'Monks and society in iconoclastic Byzantium', *Byzantine Studies* 6 (1979), 130–51.

Rio, A. (ed.), *Law, Custom, and Justice in Late Antiquity and the Early Middle Ages* (London, 2011).

Robinson, C., *'Abd al-Malik* (Oxford, 2005).

Rösch, G., *Onoma Basileias: Studien zum offiziellen Gebrauch der Kaisertitel in spätantiker und frühbyzantiner Zeit* (Vienna, 1978).

Rosen, L., *The Anthropology of Justice: Law as Culture in Islamic Society* (Cambridge, 1989).

Rosen, L., *Law as Culture* (Princeton, 2006).

Roueché, C., 'The functions of the governor in late antiquity: some observations', *Antiquité Tardive* 6 (1998), 31–6.

Rouland, N., *Legal Anthropology* (London, 1994), trans. P. Planel.

Rowe, C. and Schofield, M. (eds), *The Cambridge History of Greek and Roman Thought* (Cambridge, 2000).

Saradi, H., 'The Byzantine tribunals: problems in the application of justice and state policy (9th–12th c.)', *Revue des Études Byzantines* 53 (1995), 165–204.

Sarris, P., *Economy and Society in the Age of Justinian* (Cambridge, 2006).

Sarris, P., 'Economics, trade, and "feudalism"', in L. James (ed.), *A Companion to Byzantium* (Chichester, 2010), 25–42.

Sarris, P., *Empires of Faith: The Fall of Rome to the Rise of Islam, 500–700* (Oxford, 2011).

Scheltema, H., 'Byzantine law', in J. Hussey (ed.), *The Cambridge Medieval History Vol. IV* (Cambridge, 1967), Pt. 2, 55–77.

Schminck, A., *Studien zu mittelbyzantinischen Rechtsbüchern* (Frankfurt, 1986).
Schminck, A., 'Collectio 25 capitulorum', in *ODB* (1991) vol. 1, 480.
Schminck, A., 'Collectio 87 capitulorum', in *ODB* (1991) vol. 1, 480.
Schminck, A., 'Collectio Tripartita', in *ODB* (1991) vol. 1, 480.
Schminck, A., 'Epanagoge Aucta', in *ODB* (1991) vol. 1, 704.
Schminck, A., 'Epitome Legum', in *ODB* (1991) vol. 1, 724.
Schminck, A., 'Nomokanon of fourteen titles', in *ODB* (1991) vol. 3, 1491.
Schminck, A., 'Probleme des sog. *Nomos Rhodiōn Nautikos*, in E. Chrysos et al. (eds), *Griechenland und das Meer* (Mannheim, 1999), 171–8.
Schminck, A., 'Bermerkungen zum sog. "Nomos Mosaikos"', in *FM* XI (Frankfurt, 2005), 249–68.
Schofield, M., 'Stoic ethics', in B. Inwood (ed.), *The Cambridge Companion to the Stoics* (Cambridge, 2003), 233–56.
Setton, K., 'On the importance of land tenure and agrarian taxation in the Byzantine Empire, from the fourth century to the fourth crusade', *The American Journal of Philology* 74 (1953), 225–59.
Ševčenko, I., 'The search for the past in Byzantium around the year 800', *DOP* 46 (1992), 279–93.
Shahid, I., 'The Iranian factor in Byzantium during the reign of Heraclius', *DOP* 26 (1972), 293–320.
Shepard, J. (ed.), *The Cambridge History of the Byzantine Empire c.500–1492* (Cambridge, 2008).
Shepard, J., 'Equilibrium to expansion (886–1025)', in Shepard (ed.), *The Cambridge History of the Byzantine Empire, c.500–1492* (Cambridge, 2008), 493–536.
Shepard, J., 'General introduction', in Shepard (ed.), *The Cambridge History of the Byzantine Empire c.500–1492* (Cambridge, 2008), 2–95.
Simon, D., 'Provinzialrecht und Volksrecht', *FM* I (Frankfurt, 1976), 102–16.
Simon, D., 'Die Epochen der byzantinischen Rechtsgeschichte', *Ius Commune* 15 (1988), 73–106.
Simon, D., 'Legislation as both a world order and a legal order', in A. Laiou and D. Simon (eds), *Law and Society in Byzantium: Ninth–Twelfth Centuries* (Washington DC, 1994), 1–25.
Singowitz, B., *Studien zum Strafrecht der Ekloge* (Athens, 1956).
Sirks, B., *Food for Rome: The Legal Structure of the Transportation and Processing of Supplies for the Imperial Distributions in Rome and Constantinople* (Amsterdam, 1991).
Sirks, B., *The Theodosian Code: A Study* (Friedrichsdorf, 2007).
Sirks, B., 'The colonate in Justinian's reign', *Journal of Roman Studies* 98 (2008), 120–43.
Sivertsev, A., *Judaism and Imperial Ideology in Late Antiquity* (Cambridge, 2011).

Spain Alexander, S., 'Heraclius, Byzantine imperial ideology and the David Plates', *Speculum* 52 (1977), 217–37.

Spatharakis, I., 'The text of chapter 30 of the *Lex Rhodia Nautica*', *Hellenika* 26 (1973), 207–15.

Speck, P., *Kaiser Konstantine VI. Die Legitimation einer fremden und der Versuch einer eigenen Herrschaft* (Munich, 1978).

Speck, P., *Artabasdos, der rechtgläubige Vorkämpfer der göttlichen Lehren: Untersuchungen zur Revolte des Artabasdos und ihrer Darstellung in der byzantinischen Historiographie* (Bonn, 1981).

Speck, P., *Ich bin's nicht, Kaiser Konstantin ist es gewesen: die Legenden vom Einfluss des Teufels, des Juden und des Moslem auf den Ikonoklasmus* (Bonn, 1990).

Staubach, N., *Rex christianus: Hofkultur und Herrschaftspropaganda im Reich Karls des Kahlen* (Cologne, 1993).

Stephenson, P. (ed.), *The Byzantine World* (London, 2010).

Stoclet, A., 'From Baghdad to Beowulf: eulogising "imperial" capitals east and west in the mid-eighth century', *Proceedings of the Royal Irish Academy, Section C* 105 (2005), 151–95.

Stolte, B., 'Not new but novel: notes on the historiography of Byzantine law', *BMGS* 22 (1998), 264–79.

Stolte, B., 'The challenge of change: notes on the legal history of the reign of Heraclius', in G. Reinink and B. Stolte (eds), *The Reign of Heraclius (610–41): Crisis and Confrontation* (Leuven, 2002), 191–204.

Stolte, B., 'Balancing Byzantine law', *FM* XI (Frankfurt, 2005), 57–75.

Stolte, B., 'The social function of the law', in J. Haldon (ed.), *A Social History of Byzantium* (Chichester, 2009), 76–91.

Stolte, B., 'Justice: legal literature', in E. Jeffreys, et al. (eds), *The Oxford Handbook to Byzantine Studies* (Oxford, 2008), 691–8.

Svoronos, N., 'Notes sur l'Origine et la Date du code Rural', *Travaux et mémoires* 8 (1981), 487–500.

Teall, J., 'The Byzantine agricultural tradition', *DOP* 25 (1971), 33–59.

Thacker, A. (ed.), 'The power of the Word: the influence of the Bible on early medieval politics', *Early Medieval Europe* 7:3 (1998).

Treadgold, W., *The Byzantine Revival, 780–842* (Stanford, 1988).

Treadgold, W., *Byzantium and its Army* (Stanford, 1995).

Treggiari, S., 'Social status and social legislation', in A. Bowmanet al. (eds), *The Cambridge Ancient History, Vol. X: The Augustan Empire, 43 B.C.–A.D. 69* (Cambridge, 1996), 873–904.

Troianos, S., *Ho Poinalios tou Eklogadiou* (Frankfurt, 1980).

Troianos, S., *Oi Pēges tou Vyzantinou dikaiou: eisagōgiko voēthēma* (Athens, 1986).

Turner, D., 'The politics of despair: the plague of 746–47 and iconoclasm in the Byzantine Empire', *The Annual of the British School at Athens* 85 (1990), 419–34.

Uspenskii, F., 'K' istoriikrest'ianskogo zemlevladeniia v Vizantii', *Zhurnal ministerstva narodnogo prosveshchenia* 225 (1883), 30–87.

Van Bochove, T., *To Date and Not to Date: On the Date and Status of Byzantine Law Books* (Groningen, 1996).

Van der Wal, N. and Lokin, J., *Historiae iuris Graeco-Romani delineatio: les sources du droit byzantin de 300 à 1453* (Groningen, 1985).

Vernadsky, G., 'Sur les origines de la loi agraire byzantine', *Byzantion* 2 (1925), 169–80.

Voss, W., *Recht und Rhetorik in den Kaisergesetzen der Spätantike* (Frankfurt, 1982).

Wagschal, D., *The Nature of Law and Legality in the Byzantine Canonical Collections 381–883*, Doctoral thesis, Durham University (2010). Available at Durham E-Theses Online: <http://etheses.dur.ac.uk/468>.

Wessel, S., 'The *Nouthesia* and the law of Moses', *Byzantion* 73 (2003), 530–42.

Whitby, Ma., 'A new image for a new age: George of Pisidia on the Emperor Heraclius', in E. Dabrowa (ed.), *The Roman and Byzantine Army in the East* (Krakow, 1994), 197–225.

Whitby, Ma., 'George of Pisidia's presentation of the Emperor Heraclius and his campaigns', in G. Reinink and B. Stolte (eds), *The Reign of Heraclius (610–41): Crisis and Confrontation* (Leuven, 2002), 157–73.

Whittow, M., *The Making of Orthodox Byzantium* (Basingstoke, 1996).

Whittow, M., 'The middle Byzantine economy (600–1204)', in J. Shepard (ed.), *The Cambridge History of the Byzantine Empire c. 500–1492* (Cambridge, 2008), 465–92.

Wickham, C., *Framing the Early Middle Ages: Europe and the Mediterranean, 400–800* (Oxford, 2005).

Wickham, C., *The Inheritance of Rome: A History of Europe from 400 to 1000* (London, 2009).

Wood, P., *'We have no king but Christ': Christian Political Thought in Greater Syria on the Eve of the Arab Conquest (c.400–585)* (Oxford, 2010).

Woolf, G., *Becoming Roman: The Origins of Provincial Civilization in Gaul* (Cambridge, 1998).

Wormald, P., '*Lex scripta* and verbum regis: legislation and Germanic kingship, from Euric to Cnut', in P. Sawyer and I. Wood (eds), *Early Medieval Kingship* (Leeds, 1977), 105–38.

Wormald, P., *The Making of English Law, Vol. 1: Legislation and its Limits* (Oxford, 2001).

Wortley, J., 'Iconoclasm and leipsanoclasm: Leo III, Constantine V and relics', *Byzantinische Forschungen* 8 (1982), 253–79.

Zacharia von Lingenthal, K., *Historiae Juris Graeco-Romani Delineatio* (Heidelberg, 1839).

Zacharia von Lingenthal, K., *Geschichte des griechisch-römischen Rechts* (Berlin, 1892).

Zimmerman, R., *The Law of Obligations* (Oxford, 1990).

Zuckerman, C., 'The reign of Constantine V in the miracles of St Theodore the Recruit (BHG 1764)', *Revue des Études Byzantines* 46 (1988), 191–210.

Zuckerman, C., 'Learning from the enemy and more: studies in "Dark Centuries" Byzantium', *Millennium* 2 (2005), 79–135.

Index